FERMENTED VEGETABLES

Fermented Vegetables

CREATIVE RECIPES FOR FERMENTING
64 VEGETABLES & HERBS IN
Krauts, Kimchis, Brined Pickles,
Chutneys, Relishes & Pastes

KIRSTEN K. SHOCKEY &
CHRISTOPHER SHOCKEY
Photography by Erin Kunkel

Storey Publishing

The mission of Storey Publishing is to serve our customers by
publishing practical information that encourages
personal independence in harmony with the environment.

Edited by Margaret Sutherland and Molly Jackel
Art direction and book design by Alethea Morrison
Text production by Liseann Karandisecky
Indexed by Nancy D. Wood

Photography by © Erin Kunkel, except pages 358 and 359 by the author
Illustrations by © Daniel Everett
Hand lettering by Alethea Morrison

Storey books are available for special premium
and promotional uses and for customized editions.
For further information, please call 1-800-793-9396.

Storey Publishing
210 MASS MoCA Way
North Adams, MA 01247
www.storey.com

Printed in China by Toppan Leefung Printing Ltd.
10 9 8 7 6

Library of Congress Cataloging-in-Publication Data

Shockey, Kirsten, author.
  Fermented vegetables / by Kirsten and Christopher
Shockey.
     pages cm
  Includes bibliographical references and index.
  ISBN 978-1-61212-425-4 (pbk. : alk. paper)
  ISBN 978-1-61212-426-1 (ebook) 1. Fermented
foods. 2. Vegetables—Preservation. 3. Canning and
preserving. I. Shockey, Christopher, author. II. Title.
TX612.V4S47 2014
664'.024—dc23
                                    2014020893

Be sure to read all of the instructions thoroughly
before undertaking any of the techniques
or recipes in this book and follow all of the
recommended safety guidelines.

"Here, try this," we'd say as we thrust some new creation at our sometimes-skeptical children on the other side of the fork. It became habit for them, just something they did in our house with two fermentistas on the loose. Now and then they'd ask, hopefully, if we were ready to move on to become bakers or chocolatiers. Still, they always opened up and gave us their honest assessment and support.

Thank you, Jakob, Kelton, Dmitri, and Ariana.

LOVE, MOM & POP

Contents

Why We Ferment, 11

PART 1
Dipping into the Brine
FERMENTATION FUNDAMENTALS
— 14 —

PART 2
Mastering the Basics
KRAUT, CONDIMENTS, PICKLES, AND KIMCHI
— 48 —

Why We Ferment

THERE'S MORE TO FERMENTED VEGETABLES than probiotics, nutrient density, and food preservation. These three attributes are piquing people's interest, but to be honest, that's not enough. Just because you know something is good for you doesn't mean you're going to eat it. You have to *want* to eat fermented vegetables, to crave them, and the reason you will is flavor. You'll eat fermented vegetables because you want to, not because you should. Availability and ease of preparation are important, but incorporating fermented foods into your diet is, we believe, all about taste.

By fermenting, you'll unlock new, unimagined, complex, deep flavors. You'll experience the unique flavor that comes from time and place with each delicious batch.

We also know that no matter how delicious something is, if it's not easy to prepare at the end of a busy day, it won't make it to the dinner table. That's where fermentation comes in: You can make delicious, nutrient-dense fermented vegetables whenever you have the time. Later, when there are no fresh veggies in the crisper drawer, or you don't have the time to cook up something quick, you'll have instant side dishes, salads, or flavorful foods around which to build a meal. Fermented vegetables are the ultimate convenience food!

We were introduced to the *Nourishing Traditions* cookbook and the Weston A. Price Foundation on Christmas Eve in 1999, with an unusual gift from Kirsten's mother. This cookbook and the foundation marked the beginning of a growing interest in traditional foods such as whole raw milk, real butter, and fermented foods. That evening we'd eaten weisswurst and potato salad, a holiday tradition from Kirsten's Bavarian father. We were seated around the candlelit tree, passing around simple gifts, when Kirsten's mother handed us Sally Fallon's cookbook and a heavy box. "Be careful; keep it upright," she said, smiling. We opened the box to a crock full of bubbling fermenting cabbage. Despite her German heritage, Kirsten was a bit surprised. The fragrance soon overcame the pine scent of the tree, and the children's faces, lit by the candles, exhibited concern.

Little did we know that this was the beginning of our fermentation journey.

Five years later our homestead in southern Oregon was humming along. By then we were making our own cheeses and yogurts from the milk of our cows and goats. Our fruit trees produced enough apples, plums, and pears for long nights of canning preserves for our four children, who seemed to inhale jam. Christopher sometimes squirreled away enough fruit to make fermented libations, which helped to soothe the long hours. We were not, however, making more than simple sauerkraut.

Then *Wild Fermentation,* by Sandor Katz, arrived in the mail. We began to try different vegetables, and soon our fermentation equipment had grown from that Christmas crock to six Harsch crocks, all almost always packed with something from our kitchen garden or the farmers' market. This period centered on making nutritious, flavorful foods for our growing family.

In 2009, we were searching for a way for the farm to pay for itself. Although we'd been making cheese, bread, and cider for years, our valley was blessed with many other producers of those foodstuffs. We decided to produce interesting ferments, ones that highlighted locally grown foods and would inspire people to eat fermented vegetables daily. The beauty of the fermentation process lies in its ancient simplicity — we were able to start with very little capital compared to most small businesses.

Two years later we had a USDA-certified kitchen with two fermenting rooms built into the hillside along with five sinks, an 80-quart stainless steel bowl on wheels, a dozen 10-gallon ceramic crocks, a bunch of knives, and two large, noisy commercial refrigerators. We quickly built a loyal customer base through farmers' markets, demonstrations, classes, and selling our product in some local grocery stores, restaurants, and regional charcuteries. By all measures we were successful, a small but growing solar-powered farmstead business, sourcing local organic vegetables and producing food people loved.

That first year we developed close relationships with local farmers and experimented with making seasonal combinations. The phone would ring: "We have an abundance of garlic scapes. Can you do anything with them?" Usually the answer was, "Hmm, we can try." By the end of the season we'd produced 52 varieties of fermented vegetables that surprised and delighted our customers. Each week at the farmers' market, people were eager to discover what new flavor had emerged from the fermentation cave. It was so much fun . . .

Food processing became an important word combination to us. To move to the next level of success, we needed to standardize the food part and optimize the processing part.

The second fall, when the farmers' market ended and we began to focus on our commercial accounts, reality hit us: Grocery stores and restaurants wanted just a few consistent, inexpensive products. We started working through our production processes, looking for ways we could cut labor costs through automation. The rotary slicer that Christopher had mastered would need to be replaced with a monster food processor, capable of swallowing many whole cabbages per minute. We still needed a walk-in cooler to maximize preservation of the harvest.

The issues of scale, efficiency, and profitability pose quandaries for every small business. We thought there was something critical missing in this projected future — the artist. Our passion lies in the artistry, the attention to each individual flavor, the experimentation, and the discovery of tastes and colors that arise from concoctions that are put in the crock by either necessity or serendipity. One day we looked at each other and realized we couldn't continue down this commercial road.

We had, by this time, learned a lot about fermenting, and also a lot about what people look for in this artisan category of food. We decided to write a book to help you answer the three big questions we heard in our classes, at demo tables, and at our farmers' market stand:

What are the secrets to making a great batch?

Which veggies play well together in the crock, and which just shouldn't be fermented?

Because probiotic foods are so good for us, how can we enjoy them with every meal?

Fermenting vegetables is simple once you know the tricks. We believe that all of us should be making our own krauts and pickles and condiments.

About the Book

In part 1, Dipping into the Brine: Fermentation Fundamentals, you'll learn the scientific nuts and bolts of fermentation. You'll read about what's happening under the brine and why this salty liquid is essential. There is a discussion on salt, which is really the only ingredient you'll need other than vegetables. We'll share some thoughts on fermentation as preservation and introduce you to the tools of the trade.

Part 2, Mastering the Basics: Kraut, Condiments, Pickles, and Kimchi, is a thorough tutorial on the ins and outs of fermenting vegetables. We'll guide you with words and pictures from the traditional — mastering sauerkraut, brine pickling, and kimchi — to the more contemporary condiments. This section also provides a troubleshooting guide, one based on years of answering questions in our fermentation classrooms.

In part 3, In the Crock: Fermenting Vegetables A to Z, you'll learn how a variety of vegetables (including foraged and sea vegetables) and a few fruits perform in the crock. Along with recipes, we'll share suggestions and tips. This section will present a lot of ideas to inspire your own creations and let you in on our sometimes-humbling experiences in the kitchen and fermentation cave.

Part 4, On the Plate, gets us to the really good stuff: the eating. We had fun coming up with these recipes, sometimes just to hear our kids say, often woefully, "You're not going to put a ferment in that, are you?" We aim to rock sauerkraut's rap as a hot dog food and introduce new flavor profiles that will delight you and your family.

Throughout the book there are stories and recipes highlighting some of the professional fermentistas who bring this artisanal food to tables throughout the country.

Whether you're new to fermented vegetables or a lifelong devotee of the crock, this book has something for everyone. Let's get started.

Part 1

Dipping into the Brine
Fermentation Fundamentals

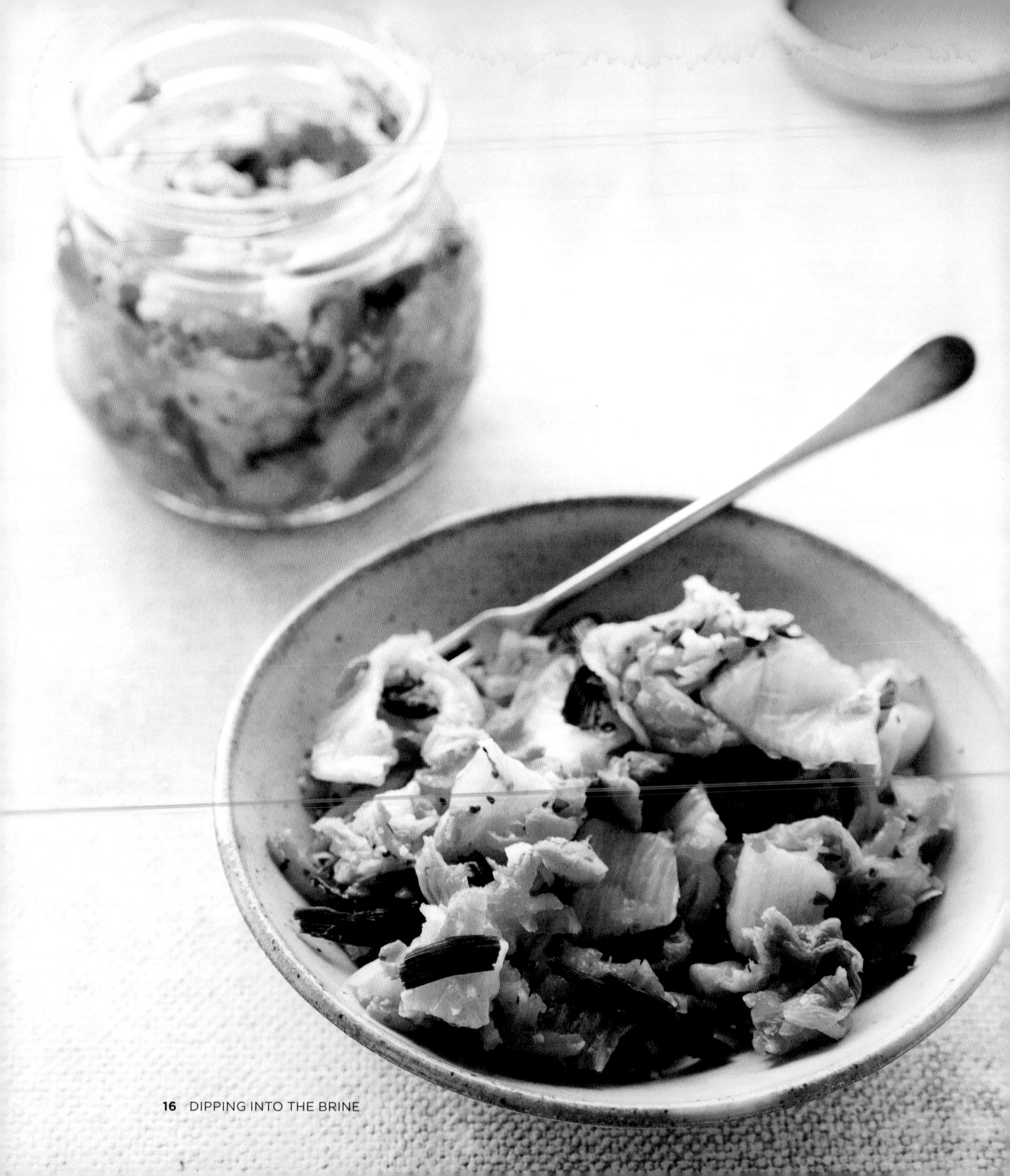

Our society is built upon a hodgepodge of eating habits and cultural traditions, both lost and found. Everything from processed foods to whole foods and empty foods is available, and we see our health growing better or worse, depending on our choices. People have made lifestyle changes and tried diet after diet to find health. The 1970s brought us the back-to-the-land movement, *Diet for a Small Planet* (by Frances Moore Lappé), and macrobiotics. More recently, people have tried high-protein, low-carb recipes with the Atkins and Paleo diets, and fruitarians eat raw fruit only. At the same time, chefs around the country are taking foods to new places with flavor and textures.

Food celebrities such as Alice Waters of Chez Panisse and the food writer Mark Bittman have shown what's possible with simple but seasonal foods cooked to perfection, and Michael Pollan continues to push us to look squarely at how we grow and consume our food. The locavore movement and farm-to-table eating aim to address everything from small-farm economics and food safety and quality to eating seasonal foods produced locally. In 1999, Sally Fallon's *Nourishing Traditions* prescribed eating traditional foods prepared in time-honored ways. That same year Hawthorne Valley Farm in Columbia County, New York, likely started one of this generation's first farmstead sauerkraut cellars. The revival of lost culinary methods and arts, like fermentation, started to attract a wide audience. Fermentation became more than just a method for making wine and cheese; it branched out to vegetables, which are now a legitimate artisanal food, honoring traditional methods and science to preserve food for flavor and color. This goes beyond keeping food from spoiling (the original use) and differs significantly from preservation techniques that erode flavor and nutritive value.

What is this book *not* about? It's not about wine and cheese, beer and sourdough, kombucha and chocolate; these are the already well-known and sexy members of the fermented-food club. It's also not about pickling with vinegar or using starter cultures and whey.

What you have in front of you is a book about lacto-fermenting modest, humble vegetables by the oldest, most straightforward method: with salt (and sometimes water). As you explore the recipes, you'll experience tang, zest, effervescence, and pizzazz.

And all you'll need to unlock the power and flavor of high-quality produce is a few jars or a crock, a bit of salt, and fresh veggies. This book is your passport to a culinary adventure. *Bon voyage*!

CHAPTER 1

Back to the Future

VEGETABLE FERMENTATION AS PRESERVATION

Fermenting vegetables is a simple, inexpensive process that was used reliably for a few thousand years. Then, in the early 1900s, technical innovations promised things the crock just couldn't deliver. Canned jars of food remain stable on a shelf for years. Blanch your veggies, toss into a bag, and store in the freezer — what could be easier? No heavy crocks to clean, no time spent monitoring and skimming off any impurities; it was all very modern and clean and safe.

Only in more recent years have nutritionists begun to understand what all that sterilizing and freezing did to the vitamins and minerals that make vegetables good for us — not to mention the flavor. Enter fermentation, or, to be accurate, reenter fermentation.

Now fermented foods are considered artisanal, a combination of traditional methods and scientific knowledge used to preserve food for flavor, color, and nutritive value.

When we bring vegetables into the kitchen, we hope to preserve them long enough to enjoy them, so we wash them and keep them at the proper temperature. Despite that, a 2004 study by the University of Arizona found that 40 percent of the food grown in the United States goes to waste, and a large portion of that is what consumers let spoil in their fridge. Every year the average household sends $600 in food to the landfill (for some of us that is actually the compost pile or out to the chickens). So if you couldn't resist that beautiful bunch of turnips at the farm stand but have no idea how to prepare them, think fermentation. Lactic-acid fermentation is an ideal way to preserve the bounty while retaining nutrients and deepening the flavor profile.

> *Sauerkraut belongs in a barrel, not a can. Our American mania for sterile packaging has removed the flavor from most of our foods. Butter is no longer sold out of a wooden tub, and a whole generation thinks butter tastes like paper. There was never a perfume like an old-time grocery store. Now they smell like drugstores, which don't even smell like drugstores anymore.*
> — CARY GRANT AS DR. NOAH PRAETORIUS,
> IN *PEOPLE WILL TALK* (1951)

Preserving the Harvest

Many batches of fermented vegetables that you make will be consumed within a few days or weeks — you won't be able to help yourself — but fermentation is also a live, nutrition-enhancing, long-term preservation method for the bounty that comes from your vegetable patch, local farmers, and the farmers' market. If you're serious about pickling everything in your garden, consider a ferment refrigerator, which is simply an old refrigerator you set in an out-of-the-way corner and fill with your finished ferments. It will allow you to catch your ferments' flavors just where you like them and effectively keep them there.

Two refrigerators might seem lavish, but it's cheaper than digging a root cellar. And it's all relative: modern Koreans, who traditionally buried their *onggi* pots in soil or under straw for preservation, consider their kimchi refrigerator a basic household appliance.

At our stand at the farmers' market, customers told us many a story about barrels of kraut in their grandparents' basement. One woman said that when she was a child in Wisconsin, her grandmother would give her a bowl and send her down the stairs, through a dark cellar, to get a portion of sauerkraut. She remembered removing the lid of the sauerkraut barrel and then carefully folding back a thick mat of mold. She'd fill the bowl, pat down the remaining kraut, carefully replace the mold mat, and cover with the lid. This mold mat sounds awful, right?, but it kept the kraut anaerobic — that is, alive without oxygen — and therefore safe to eat (see Going Off the Grid: Non-Refrigerated Storage, page 97).

Christopher Writes

It was at our first farmers' market that the questions started coming. "So are you guys sauerkraut makers?" people asked. The question stumped us. Technically yes, but we also made kimchi. Later in the summer we added a line of crackers made from brine. More questions arose when we began serving assorted brines in shot glasses; at that point we were makers of sauerkraut, kimchi, and crackers and bartenders of the brine.

"Traditional food preservationist" seemed like someone who would work in a museum. I've seen "fermentationist," but that's quite a mouthful. A "zymurgologist"? Zymurgy is the branch of chemistry relating to fermentation, and although the word is super cool, it's appropriate for the brewing arts. "Pickler" is the traditional word for the occupation, but that only confused folks. People assumed this meant we made cucumber pickles. Which would mean that for most of the year we were picklers sans pickles.

One frosty day, after we'd set up for the day's market, I headed to Noble Coffee for our morning brew. As Daniel prepared the drinks, he asked what I did. I told him we followed the season, combining the best of the vegetables as they came in from the fields. I rhapsodized about the difference between an early crisp beet and one overwintered and oozing sugars.

"Sounds like a barista to me," he said, as he handed me two steaming cups.

"You know what we are?" I asked Kirsten, as I handed her a cup of coffee.

"Hungry?" she guessed, passing me a breakfast burrito.

"Fermentistas," I said proudly.

Health and Well-Being

Science is in the nascent stages of understanding how our physical and mental health is interlocked with the vitality of the population of bacteria that live with us. We know fermented vegetables are a piece of the puzzle not only in keeping probiotics in our diet, and therefore in our gut, but also in the changes that overcome the vegetables that make their nutrients more available for our bodies to absorb.

Many discussions of vegetable fermentation mention that Captain Cook kept scurvy at bay on his ships with mandatory servings of sauerkraut; it worked, as we know now, because fermentation increases the cabbage's vitamin C. Now we also know that fermentation increases other vitamins and minerals as well. For example, in 2005, a study published in *Food Microbiology* found that when homemade vegetable juices are fermented, their iron is 16 percent more soluble than in the raw juice.

Among many other nutrients critical for the body's well-being are B_{12} and folate. Vitamin B_{12} is difficult to come by for people on a strict vegetarian or vegan diet, as it's present only in animal-based foods. Fermented vegetables, however, contain B_{12}; the bacterium *Lactobacillus reuteri* produces it during the process. This friendly microorganism also munches away on the vegetable sugars, converting the carbohydrates into acid, which is important for people watching their blood sugar.

There are social benefits attached to this culinary art as well. When you cook with family or friends you create a bond — from the food preparation (which can start as early as choosing seeds to grow) to gathering daily at the table. Food keeps us connected both tangibly and immeasurably.

Consider fermenting vegetables as a group activity. Enlist the kids, your significant other, friends, and guests to chop, slice, or grate; salt; and massage, pound, or press vegetables into a crock. No experience is necessary, so even the youngest member can participate. And for the I-don't-like-kraut set, they're sure to at least taste the ferment they helped make.

The Perks of Fermenting Vegetables

Fermentation preserves vegetables raw and without heat, so it retains their vitamins, minerals, and enzymes. But did you know it often enhances them? And the organisms that enable fermentation are themselves beneficial. Here's how fermentation helps:

- » It preserves and enhances B and C vitamins.
- » It makes nutrients more readily available.
- » It aids in digestion.
- » It doesn't call for chemical preservatives.
- » It supports the immune system.

CHAPTER 2

The Inner Life of Pickling

THE SCIENCE BEHIND VEGETABLE FERMENTATION

The recipes in this book all use the simple process of lacto-fermentation to acidify vegetables, not culturing. Yes, these pickled veggies develop flavor and a healthy population of probiotic goodness — they have got culture, for sure. However, semantically speaking, "culturing" implies the adding of a culture, a starter dose of a desired strain of bacteria. This is quite important in cheese making, especially if you are looking to make a specific variety. But in pickling, with the simple encouragement of salt, everything you need is right there on the (preferably organic) fresh vegetable.

Within vegetable fermentation there are three slightly different procedures that will give you the same end result — a lacto-fermented pickled vegetable. First there is kraut making (sometimes called dry salting, which can seem like a misnomer because it is anything but dry) and its condiment variations, described in chapters 4 and 5; the second is brine pickling, in chapter 6; and the third procedure is a melding of the two, which you will learn about with kimchi in chapter 7. In this chapter,

we'll explain how these processes work, what is really going on in your crock, and why it is safe.

Vegetables + Microbes: A Lacto-Fermentation Starter Kit

Fresh fruits and vegetables are naturally covered in microorganisms, especially those grown using organic methods. That is a good thing. These little guys come from plant surfaces, soil, water, and air. Some of them are pathogens. It's not just bacteria, mind you, that are clinging to our future meals. Molds and yeasts are there too, in fact in larger numbers than the friendly lactic-acid bacteria that we want to encourage in our lacto-fermented vegetables. All are held in check while the plant is living. But as soon as it's harvested, it's a race against time as these microorganisms cling to and grow on any place on the plant that's cut, damaged, or bruised. That's why it's so important that the fruits and vegetables are washed well and kept cold to retard the microorganisms' growth.

When we bring these veggies in from the garden or home from the market, it is our responsibility to preserve the nutrients until we eat them. Lactic-acid fermentation is a noble way to deal with nutrient and flavor preservation. Once vegetables are preserved this way, you can eat them as slowly as you like, and here's why: All those microorganisms we mentioned clinging to the plant, good and bad, are just waiting for their turn to alter the vegetables. When you ferment vegetables, you are choosing sides; you are electing the "good guys." Through a simple process that hasn't changed in thousands of years, we allow the lactic-acid–forming bacteria to take over permanently.

For krauts, kimchis, and condiments, we will shred (or micro-thin slice) these vegetables. We do this to break down the cell structure, which helps the salt do its job more efficiently. Shredding also frees up the plants' sugars, which is what lactic-acid bacteria (the good guys) feed on. For brine pickling, we use the vegetables whole or cut in larger pieces.

How Salt Works

How cool is it that just a little salt can preserve fresh vegetables with vitamins intact for months, even years? But don't let this simple ingredient cause confusion; it is actually not very complicated. The first purpose of salt is to draw juices out of the vegetable's cells, which is how our all-important brine is created. This brine is crucial because the lactic-acid bacteria (LAB) are anaerobic, meaning they don't need oxygen. Because many of their competitors need oxygen, we want to move this whole operation underwater or, in this case, under brine.

Salt also acts to enhance the texture of your preserved vegetables because it hardens the pectin in the cells of the vegetables; this helps retain crispness.

Another purpose of salt is to increase salinity, which gives the bacteria we want the upper hand, as the correct saline environment does not inhibit the LAB we are encouraging but does inhibit the forces that decay (or possibly make us sick) — that is, undesirable bacteria and yeasts. This bacterial

LACTOSE INTOLERANCE AND LACTO-FERMENTATION

We get this question a lot: "I am lactose intolerant. Can I eat lacto-fermented vegetables?"

The answer is yes. Fermented vegetables contain no lactose or casein. The term *lacto-fermented* causes a lot of bewilderment to people trying to navigate food intolerances. To begin with, the words are similar. *Lactose* is milk sugar. *Lacto* refers to the lactic acid that is produced by the action of the lactobacillus bacteria. Additional confusion arises because it is the lactobacillus family of bacteria that make milk acidic to form dairy ferments such as yogurt and cheese.

Many sauerkraut recipes, in other publications or on the Web, further the confusion for fermented vegetables because they call for whey (see page 56) as a starter culture, because it contains lactic acid. Since whey is not needed, no dairy need ever get near a lacto-fermented kraut, kimchi, or pickle.

process, which begins with salting, is what produces enough lactic acid to preserve and enhance our vegetables.

Remember that sugars are breaking down, or decomposing as some like to point out, to create lactic acid. Proteins, carbohydrates, and bacteria are being created. Without salt this list of variables has a higher likelihood of causing putrefaction. Salt also inhibits yeasts, which break down the sugars into alcohol instead of lactic acid. A mere 0.8 percent salt to vegetable weight will prevent the type of decomposition you don't want. Ideally this percentage is kept a little higher; otherwise you will risk a softer texture. Our standard is around 1.5 percent, which for a hundred pounds of shredded cabbage (a mountain heaped way above the rim of an 80-quart bowl) means a little more than 2 cups of salt. For comparison, the salinity of seawater is 3.5 percent.

It is also important to understand that too low a sodium content doesn't provide the advantage for the friendly microorganisms, and you can end up with a rotting crock; conversely, too much salt will stop lactic-acid bacteria in their tiny tracks, inhibiting fermentation. With salting, moderation is the key, and your taste buds are your best guide (see page 44).

SALT IN BRINE PICKLING

Vegetables for brine pickling are either whole or cut into larger pieces. These are then immersed in a prepared salt brine. Unlike shredded or thinly sliced veggies, these whole vegetables cannot create their own brine. The vegetables suspended in the salt water interact with the brine in the process of osmosis, which dehydrates the vegetables' own cells, such that the water is replaced by salt water; this begins the lactic-acid fermentation process.

WHOLE VEGETABLES IN SALT BRINE

So You Want to Ferment without Salt?

Any serious fermentista will encounter salt-phobic people who try to make salt-free sauerkraut or want to convince you to do the same. There are certainly a lot of recipes out there on the Web; some require a blender, some use seaweed or celery seeds in place of salt. With care and luck, fermentation can be accomplished without the salt, and some people do so successfully. Expect these ferments to be softer and at times mushy.

But why not use salt in your ferments? Our bodies need salt anyway. Without it we die. A study published in the *American Journal of Medicine* in 2006 reads, "Sodium intake of less than 2300 mg [the daily recommended allowance] was associated with a 37% increase in cardiovascular disease mortality and a 28% increase of all-cause mortality." In other words, without the correct balance of salt and water, the systems in our body stop functioning. As with most things, common sense and balance are key.

For brine pickling, brine strength needs to be more exact and salt content a bit higher than for krauts. For example, cucumbers in too weak a salt brine solution will probably have a soft instead of crunchy texture due to the cucumbers' own enzymes or yeasts and molds getting too much of a foothold. They also will not last as long under cold storage. Too high a salt percentage (say, over 10 percent) can also prevent proper fermentation. These cucumbers not only are very salty but will take much longer to ferment, develop a harder texture, tend to bloat, and become hollow inside. The sweet spot for a crunchy, tasty, sour cucumber pickle that will stand the test of time is salinity around 3 percent — that is, ¾ of cup salt per gallon of pickles.

We've come across a lot of salt-averse folks in our time as fermentistas, and to them and to you we say: combining good vegetables with good salt keeps the process simple and safe. We need salt to survive. This is as good a place as any to get it. Let's not forget the simple fact that salt is a flavor enhancer; fermented vegetables taste so much better with a little salt. Besides, there are so many other processed, corporately produced, salt-laden

PACKING IT IN: MORE SALT IS NOT BETTER

You've probably seen recipes or descriptions of fermented or pickled foods that contain the phrase "packed in salt." Many recipes suggest layering salt and the vegetable; this inevitably leads to a kraut or pickle that is way too salty, even inedible. There are two things at play here. One is that our forebears made saltier krauts, as they had no refrigeration and their health and nutritional needs often depended on the salt in their preserved foods. These salty preserves were also an important flavoring component of the bland, unsalted starches that were the bulk of their meals.

The second factor is that fledgling sauerkraut makers often think that more salt will assure safety. It is a misconception that salt alone preserves. Let's forget about "packed in salt" and remember that salt draws out the liquid from what is being preserved. This liquid becomes the brine, and only enough salt is required to make the brine more hospitable to friendly lactic-acid bacteria that acidify the vegetables. This acidification is the preservative.

More than once, folks came to our market stand asking if we gave advice. They'd confess they'd made a batch of kraut on their own that was too salty to eat, and they were still waiting for it to mellow out. In one case a husband needed us to tell his wife to throw away the salty kraut that had been in a crock in the basement for three and a half years. It's always hard to break the news that this kraut isn't going to get any more palatable. It does not get less salty as it ferments and ages; if anything, as brine evaporates, the salt becomes more concentrated.

If you have a too-salty batch in your history, or if you've never made sauerkraut, the recipes in this book will guide you to the proper amounts of salt. Know that the key to success is to add salt gradually and taste as you go. You'll read more about this in chapter 4's Adding Salt section.

foods that are less worth eating if you're trying to reduce salt intake.

Thinking Outside the Crock: Your Fermenting Environment

The environment for your active ferment (prior to storage) includes temperature, light, oxygen, pH, and time. Temperature and light are the external conditions that affect all the magic going on inside the crock. Within the crock, we will explore the significance of oxygen, pH, and that ever-slippery fish: time. These elements are not only a part of the fermentation process, they are the steps in the recipes you'll follow later in the book.

TEMPERATURE AND LIGHT

Most recommendations for temperature are to ferment between 55 and 75°F; this range is especially conducive to *L. plantarum* and *L. brevis*, some of the rock stars of the lactobacillus community. Keeping the temperature relatively consistent is important to encourage fermentation. The higher the temperature, the quicker the acid develops, resulting in a shorter fermentation time. When the temperature is too high, everything speeds up and the organisms don't have time to develop properly, which is evident in underdeveloped acidity and off-flavors. Conversely, when the ferment is too cold in the early stages, the LAB are sluggish and can't reproduce fast enough to develop the acidity that keeps the rotting organisms out of the crock.

Ideally it is best to keep your ferment in a dark place and certainly out of direct sunlight, which could cause light damage and temperature fluctuations in your crock and thus disrupt the bacteria's work. Dark doesn't have to be pitch black and in a cave (though cave fermenting is nice); the ferment can be in the corner of a counter, out of direct sunlight. Despite the imperfections of a counter for fermenting, we still recommend having the crock or jar nearby so you can easily keep an eye on it, especially when you're first learning. They say a watched pot doesn't boil, but an unwatched crock *will* bubble over.

EXHALING: CO$_2$, OXYGEN, AND YOUR FERMENT

As we discussed in the salt section earlier, we need to keep our veggies submerged in brine in order to create an oxygen-free environment where the lactobacilli can thrive and the undesirable bacteria and yeast cannot. Pickles are periodically topped up with fresh brine, and krauts are sometimes repeatedly pressed down to keep them submerged. Additionally, if the brine surface is not tightly covered, yeasts, molds, and aerobic (air-requiring) bacteria will form. Most of the time any mold and bacteria (in the form of scum) can be skimmed off, leaving a safe and fresh ferment underneath. But here is the balancing act during this process: we don't want to disturb the ferment too much, as this can also invite yeast spores and oxygen. At a certain point, the aerobic bacteria will lower the brine acidity by eating the lactic acid, and the result will be a spoiled jar or crock.

During fermentation, the most important task is to show the CO$_2$ out the door, usually by pressing on the weight (see Followers and Weights, pages 36–39). When the air bubbles are pushed out, brine replaces that space, keeping oxygen from moving in.

A TICKING CROCK: TIME AND YOUR FERMENT

Fermenting takes time, and time is the *cooking* in terms of fermentation. It is with time that the chemistry silently changes, melding flavors, breaking down starches, and enhancing the food's digestibility. Think about the bread-making process as an instructive analogy to the curing times of your fermentations. In a bread recipe there is the fairly concrete baking time — *45 minutes at 350°F* — but then there is the rise time, when the dough must rise *in a warm, draft-free place until it has doubled in size.* If you bake bread you know this amount of time depends on the temperature, quality of yeast, quality of water, and other factors. In both cases you are waiting for a live biological process to work diligently at what it does best — process sugar. So, instead of *until doubled*, you will have *until sour* as your guide. For example, smaller vessels at warmer temperatures will mean shorter fermentation cycles; larger crocks and cooler temperatures will take longer.

We are often asked when optimum probiotic content is achieved. It seems there is not a standard formula. There is a progression of diverse bacterial species as they move through the cycle. Different colonies peak at distinctive points during fermentation. There are also seasonal conditions and types of vegetables to consider. Ultimately the thing to understand is that you will get the benefits whenever you choose to eat your fermented vegetables. If they taste great, then you will eat them, and that alone will make them infinitely healthier than anything that the curing time or process can deliver.

In technical terms, your vegetables are considered properly fermented when they are below a pH of 4.6. Remember from science class that pH is a measure of the acidity and alkalinity of a solution — in our case, the brine — that is a number on a scale of 0 to 14. The value of 7 represents neutrality; the lower numbers indicate increased acidity, and higher numbers, increased alkalinity. When the pH is closer to neutral, the solution is more welcoming to the growth of many microorganisms, though not always the ones we want; we want only the acid-loving LAB to find the brine hospitable, so we are aiming for numbers below 4.6.

While acidity level can be objectively determined with a pH test, in our experience the proper acidity development is clear to the taste buds (and incidentally, all the ferments that we've double-checked with pH strips were well below 4.6). That said, we want you to be comfortable and successful, so if it will put you at ease to know the pH level, consider using pH test strips (see page 44).

LET'S HEAD TO THE KITCHEN

You may be new to vegetable fermentation. Maybe you've heard rumors of nasty smells and scum. You know there are bacteria, and haven't you been told your whole life bacteria make you sick? Turns out, science tells us, we are the sum of all of our good bacteria, and not enough of it in our system can make us sicker. Fermented vegetables are a live food and sometimes react in ways you may not expect. You may encounter unfamiliar odors, tastes, and textures. Throughout this book we will present you with information that will give you the opportunity to understand your experiences and learn the artistry of vegetable fermentation.

CHAPTER 3

Crocks and Rocks

THE TOOLS OF THE TRADE

One of the attractive qualities of vegetable fermentation as a culinary art is its minimalism. Less kitchen equipment is required than for most culinary pursuits — no special pots, pans, or kettles, not even a stove. To pickle, you need only a bowl, a knife, a cutting board, a jar or crock, some kind of weight, and a bit of salt. (Okay, you will need some vegetables too.) You can of course elaborate on this list and buy the swanky homemade crocks, hand-turned hardwood tampers, and round glass weights. This section will help you navigate the tools of the trade, including salt, the only rock you can eat.

Material Considerations: Preparing, Curing, and Eating Fermented Foods

You will often hear *never touch your sauerkraut with metal,* or some such warning. Why? Fermentation works as a preservative by acidifying. As vegetables ferment and become acidic, certain kitchen implements may chemically react with the developing acid. This can cause strange flavors, off-textures, or bad kraut. Metal and plastic are two common materials in the kitchen that can work for and against the fermentista.

METALS

Let's start with preparation. When you are preparing vegetables they are not acidic and therefore won't react with your utensils. At this point it is nice to have a container big enough to toss, mix, massage, or pound the ingredients in, since your initial vegetable volume is often double that of your final product. Go ahead and use your large stainless steel bowl.

The next phase of concern is during fermentation. The acidifying process is beginning, so until your ferment is ready to eat you want to make sure you use nonreactive materials; these are often stoneware (the crocks), glassware, wood, hard plastics, silicone, and high-quality stainless steel.

So let's talk about what not to use. Common reactive metals to avoid with acidified foods are aluminum, copper, cast iron, and low-grade stainless steel. Because stainless steel is an alloy, the quality of metals used in its composition can vary. Much of the stainless cookware available will react with the salts and acids in fermenting food. The best type of stainless steel for the fermenting stage is a high-grade surgical quality.

Some housewives are in the habit of using copper vessels for pickle making because copper gives a good color to pickles. Never use a copper kettle because the copper salts which give this color and which are transferred to the pickles are poisonous. . . . If proper methods are followed, the salt and acids in the brine produce the desired firmness without any additions.
— A 1918 TENNESSEE EXTENSION PUBLICATION

Using pots or implements made of these reactive materials will result in metals, like chrome and nickel, leaching into your ferment. Don't use them during fermentation, for storage, or when cooking this acidic food. We once cooked a potato soup using brine broth in our favorite cast iron soup pot. The soup turned gray-lavender and tasted like metal; it was inedible.

However, when it's time to eat your creations, there's no need to hunt for wooden forks every time — once your ferment is done, serving and eating with stainless steel cutlery is fine.

PLASTICS

Plastics are next in the group of reactive materials. In the simplest terms the more malleable a plastic, the more volatile it is. For example, soft flexible plastic wrap exchanges synthetic ions with food more quickly than a #2 plastic water jug, and a more rigid plastic bowl is even less reactive. It is the polyvinyl chloride (PVC) typically found in plastics, especially wrap, that leaches toxins, including the hormone-disrupting toxin diethylhexyl adipate (DEHA), into the surface layers of food. Another ingredient in many plastics is bisphenol A (BPA), which has received a lot of press for the damage it can do to our health.

In this book we use plastics sparingly, especially since it is a nonrenewable resource. In some cases plastic products can be the simplest choice for a successful ferment — in some condiment recipes, we use water-filled ziplock bags as a weight. Freezer bags don't contain phthalates or BPA (they are actually a rigid, not stretchy, plastic) and won't degrade in acid or salt. Heavy-duty freezer bags can be carefully washed and reused.

If you want to get away from plastic altogether, with a little ingenuity you can ferment without it. For the flexibility of plastic you might try nonreactive silicone for strainers and other utensils used with acidic krauts and pickles. We have also used round silicone mats, which have a long, reusable life, as primary followers directly on top of the ferment. Silicone is sold in different shapes and sizes and you can cut it to fit your crock if you can't find the right size. Small glass or ceramic disks that fit in jars (see the resources, page 360) can replace plastic in smaller ferments.

Fermentation Vessels

As with any trade, having the right tool for the job can save a lot of frustration. Outfitting your kitchen for fermenting vegetables is easy. There is a lot of bling available, but ultimately all you need is a vessel — whether it's a glass jar or one good crock.

Ceramic vessels have proven themselves over time for the art of fermenting. They keep your ferment in a cool and dark environment, which is just what the bacteria need to survive. That said, you might not want to use your grandparents' old stoneware crock that has been holding utensils or dried flower arrangements, at least without testing it for lead first (many older glazes had lead in them). You can take your crock to a lab near you

for a test or do it yourself. Follow the instructions on a lead paint test kit, available at a hardware store. Find an area on the outside of the crock, preferably along the bottom, and scratch the surface to take a sample for testing. Also check your crock for hairline cracks, as they can be a source of contamination.

A few years ago new crocks were difficult to obtain, but now there are crocks available in many sizes at many hardware, garden, and cooking stores. Unfortunately, not all of them come with lids or followers, which we will explain in a moment. For large batches, straight-sided crocks are your best bet for a low-cost, large vessel that is not plastic. They are a great medium for excellent flavor, but they are heavy. Simple furniture dollies work well for moving crocks when they are crammed full and for keeping the more porous unglazed crock bottoms off the ground, preventing moisture collection and the formation of mold there; this mold shouldn't affect your ferment but is no fun to deal with.

One thing to consider when shopping for a crock is how much upper-body strength you'll need to move your crock around. Crocks are heavy. Our 7.5 L Gärtopf crock weighs 19 pounds empty; completely full, we are lugging 33 pounds.

WATER-SEAL CROCKS

For the serious fermentista, or the cook who enjoys the beauty of tools, there are the Cadillacs: German and Polish water-seal crocks. These vessels have an outer deep rim with a trough that holds water. When the lid is placed in the trough, the water creates an airlock. The lid has a small hole in the rim that allows carbon dioxide to escape without allowing air into the crock. They come with heavy followers (see page 36) that nest into the pot, making the crock almost foolproof. Compared to a simple straight-sided stoneware crock they are expensive, but they do eliminate some of the difficulties around controlling the fermentation environment.

Some management of the trough is required. The water trough can also take some finagling when you are removing your fermented goodies, especially if the water has gotten murky. When the lid and trough are both clean, it is simpler to remove what is in the crock without contamination. Here's how:

» Have a plate ready to slip under the lid as you lift it to prevent trough water from dripping back into the brine.

Looking into a water-seal crock; water in the rim creates an airlock when the lid is in place

» Clean out the water. The easiest way to do this is with a turkey baster and a towel to sop up the rest.

» When there is brine to remove, use a ladle instead of trying to lift the crock to pour it off.

ONGGI POTS

For making kimchi the traditional vessel is called an *onggi* pot. The type of soil used to make the clay, which is worked by hand, leaves small air pores. This creates a breathable pot, which is one of the unique characteristics of onggi pottery. Pores in the clay allow fermentation gases to leave, taking smell and any bitter taste with them and ensuring the quality of the fermented food inside.

The one drawback is that it's difficult to find a follower for these pots, as the opening is smaller than the surface area you must cover inside. Traditionally rocks are used.

Until recently these pots were only available in Korea, but now potters throughout the United States are creating fermenting crocks of various types. Our favorites come from Adam Field Pottery. (See the resources, page 360.) If you find one that speaks to you, it is like having a friend in the kitchen.

JARS

The advantage of using glass jars, rather than crocks, is that they are cheap, you can watch what is happening, and you can make small batches. You can also try unusual vegetable combinations without committing to a large amount. For this purpose we almost always use jars. We also like to use them when the cucumber plants are giving just enough for a jar of pickles every day, but not enough to make a full crock. As a day's worth of

TRADITIONAL ONGGI POTS

cucumbers matures to pickles, it can get sealed and stored in the same jar.

Jars require some babysitting to keep the ferment under the brine and the brine in the jar. Jars are harder to weight sufficiently to keep the CO_2 from creating air pockets. The tendency is for the gas to push the brine up and out of the jar. In the early stages of an active ferment you will have to gently press on your weight (often several times a day) to get the brine back down between the vegetables. The advantage of a jar is that you can see whether your ferment needs tending. (Alternatively, in a well-packed water-seal or onggi-type crock, this constant pressing is not an issue.) Because we want to keep our light-shy bacteria out of direct light, it's a good idea to cover glass vessels that are actively fermenting with a clean towel.

Jars can also present a disadvantage in a large-batch situation. It can be unwieldy and time-consuming to monitor a bunch of individual ferments of the same batch; you are dealing with more variables and more surface area, the latter of which can cause more loss to spoilage. It is more practical and makes for a more consistent product to make one large batch of pickles, kraut, or kimchi and then transfer the ferment into smaller jars for long-term storage in the refrigerator.

FOOD-GRADE BUCKETS

While 5-gallon plastic food-grade buckets are a popular and inexpensive choice for larger home-scale batches of kraut or pickles, they are not our first choice as a fermentation vessel. We can taste a subtle difference in krauts fermented in stone or glass versus plastic. We do, however, store and transport large batches of finished ferments in plastic buckets — sealed lids and handles are not overrated.

Followers and Weights

Because keeping your vegetables submerged in brine is crucial to success, it is essential to find a method that works best for you to maintain this anaerobic environment.

In the recipes, we will refer to *primary followers*, *secondary followers*, and the *weight*, which includes *weighted followers*.

PRIMARY FOLLOWERS

The primary follower goes right on top of your ferment. It acts as a barrier, keeping any small bits of vegetable from floating out from under the brine. This can be an outer cabbage leaf, or for a large crock a few leaves, to create a blanket. Usually this cabbage-leaf blanket will keep all the small shreds submerged under the brine. There are many other acceptable leaves, which you will learn about in the recipes, but grape or horseradish leaves also are large and work well (see also page 79).

A primary follower might also be a bit of plastic wrap, some cheesecloth, or a piece of silicone mat or food-grade plastic drying screen, like you would see in a food dehydrator, cut to the size of your crock. Any of these can be tucked under the secondary follower to keep the vegetables from floating up out of the brine.

SECONDARY FOLLOWERS

Unless you have a water-seal crock, you will need to come up with your own solution for a secondary follower. It will need to fit the opening of the container and nestle over as much of the top of the ferment as possible. Its purpose is to provide weight to keep the vegetables submerged. For most crocks, a plate can work; for a larger opening, check at thrift stores, where you might find the flat glass plate from a microwave. The direction the plate is used, right side up or upside down, depends on the shape of the opening and whichever direction will assist you most in keeping that ferment tucked in place.

You can make your own follower out of wood by cutting a round piece from a solid piece of hardwood such as maple, but not aromatic wood like pine or cedar as this will affect flavor. You'll also need to take into consideration that the wood will soak up brine and expand in the crock.

Christopher Writes

One man shared a sad story with us of his first and only batch of sauerkraut that ended in a shattered mess. He had inherited a beautiful crock from his grandmother and needed a follower. He cut one from wood to fit his crock's opening, made the batch of kraut, and tucked it out of the way. A few days later he found a pool of brine accumulating outside his closet door and a prominent crack running down his beloved heirloom. The custom wooden follower had swollen in the brine and eventually cracked the sides of the crock. "I had to throw it all out," he told us, "and I never had the heart to try it again."

To make a wood follower, mark the dry wood about ½ inch smaller than the diameter of the inside of your crock. Drill a small hole in the center of the round to allow brine to flow through and give you something to hold onto when you want to remove it. Soak the new follower in water for a day or two to gauge expansion before you try it in your crock. We like to keep our wooden followers conditioned by periodically rubbing them with an ointment made from a little olive oil in melted beeswax at about a 50:50 ratio.

VARIOUS FOLLOWERS
Wood, Stone, a Plate

The German and Polish water-seal crocks come with a two-piece ceramic follower that fits snugly down into the crock. These don't require extra weight, as the followers are snug and the carbon dioxide is able to escape cleanly through the seal created by the water trough. These are porous and when not in use need to be stored upright in a way that allows airflow; otherwise they can become musty. For most other followers, you will still need some weight (see below).

WEIGHTS

When fermentation begins, the lactic-acid bacteria (LAB) are producing not only lactic acid but also an abundance of carbon dioxide. That carbon dioxide will lift even heavy granite followers. The more weight you have, the better you are able to keep the brine in the vegetables and not flowing over the top of the jar or crock.

Options for weights will vary with the size of your crock or jar. Remember not to use reactive materials, like that heavy can of organic tomato paste you got through a buying club. For a wide-mouth pint or quart jar you can use a water-filled, sealed pint jar over the primary follower. In this situation the jar acts as follower and weight.

Some people like to use a beautiful round river stone. If you find one, just remember you don't want one with high lime content. Sterilize it by boiling it for 10 minutes.

The larger the crock, the more weight you will need. We initially thought our heavy handmade granite followers would have enough weight on their own, but as the carbon dioxide was created our stone began to lift off the kraut and we had to place three water-filled gallon jars on top of the stone followers.

THE ZIPLOCK BAG METHOD

One popular way to make a combination follower and weight is the ziplock bag method. Filled with liquid and zipped tight, the plastic bag seals like the primary follower and keeps everything tidy and weighted down. This all-in-one solution works extremely well for jars and other small vessels and is our favorite method for our concentrates, pastes, chutneys, or any ferment with very little brine. That said, if you like this method, you can use it on large ferments, too. We have seen it used on 55-gallon barrels with much larger bags.

It's best to use the heavier-gauge freezer bags. The quart size works well as a weighted follower for half-pint, pint, and quart jars. A gallon jar requires a gallon-size bag. Half-gallon jars can use either size, but if you have enough room, the extra weight the gallon bag provides is helpful. For larger crocks, use a 2-gallon or larger bag. To employ, open the bag and place it in the jar on top of the vegetables, pressing it onto the surface and wedging it around the edges. To add weight, fill the bag with water until there are no more air pockets; then seal the bag. You can also fill the bag with brine so that if the bag leaks it won't contaminate your ferment as fresh water will; if you are concerned about leaks, you can fill the bag over the sink first to test. We have only had a leak once or twice. If you do experience a leak, the ferment may not be ruined; only the flavor and texture will be affected.

Alex Hozven of Berkeley's Cultured Pickle Shop shared a technique that provides the weight needed but ensures that liquid will not accidentally leak into the ferment: rather than water or brine, she uses clean pebbles in the bag.

As interest in the fermentation arts grows, so does creativity around it. There are artists making handmade weighted followers for small jars, and small glass fermenting weights are also abundantly available (see the resources, page 360). If you are an avid fermentista, these reusable followers are worth the investment.

Coverings

A covering is something that goes over the whole followed-and-weighted affair. It lets the air escape while keeping out dust, bugs, or other contaminants while you're actively fermenting. Cheesecloth, muslin, a kitchen towel, or another clean cloth, draped over the top of the crock, is a simple solution. Sometimes, when using a jar, you can use the lid as your covering, placed on top but not tightened. We have seen lids made from wood, which are beautiful, but the downside is that they cannot cover a weight that might be sticking above the rim of the crock. Our solution: homemade cloth shower caps!

Christopher Writes

My mother offered a dozen times to help in any way she could with our farmstead kraut business. We hadn't come up with anything for a retired high school art teacher to do. Mom had sewn for years. So one day when we were trying to figure out how to make giant shower caps, Kirsten came up with the idea of asking my mom to sew these bonnets for us. Mom was thrilled to help us out. We got cute and functional caps made from vintage patterned material. They were so charming that when we commissioned smaller ones for the 1-gallon crocks for one of our classes, we had a bit of a tussle amongst the students for their favorite patterned caps. Some fabric, elastic, and a needle and thread are all you need.

Airlocks

Airlock systems are gaining popularity; as a friend pointed out, "I find they allow me to neglect my ferments." These airlocks affix to the lid of a jar, keep any new air out of the fermentation environment, and give the CO_2 an opportunity to escape, often without spilling the brine. Without the airlock, you must leave your lids loose to let CO_2 escape, which means keeping a closer eye on oxygen contamination and brine loss. An airlock certainly can make the job of babysitting your jars simpler. It can also improve the flavor quality of the ferment because introduction of "outside influences" are kept in check.

Well then, you ask, why wouldn't we just always use an airlock? Because fermentation is so simple that you truly don't need one, and we want to make sure everyone understands how the process works. Plus, some of us just don't want to purchase, clean, or find room in the drawer for one more gadget.

There are many commercially available jar lids with built-in airlocks that are easy to use, though a little pricier (see the resources, page 360). One brand, Perfect Pickler, fits quart-sized mason jar lids. Another jar system, called Pickl-It, uses bail-style glass jars outfitted with an airlock. We experienced corrosion of the bail wire, but the wire does not come in contact with the ferment, so it will not affect the food.

When filling a jar with an airlock, you will still need to make sure you have not over- or under-filled the jar. Everything must be snugly pressed into the jar with a follower to help keep things in place.

Tampers

Tampers, also called pounders, are often turned blocks of wood that are used to press the ferment into the vessel. Having something to help compact your ferment is very helpful, as it can be difficult to maneuver your hand in a small jar and can turn into a small workout in a larger crock (see sidebar). In some cases this tool can also be used to bruise the shredded and salted vegetables to further release brine. This is a handy tool; however, as in most things, a little ingenuity and a look through your utensils can produce a suitable

tamper. For example, the plunger from a Vitamix blender will work, as will a solid straight-sided (French or Asian-style) rolling pin.

Kirsten Writes

Tamping is always my job. Let me tell you, pressing kraut into a 10-gallon crock is quite a workout. And note: I said pressing, not pounding. Pressing is using most of your weight and strength to push on the kraut to remove air pockets and bring the brine to the surface. I like to use my fist, which is pretty demanding. Pressing kraut in a small jar can be equally as demanding, but on your fingers instead of your fists, as most people's hands don't fit inside the jar.

Our dear friend Jerry, a retired engineer and avid whitewater river guide, made our first tamper from a wooden canoe paddle by replacing the wide part of the paddle with a beautiful rounded wooden pounder. Two tools in one! He now sells his tampers and pounders in a variety of sizes (see the resources, page 360). You can also sometimes find pounders in antique stores or from local or online woodworker-fermentistas.

Slicing, Shredding, Chopping

Much of the success of a good batch of kraut is its finished texture, which is related to how you prep your cabbage. We had never given texture much thought when we bought a hand-cranked rotary slicer; we bought it to avoid hurting ourselves shredding case after case of cabbage with a 14½-inch blade of sharpened steel, a knife just short of a machete. With some of our first earnings we set out to find something safer, and we discovered a hand-cranked rotary slicer called the Nemco Easy Slicer.

The Nemco was perfect: versatile, affordable, accommodated most vegetables, and came with a number of slicing and shredding plates. It was made in the USA, quiet to operate, and definitely fit our green, off-the-grid technology.

When the cabbage quarters lined up just right in the hopper, the slice was beautiful, but we were left with all the extra bits that didn't quite go through, so the total effect was not uniform. We called the texture "farmhouse," indicating its rustic handmade character. Our customers told us many times that they especially liked this texture.

All of this is to say that the people who enjoy your crock's bounty will notice and appreciate the consistency of your kraut. So when you think about slicing your vegetables, consider the texture you like. A thin slice is easy to brine but may produce a soft ferment. A large, chunky chop provides a hearty finish but is difficult to bring to brine. Find the in-between that works for you. Meanwhile, let's look at some of the other tools you'll need.

KNIVES

A few good-quality sharp knives are all you need. The traditional chef's knife comes in a few sizes. The larger 10- or 12-inch sizes are nice for cutting through cabbages and thick-skinned squash. A smaller chef's knife is good to have for general chopping, slicing, dicing, and mincing. We also always keep a good paring knife alongside the cutting board for cutting out blemishes or other small tasks.

SLAW BOARDS

Every fermentista gets to a point when the question of slaw boards comes up. This happens when your batch sizes have moved beyond a knife and a cutting board. When we started making sauerkraut, everyone with an old slaw board they had picked up at a yard sale "donated" it to us. They are easy to find in antique stores, often without the sliding box that holds the cabbage while you move it across the series of blades. They look good hanging on the wall but can be a danger to the fingertips when in use.

You can find beautiful new slaw boards in kitchen stores and online. These boards are the same as the traditional design, just shiny, complete, and sharp. Unless you find one with a hand guard you may want to pick up a pair of sturdy slash-resistant gloves while you are shopping.

HAND GRATERS AND PEELERS

Hand graters and slicers come in every shape and size. We use ours for grating vegetables. A microplane grater/zester is wonderful for garlic cloves, citrus zest, or ginger and turmeric root.

Peelers are good for making ribbons of hard vegetables, such as carrots, daikons, beets, or any other root. We use these ribbons to add whimsical strips of carrot color to a kraut or to mix up the texture of a kraut or condiment. Let your imagination guide you.

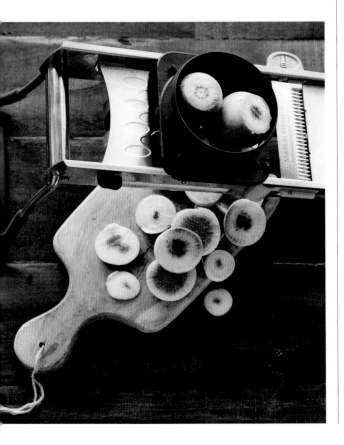

MANDOLINES

Mandolines allow the fermentista to experiment with vegetable texture and to create unique ferments. We have come to love the versatility of the mandoline with its many attachments, especially for the demands of our many condiments (relishes, chutneys, and salsas) that require, for example, micro-thin slices and tiny dices (see Mastering Condiments, page 65).

Mandoline slicers, with their shiny, sharp series of blades, can be intimidating, but most come with a hand guard that when used properly makes them safer than a knife. If you have a mandoline without a hand guard, again we suggest you seek out the sturdy slash-resistant gloves available in kitchen stores.

FOOD PROCESSORS

Food processors are convenient for various aspects of grating and slicing certain vegetables. The grating attachment is perfect for harder root vegetables like beets, carrots, and celeriac.

We find it doesn't save any time to slice cabbage with the food processor, as it's a battle just to get the cabbage small enough to fit down the hopper and through the slicing blade, at which point you might as well have sliced it with a knife. The slicing disc is useful, however, for thinly slicing vegetables and offering texture options (like a mandoline).

The chopping blade is useful for chopping herbs and making pastes. For the kimchi seasoning paste, for example, we like to mince the garlic and ginger with the pepper flakes in a food processor.

Other Equipment

Here are a few other gadgets you may want in your fermentation tool kit.

DEHYDRATORS

Dehydration opens up a whole range of ingredients that otherwise would spoil a ferment. For example, fruit, in general, has too much sugar to ferment well; however, dried cranberries, dried pears, or raisins are delicious in many ferments. Tomatoes or mushrooms will taste off if they're fermented fresh, but the concentrated dehydrated flavor of these items is delicious in a ferment. Many fresh fruits and vegetables can be purchased already dehydrated, but what about fermented veggies? You might enjoy making your own probiotic-rich seasonings by dehydrating already fermented veggies either to sprinkle on a salad or to flavor a meal (see Seasonings, page 75).

KITCHEN SCALES

Using scales to measure ingredients has become much more common in the United States, yet it is still not a widespread trend, a conundrum which Farhad Manjoo aptly describes in a 2011 *New York Times* article: "This creates a chicken-and-egg problem for the kitchen scale. Cooks don't own scales because recipes don't call for one, and recipes don't call for one because cooks don't own one."

We used a scale for measuring ingredients in our large commercial batches, but we want these recipes to be accessible to everyone. So for larger quantities of vegetables, we give measurements by weight because that is often how they are purchased, but for smaller quantities of herbs and salt, we stick to standard volume measurements.

pH TEST STRIPS

Although we don't use them, if you are new to fermentation or are extra cautious, you can make sure kraut is acidic enough by checking the pH level. A simple way to do this is with pH litmus strips. They are sold online and in brewing supply stores as dip sticks in a pack or in a small tape-dispenser-like roll. These testers come in all different ranges; make sure to find the ones that measure with some degree of accuracy in the acidic range (below 5). The full-range types aren't always specific enough. The strips are simple to use: just dip the end in your kraut and match the color of your strip to the color chart on the box. These are inexpensive compared to a pH meter, which is a very complicated and unnecessary tool for home fermenting (for more about pH, see A Ticking Crock on page 28).

Salt: Shaking Out the Differences

With just salt (and not very much of it) you can preserve fresh vegetables and their nutrients for months, even years. Our ancestors thought this was pretty great, so much so that armies marched across ancient landscapes just to be paid in salt. (Yep, salt is where our word *salary* comes from.) In this section you'll find out which salt to put in your toolbox for the job of brining and about some of the many varieties available for the task.

ISN'T ALL SALT THE SAME?

Not too long ago, kosher pickling salt and sea salt in the bulk bin of a health food store were the only salt choices. Now we can taste our way around our planet with the salts of the earth and sea. Salts of all colors and flavors are available in even the most common of grocery stores. We can choose red or black, finishing, milling or cooking salts, in small crystals or large blocks.

NOT ALL SALTS ARE CREATED EQUAL

With these amazing varieties, there is no reason to settle for kosher pickling salt or other highly refined salts, which contain additives that are not helpful to your ferment. These refined salts are salty in a way that assaults your taste buds. When people come to us with tales of too-salty kraut, the first question we ask is, what kind of salt did you use? The answer is almost always pickling salt. Many salts contain a different ratio of sodium chloride to minerals, which changes the flavor drastically. In our classes we often begin by passing around different salts to taste. People are often surprised at how sweet they can be. All salts are not created equal. Have fun discovering salts. Find a good-quality mineral-rich salt that suits your palate.

The subject of minerals is important in this time of depleted soils. The foods we have are no longer as rich in essential elements as they were previously, and it can be challenging to nourish ourselves properly. We even see it in our farm animals — keeping a small herd of dairy goats healthy became all about getting enough minerals into their systems. It stands to reason that we humans, eating from the same soil, should make sure our diets are mineral-rich. Mineral-rich salt added to nutrient-dense food is a good solution.

Because all salts are not the same, density, and therefore weight, will vary according to mineral content and coarseness. That is partly why the amount of salt given in these recipes is not exact. We have made the same recipe, changing only the salt variety, and had very different results — another good reason to taste your ferments when salting.

WHICH SALT SHOULD I USE?

We like to incorporate mineral-rich salts into our ferments and our diet and try to stay away from salts with unnecessary additives. Here are some of the salts we like to use and those we don't.

Mineral-Rich Salts of the Land. *Redmond Real Salt,* rock salt mined in central Utah, and *Himalayan Crystal Salt,* mined in and around Pakistan, are both salts from remnants of ancient seabeds. These deposits were subjected to considerable heat and pressure to form densely compacted crystals that contain many beneficial trace minerals. These salts of the earth have a very low moisture content. Both of these have a beautiful pink color and are finely ground, which works well for krauts. We used Redmond salt in our business as it was more affordable and "local" compared to salt from Europe or Pakistan. We also delighted in the subtle sweetness that it gave our krauts. Rock salt will make pickling brine that is a bit gritty, but this grit will sink to the bottom of the crock and will not affect the quality of the vegetable.

Mineral-Rich Salts of the Sea. The most common artisan sea salts are *sel gris,* which means gray salt in French, and *fleur de sel,* literally flower of salt. These are commonly known as Celtic sea salt. They are harvested by evaporating seawater in large pans, leaving the salt behind. Also left behind in this unprocessed sea salt are microscopic bits of plankton, minerals, and micronutrients that are made more available to our body through fermentation. These salts have a much higher moisture content. They are quite sweet and wonderful to ferment with. Often, however, these salts are coarse, which means they are slower to break down as you work them into the kraut and build the brine. This can make your job of getting the vegetable to release the brine more difficult. This is simply solved by first giving the coarse salt a light crushing.

Iodized Salt. There is some confusion around how iodized salt affects fermentation. It is said that the antimicrobial properties of iodine inhibit the very bacteria we are seeking to encourage. Technically it is possible that industrialized refined salt with added iodine could inhibit fermentation and cause a discolored product. A refined salt has had the minerals leached out, and the amount of iodine added can be up to 300 percent more than the amounts occurring naturally in unrefined salt. Even the unrefined solar-evaporated sea salts lose a lot of their native iodine through long periods of exposure to the sun. We are not concerned with the trace amounts of iodine in unrefined salts.

Kosher Pickling Salt. We believe most recipes call for kosher pickling salt simply because it has become convention and the label on the box tells us it is for pickling. These flaked crystals have more surface area and are intended to draw the moisture more efficiently. There is also the notion that kosher = pure and therefore there are no additives. True, no iodine has been added. True, it is 99.9 percent refined sodium chloride. So is it pure? The key word in the last sentence is *refined*. The salt begins in a salt deposit in the earth or is dehydrated out of the seawater. A brine is made by pumping water into the raw salt. The resulting salt water is treated with carbon dioxide and sodium hydroxide to separate out the undesirable solids like calcium. This refined liquid is boiled off at high heat in open pans until flaky salt crystals form. Some brands of kosher salts then add sodium ferrocyanide and other chemicals as "anti-caking agents." This does not sound pure to us.

Part 2

Mastering the Basics
Kraut, Condiments, Pickles, and Kimchi

Eat some foods that have been predigested by
bacteria or fungi.

— **MICHAEL POLLAN,** *FOOD RULES: AN EATER'S MANUAL*

When we began selling sauerkraut at the market, people sought us out, and it wasn't always to buy kraut. Sometimes they just wanted to taste our samples, chat, or learn. We were happy to oblige, as we encourage people to take an active role in their food. Our classes were born from this experience, and so was this book.

In this section, you'll encounter the soul of fermentation and the core of what we share with customers and students. Mastering the techniques will ensure success whether you want just plain sauerkraut or to create recipes.

You'll also find the master processes, illustrated step-by-step with photos, for each type of ferment: kraut, condiments, brine pickles, and kimchi. (Throughout part 3, we'll refer you to these chapters for details and guidance, although once you've made the basic recipes a few times, you won't need much help.) You'll also find storage directions, a troubleshooting section, and an appendix on page 356 to visually guide you through this thing called scum!

Before You Get Started

Before beginning a fermentation project, wash your hands well with regular soap and warm water; avoid using antibacterial soaps, as these could inhibit the fermentation process (especially once you have both hands elbow-deep in cabbage). Nor do you want to clean your vegetables with soaps, vegetable washes, or antimicrobial rinses, as these can wash off the good bacteria that fermentation requires.

And remember, we are not canning here, so there is no need to sterilize your vessels or tools. Your equipment should be cleaned with warm soapy water, though not with antibacterial or other products that will kill our friends — the lactobacilli. Many people do not use anything but warm water to rinse out their stoneware crocks, believing that this promotes the most amiable environment — perhaps even aiding in the microbial process.

The Fermentista's Mantra: The Path to Success

We give to our students a mantra that helps them with their early batches:

> ## Submerge in brine and all will be fine.

This simple phrase is all you need to remember to keep your ferments safe to eat. We submerge in brine because good bacteria don't need oxygen. Many of the bad guys do, however, so we keep veggies well under the brine.

It's Just a Crock: Your Safety Checklist

Fermenting is a simple process. With some minor variations, all you need is a jar, some salt, and veggies. Things can go awry (see the Scum Gallery, page 358, for examples), but if you follow the directions, you'll end up with fermented vegetables (and some fruits) that are safe and delicious.

Along with the mantra, keep this checklist in mind.

» Clean all work surfaces, tools, and your hands with warm soapy water.

» Rinse vegetables in cool water without soap.

» Keep everything below the brine.

» During fermentation, put the jar or crock where the temperature is a relatively constant 55 to 75°F.

» Store cured ferments in the refrigerator.

» Don't eat if it smells rotten or looks slimy.

Use good water! Really what that means is to use water that is unchlorinated, as chlorine can inhibit fermentation. Increasingly, municipal water systems are adding a combination of chlorine and ammonia that does not evaporate out, called chloramine. To remove chloramine one must use a system that first employs a carbon filter to remove the chlorine in the chloramine molecule, and then a reverse-osmosis filter to remove the remaining ammonia.

CHAPTER 4

Mastering Sauerkraut

In this chapter you'll learn everything you need to know about making sauerkraut, and in the next, its variation, condiments. We'll walk you through the process, showing you the steps in photographic detail, to set you on the path to becoming a fermentation (c)rock star. When you understand how the ingredients work, you can make any variations that strike your fancy.

Kraut making is wonderful for people who don't like to measure, who use formal recipes as a jumping-off point. That said, our recipes do include measurements, but if you have a bit more cabbage than the recipe calls for, toss it in; the ferment won't suffer.

The ingredients are cabbage and salt. As a matter of fact, one of us — we won't name names — would jump feet-first into the cabbage and make a barrel of kraut without knowing any more than that. We want you to make a life-changing first batch, however, so read on before you tackle any of the kraut recipes.

We'll start with the cabbage, then delve into salting, brining, and curing your budding ferment.

Cabbage: Your Raw Material

Our essential vegetable, the cabbage, comes in a variety of sizes. It ranges from a tiny, dense head bred for single-person households to the size of a soccer ball.

For our purposes, one cabbage assumes a 2-pound, tightly packed head. If the heads you have are loose, adjust with some extra leaves. If the heads are exceptionally large and heavy, use one and some extra leaves in a recipe that calls for two.

Then there's the giant, homegrown cabbage that's about to set seed and is loosening for that reason. The head becomes slightly cone-shaped and will eventually open, when the core develops into a flower shoot. At the cone-head stage, you can still make kraut. If it opens too much, though, the leaves are drier, tougher, and greener, and the flavor is different. At that point, it's just not kraut-worthy.

SELECTING THE CABBAGE

Through the miracle of cold storage and refrigerated shipping, you can always find cabbages. They're a staple. Unglamorous. Peasant food. But they're also quite amazing in their variety: there are summer cabbages, fall cabbages, and winter cabbages. Cabbages are a hardy cool-season crop. In northern climates the season begins as the spring-planted cabbages ripen in June and July. This season can last through January or February, but by April cabbages are being shipped from southern farmlands. This is something to be aware of when you want to make a big batch of kraut and are looking for the freshest cabbage possible. Out-of-season cabbages are likely more expensive, and they may be dry from long hauling and storage times.

So what do you look for? You want firm heads with crisp, shiny leaves. (They look dull as they lose vitality.) Check for damage on the outer leaves. If a head is cracked or bruised, chances are there's interior damage. Bypass pre-cut, plastic-wrapped cabbages; they're already losing nutrients.

If you're harvesting from the garden, cut a head right off the root but let some outer leaves remain. It'll sprout baby cabbages from the sides of the root core.

Adding Salt

After coring and shredding the cabbage, it's time to add salt. Don't let this cause you anxiety. While encouraging bacteria seems like a project for the science lab, it is an organic process that has a very tolerant range of what is acceptable. Just as in cooking, there is a degree of flexibility in the amount of salt that tastes right in a dish.

Though these recipes all contain a recommended amount, it is best to begin with half that amount. Taste. You want to taste the salt, but not be overwhelmed by it. Slowly build up to the recommended amount, but don't be afraid to stop if your mixture is beginning to taste too salty. If you find it too salty, add more cabbage. If it's tasty fresh, it will be delicious fermented.

> **FERMENTISTA'S TIP**
>
> ### Taste before You Pack!
>
> *Please, please, please taste your kraut while you are making it. It is the simplest way to ensure success. Make sure you can taste the salt, but it should not be "briny," "salty," or in any way unpalatable. Remember: If it is good fresh, it will be excellent fermented.*

If it's a regular or small batch, you can add the salt after all the cabbage and any accompanying veggies are shredded. If you're doing a very large batch, sprinkle in the salt as you shred and transfer the cabbage to a bowl. This will begin to break down the cell walls and release the juices even before mixing and will help ensure that the salt is spread throughout the batch.

Once the salt is added you'll massage it in with your fingers. Be sure you have washed your hands well in warm soapy water (remember, don't use antibacterial soap, as it can interfere with the fermentation process). Don't be afraid to use your fingers. The process of massaging cabbage is similar to kneading bread dough. Pick some up in your hands and squeeze it. Think deep-tissue Swedish massage, not a gentle back rub. Repeat this process, working through the entire batch. Almost instantly, the cabbage will start glistening, looking wet and limp. There will be a puddle of liquid pooling at the bottom of the bowl. For a large batch, massaging is more of a workout.

When we make 10-gallon crocks of kraut, we thoroughly work in the salt and let the batch sit, covered, so that exposure to air doesn't dry it out. After about an hour we toss and massage it again for a few minutes just to get everything mixed. At this point there is brine building at the bottom. We then let it sit again, often through the rest of the day. Periodically we mix it a bit. At the end of the day it has produced a lot of brine and is ready to be pressed into the crock — the salt does the work.

Help! I Don't Have Enough Brine in My Kraut

You have salted, mixed, and massaged your shredded kraut, but when you squeeze, it is like milking the proverbial turnip. No liquid. Sometimes this happens when veggies are simply drier than usual, which can happen with long refrigeration periods. Sometimes it's because the veggies were not sliced thin enough. Here are some solutions.

First, taste it one more time. If you think it can take more salt, sprinkle in just a bit. If adding more salt was the answer, it's time to pack. If you still don't have enough brine, there are a few more tricks.

With or without added salt, maybe just a little time apart will help the relationship. Cover your bowl and set it aside for about an hour. When you return, the salt should have continued to break down the cell walls of the cabbage, and you should have more brine.

Now massage your kraut again. It should be wetter, but if you are thinking, "So that didn't work, now what?" you could try packing the kraut and pressing it into a crock or jar. You might find a thin brine layer at the top; thin is enough, as long as the cabbage is submerged. If there is still not

enough, put it all back in the bowl. Now you have some choices.

Do not add salt water to sauerkraut! Other kraut makers might tell you otherwise, but in our experience this can cause a discoloration and possibly a mushy kraut. (As you will read later, this rule does not apply to kimchi or pickles.) The simplest option is to add other veggies that are known to give off a lot of liquid. Believe it or not, turnips are one of them. (Maybe you *can* milk a turnip!) Grate your turnips, or use very thinly sliced onions, grated carrots, or beets. In this book we are defining grated, or sometimes shredded, as processed with a medium grater blade, unless otherwise specified.

The next option is to find another kind of liquid that will enhance the quality of your kraut. A few tablespoons of lemon juice, bottled or fresh, can save the day. The lemon flavor will be subtle, as it gets lost in the acidity that you are creating with the fermentation. If you want to taste the lemon, add the zest also. You can also use fresh-squeezed orange, lime, or grapefruit juice. If you have leftover fermented brine from previous batches of krauts, or pickle juice, you may use that as well, keeping in mind the potential effect on flavor.

If you really want simple unadulterated cabbage sauerkraut, then there are two more possibilities for creating more brine. One is to bring out the pounder and beat more liquid out. With too vigorous an effort you risk softer kraut, but this is a time-honored practice. Another method many people use is to take a bit less than a quarter of the volume of your batch and blend it. Return this kraut "smoothie" to your batch and proceed. This is not our favorite solution; we find the crisp, crunchy texture suffers.

No Whey?

You might be wondering about whey. A lot of sauerkraut recipes call for whey to inoculate the vegetables. This will help add to the brine volume.

However, good-quality raw whey can be difficult to find and we generally don't recommend it anyway. It is an unnecessary extra step. Remember, vegetables already have the necessary bacteria for fermentation. To use an inoculant such as whey might in the beginning speed up the process by which the lactobacilli overwhelm the undesirable bacteria, but it is by no means necessary. The process will continue through the same progression of the different members of the lactic-acid bacteria family without adding whey. We also avoid using whey because our priority is flavor, and sometimes whey can leave a slightly "cheesy" or "sour milk" flavor.

Packing the Crock

Don't be concerned if the vast contents of your bowl look like they will never fit into your crock or jar. Start by placing a small amount in the bottom of your crock, about an inch or so. Compress this with your fist, or a flat-bottomed kitchen utensil, like a straight-sided (French-style) rolling pin, the plunger from a juicer, or a potato masher (see Tampers, page 41). When this is compacted, add a bit more and press again. Make sure that you are forcing the air bubbles out as you go. As you move up through the vessel, you will notice that the liquid is increasing. Meanwhile, the volume in your bowl is decreasing, and you might be wondering if you made enough. Keep pressing.

Your crock will be full when you have around 4 inches of space between the brine and the top rim; this is called *headspace*. In a 5- or 10-gallon crock, you should aim for around 6 inches of expansion room. In a jar, the vegetables should reach just below the shoulder. You need 2 to 3 inches from the top of the jar rim to the top of the brine — enough room so that even with a follower and a weight, all your hard-fought-for brine doesn't bubble out onto the counter.

FERMENTISTA'S TIP

No room left in the crock and still half a bowl of limp vegetables? Find an appropriate-sized jar and follow the same instructions. Or if you like the taste, it might just be the vegetable salad side dish you needed for dinner, or a pre-chopped vegetable for soup.

This is the time for the *primary follower* (see page 36), which in this case can be a large outer cabbage leaf (or a small sheet of plastic wrap); it will keep the shredded bits from floating above the brine. Tuck the leaf under the shoulder of the jar or crock to secure it.

Place your *secondary follower* and a *weight* in your crock or jar. Wedge it into place, with the brine covering it. Keep that oxygen out. You should be thinking, "Submerge! Conquers evil every time."

If you have a crock with a lid or a jar with an airlock, you will put this in place. The airlock is designed to let the CO_2 escape. Otherwise cover the top of the jar or crock loosely with a clean tea towel or muslin to keep out fruit flies or anything else that could fall into the brine. If you're using a regular jar lid, don't clamp it down; you want the CO_2 to be able to escape.

Even if you left a lot of headspace, put your crock or jar on a plate or cookie sheet to catch escaping brine. Never underestimate the power of exhaling bacteria. In fact, carefully watch for the level of kraut rising above the brine. Check every day during the active phase at the beginning. You will need to apply pressure to force the air out and allow the brine to return to the top of the kraut. A small jar will need to be watched more carefully to keep the brine over the cabbage.

Placing the Crock

Now there is nothing left to do but to place your nascent kraut in a corner of your kitchen and wait. Keep it out of bright or direct light, though we find it's better to expose your ferment to a little bit of light in your daily space than to keep it in an out-of-the-way closet where it will be forgotten, especially the small batches.

Most recommendations are to ferment between 55 and 75°F. Our preferred fermenting temperature is around 65°F because the ferment moves more slowly, stays crunchy, and develops good flavor before eventually becoming very sour. That said, we have found that if the ferment starts in the sweet zone for a few days, it can be moved to below 55°F (in a cellar or garage) and will keep fermenting at a slower rate, which can have advantages in developing the flavor. If you get below 45°F for sustained periods, it will hold slow and steady as if it were in a refrigerator.

Practically speaking, what does this mean in your home? No one knows the climate of your home better than you. If your kitchen counter is too warm in the height of summer, then look for a closet or basement that is cooler. One of our students puts his crock on a tile floor where the thermal mass of the floor is enough to keep the temperature constant. In winter, a crock on the top of a water heater could help keep fermentation active in a cold climate.

Curing Your Kraut: Maintaining the Active Ferment

Your crock or jar is in a corner. Things are happening. You wake up to a pool of brine on your counter; the bubbling is active. This sign of fermentation is comforting and easy to read. But for the novice fermentista, questions begin to arise. Perhaps the bubbling has stopped, or nothing is happening, or the bubbling never started as far as you can tell. Possibly something questionable is forming on top (for this we have provided a scum gallery; see page 358).

In a perfect world you will begin to see action in your kraut the day after you've packed it. If you're fermenting in a jar, you will see the little bubbles moving up through the cabbage similar to champagne. If you're lucky enough to own a crock with a water seal, you will begin to hear an occasional *bloop* as the CO_2 escapes. Sometimes, even though the kraut is actively fermenting, these signs are less obvious, or they don't last very long. This is all within the range of normal.

Krauts can be anything from explosively active to seemingly dead, and both are fine in the end.

Your job during active fermentation is a bit of a balancing act: you're responsible for keeping those veggies submerged, so you'll need to check your crock regularly, but at the same time you must try not to disturb it too much, as this can invite in unwelcome microbes and oxygen.

The Waiting Period

How long you'll have to wait depends. A very small batch of kraut will be ready much sooner than a larger batch in a crock. If you're making a small batch, watch it carefully, keep it pressed down under the brine, and taste it soon. It is these small batches that often get novice fermentistas into trouble. Since it is widely believed that kraut needs to sit for a week or three, the unsuspecting fermentista can easily let a batch spoil because small batches are difficult to keep weighted under the brine. In warm weather a small batch might be ready in as little as three days. Large crock sizes can take three weeks to a month or more.

Warmer incubation space and vegetables with a higher sugar content are often more active and require that you watch them a little more carefully to make sure everything stays submerged. Generally these are "ready" sooner. Remember, this is a live food exhibiting its *terroir*, or sense of place, climate, and season. This means that even when you follow the exact same procedure, your ferments will be different each time. This is the beauty and excitement of the art.

Knowing When It's Done

There are two things to consider: acidity level and taste. Acidity level is a clearly defined goal — anything below a 4.6 pH level (see A Ticking Crock, page 28). Taste is a matter of personal preference. There are as many opinions about active fermentation length as there are kraut makers. Some people will not even consider eating anything short of a six-week cure time, either because they like it sour, or perhaps more often because they have heard that the longer it ferments, the more probiotics there are in the crock. On the other hand, one person wrote in an online forum that she never left something on the counter for more than four days (keep in mind, this short a curing length may compromise the acidity level on some batches). The real answer to the question of how long to ferment your vegetable is most irritatingly vague: It depends.

> *How long do you ferment your pickles? 'Til they're perfect. Depending on the type of pickle, this can be anywhere from 24 hours to a year or more.*
>
> — ALEX HOZVEN, OWNER, CULTURED PICKLE SHOP, BERKELEY, CALIFORNIA

A small crock in a deep-summer kitchen will probably be acidic enough in as soon as three days. The larger the crock, or the cooler the room temperature, the longer it will take to reach a 4.6 pH or lower. Early on in the fermentation process, vegetables will taste acidic, as though lemon has been squeezed into them. You will also know your ferment is not quite there because it will taste dull, like a wilted salad. Although 4.6 pH is your goal, we have found most finished krauts are even more acidic — below 4 pH. And once you have reached that acidity level, "done" is again subjective. Let your senses make the decision for you.

When Is the Ferment Ready?

» **Look:** somewhat translucent and the color of cooked cabbage (more yellow than green)
» **Smell:** sour
» **Touch:** firm to soft, but not slimy
» **Taste:** pleasingly sour and pickle-y, but without the strong acidity of vinegar

After a few days, you can do your first taste-test on smaller batches. On multi-gallon batches this will be in one to two weeks. Carefully lift your weights and follower with clean hands. With a clean nonreactive utensil (stainless steel is fine), remove some of your veggies and taste them. Replace it all carefully, keeping everything submerged. Your weight will probably have some sediment on it; rinse it off with hot water before replacing.

Your kraut should already taste a bit sour. But it may still be a bit "green." In other words, it will be like a half-sour pickle, without the full-bodied rounded flavor of the acidity and spices that a pickle develops, somewhere between the cucumber and the pickle it is becoming. Young sauerkraut is the same way. If you prefer this "half" flavor, you can put the ferment in the refrigerator to arrest the process. The spices will still deepen as it sits in the refrigerator. We think the best answer to the question "When is my kraut done?" is "When it tastes great."

FERMENTISTA'S TIP

When fermenting in the kitchen, make sure your jar or crock isn't too close to a refrigerator's motor or fans; they could heat up your ferment without you knowing it.

▶ Rinse the vegetables in cool water and prepare according to the recipe directions; transfer to a large bowl.

▶ Add half the salt in the recipe and, with your hands, massage it in (as if you were kneading dough), then taste. You should be able to taste salt, but it should not be overwhelming. If it's not salty enough, continue adding small amounts and tasting, until it's to your liking. Remember: If it's tasty fresh, it will be delicious fermented.

▶ The vegetables will quickly look wet and limp. Depending on the amount of moisture in the vegetable and your efforts, some amount of liquid will begin to pool in the bowl. If you've put in a good effort and don't see much brine, let the vegetables stand, covered, for 45 minutes, then repeat the massage.

▶ Transfer the vegetables to a crock or jar. Press down on the vegetables with your fist or a tamper; this will release even more brine. There should be some brine visible on top of the vegetables when you press. (Don't worry if the brine "disappears" between pressings.) If not, return the vegetables to the bowl and massage again.

▶ When you pack the vessel, leave 4 inches of headspace for a crock, and 2 to 3 inches for a jar. (*Headspace* is the area between the brine and the top rim of the vessel.)

(CONTINUED ON NEXT PAGE)

▶ Top the vegetables with one or two leaves, if using, or a bit of plastic wrap. This *primary follower* keeps the shreds from floating above the brine.

▶ Top with a *secondary follower* and *weight*. For a crock the follower may be a plate that fits the opening of the container and nestles over as much of the surface as possible; then weight down the plate with a sealed water-filled jar. For a jar, you can use a sealed water-filled jar or ziplock bag as a follower-weight combination. (*Note:* Use a ziplock bag that fits the diameter of the vessel and is large enough to submerge the vegetables.) Then cover it all with a large kitchen towel or muslin.

▶ Set aside the jar or crock on a baking sheet, somewhere nearby so you can keep an eye on it, out of direct sunlight, in a cool area (anywhere that is between 55 and 75°F will work, but the cooler the better). Ferment for the time indicated in the recipe.

▶ Check daily to make sure the vegetables are submerged, pressing down as needed to bring the brine back to the surface. You may see scum on top; it's generally harmless, but if you see mold, scoop it out.

▶ Using a clean, nonreactive utensil, remove some of the kraut and taste it when the recipe directs. It's ready when:
  » It's pleasingly sour and pickle-y tasting, without the strong acidity of vinegar.
  » The flavors have mingled.
  » The veggies have softened a bit but retain some crunch.
  » The color is that of the cooked vegetable.

If it's not ready, rinse the followers and weight, put everything back in place, and continue monitering the brine level and watching for scum and mold.

▶ When the kraut is ready, carefully skim off any scum on top, along with any stray bits of floating vegetables. Transfer the kraut into a jar (or jars) if you fermented in a crock. If you fermented in a jar, you can store the kraut in it. Leave as little headroom as possible, and tamp down to make sure the kraut is submerged in its brine. Screw on the lid, then store in the refrigerator.

1. Thinly slice cabbage.

2. Work in salt with your hands.

3. Massage the cabbage until brine develops.

4. Press cabbage firmly into fermenting vessel, pressing out air pockets.

5. A properly stuffed crock.

6. Place a primary follower on the surface.

7. Add a follower and weight, forcing the brine to the top.

8. Cover with a cloth and set aside in a cool place.

9. During fermentation press to release CO_2 and maintain brine coverage.

10. Taste to test doneness.

11. Firmly pack storage jars and refrigerate.

CHAPTER 5

Mastering Condiments

VARIATIONS ON KRAUT

Exploring the breadth and depth of the vegetable fermentation art is an endeavor of infinite possibilities. We love fresh flavor and whole foods, but a lot of what we do is because when it comes to the dinner crunch time, we are lazy cooks. We use fermented condiments to jazz up our meals. Relishes, chutneys, and salsas act as fresh flavorful sides to perk up any meal.

Whole-leaf fermenting of herbs is another tasty way to preserve the bounty and create delicious garnishes for a cook's arsenal. Fermented pastes and bases can function as a seasoning foundation on which to build a meal. Think whole-food seasoning packets — a dollop or dash of leek, garlic, or another herbal paste added to a soup, sauce, or dressing at the end of the cook time provides a final burst of flavor to your meal. These two types of ferments have become convenience foods for us, very useful to have on hand — one shelf in the door of our fridge is now dedicated to fermented herbs and pastes. This is essentially a second spice cabinet. Using fermentation to provide instant fresh summer flavor year-round has been our best discovery in this culinary journey.

As you explore this chapter, you'll see the process is no different from kraut (chapter 4); the secret to success is still getting your ingredients immersed in brine, keeping them under that brine, and letting the lactic-acid bacteria do the work.

With condiments, the biggest challenge can be obtaining enough brine. There are a few reasons for this: In some of these recipes the larger vegetable pieces have less "damaged" surface area than shredded veggies and will weep less brine; some of the ingredients, like fresh leafy herbs, simply don't have as much moisture content; and lastly, condiments are often small-scale ferments, and when there is not a lot of vegetable there is not a lot of brine. These ferments require a conscientious effort in order to keep the vegetables under the smaller amount of brine. The recipes will guide you through these conditions to a successful result.

Relishes, Chutneys, Salsas, and Fermented Salads

The distinction between these four types of condiments is in the size and shape of the produce and the spices and herbs you use. Essentially they are all fermented or "sauered" vegetables that don't contain cabbage, and the vegetables are not shredded or grated; rather they are sliced, chopped, diced, or pulsed in a food processor, depending on the texture desired. For example, a salsa would call for the combination of vegetables to be roughly chopped or pulsed in a food processor, producing a chunky sauce-like condiment, like Sweet Pepper Salsa (page 215). Chutneys and relishes are similarly diced or sliced, and the distinction lies more in the type of spices used. We often add dried fruits to concentrate the flavors and make a thick condiment that can be dolloped on the plate such as Squash Chutney (page 251) or Rhubarb Relish (page 223).

You can also use your ferments to create condiments. For example, use part of a batch of already fermented pickles — adding extra sugar, spices, or vinegar that won't turn sour through fermentation — to create a sweet pickle relish, as in Sweet Dill Relish (page 171).

Use condiments as a strategy to rescue a ferment that didn't quite live up to your expectations. The inadequacy could be about texture, such as a limp pickle (see Sweet Dill Relish, page 171, again), or a dull flavor, where adding spices or dried fruit can brighten it up. Or it could be too much flavor: We once made a pickle medley with jalapeños that was too spicy to eat. We blended the entire batch of vegetables, added brine, and *voilà!* Hot sauce.

The process for making these types of fermented recipes is essentially the same as for kraut (see page 59), with a few variations illustrated in the photos that follow.

▶ Vegetables in these types of recipes will be sliced, diced, or pulsed in the food processor rather than shredded.

▶ Getting the brine may take a little longer than for shredded vegetables. You may need to let the salted produce sit, covered, for 30 to 45 minutes for the brine to build.

▶ When you press the vegetables into the crock or jar, you should see brine above the veggies. Don't worry if it "disappears" between pressings. As long as it rises up when pressing, you have enough.

▶ Top the ferment with a *primary follower* (a leaf or piece of plastic wrap). Then add a *secondary follower* and *weight*. For a crock, you can use a plate topped with a sealed water-filled jar. For a jar, you can use a sealed water-filled jar or ziplock bag as a follower-weight combination.

▶ During storage, the less airspace above a ferment, the longer it will last, so fill each jar to the rim and transfer the ferment to a smaller jar as you use it. Keep a small round of plastic wrap or wax paper directly on top of the ferment to prevent evaporation and contamination.

1. Thinly slice the vegetables.

2. Work in the salt.

3. Cover the vegetables and set aside to allow brine to develop.

4. Press the vegetables under the brine.

5. Submerged and weighted = healthy environment for fermentation.

6. Ready for long-term storage, with a piece of waxed paper in place to impede evaporation.

Pastes and Bases

Many worldwide gastronomic traditions are based on thick, robust pastes. Herbs and spices are ground together and used to flavor sauces to be served over grains. In Thailand red or green curry pastes are the basis for many dishes. In North Africa it is the berbere chili pastes, and in Indonesia it's sambal pastes that instantly add bling to the meal. In these pages you'll find, for example, Thai Basil Paste (page 115), Garlic Scape Paste (page 183), and Pepper Paste (page 213).

One or all of these, combined with coconut milk, can turn a simple stir-fry into a Thai-style curry.

You could make pastes or bases by "pounding fragrant things," which is how it has been done for many generations; however, since we are now fortunate to have food processors, it is the tool we recommend. The ingredients, which are generally the aromatics, are put into a food processor and chopped to a paste, salted, tightly packed, and fermented.

Pounding fragrant things — particularly garlic, basil, parsley — is a tremendous antidote to depression. But it applies also to juniper berries, coriander seeds and the grilled fruits of the chile pepper. Pounding these things produces an alteration in one's being — from sighing with fatigue to inhaling with pleasure. The cheering effects of herbs and alliums cannot be too often reiterated. Virgil's appetite was probably improved equally by pounding garlic as by eating it.

— PATIENCE GRAY, FOOD AND TRAVEL WRITER (1917–2005)

The process for making these types of fermented recipes is essentially the same as for kraut (see page 59), with a few variations illustrated in the photos that follow.

▶ Pastes and bases are pulsed to a paste consistency in the food processor. When you mix in the salt, the vegetables will become juicy immediately. There is no need to massage to get the brine.

▶ When you press the vegetables into the jar, there will be only a small amount of a thicker, sometimes syrupy brine that may be hard to distinguish from the vegetables. Don't worry if it "disappears" between pressings. As long as the paste is juicy, you have enough.

▶ Pastes need to be carefully packed and weighted in order to keep the vegetables under the brine and protected from the air. The best method for this is the water-filled ziplock bag, which acts as *primary follower*, *secondary follower*, and *weight*. Press the plastic down onto the top of the ferment and around the edges before you fill it with water and seal.

▶ During storage, the less airspace above a ferment, the longer it will last, so fill each jar to the rim and transfer the ferment to a smaller jar as you use it. Keep a small round of plastic wrap or wax paper directly on top of the paste to prevent evaporation and contamination.

When taste-testing a paste, be aware that it will taste somewhat saltier than a kraut or relish because it's meant to be a concentrate, like bouillon.

1. Chop or pulse the veggies to a fine consistency.

2. Press the paste to remove air pockets and bring brine to the surface.

3. Place a ziplock bag on the surface of the ferment, and fill the bag to the jar rim with water to create weight.

4. Ready for long-term storage, with a piece of waxed paper in place to impede evaporation.

Whole-Leaf Ferments

Think of whole-leaf ferments as an alternative to drying aromatic leafy herbs from the garden. Some herbs, like basil, lose their flavorful volatile oils to the drying process. Fermentation instead captures and intensifies these flavors.

Whole-leaf ferments are made by salting the whole leaves, which shrink considerably — a bushel of leaves will shrink to a height of 2 inches in a 2-gallon crock. Don't expect a lot of brine in these recipes; they can seem nearly dry, but if you follow the recipes with care, they will ferment beautifully.

Use fermented whole leaves as you would fresh herbs — as a garnish. Or you can process the leaves and stems to more of a paste consistency to use in any sauce or stir-fry, on pasta, or even in soups — though it's best to add at the end of the cooking time to retain the raw benefits.

The process for making these types of fermented recipes is essentially the same as for kraut (see page 59), with a few variations illustrated in the photos that follow.

▶ Remove the leaves from the stems.

▶ After salting, gently toss the leaves. They will wilt immediately and start to brine. Don't expect a lot of brine; this can be an almost dry ferment.

▶ Press the leaves into a jar, tamping to remove the air pockets. The leaves will become a deep green wilted color, and you will get a tiny amount of a dark-colored brine.

▶ When this ferment is ready, you won't see much visual change, and because of the aromatic nature of the leaves, when you taste-test it the sour is not as obvious as the salt.

▶ During storage, the less airspace above a ferment, the longer it will last, so fill each jar to the rim and transfer the ferment to a smaller jar as you use it. Keep a small round of plastic wrap or wax paper directly on top of the ferment to prevent evaporation and contamination.

1. Fresh leaves before salt is added.

2. Leaves wilted by salt.

The Taste Test: Navigating through the Scum to the Kraut on the Other Side

When it's time to taste-test your ferment, be warned: there may be scum, blooms of yeasts, or molds on top of your followers, or even on your ferment. Take your time and follow these directions.

1. Remove the weight.

2. Wipe the insides of your jar or crock with a clean towel carefully so as not to disturb the ferment or the scum.

3. Gently remove the follower. There is often sediment on top of the follower; try not to disturb it too much.

4. You will be looking at the primary follower; if it is leaves, lift them out carefully, collecting any stray floating vegetable bits in with them; discard. If it is plastic wrap and there is brine on top, ladle out any extra floating vegetable bits. Pull out the plastic wrap, folding it over to catch any sediment (this sediment is not harmful but may impart a flavor).

5. If the ferment is completely under the brine, it will be good. If the brine level is low and close to the surface of the ferment, there may be some soft or off-color areas; simply remove these parts. The ferment underneath will be fine and ready to taste.

3. Press the leaves to remove air pockets and bring brine to the surface.

4. Fermented leaf, ready to taste.

5. Ready for long-term storage, with a piece of waxed paper in place to impede evaporation.

SEASONINGS

You can make simple savory seasonings by dehydrating fermented veggies and grinding them in a blender. When the brine is evaporated, you are left with the original salt and the concentrated flavor of the vegetable. For example, the Simple Beet Kraut pictured below (page 120) makes a lovely deep pink tangy spice, which is not only stunning sprinkled on top of a salad but also delicious. If you don't eat it too quickly, dehydrate your kimchi for instant kimchi spice. Many a ferment can make a perfect seasoning dehydrated as is. Some ferments are fun to jazz up even more with other herbs and spices, or even sesame seeds, like Shiso Gomashio (page 229). And these seasonings are shelf stable, so they can live and probiotically season your food straight from the cabinet for months. Dehydrating can also be a strategy for clearing out older krauts from the fridge when you are ready to make more. To make seasonings:

1. Drain the brine from the ferment by letting it sit in a strainer over a bowl for 30 minutes, or by putting it in cheesecloth and actively squeezing out the juice. You want to get the loose drippy moisture out; you don't need to squeeze it completely dry.

2. Spread the ferment out on a tray or baking sheet and dry for 8 to 10 hours or overnight in a dehydrator at 100°F.

3. Shelf life for dried krauts is 6 months at room temperature. The lower the temperature, the longer the shelf life (for example, 60°F increases viability to 12 to 18 months). Refrigerate or freeze in airtight containers for long-term storage.

CHAPTER 6

Mastering Brine Pickling

Most people think of pickles as chunks of vegetables floating in vinegar, which is one type of pickle, but it's not the only kind. Technically *everything* that we are talking about in this book is pickling. When we ferment and produce brine, we are generating the environment for an acidic solution that preserves.

For the purposes of this book, we will define pickles as vegetables that are either still whole or cut into larger pieces. Unlike shredded, thinly sliced, or finely diced veggies, these vegetables cannot create their own brine, so we add a prepared salt brine and submerge the vegetables in it. The vegetables suspended in the salt water begin to interact with the brine in the process of osmosis (see page 25), which begins the lactic-acid fermentation process.

Remember the mantra: *Submerge in brine and all will be fine*. The rule is still the same: Keep those veggies submerged.

Understanding Brine

To make brine, always use the best water you can find, preferably unchlorinated spring water. Many books recommend boiling the water before making brine. When we are confident that our water source is pure, we skip this step.

You don't want to use kosher pickling salt. It is refined and contains anti-caking agents, which do not help your pickles. We like to use salts that have a lower sodium chloride content and higher mineral content, because high-quality, unrefined salts that contain trace minerals and enzymes help your body maintain a proper balance (see chapter 3). The other benefit is the pickles taste less salty.

For cucumbers (see page 166), the ratio of salt to water is different from what is appropriate for other vegetables; it is important for proper preservation and to achieve that deli taste. This has to do with the enzymes in cucumbers that are prone to break down and soften the vegetables. Cucumber brine is ¾ cup salt to a gallon of water. If you want less salt, you can experiment with reducing the amount a little, but don't go lower than ½ cup salt to a gallon of water. On other veggies, especially roots and more dense vegetables, you can use a more dilute brine solution, which we call the Basic Brine.

Unless otherwise indicated in a recipe, these are the two main brines you'll need throughout the recipes in this book; for both, simply stir the salt into the water until it is dissolved.

BASIC BRINE
  1 **gallon water**
  ½ **cup salt**

CUCUMBER BRINE
  1 **gallon water**
  ¾ **cup salt**

KIMCHI BRINE
  1 **gallon water**
  1 **cup salt**

PICKLE FACTS TO IMPRESS YOUR FRIENDS
  » Pickling cucumbers began in India 4,000 years ago.
  » *Pickle* comes from the Dutch word *pekel*, which actually means "brine."
  » Traditional pickling herbs like mustard seed and cinnamon are antimicrobial.
  » Pickles are like kraut or kimchi: they introduce vitamin B into the food.
  » George Washington is said to have had a collection of 476 varieties of pickles.
  » When both salt concentration and temperature are low, the dominant bacteria at work are *Leuconostoc mesenteroides*. This strain produces a mix of acids, alcohol, and aroma compounds. At higher temperatures, we see *Lactobacillus plantarum*, a.k.a. lactic-acid bacteria. Many pickles start with *Leuconostoc* and change to *Lactobacillus* at a progressively higher level of acidity.

We suggest making a little more brine than you will need because when fermenting your pickles (and even once they're stored in the fridge), you often need to top up the jar or crock to keep the vegetables submerged; keep the extra brine in the fridge for about a week.

FERMENTISTA'S TIP

A Note on Brine Solutions with Added Vinegar

There are as many family recipes for pickles as there are grandmothers who made them. In our classes we have been asked about brine solutions that contain both salt and vinegar for fermentation. It's important to understand that fermentation takes place naturally and beautifully without the added acid of vinegar. It's not a good idea to use both. The salt solution is ideal for promoting the succession of lactic-acid bacteria. While there is a bit of acetic acid (vinegar) that is created during the fermentation, the ratio works. When acetic acid is introduced from the outside, the balance is disrupted and this can stunt the development of the pickles.

But what about that classic bread-and-butter pickle flavor — all vinegar and sweet? This cannot be achieved by fermentation alone. Instead, ferment your cucumbers fully, remove some of the brine, and replace with a 50:50 solution of raw vinegar and honey or sugar.

LEAVES

We add leaves to pickles for two reasons: to keep the veggies under the brine and to help keep veggies crisp. The leaves to use are those that contain tannins, which is what encourages crispness. We generally use horseradish or grape leaves for their size. The grape leaf is so conveniently shaped and just plain looks good. The horseradish adds a wonderful flavor; the large leaf also keeps your pickles from floating up. Other options include raspberry leaves, currant leaves, sour cherry leaves, and oak leaves. Oak leaves are high in tannins and can add a little more bitter than you are looking for, so use them sparingly. Find leaves that have not been sprayed.

These leaves all come from perennial shrubs, vines, and trees, so if you plan to pickle in the winter you might consider preserving some grape leaves just for this purpose (page 184).

ABOUT PICKLE MEDLEYS

You can use just about any vegetable to make brined pickles, just not necessarily together. There are some things to keep in mind when making medleys:

» Consider the type of vegetables. You want the textures to be similar; for example, you don't want to use zucchini and beets in the same ferment, as the rate of fermentation is different.

» Alliums such as onions and garlic work well in any pickle.

» Sliced peppers tend to get very soft. If you want to add sweet or hot peppers, use the dried ones, or the small whole pickling varieties, such as pimientos.

▶ Prepare a salt-water brine according to the recipe directions.

▶ Rinse the vegetables in cold water and prepare according to the recipe instructions.

▶ Combine the vegetables (and any spices) in a large bowl and mix thoroughly.

▶ Pack the vegetables into a crock or jar, leaving 4 inches of headspace in a crock (*headspace* is the space between the vegetables and the top of the vessel) or wedging them under the shoulder of the jar (this will help keep them submerged in the brine).

▶ Pour in enough brine to cover the vegetables completely. In a jar this may be quite close to the rim; in a crock you'll need to leave room for the follower. (Remember the pickling mantra: *Submerge in brine and all will be fine.*) Reserve any leftover brine in the fridge (it will keep for a week; discard thereafter and make a new batch, if needed).

▶ Place grape or other tannin-rich leaves (oak, horseradish, sour cherry, currant, and so on), if using, over the vegetables as a *primary follower*.

▶ If using a crock, add a *secondary follower*, such as a plate that will rest atop the pickles, and a *weight*, such as a sealed water-filled jar, to keep things in place. If using a jar, the tightly wedged vegetables usually stay in place so you won't need a *secondary follower* or *weight*. Just loosely cover the jar with the lid; that is, don't clamp down a bail-style lid or tighten the band of a canning jar lid. This enables the ferment to release CO_2. Then cover the crock or jar with a clean towel.

▶ Set aside the crock or jar on a baking sheet, somewhere nearby and out of direct sunlight, in a cool area (anywhere that is between 55 and 75°F will work, but the cooler the better). Ferment for the time indicated in the recipe. *Note*: The baking sheet will catch any brine that spills out; periodically discard the liquid.

▶ During the fermentation period, monitor the brine level and top off with the reserved brine solution, if needed, to cover. You may see scum on top; it is generally harmless, but if you see mold, scoop it out. Veggies peeking up out of the brine will quickly get soft and spoil. If you see anything even *a tiny bit* out of the brine, use a utensil to just poke it back under or, if it's begun to soften or turn pinkish, pluck it out. Everything else should stay under the brine.

▶ As the vegetables ferment, they begin to lose their vibrant color and the brine will get cloudy. This is when you can start to test your pickles. Using a clean, nonreactive utensil, remove some of the vegetables and taste. They're ready when:
  » They're pleasingly sour and pickle-y tasting, without the strong acidity of vinegar.
  » The flavors have mingled.
  » They're softer than they were when fresh but retain some crispiness.
  » The colors are muted, even dull.
  » The brine is cloudy.

If they're not sour enough for your palate, rinse the followers and weight (and replace the grape leaves with fresh ones, if using), put everything back in place, and continue monitoring the brine level and watching for scum or mold.

▶ When the pickled vegetables are ready, carefully skim off any scum on top, along with any stray bits of floating vegetables. Transfer the pickled vegetables into jars if you fermented in a crock. If you fermented in jars, you can store the vegetables in them. Pour in enough brine to completely submerge the vegetables. Cover with fresh grape leaves, if you have some, then screw on the lids and store in the refrigerator.

▶ After about 1 day check to be sure the pickles are still submerged, topping off with more brine, if necessary.

1. Make the brine.

2. Cut veggies into chunks.

3. Mix veggies and spices together to distribute evenly.

4. Pack the mixture into a jar.

5. Pour in brine until veggies are submerged.

6. Place a leaf or other follower on the surface.

7. The leaf is over the veggies and below the brine.

8. Cover with lid but do not tighten. You want CO_2 to escape.

9. Cover with a cloth and set aside to ferment.

10. Taste the veggies when the brine begins to appear cloudy. Often spices will settle to the bottom.

11. Finished pickles.

12. Transfer to smaller jars for long-term storage.

13. For storage, pickles should be fully submerged.

CHAPTER 7

Mastering Kimchi Basics

Preserved in soybean paste kimchi tastes good in the summer, whereas kimchi pickled in brine is served as a good side dish during the winter. When the root of the Chinese cabbage grows larger in the ground, it tastes like a pear, especially after the first frost in the autumn harvest season.

— FROM THE POEM "SIX SONGS ON THE BACKYARD VEGETABLE PLOT," BY LEE GYU-BO (1168–1241), IN *GOOD MORNING, KIMCHI*, BY SOOK-JA YOON

The quote above is the first written record of kimchi pickled in brine. Lee Gyu-bo was a twelfth-century Korean senior government official who left his work behind for a simple life in the woods as a poet. His story is one that is still being played out. Trying to get back to the land, it turns out, is nothing new.

Kimchi probably most famously hit the world media in 2008 during the outbreak of avian flu. There was not one recorded case of the flu in Korea, which was attributed to kimchi consumption.

This magical "soul food" of Korea often appears on "super food" lists. It is believed the properties of the combination of garlic and pepper, magnified by fermentation, is what gives kimchi its immune-boosting power.

The product that is now known as kimchi developed on the Korean peninsula. It is distinguished by its staple ingredients: Chinese or napa cabbage, radish, garlic, scallions, ginger, and red chile pepper.

Neither of us has a Korean background, nor did we apprentice with a master kimchi maker to learn the art. Our kimchi résumé is simply that we read as much as we could, we made a lot of it, and many people enjoyed what we created and sold. From that experience we hope to provide a basic primer in this chapter.

As with other ancient domestic arts, there are as many correct ways to make kimchi as there have been mothers passing down knowledge to their daughters. The exacting recipes that we are accustomed to today would not have been an option for most families. Through much of history, people haven't had the luxury that comes with supermarkets and year-round vegetables. The variability of each year's harvest season dictated the composition of kimchis.

As we trend toward more local food systems, we are returning more to the old ways. The home cook realizes that though there is no daikon available, for example, the farmers' market is bursting with red, purple, and pink Easter egg radishes. And so the recipe shifts and the flavor of that moment is captured. Next time, it might be turnips that take center stage.

Understanding Kimchi

Kimchi is the common name for *any* vegetable pickled in the Korean style of lactic-acid fermentation. The most familiar type of kimchi in the United States is a dazzling sunset orange color with a fiery spicy flavor to match. It's called *tongbaechu* and its main ingredient is napa cabbage.

In Korea there are nearly 200 documented varieties of kimchi, and probably an exponential quantity of family recipes. Kimchi is more than a side dish or condiment, it's a cultural symbol and a great source of national pride, as evidenced by the national museum dedicated to the dish.

In this book we've included recipes for the two broad types of kimchi: the regular type of kimchi, like *tongbaechu*, which is similar to kraut in consistency, and water kimchi, which is a vegetable

pickle in prepared brine. Water kimchis are made by following the same process as brine pickling (see chapter 6). The biggest difference between water kimchi and its Western pickle counterpart is the spice profile. Instead of dill and mustard seed, water kimchis often include ginger, chile pepper, garlic, and sugar in the brine, which adds extra effervescent sparkle. We have found that using this array of ingredients allows for a lot of experimentation. Changing the ratios can radically change a recipe, although you almost can't go wrong with variations on ginger, garlic, and chile pepper.

Some traditional recipes contain a starch, often rice or wheat flour, which is made into a paste to act as a thickener. We have chosen to keep the kimchi recipes in this book simple, and so we do not use starches.

A few of our kimchi recipes are adapted from a book by Sook-ja Yoon called *Good Morning, Kimchi!* If you are serious about kimchi, this can be an inspiring book, though at times the translation requires a bit of interpretation.

Getting Started

The traditional process for kimchi can be thought of as a hybrid of brine pickling and sauerkraut making. The napa cabbage soaks in a brine solution for 6 to 8 hours; then it is mixed with spices and other vegetables that have not been in brine. This is an extra step that takes some time and planning.

Before we made kimchi commercially, we tried to cheat tradition and just process kimchi ingredients as in any mixed-vegetable sauerkraut. This is valid and tasty, as you can try for yourself in a favorite recipe contributed by the fermentistas at Spirit Creek Farm (page 143). We prefer the flavor we get when we take the extra brining step, though we suggest you try both methods to see which one you prefer.

The process is also different scientifically. As the cabbage soaks in brine, salt penetrates it by osmosis and dehydrates the cabbage, whereby the water is replaced by salt. Now there is salt both inside and out.

Korean Pepper Powder, a.k.a. *Gochugaru*

The traditional red chile pepper in kimchi is *gochugaru* (*gochu* means chile; *garu* means powder). It's a vibrant red and has a bit of sweetness, like Hungarian paprika. Unlike paprika, however, *gochugaru* is hot.

You'll find this imported Korean chile powder at Asian markets. Most of the ones we can find contain salt and other additives, which we don't want. When we cannot find pure chile powder we substitute red chile pepper flakes. For an authentic look and feel, grind the flakes into a finer powder.

SPRING RADISH PICKLES

▶ In a crock or large bowl, combine the brine ingredients according to the recipe directions, and stir to dissolve.

▶ Rinse the vegetables in cold water and prepare according to the recipe directions.

▶ Submerge the vegetables and leaves you'll use as a *primary follower* in the brine. Use a plate as a weight to keep the vegetables submerged. Set aside, at room temperature, for 6 to 8 hours.

▶ Drain the brined vegetables for 15 minutes. Reserve about 1 cup of the brine solution. Meanwhile, combine the seasonings and any unbrined vegetables, blending thoroughly.

▶ Chop the brined vegetables according to the recipe instructions, then put them in a large bowl. Add the seasoned vegetables and massage together thoroughly.

▶ Transfer the vegetables into a crock, jar, or onggi pot, a few handfuls at a time, pressing with your hands as you go. Add reserved brine as needed to submerge the vegetables and leave about 4 inches of *headspace* for a crock or onggi pot, or 2 to 3 inches for a jar. (*Headspace* is the space between the top of the brine and the top of the fermentation vessel.)

▶ Cover with any reserved leaves (the *primary fol-lower*). Add a *secondary follower* and *weight*. For a crock, the follower may be a plate that fits the opening of the container and nestles over as much of the surface as possible; then weight down the plate with a sealed water-filled jar. For a jar or onggi pot, use a sealed water-filled jar or ziplock bag. Then cover it all with a large kitchen towel.

▶ Set the fermenting vessel somewhere nearby so you can keep an eye on it, out of direct sunlight, and cool (anywhere that is between 55 and 75°F will work, but the cooler the better). Ferment for the time indicated in the recipe.

▶ Check daily to make sure the kimchi is sub-merged, pressing down as needed to bring the brine back to the surface. You may see foam on top; it is harmless, but if you see mold, scoop it out.

▶ Using a clean, nonreactive utensil, remove some of the kimchi and taste it when the recipe directs. It's ready when:
» It's pleasingly sour and pickle-y tasting, without the strong acidity of vinegar.
» The flavors have mingled.
» The vegetables have softened a bit but retain some crunch.

If it's not ready, rinse the followers and weights, put them back in place, and continue monitoring the brine level and watching for scum and mold.

▶ When the kimchi is ready, carefully skim off any scum, along with any stray bits of floating vegetables. Transfer the kimchi into small jars for storage. Tamp down to make sure the ferment is submerged in its brine. Leave as little head-room as possible. Screw on the lids; store in the refrigerator.

1. Make the soaking brine.

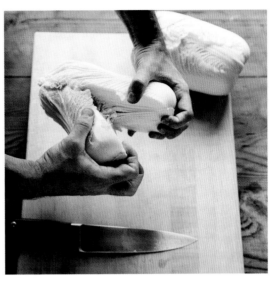

2. Cut through the end of the cabbage and pull apart to split in half.

3. Submerge the cabbage in the brine, weighing it down to keep it submerged.

4a. Drain the cabbage after 6 to 8 hours of soak time.

4b. Prepare the remaining vegetables and seasoning mixture.

5. Combine the brined and seasoned vegetables and massage together.

6. Press the kimchi firmly into the fermenting vessel to remove air pockets and bring brine to the surface.

7. Add a follower and weight.

8. Cover with a cloth and set aside to ferment.

9. Carefully scoop off any mold if it develops.

10. Rinse off the weight before replacing for further fermentation time.

11. Transfer to smaller jars for long-term storage or to give as gifts.

CHAPTER 8

Practical Matters

STORAGE AND TROUBLESHOOTING

Now that you're well on your way to mastering the processes of basic fermentation, there are a few more things you may be wondering about. How long and what's the best way to store your creations? What if something looks like it's going wrong? And what if, along the way, you still have unanswered questions? You'll find answers in this chapter.

Nurturing Ferments: Storing Considerations

In this section you'll find out how long you should store your ferments and get tips on the best way to keep and prolong the life of your creations, both in the fridge and out.

HOW LONG CAN I STORE MY FERMENT?

Because sell-by dates appear on most products, this is a common question. The answer is not straightforward — it depends. The developed acidity is what preserves the vegetables. Sometimes people eat very "young" ferments as a quick pickle or slightly fermented salad. These crisp, slightly sour ferments may not be at 4.6 pH. When storing ferments you will want to make sure they are fully

soured. If you're not confident that you can tell the proper acidity by taste, use pH strips to test your ferment (see page 44).

The most important thing to remember here is that fermented vegetables are a live food, so the rules are different than for, say, a jar of home-canned strawberries. The strawberries sit sealed and relatively stable on the shelf until opened, when the enzyme action toward spoiling is once again set into motion. Fermented vegetables are always changing; even when the jar is sealed in the refrigerator, the bacteria are ever so slowly continuing to acidify your food. This doesn't mean it's spoiling or going bad, so you have to change your idea of what is no longer fit to eat — as long as it still tastes fresh and crunchy, it is good.

Any ferment contaminated by mold or yeast should not be eaten, but as a general rule of thumb, fermented vegetables will keep for 6 to 12 months. Keep in mind that we have certainly thrown out things that have gotten soft early in the storage period, and there is no reason to toss something out at year's end if it is still tasty and viable. We have containers of Sweet Pepper Salsa (page 215) that are two years old and more delicious than ever. The shelf life on dehydrated krauts (for use as seasonings) is 6 months at room temperature. The lower the temperature, the longer the shelf life. Refrigerate or freeze all ferments in airtight containers for long-term storage.

Don't forget that fermented vegetables can vary from batch to batch because of the season, the crop, unknown forces at play in your kitchen, whatever. It's not always predictable, but that is what makes it fun. We just have to reclaim our own judgment skills: observation and taste have served humans well for a long time.

There are a few ferments in this book that are "quick ferments" meant for consumption within a few weeks, and these are noted in the recipes.

KEEPING LIVE FOOD ALIVE: HOW TO STORE FERMENTS

We choose to store our ferments in the fridge to capture the bounty of each season and preserve the flavor at its peak, for both the short and long term. For us it means having a second refrigerator standing by. This may seem extravagant, but we have found over the long haul that it not only has proven a thrifty measure but has also enhanced our family's diet in priceless ways.

That said, this is a pre-refrigeration preservation technique after all, right? If you're interested in long-term storage without refrigeration, see the sidebar on the facing page. Otherwise, here are some storage tips.

Refrigerated Storage for the Short Haul
» Any ferment that is being consumed on a somewhat regular basis keeps best in your refrigerator.
» Ferments stay freshest if you tamp down the vegetables tightly in the jar after each use.

If the ferment doesn't have a lot of brine it's okay. Use a nonreactive (wood or stainless) utensil, slide down any stray pieces on the side of the jar, and press it all down. You tamp to remove air bubbles — compressed kraut stays fresh.
» For brine pickles, make sure none of the vegetables are bobbing above the brine.
» Rotate your ferment into smaller jars as it is consumed. Less airspace increases the freshness and longevity of your ferment.

Refrigerated Storage for the Long Haul
» Transfer ferments that will be stored in a refrigerator to appropriate-sized jars for the batch. This can be gallon jars or a series of small pint jars. Just make sure the jars are firmly packed to within an inch of the top.
» For dryer ferments, like whole leaves, press a small round of plastic wrap or waxed paper on top of the vegetables. This will help keep everything under the brine and slow down evaporation over the long haul.
» For brine pickles, position a leaf or a small piece of plastic wrap on top to keep everything submerged.
» Brine evaporates. For pickles, check the level every few months and top with fresh, unfermented brine solution to cover. This isn't usually a problem for krauts. If it is, top only with previously fermented brine.
» Most jar lids are metal. For storage lasting a number of months or longer, place a bit of plastic wrap or wax paper over the top of the jar before screwing on the lid or ring. This keeps rust from forming on the inside of the lid or along the ring.

» Ball makes and sells white plastic lids that fit both their regular and wide-mouth jars. These lids work fine in the refrigerator but can leak if you take your ferments mobile. Tattler makes reusable BPA-free plastic canning lids in both sizes that you can use with the common metal bands; they have a rubber gasket and seal nice and tight. This tight seal usually prevents the band from corroding. (See the resources, page 360.)

Troubleshooting Your Ferment: FAQs and What-Ifs

Because fermented vegetables are a live food with all the quirks and personality of any live being, there can be many variations of normal. Often the fermentista (even one with years of experience) will look into a crock and wonder, "What in the heck?"

And if something looks especially dubious, do consult the scum appendix (page 356), where we've compiled mug shots of the most common culprits of the crock.

GOING OFF THE GRID: NON-REFRIGERATED STORAGE

Here are some thoughts for those who want to preserve their ferments "old school":

» Don't forget that "old school" often means tastes and textures that we are no longer accustomed to, having grown up with refrigeration. You need to know that the fermentation process keeps working, even in the refrigerator. It is just cool enough that it is slowed to a point of suspended animation and therefore can go months without perceptible changes. In other words, your flavors will not stay intact using old-school methods in the same way that they will with refrigeration.

» Don't put your efforts into small jars; larger batches preserve better. Our best unplugged storage results are with bulky 10-gallon crocks topped with generous amounts of brine in a space that stays under 55°F. Ideally this temperature is consistently under 50°F and above freezing. (As we know from every jar of kraut that left our farm, the USDA recommends under 42°F.)

» You can also work with water-seal crocks (see page 34) or jars with airlocks (see page 39). Again this option requires a consistently cool root-cellar-type space.

» Water-bath canning is another option. Keeping the probiotics intact by not heating your pickles or krauts may be your first choice, but if that's not possible, then water-bath canning still offers a way to safely preserve the low-acid vegetables that would otherwise need pressure canning. By preserving your locally grown harvest of fresh veggies, you are still capturing the peak energy of the vegetable, and you can't do better than that for good, clean food. You'll want to ferment your vegetables to an acidity of 4.6 pH or lower (see pH Test Strips, page 44). Then follow the USDA guidelines for boiling-water canning for both raw- and hot-packed vegetables. See the ferment and pickle pages at nchfp.uga.edu, where you can also download a PDF of the USDA's *Complete Guide to Home Canning*.

This section has grown from the hours we spent teaching fermentation, standing at sample tables with sauerkraut, or answering phone calls, e-mails, and Facebook messages. As we wrote this book, each time we got a query we had not thought of, this section grew. We are sure there are many more questions out there, but this is a list of the most common issues faced by fermentistas who are teaching themselves this skill.

Our children have grown up with fermentation in the kitchen, as have many young people. However, collectively as a society we do not yet have a shared story of fermenting with our grandmothers. We will, but until then we must all share our experiences as we rediscover and reinvent this culinary art. Remember: Be brave and trust your gut. If it truly feels, tastes, and seems wrong, take it to the compost to build soil, and try again.

Should I sterilize my crocks and jars?

It's not necessary to sterilize by boiling your jars, as you would in canning. However, good hygiene is always important. You will avoid chances of yeast and other contaminants just by making sure your work surfaces, implements, jars, and vegetables are clean. However, do not wash your vegetables with antimicrobial soap, extract, or any of the commercial vegetable washes on the market. These products remove the good bacteria along with the bad, essentially throwing out the baby with the bathwater, which could ruin the fermentation process.

Oops! I've over-salted the kraut.

It happens. This is probably the most common problem. Take the portion you plan to eat from the briny kraut and soak it in clear, cold water. Pour this off. Repeat this process until enough of the salt has been washed away. Let it sit in a stainless steel or plastic strainer for about half an hour. We honestly haven't done the lab work required to know whether all the probiotic benefits go down the drain with the salt, but more than likely some of the advantages of fermented food do stay intact.

Another use for over-salty kraut is to make a stew and, instead of adding salt, add some of the salty kraut near the end of the cooking time. Think of it as adding a bouillon cube to enhance flavor.

Sometimes after trying these suggestions you'll realize there's no hope. We encourage you to release your guilt and liberate the offending kraut. Find a weedy spot in your yard and dump it there. It may not be aesthetically pleasing, but you will be freed from the briny torment and the weeds will be killed, too. Salting the fields was an ancient practice that seemed to work for oppressors . . . just ask the Romans.

As we have said, ultimately the best way to make sure this does not happen is to taste your ferment as you make it. If it is too salty, add more vegetable matter, instead of trying to rinse the salt out once the process has started; you risk washing out too many of the active organisms and causing an improper ferment.

The kraut tastes too sour.

This is a matter of personal preference. If it is too sour, it has probably fermented too long. Taste the next batch sooner and more frequently during the curing time; that way you will know when you like it best.

The kraut tastes bad and weird.

Unwanted bacteria may have found their way in. Trust your gut. If it tastes bad, compost it, and don't be discouraged from trying again.

What if my brine is too thick or gelatinous?

Sometimes brine can be viscous or stringy. In our experience the slime often disappears when the ferment is allowed to age longer. We have also experienced this when temperatures have been too high. As long as all other signs are fine — it smells good and the veggies are crisp — try giving your ferment a little more time in a cool spot. We have seen a gluey kraut turn around with a month in the refrigerator.

The kraut isn't sour enough.

Repack and re-weight your ferment and continue to ferment outside of the refrigerator. Check again in a few days. If you like things "super sauer" you can add a touch of sugar to your ferment as you are making it — ½ teaspoon for 2 pounds of vegetables should do it.

There's mold!

Believe it or not, greenish or grayish mold on the top layer of ferments is relatively normal. Just scrape off the moldy layer. But if the mold is black, pink, or orange, or your ferment smells or tastes off, then send it to the compost pile.

The jar won't open.

There are two possibilities: 1. Active ferments can continue to build up CO_2 pressure that can make them a challenge to open. 2. Salt can cause corrosion that makes the jar band stick. In either case run the lid under a bit of warm water. Try again with a cloth for traction. Corroded bands are difficult to remove but generally don't affect the contents of the jar. If you are faced with a corroded lid, use your best judgment as to the whether the ferment is edible. For example, a small spot of rust on the bottom of the lid has likely not done anything to taint the ferment.

The kraut is too dry.

Maybe it seems all your brine went away when you put it in the refrigerator. The brine doesn't go anywhere, but as the ferment chills, it contracts. Just compress the kraut. As you eat kraut from your jars, always tamp back to a tight pack. You can always add a little fermented brine from another batch, but remember not to add water.

The kraut is too soft.

The fermentation may have happened too quickly, or the salt strength was insufficient, or the salt was not evenly distributed. Soft kraut can also result from kraut that was not packed properly, leaving air pockets. Air pockets can develop when the weight atop the ferment is not heavy enough to keep the brine in the vegetables during the most active stages of fermentation.

> **FERMENTISTA'S TIP**
>
> *If your kraut is soft but otherwise fine, you can still eat it. If you don't find soft kraut pleasing, you can use it to cook with: in a frittata (page 285), a chocolate cake (page 351), and any long-simmered soups and stews.*

The pickles got soft in storage.

This means they were exposed to air. Remove soft pickles from brine or toss everything into the compost if the whole batch is soft. To avoid this, keep the pickles covered and safe from oxygen exposure to reduce spoilage. Add a bit of brine to top off the jar, seal tightly, and return it to the refrigerator. This should stabilize and last for months. As you eat, the amount of liquid decreases, or the balance of veggie to brine is upset. But your refrigerated pickled veggies will survive out of the brine for the few weeks it takes to eat the jar.

The kraut is a funny color.

Over a period of time, kraut will darken. It will also turn dark if the storage temperature is too warm. With a young kraut, a dark color could indicate uneven salting, elevated curing temperature, or merely that the cabbage was not trimmed completely, leaving the darker outer leaves. Pink? Some spices and vegetables will give the kraut a pink hue, for example shiso. Otherwise, pink is yeast. Surface pinkness indicates that the ferment has not had enough covering or weight. Remove the discolored kraut, or compost the whole batch if it occurs throughout.

The refrigerated jars pop and fizz when I open them.

That is okay. This is a live food and the CO_2 is escaping. The microculture is just continuing its natural cycle. Pressure increases when carbon dioxide builds in a jar without an escape route. Even when a ferment is technically done, as defined by correct acidity and good flavor, it can still be quite active, which can cause a ferment

literally to bubble and climb out of the jar. Here's where we tell you: All of this is okay. Your loved ones won't get sick from eating this food. (Rest assured even when your jar is quiet, it is still full of live cultures.)

When you realize you're opening a hissing, fizzing jar, clamp the jar down and then open it over a clean bowl so that if the brine bubbles out you will be able to rescue it and pour it back into the ferment.

> **FERMENTISTA'S TIP**
>
> ### It's Alive!
> *Why are some ferments more alive and effervescent than others? Here's what's happening in the crock: In the early stages of fermentation, called the heterofermentative stage, the microbes produce a lot of lactic acid and significant amounts of carbon dioxide. These early colonizing species of lactobacilli that move in are very active. They are also a little more heat sensitive and less tolerant of the lower acid levels they are producing. This sends the ferment on to the next wave of microbes that continue to produce lactic acid and carbon dioxide, though at much lower levels. This is called the homofermentative stage.*

The kraut smells like dirty socks.

When this comes up, our first question is: Does it smell putrid? Putrid is an unmistakably awful odor. Putrid can smell like rotting potatoes. Putrid can make your eyes water and your stomach turn. Other indicators, like a slimy texture, mold growth, or an off-color, often accompany this kind of stench. If it's not slimy, moldy, and putrefied, chances are it is just the perfume, fragrance, bouquet, or stink, if you will, of the fermenting vegetables. This is subjective.

There are three ferment perpetrators that can cause the offending odor. These are naturally occurring fatty acids. For reasons unknown, some batches produce one or more of these acids in quantities that affect the smell. (Don't forget: vegetable ferments also experience what the wine world calls *terroir* — the flavor and mood is affected by season and place.) These acids are present in other foods and, in many cases, used in the food and flavor industry. You can be assured their presence does not make your kraut unsafe.

The first is *n-propionic acid*, a fatty acid produced naturally by *Propionibacterium* during in the fermentation process. (It is a member of this family that causes the holes in Swiss cheese.) These bacteria break down the lactic acid and are often described as smelling like human sweat or dirty socks. The good news is that propionic acid has antimicrobial properties, which is why it is also used in bread making.

The second offender on this list is *n-caproic acid*. This fatty acid smells like goats, so much so that it was named after the Latin word for goats, *caper*.

The last in our list of most common stinkers is *n-butyric acid*. This fatty acid smells like rancid butter. Again, it is harmless, and from the scientific research that we consulted — the kind where everything is done under intense scrutiny in sterile laboratory conditions — it is unclear to scientists why some batches develop this compound.

If the ferment smells of sulfur, these are different compounds that will dissipate in the steam when the kraut is heated to 158°F. Our guess is that this is why many traditional recipes are cooked.

Alleviating Fermentation Fragrance in Your Kitchen:
- » Find a place to age your ferments that is out of the way, or slightly ventilated.
- » Work with a water-seal crock or airlock lids.
- » Even the strongest-smelling krauts often lose a lot of their nasal punch when refrigerated. Chilled kraut tastes and smells milder than room-temperature kraut.

I have to go away — what then?

Sometimes things come up that won't allow you to tend to your curing ferment. If your ferment is immature and needs babysitting, taste it before you leave; if it is not ready but you are afraid it will bubble away the brine or be overly sour, you can put it in the refrigerator for a week or two — followers, weight, and all. It will slow way down (think suspended animation), and when you come back you can put it back on the counter. As it warms up, it will also wake up and continue fermenting.

Part 3

In the Crock
Fermenting Vegetables A to Z

YOU CAN PROBABLY BRING UP A MEMORY of something you put in your mouth that surprised and delighted you. Your eyes closed in a slow-chew moment.

That's what this section is about: enjoying new flavors that also happen to be good for you. For some, that new flavor is tasting fresh lacto-fermented cabbage sauerkraut for the first time. For others, the addiction to lacto-fermented vegetables is already in place and they're ready to go beyond — way beyond — green-cabbage sauerkraut, kimchi, and brined pickles. This section provides recipes and complete instructions for both — from archetypal ferments to unusual single-vegetable recipes to creative combinations and spins on the classics.

We invite you daring fermentistas to come up with your own combinations, using this section to help guide you. Technically, you can ferment any vegetable, but through trial and error and countless hours in the kitchen and our fermentation cave, we've saved you the agony of attempting the few that just aren't worth it.

This part of the book is designed for exploring — a source for culinary discovery. We hope it inspires you to take our ideas and, well, ferment them. Let the journey begin.

How to Use This Section

We designed part 3 to be useful in several ways. For example, if you're a gardener and find yourself with an abundance of, say, spinach, flip straight to the spinach pages, where you'll discover ways to work with that veggie. Or if you're at the farmers' market and see a vegetable you'd like to prepare in not-the-usual way, buy it and then turn to the pages here that give you fermenting recipes for that vegetable. Each garden vegetable and herb, presented alphabetically, has its own section, followed by two smaller sections on foraged wild veggies and a few fruits that lacto-ferment well.

Within each vegetable section you'll see **Your Raw Material**, which provides information specific to the fresh vegetable, perhaps about nutrients, or maybe tips for selecting. **In the Crock** tells you how to use the vegetable shredded, sliced, or diced and fermented without the addition of a brine solution. **In the Pickle Jar** is for pickling or brining whole vegetables, which of course you can do in a jar or a crock, and **Create Your Own Recipes** presents ideas for inventing your own ferments.

Our passion for simple good food and delicious flavors and aromas has driven this book. When you ferment garden-fresh veggies, you're part of the renaissance in using an ancient culinary technique that is now coming into its own as micro-krauteries throughout the country are creating this artisanal food.

About the Recipes

Vegetable fermentation is like putting on a play.

In both there's a cast of characters. Some, such as the vegetables, the salt, and the spices, are onstage, in the spotlight: they're the leads. The majority, though, do their work behind the scenes. *Lactobacilli* ride into a crock on the coattails of the stars, but like set designers, costumers, and the director, they're just as important. Regardless of the role, each performer has her own personality. It's the same with ingredients: they each have a special aroma, texture, taste, which may change according to the season, the soil, your climate, and the ambient temperature of your home. Thus, as in a play, no two performances are identical.

FERMENTATION TIME

Fermentation times as shown in the recipes can be only approximate. Use them as a guide or suggestion, but rely on your own senses to tell you when a ferment is ready: watch for changes in the vegetable's appearance; taste and smell for that telltale pickle-y sourness.

In each recipe you'll see a range of time. Many factors can affect the time it takes your produce to ferment, but as a rule, the first number in the range is your minimum *warm-temperature* fermentation time and the second number will be your minimum *cool-temperature* time. So when the recipe suggests fermenting for 5 to 10 days, consider the temperature of your room and know that your veggies will take longer to get "sauer" in a cool room than in a warm one.

VEGGIE WEIGHTS AND MEASURES

Unlike the chemistry in baking, which requires exact measurements — get the baking soda wrong, and there are repercussions — vegetable pickling leaves room for divergence, variation, and adaption. In most of the ingredient lists we refer to the whole vegetable. Although this may seem unconventional, we found a few problems when we tried using precise measurements.

The first is the springy nature of sliced cabbage: consistent measurement in a cup is difficult (and savoy cabbage has even more bounce). We tried measuring by weight, but then what to do with the bit of cabbage left over? Worse is if there's more waste in the outer leaves than anticipated and you don't have enough to meet the weight requirement. Recipes based on quantities of whole vegetables minimizes waste of both vegetables and energy. You'll know how much to pick or buy, and you'll use it all.

Note: If you're using a grater or a food processor, use the medium grater blade when a recipe calls for grating or shredding, unless specified otherwise.

YIELD

Recipe yields are all approximate because you're working with different-sized vegetables and varying water contents, often determined by season and freshness.

We offer a recommended fermenting vessel size for each recipe because while we assume you'll use your crock if you have one, we want to give you an idea of the size vessel you'll need if you don't, and make sure that whatever vessel you use will accommodate the ferment with enough room for the brine to bubble and grow.

SALT

We use fine Redmond Real Salt, which is a sea salt with a bit lower sodium chloride content and a subtle sweetness due to its higher natural mineral content. While most salt choices will work, we recommend that you use a salt with a similar grain size (not coarse) that is unrefined and without additives (see page 44).

How much salt is right? Something as seemingly simple as salt has variation in weight, sodium chloride content, and flavor. This is in addition to the varying moisture contents in the vegetables and differing climates. So here's what to consider when you salt your ferments:

» In most of the recipes we ask that you taste for salt to accommodate different palates and varieties of salt. Let the amount in the recipes guide you. Add salt gradually and keep tasting, and you won't go wrong.

» If you know your fermenting environment will be consistently on the warm end of the 55 to 75°F range, you might want to sprinkle in just a little more salt than the recipe suggests; this will help maintain the texture and develop the flavor. Otherwise, the kraut will be more acidic and somewhat softer, but still safe to eat.

» Note that for brine pickles, you're working with a salt brine recipe, so you won't be tasting for salt.

The amount of salt needed in the recipes is not always precise because there's a range in which the magic in the crock takes place. For krauts, that range is a salt content equal to 1.5 to 3 percent of the weight of the vegetable (brine pickles and brined kimchis require a higher salt content, at about 3 percent).

Our kraut and condiment recipes use salt amounts on the low end of the range, generally around 1.5 percent, which is where we think the texture and flavor are best (thanks to refrigeration we can use lower, healthier levels of salt and still be successful); commercial krauts generally use a 2.2 to 2.5 percent ratio of salt; and each of the recipes from our guest fermentistas uses salt differently — illustrating that this is more than just science in the kitchen, it's culinary art. But there's no need to do any math here; just follow the recipes, letting your taste buds guide you.

MANTRA FOR SUCCESS

If you remember this phrase, you won't go wrong:

{ Submerge in brine and all will be fine. }

Christopher Writes

✳ "I hate my sauerkraut!" someone behind me blurts out. It's a cry that would make any sauerkraut maker cringe.

I'm solo this Saturday. I'd told Kirsten I could handle everything today, but I'm regretting that decision.

My mind is racing as I fasten a cooler lid. Flight seems like a good idea, as does hiding under the table, but neither would be easy to explain to Kirsten later, so I try to compose myself before standing up to face my accuser.

Peering up at me is a sweet-looking woman with her hands placed firmly on the sides of our tasting tray. She's waiting for a reply.

"What don't you like about it?" I ask.

"It's wrong. It's just not, you know, good. I've followed the instructions in my cookbook and am just so damn frustrated that I thought I'd ask you what to do before I throw out this batch," she said. Then she noticed our tasting jars: six different krauts and kimchis. "Are all of these sauerkrauts?"

I stare at her while it slowly dawns on me that it's not one of our ferments she hates; it's hers. I start asking questions and learn that she's been using a simple recipe in a popular book on traditionally prepared foods. It's a recipe that forgets to mention that ferments must remain below the brine line, which calls for a weight of some type. Without it, the vegetables eventually rise above the brine, and with exposure to the little bit of air in the closed jar, even in a refrigerator, undesirable microbes get in, causing the whole thing to go bad.

I explain this omission to her and encourage her to buy a couple of organic cabbages from one of the stands and give it another try.

"Would you like to try some samples to get an idea of what you want to create?"

Looking over our jars of Curtido, Lemon-Dill Kraut, Golden Beet Kraut, and Spicy Kimchi, she turns back to me: "Don't you make plain old sauerkraut?" We do, but it's sold out.

Other people push past her to taste, and I watch as she wanders over to our neighbor's produce stand.

The next week she returns and reports that her latest batch looks great. It's bubbling away, she tells me, and smells wonderful, but she's not convinced it'll be tasty. I hand her a bamboo skewer and point to a sample jar of our Naked Kraut (page 132), which is just cabbage and salt, glorious in their simplicity. She stabs at it, puts it in her mouth, then closes her eyes and slowly chews.

"That," she proclaims, "is what I want mine to taste like. I want to make that," she says, pumping the skewer at the sample jar for emphasis.

I forget about the interaction until late October, at the end of the market season, when she returns. She tells me she has her recipe down pat and produces so much fermented goodness that she shares it with her coworkers.

"I'm ready to try something new now," she says. Beginning with the closest jar, she tastes what we have out, eyes closed, chewing slowly, sighing with every bite, smiling.

Not every aspiring fermentista has this woman's drive to push through a summer-long learning curve. We like to think she persevered because of flavor.

Garden Vegetables and Herbs

ARUGULA

Arugula, native to the Mediterranean basin, is popular in Italian cuisine, which makes sense: Ancient Romans regarded it as a valuable green for its peppery leaves, and they used the seed as a spice. Believing arugula to be an aphrodisiac, they recommended it as a side dish to accompany any meal.

YOUR RAW MATERIAL

Though it looks like a leafy green, arugula (also known as salad rocket) is a member of the crucifer family, along with broccoli, cauliflower, and our fermentation star, cabbage. Cooking destroys the enzymes that activate important sulfur-rich phytochemicals; fermenting enhances them.

Sounds great, but here's the thing: When we experimented with using it in a Korean water kimchi (a.k.a. brine pickle), we discovered that arugula's nutty-peppery flavor, so tasty in a mesclun salad, when fermented first becomes quite bitter. Even the pluckiest of palates might be turned off.

Now for the good news: As this ferment sits in the fridge, the bitterness mellows, and it actually disappears over time.

Another way to ameliorate the bitterness is to chop the arugula and add it to a combination kraut, or to use it instead of mustard greens in a kimchi.

IN THE PICKLE JAR
Arugula Kimchi

yield: about 1 pint
(fermentation vessel: 1 pint)
technique used: Mastering Brine Pickling (page 77)

This ferment is a water kimchi (which uses the same process as brine pickling). The brine boasts a lot of flavor and is good all by itself as a brine shot or for making crackers (page 293). (This recipe is adapted from the cookbook *Good Morning, Kimchi!* by Sook-ja Yoon.)

- 2 cups unchlorinated water
- 1 tablespoon unrefined sugar
- 1 teaspoon unrefined sea salt

- 1–2 bunches arugula
- 3 thin slices fresh ginger
- 3 cloves garlic, sliced
- 1–2 dried red chiles or 1–2 slices dried sweet red pepper
- 1 grape leaf (optional)

1. To make the brine, combine the water, sugar, and salt, and mix to dissolve. Set aside.

2. Gently form the arugula leaves into little bundles (the stems are brittle and won't be easy to curl into a jar). Put the bundles in a pint jar and add the ginger, garlic, and chiles. Pour in enough brine to cover the arugula. Top with a grape leaf, if using, or a piece of plastic wrap as a follower; place a sealed water-filled jar on top to keep everything in place. Store any leftover brine in the fridge (it will keep for a week; discard thereafter and make a new batch, if needed).

3. Set aside on a baking sheet to ferment, somewhere nearby, out of direct sunlight, and cool, for 4 to 5 days. During the fermentation period, monitor the brine level and top off with the reserved brine solution, if needed. You may see scum on top; it's generally harmless, but consult the appendix if you're at all concerned.

4. When the brine is cloudy with a reddish tint from the chiles, and the leaves are faded, you can test it. Remember, the arugula will be a little bitter at first, but beyond that you will want to make sure there is a pleasant sour flavor.

5. When it's ready, screw on the lid and store in the refrigerator. This pickle will keep, refrigerated, for 6 to 8 months. The bitterness in the arugula softens over time.

Create Your Own Recipes

Fresh arugula makes a wonderful pesto. Try fermenting the leaves as a paste with garlic, a little cracked black pepper, and lemon as the base, following the instructions for making pastes (page 70). To serve, mix in some chopped pine nuts and grated Parmesan.

ASPARAGUS

The ancient Romans had a saying to describe a task swiftly accomplished: "as quick cooking as asparagus."

How times change! That wasn't the prevailing opinion in the United States of 1871. *The White House Cook Book: A Comprehensive Cyclopedia of Information for the Home*, a book thick with advice to the homemakers of the era, claimed to "represent the progress and present perfection of the culinary art." Treasures abound within old, forgotten books; this one, however, recommended boiling asparagus for 20 to 40 minutes! One recipe suggested the cook "lift it out gently, as it will be liable to break."

The Romans had the right idea. Reputedly, their royalty prized asparagus enough to keep a fleet just to fetch it. They would have liked the slightly crisp, al dente texture of our pickled asparagus.

YOUR RAW MATERIAL

Ferment asparagus in the spring, when it's in season; the sooner these spears go from ground to jar, the better. (Off-season asparagus has a duller flavor and a denser, less desirable texture.) The diameter of the spears, pencil thin or thumb thick, doesn't matter. What counts is that within a batch they're of uniform size.

IN THE PICKLE JAR

Asparagus Pickles

See photo on page 231

yield: about 1 quart

(fermentation vessel: 1 quart)

technique used: Mastering Brine Pickling (page 77)

These are the pickles to bring to a potluck when you want to show off — they're food art, in both flavor and appearance, and easy to make. You'll need to trim the spears to fit into a 1-quart jar, but you can use any leftover nonwoody pieces to make a jar of bite-size pickles. To fill two narrow-mouth pint jars instead, cut the spears to 3¾ inches long.

1–2 **pounds asparagus spears**
3–4 **cloves garlic**
  1 **teaspoon black peppercorns**
  ½ **teaspoon chile pepper flakes**
  1 **bay leaf**
3–4 **dried red chiles (cayenne if you want spicy; sweet if you want pretty without heat)**
  1 **grape leaf (optional)**
2–3 **cups Cucumber Brine (¾ cup unrefined sea salt to 1 gallon unchlorinated water)**

1. Snap the woody ends off the spears and then cut them to fit in a 1-quart jar or crock; 5 inches is about right to leave room for the brine to cover them. Crush the garlic cloves with the flat side of a knife, just enough to break them. Put the peppercorns, pepper flakes, and bay leaf in the bottom of a 1-quart jar or crock. Arrange the spears upright, wedging the garlic and dried chiles between the spears. Put the grape leaf, if using, on top of the spears. Pour in enough brine to fully cover the spears and grape leaf, if using. When the spears are tightly packed they tend to stay in place, so you won't need a weight, which could damage the delicate sprout ends. Cover loosely. Store any leftover brine in the fridge (it will keep for a week; discard thereafter and make a new batch, if needed).

2. Set aside on a baking sheet to ferment, somewhere nearby, out of direct sunlight, and cool, for 5 to 8 days. During the fermentation period, monitor the brine level and top off with the reserved brine solution, if needed. You may see scum on top; it's generally harmless, but consult the appendix if you're at all concerned.

3. The pickles are ready when the spears are a dull olive green and the brine is cloudy. We generally don't taste-test these if we are going to store them in the jar because we want to keep all the spears tightly packed. These will be softened (but not mushy) and have a pickle-y but not vinegary flavor.

4. Store in jars, with lids tightened, in the fridge. After about 1 day, check to be sure the pickles are still submerged, topping off with the reserved brine, if necessary. These pickles will keep, refrigerated, for 12 months. The flavor intensifies over time.

IN THE CROCK

Asparagus Kimchi

yield: about 1 quart
(fermentation vessel: 1 quart)
technique used: Mastering Brine Pickling (page 77)

In this recipe the "kimchi" vegetables and spices are packed around the whole asparagus spears, then a little brine is added to make sure there is enough liquid to keep everything submerged. Serve a few spears topped with the shredded veggies as a pungent fermented side salad to an Asian meal.

- 1–2 **pounds asparagus spears, woody ends removed**
- ½ **cup grated carrot**
- ½ **cup grated radish (any variety)**
- 1 **tablespoon chile pepper flakes or crushed red pepper**
- 1 **tablespoon grated fresh ginger**
- 4–5 **cloves garlic, grated**
- 1–2 **cups Cucumber Brine (¾ cup unrefined sea salt to 1 gallon unchlorinated water)**
- 1 **grape leaf (optional)**

1. Cut the spears to fit in a 1-quart jar or crock; 5 inches is about right to leave room for the brine to cover them.

2. Make a paste in the food processor with the carrot, radishes, chile pepper flakes, ginger, and garlic, or hand-grate and massage together.

3. Arrange the spears upright in a crock or jar, wedging them in and packing the paste around them as you go. Add brine, making sure all the tender tips are covered with liquid. Top with a grape leaf, if using, or a piece of plastic wrap to keep the paste under the brine. When the asparagus spears are tightly packed they tend to stay in place, so you won't need a weight, which might damage the delicate sprout ends. Cover loosely. Store any leftover brine in the fridge (it will keep for a week; discard thereafter and make a new batch, if needed).

4. Set aside on a baking sheet to ferment, somewhere nearby, out of direct sunlight, and cool, for 5 to 8 days. During the fermentation period, monitor the brine level and top off with the reserved brine solution, if needed, to cover. You may see scum on top; it's generally harmless, but consult the appendix if you're at all concerned.

5. These pickles are ready when the spears are a dull olive green and the brine is cloudy. We generally don't taste-test this ferment if it is in a jar, because it is nice to keep all the spears tightly packed. But if you are using a crock, you will want to taste-test them as you transfer them to jars for storage (or if you plan to eat them soon). The pickles should be pleasingly sour and pickle-y tasting, without the strong acidity of vinegar, and softer than they were when fresh, like lightly cooked asparagus.

6. Store in jars, with lids tightened, in the fridge. After about the first day, check to be sure the pickles are still submerged, topping off with more brine, if necessary. These pickles will keep, refrigerated, for 1 year. The flavor intensifies over time.

BASIL

It was only after years of fermenting that we tried the process with basil. We didn't have a lot of confidence in the resulting texture and flavor. When we finally tried it, we quickly learned two things: We weren't enthusiastic about the flavor of basil in sauerkraut, and we were pleasantly wrong about fermenting the leaves.

Every summer we grow a flat of sweet basil and a flat of Thai basil among our flowers. We used to make pounds of pesto to freeze, but it was expensive to invest in all the ingredients that accompany the basil; aged cheese, nuts, and olive oil are not cheap. Now we make some pesto, but we save money, time, and freezer space by preserving the basil in a ferment.

Drying diminishes this herb's aromatic volatile oils. Fermenting, on the other hand, retains the essential basil flavor while unleashing a unique pickled quality — a fresh yet concentrated flavor. We ferment whole leaves to toss in a dish at serving time, and we make concentrated spice pastes to use during meal preparation.

YOUR RAW MATERIAL

Humans have enjoyed basil's fragrant flavor for more than 5,000 years. This member of the mint family is native to India and Asia. There are over 40 varieties of basil — colors range from pale to deep green, rich aubergine purple, and a variegated lace of golden yellow. With this variety comes a range of texture, fragrance, and flavor. The most commonly known is sweet basil (*Ocimum basilicum*).

The leaves are tender and easily bruised. Harvest basil early in the morning just after the dew dries and use as soon as possible. If purchasing basil, choose bundles with vivid green leaves that are not wilted and don't have any black spots.

WE ARE FAMILY: MINT

Mint, like its family member basil, has played a significant role in traditional herbal pharmacopoeias throughout history. Its wonderful scent and flavor have also made it a leading player in the kitchen, adding a cool refreshing taste to dishes as well as ferments. Of the many varieties of mint, spearmint, curly mint, and peppermint (the strongest flavor of the three) are the most common culinary types, but there are also fruity varieties, such as apple, pineapple, and orange mint. The flavor of the various mints holds up well in fermentation. If you are creating your own recipe, use quantities similar to what you would in a fresh salad or veggie dish. Choose the type of mint that you have available or like best and add it to the ferment when you combine the rest of your vegetables, just before salting. Chopping the leaves will release a little more flavor in the ferment. Mint also lends itself well to whole-leaf or paste preparations (see chapter 5, Mastering Condiments). Our favorite way to use mint is in Greek Lemon-Mint Kraut (page 134).

Whole-Leaf Fermented Basil

technique used: Whole-Leaf Ferments (page 72)

These whole leaves are wonderful to have on hand; they retain texture and shape and can be used in any of the same applications as whole fresh leaves. Toss some fermented leaves in a salad, stir-fry, or pasta dish (after the dish has been removed from the heat).

In this recipe you can use any quantity of leaves and any kind, or mix and match: lemon, cinnamon, sweet, Thai, you name it.

Any quantity of leaves, in ¼-pound bunches
¼ teaspoon unrefined sea salt per bunch

1. Lightly sprinkle the leaves with salt until you can taste it. (It takes very little.) Massage the salt into the leaves; they'll quickly bruise and turn dark. There's no waiting time for the brine to develop. *Note:* The leaves will shrink down to what seems like nothing — that's okay, because the flavor is concentrated.

2. Press the leaves firmly into a crock or jar. You will get a small amount of deeply colored liquid. Tamp down to remove all the air pockets, then top the ferment with an appropriately sized ziplock bag (a quart-sized bag is perfect for a wide-mouth jar). Press the open plastic bag down onto the top of the ferment, then fill it with water and seal.

3. Set aside on a baking sheet to ferment, somewhere nearby, out of direct sunlight, and cool, for 7 to 10 days. Check daily to make sure the leaves are submerged.

4. You may see scum on top; it's generally harmless, but consult the appendix if you're at all concerned. The leaves will become a deep green wilted color. You can start to taste-test the leaves after 1 week; you'll find the sour is not as obvious as the salt. Ferment longer if more acidity is desired.

5. Store in small jars, lids tightened, in the refrigerator. Leave as little headroom as possible, and press a small round of plastic wrap or wax paper directly on top of the ferment in each jar. This ferment will keep, refrigerated, for 1 year.

Basil Paste

technique used: Pastes and Bases (page 69)

This paste ferments in the same way as the whole-leaf basil. The advantage in making the paste is that you can use some of the stem, which increases your yield and decreases any waste. (We don't recommend using the flower, as it imparts a bitter taste.) Add this paste at the end of your cooking time to sauces or soups. It can also be mixed into a salad dressing.

Any quantity of leaves, in ¼-pound bunches
¼ teaspoon unrefined sea salt per bunch

1. Put the leaves and nonwoody stems into a food processor and pulse to make a paste. Sprinkle in the salt. The veggies will become juicy immediately. Press the vegetables into a small jar. More brine will release at this stage, and you should see brine above the vegetables.

2. Top the ferment with an appropriately sized ziplock bag. Press the open plastic bag down onto the top of the ferment, then fill it with water and seal; this will act as both follower and weight.

3. Set aside on a baking sheet to ferment, somewhere nearby, out of direct sunlight, and cool, for 4 to 10 days. Check daily to make sure the vegetables are submerged. You may see scum on top; it's generally harmless, but consult the appendix if you're at all concerned.

4. You can start to taste-test the ferment after 4 days. It's ready when the flavor has developed a pickle-y quality and has a nice herbal bouquet.

5. Store in jars, with lids tightened, in the fridge, leaving as little headroom as possible and tamping the ferment down under the brine. This ferment will keep, refrigerated, for up to 1 year.

VARIATION: Pesto Base

If you add a few cloves of garlic to the food processor in the Basil Paste recipe, what you have is, in effect, a great pesto starter kit. After fermentation, add to the paste a few tablespoons of olive oil, shredded Romano cheese, and ground pine nuts or almonds.

Thai Basil Paste

technique used: Pastes and Bases (page 69)

This paste is handy and tasty to add to a coconut milk–based vegetable dish or to dollop onto rice or Asian noodles. This is one of our homemade convenience foods, and we invite you to play with it.

The bottled fish sauce in this recipe provides the salt necessary to start the ferment. You won't need additional salt.

Any quantity of Thai basil leaves, in ¼-pound bunches
2 cloves garlic per bunch
1 tablespoon grated galangal root (or grated fresh ginger) per bunch
½ teaspoon fish sauce per bunch

To make this ferment, pulse all the ingredients to a paste in a food processor and then follow the directions for Basil Paste (page 114).

THAI BASIL

There is a bit of confusion about Thai basil. The culinary Thai basil that one normally finds at the market or in the seed section of the garden center is a purplish variety of sweet basil, *Ocimum basilicum*. It has a distinct flavor that shows notes of licorice, cinnamon, and a hint of mint.

Thai holy basil, sometimes called tulsi, is a variety of *Ocimum tenuiflorum* that has a minty flavor with a peppery kick. The variety of tulsi commonly found in stores has a sweet floral flavor with a delicate mint quality. This rich antioxidant and digestive aid is said to be a balm for mind, body, and spirit. Fresh and dried leaves of any variety of tulsi enhance many ferments.

BEANS, GREEN

Common wisdom has it that green beans should not be consumed raw, due to varying concentrations — less in young beans, more as they mature — of lectins, potentially toxic proteins (see the sidebar). It's a matter of balance: Enjoy young, succulent green beans as a fermented pickle; don't make them a staple in a raw-food diet.

Plant breeders have developed fleshy and tender beans that are often string-free.

YOUR RAW MATERIAL

There are many beautiful varieties of green beans, among them some that aren't even green. Yellow wax beans and green beans retain their colors when fermented, but the purple beans and the beautiful pintoed red-and-white beans turn drab during fermentation, their colors bleeding into the brine.

Choose pods that are firm and slim, with a slightly downy bright skin — indicators of a young bean. As the green beans mature on the vine they become tough and will not break down properly in fermentation. If the shape of the seeds is evident through the skin, they're too mature.

Lectin Facts

There's a lot of information (and misinformation) on the subject of eating raw green beans, from touting their health benefits to the warning that they're anti-nutrient thugs you should stay clear of. Conflicting information can make us afraid of our food.

The fact is that much of what we eat contains something "toxic" along with the benefits. As it happens, lectin proteins are present, in varying concentrations, in almost everything we eat.

According to T. Shibamoto and L. Bjeldanes, the authors of *Introduction to Food Toxicology* (Salt Lake City: Academic Press, 1993), "Toxicity has been shown in feeding studies with the pure lectin comprising 0.5–1.0% of mice or rat diets. Lectins appear to inhibit nutrient absorption in the intestine and inhibit growth of the animals. Meals that contain raw or fermented green beans should be of no cause for concern, as any lectins present would be too small of a dose to have any effect on nutrient availability. It is unknown if lactic acid fermentation has any effect on lectin content of green beans, since lectins are a group of proteins and glycoproteins."

Christopher Writes

Snapping beans was the task my brother and I did every summer. The job description was simple: Pinch one of the pointy ends and pull the string along the side of the bean and off. Then snap the beans into pieces.

This garden bounty was canned and stashed in our basement and it was my job to go down there to fetch a can or two for dinner. The monsters I knew lived there might grab my legs from under the stairs, or drop on me from the exposed floor joists, or best yet reach out and grab my hands as I reached for a jar . . . I really did see eyes and often heard breathing, and more than once I dropped and broke a jar as I sprinted for my life up the stairs.

Whatever bounty my mother sent me to get, it was always the green beans that died at my hand, and here's where it gets weird. My mother would go into hazmat mode: She'd direct the family to go behind the tape and with bright yellow dishwashing gloves she'd meticulously clean up and then douse the crime scene with Pine-Sol or bleach or both. I remember wondering, "Why are those green beans radioactive when the jar breaks, but otherwise we just dump them in a pot and eat them?"

IN THE PICKLE JAR

Dilly Beans

See photo on page 216

yield: about 1 gallon
(fermentation vessel: 1 gallon or four 1-quart jars)
technique used: Mastering Brine Pickling (page 77)

Dilly Beans are the gold standard of green bean pickles and that is the recipe we've included, but don't feel limited. If you want to try something else, we encourage you to use this process along with your favorite spice combination. For example,

we think green bean pickles are great with curry powder added to the brine. You can also include green beans in our Edgy Veggies recipe (page 155).

> 15 **cloves garlic**
> 6 **pounds green beans, trimmed**
> 1–2 **dried red chile peppers**
> 6 **bay leaves**
> 2 **tablespoons pickling spice,** *or*
>   2 **teaspoons dill seed (or, better, 3–4 fresh dill seed heads),**
>   1½ **teaspoons whole black peppercorns,**
>   1½ **teaspoons mustard seed, and**
>   1 **teaspoon coriander seed**
> 1 **gallon Basic Brine (½ cup unrefined sea salt to 1 gallon unchlorinated water)**
>   **Grape, oak, or horseradish leaves, enough to top the jar or crock (optional)**

1. Lightly mash the garlic cloves with the side of a knife, just enough to break them. Layer the beans in the jar (the visual effect is stunning if you can arrange them vertically). Incorporate the garlic, chile peppers, bay leaves, and the spices as you go, distributing equally into four wide-mouth quart jars or a 1-gallon jar or crock.

2. Pour enough brine over the beans to cover them. Tuck the grape leaf, if using, or a piece of plastic wrap over the top of the beans. Cover loosely. Store any leftover brine in the fridge (it will keep for a week; discard thereafter and make a new batch, if needed).

3. Set aside on a baking sheet to ferment, somewhere nearby, out of direct sunlight, and cool, for 6 to 10 days. During the fermentation period, monitor the brine level and top off with the reserved brine, if needed, to cover. You may see scum on top; it's generally harmless, but consult the appendix if you're at all concerned.

4. If you're fermenting in clear containers, you'll see the beans begin as a vibrant green. As fermentation begins they turn a drab olive, a result of the acids interacting with the chlorophyll. The brine will become cloudy; this comes from the production of lactic acid. On day 6 you can start to taste your beans. They're ready when the brine is cloudy, the color is drab, and they taste like cucumber pickles.

5. When the beans are ready, store in jars, with lids tightened, in the fridge. These will keep, refrigerated, for 1 year.

FERMENTISTA'S TIP

Fermentation and Botulism

Clostridium botulinum, *which manifests as botulism, is rare but still is the bogeyman of canning, both home canning and commercial-scale canning. As recently as 2007,* C. botulinum *was discovered in commercially canned green beans.*

We don't worry about botulism because fermentation uses acidity to preserve vegetables (and control microbes), which happens at below 4.6 pH, an acidic environment where the C. botulinum *spore cannot hatch or grow.*

Kirsten Writes

When Christopher and I first were married I remember his mom lamenting that it was too late for canned green beans one night. Dinner was still an hour away, but she explained that it would take a minimum of two hours to cook them. I had no idea what she meant. It turns out that my new mother-in-law was concerned about botulism, which is a rare form of food poisoning but nonetheless can be a real threat in canned, low-acid foods.

As with any "threat," we all learn to respect it and live by the rules. My lesson came when we started our commercial kitchen, 20 years later; I had to spend two days memorizing everything about botulism in order to get certification (part of our state's licensing requirements).

My mother-in-law was right, if overcautious with two hours of cooking time. Heat does kill the botulism bacteria at the boiling point, and generally people are told to boil for 10 minutes to make sure the entire batch has cooked evenly.

BEETS

The beet is the most intense of vegetables. The radish, admittedly, is more feverish, but the fire of the radish is a cold fire, the fire of discontent, not of passion. Tomatoes are lusty enough, yet there runs through tomatoes an undercurrent of frivolity. Beets are deadly serious.

— TOM ROBBINS, *JITTERBUG PERFUME*, 1984

People seem to have a strong opinion about beets. It's either love — "I adore the earthy flavor of beets" — or hate — "Beets taste like dirt."

In a ferment, love them or hate them, most people expect the sweetness of roasted beets and are surprised by the tang, which comes with the conversion of sugars into lactic acid. Even so, most beet lovers still feel the love, and even the naysayers often, again to their surprise, can develop a taste for them.

One thing we all agree on is the health claims. High in vitamin C and folate and famous for their ability to cleanse the blood, beets are also loaded with minerals that support the liver and gallbladder. Fermented, shredded beets also seem to have properties that lower the risk for certain cancers and help cure others.

YOUR RAW MATERIAL

As far as flavor is concerned, there's a huge difference in how spring beets and the overwintered roots ferment. It's in the sugar. Once beets freeze in the ground, the roots develop a lot more sugar; this affects the result of the ferment — the bubbling and what we call life energy are amazing. The brine is also thick and syrupy. Wonder why your beet ferment didn't work? The answer probably lies in when you made it, and thus the sugar content.

Fermenting beets by themselves makes them thick and syrupy, tasting somewhat alcoholic. Thus, we like to ferment beets with cabbage, half and half. Spring-beet kraut is light and bright, like the days. When using overwintered beets, increase the amount of cabbage to lighten the taste.

Undeniably, fermented red beets are beautiful, a rich and deep crimson. When you start with other types of beets, the colors won't always be what you might expect. For example, golden beets don't retain their original sunset gold. Be aware, too, of Chioggia beets. They'll lure you with their concentric, candy-cane rings. You'll think about how sexy they'll look in the jar. You might take the candy-cane image further — sugar and spice and everything nice — and make a Chioggia pickle with cinnamon sticks and whole cloves. You'll pour in the brine, and your great idea will be confirmed . . .

Fast-forward a few days, when you check the jar and see gray slices of those once candy-cane beets: The beautiful pink stripes have fallen out of the beets and into the brine. Oh, the disappointment! Your only consolation is that the flavor is still good. All right, we confess: The reviews were mixed — still love or hate.

IN THE CROCK

Beets blend nicely with a lot of other vegetables, but they'll turn everything else fuchsia. (Even the smallest addition of beet is dominant.) And your hands will also turn red. Use gloves if you're going out . . . it takes a lot of scrubbing to remove the stain, and the staining can last a few days.

Peel beets; no matter how well you wash them, a "dirt" flavor (more than earthiness) comes through when the skins are intact.

In general, beets are tough to grate. After peeling, quarter them and run them through the grater attachment of the food processor. If you do not have a food processor, hand grating works and will build up your muscle strength.

Simple Beet Kraut

See photo on page 123

yield: about 2 quarts
(fermentation vessel: 2 quarts or larger)
technique used: Mastering Sauerkraut (page 53)

The nature of beets might cause the brine to be heavier than usual, more like a syrup. This is normal. If it's too thick for you, use more cabbage than beets.

> *The beet kraut is a monster! Keeps exploding and knocking the jars sideways and burping over. I punch it down and add some kraut brine to try to thin the syrup a bit. Gad!*
> — MARY ALIONIS, WHISTLING DUCK FARM, GRANTS PASS, OREGON, MAKING HER FIRST BEET KRAUT TO SELL AT HER FARM STAND

1 **head cabbage**
1½ **pounds beets (2 medium-size beets)**
1–1½ **tablespoons unrefined sea salt**

1. Remove the coarse outer leaves of the cabbage. Rinse a few unblemished ones and set them aside. Rinse the rest of the cabbage in cold water. With a stainless steel knife, quarter and core the cabbage. Thinly slice (or shred) with the same knife, or a mandoline, then transfer the cabbage to a large bowl. Peel and rinse the beets. Use a mandoline, box grater, or food processer to grate the beets. Add the beets to the cabbage.

2. Add 1 tablespoon of the salt and, with your hands, massage it into the vegetables, then taste. You should be able to taste the salt without it being overwhelming. Add more salt if necessary. The beets are especially quick to release brine and will look wet and limp, and liquid will begin to pool. However, if you don't see much brine in the bowl, let it stand, covered, for 45 minutes, then massage again.

3. Transfer the cabbage-beet mixture to a crock or 2-quart jar, a handful at a time, pressing down with your fist or a tamper to remove air pockets. You should see some brine on top of the vegetables when you press. When the vessel is packed, leave 4 inches of headspace for a crock, or 2 to 3 inches for a jar. Top the cabbage with one or two of the reserved outer leaves. For a crock, top the leaves with a plate that fits the opening of the container and covers as much of the vegetables as possible; then weight down with a sealed, water-filled jar. For a jar, use a sealed, water-filled jar or ziplock bag as a follower-weight combination.

4. Set aside on a baking sheet to ferment, somewhere nearby, out of direct sunlight, and cool, for 4 to 14 days. Check daily to make sure the vegetables are submerged, pressing down, as needed, to bring the brine back to the surface. The foam may look a little brackish after a few days; this is within the realm of normal. Just skim off the foam; underneath it the kraut will be perfect.

5. You can start to test the kraut after 4 to 5 days. It will be a little raw tasting at this point, but this is preferred for some people. We find that beet kraut is tastier after 2 weeks. You'll know it's ready when it's pleasingly sour and pickle-y tasting, without the strong acidity of vinegar; the veggies have softened a bit but retain some crunch; and the color is a rich deep fuschia.

6. Store in jars, with lids tightened, in the fridge. This kraut will keep, refrigerated, for 6 months.

FERMENTISTA'S TIP

All in Good Time

A longer ferment will give you a more sour flavor. Sometimes red beet kraut will also take on a faint orange color with age. This is okay, but with time the beet kraut can take on yeasty or alcoholic flavors. Experiment to find the perfect beet kraut for your palate.

Curtido Rojo

yield: about 1 gallon
(fermentation vessel: 1 gallon or larger)
technique used: Mastering Sauerkraut (page 53)

This is Guatemala's version of sauerkraut. It's usually served as a quick fresh side dish, pickled with vinegar. This is our take on it, fermented. It is a variation on the Simple Beet Kraut recipe at left.

 1 head red or green cabbage (either will turn a beautiful purple)
 2 beets, shredded
 1 large red onion, thinly sliced
 ½ pound green beans, sliced in ½-inch pieces
 2–3 cloves garlic, minced
 1–2 fresh jalapeños, seeded and minced (for extra heat, keep the seeds)
 1 tablespoon cumin seed
 1 tablespoon grated orange zest or lime zest
 1 tablespoon dried oregano, crumbled
 ½ teaspoon red chile flakes
 1–2 tablespoons unrefined sea salt
1 or 2 bay leaves

Follow the recipe for Simple Beet Kraut, at left, adding the beets, onion, beans, garlic, jalapeños, cumin seed, zest, oregano, and chile flakes to the cabbage. Massage in the salt. When the brine has developed and it's ready to pack, lay the bay leaves in the bottom of a 1-gallon jar or crock and continue with the recipe instructions.

Kirsten Writes

When a farmer friend called and asked if we would like to make kraut with golden beets, our immediate reaction was: absolutely. We envisioned a radiant yellow, like van Gogh's sunflowers, beaming beet love throughout the market, pulling customers to our table. Later that week, as we enthusiastically peeled and grated beets, their vibrant color was fading before our eyes, fading into a rather unappetizing grayish-brown. Oxidation was taking place before fermentation's anaerobic acidity could save the color. Then we had a "eureka" moment: "Turmeric!" The beets fermented thick and syrupy and the color of saffron. We were sold out of 6 gallons' worth in 2 weeks.

PICKLED GARLIC SCAPES, *page 184*

ONION AND PEPPER RELISH (made with habanero), *page 203*

NAKED KRAUT, *page 132*

SWEET PEPPER SALSA, *page 215*

FENNEL CHUTNEY,
page 178

SIMPLE BEET KRAUT,
page 120

FERMENTED SHISO
LEAVES, *page 228*

CHIPOTLE SQUASH
KRAUT, *page 249*

Curried Golden Beets

See photo on page 172

yield: about 2 quarts
(fermentation vessel: 2 quarts or larger)
technique used: Mastering Sauerkraut (page 53)

Shred the beets for this recipe at the last minute, as golden beets will start to oxidize as soon as you cut into them. Work quickly once the beets are shredded; they'll retain more of their golden color the sooner you can get this ferment tucked under the brine. The optional dried currants in the recipe make this ferment thicker and sweeter.

1 **head cabbage**
2 **golden beets**
1–1½ **tablespoons unrefined sea salt**
1 **teaspoon curry powder (or make your own; see recipe at right)**
½ **cup dried currants (optional)**

1. Remove the coarse outer leaves of the cabbage. Rinse a few unblemished ones and set them aside. Rinse the rest of the cabbage in cold water. With a stainless steel knife, quarter and core the cabbage. Thinly slice (or shred) with the same knife or a mandoline, then transfer the cabbage to a large bowl. Grate the beets and add to the cabbage.

2. Massage 1 tablespoon of the salt and the curry powder into the cabbage and beets, then taste. You should be able to taste the salt without it being overwhelming; add more salt if necessary. When the brine has developed, add the currants, if using.

3. Transfer the cabbage-beet mixture to a crock or 2-quart jar, a handful at a time, pressing down with your fist or a tamper to remove the air pockets. You should see some brine on top when you press. When the vessel is packed, leave 4 inches of headspace for a crock, or 2 to 3 inches for a jar. Top the vegetables with one or two of the reserved outer leaves. For a crock, top the leaves with a plate that fits the opening of the container and covers as much of the vegetables as possible; weight it down with a sealed, water-filled jar. For a jar, use a sealed water-filled jar or ziplock bag as a follower-weight combination.

4. Set aside on a baking sheet to ferment, somewhere nearby, out of direct sunlight, and cool, for 4 to 14 days. Check daily to make sure the vegetables are submerged, pressing down as needed. This beet kraut foam may look a little brackish after a few days, which is normal. Just skim off the foam; underneath it, the kraut will be perfect.

5. You can test the kraut after 4 to 5 days. This kraut has a rich, deep flavor, and the sweet curry and currants add complexity. You'll know it's ready when these flavors are developed with an acidic or pickle-like undertone.

6. Store in jars, with lids tightened, in the fridge for up to 6 months.

MAKE-YOUR-OWN
Curry Powder

¼ **teaspoon cumin seeds**
¼ **teaspoon mustard seeds**
1 **teaspoon ground turmeric**
½ **teaspoon grated fresh ginger**
⅛ **teaspoon black pepper**
⅛ **teaspoon ground cayenne**
⅛ **teaspoon cinnamon**

In a dry skillet, toast the cumin and mustard seeds; transfer to a bowl, then stir in the rest of the spices. Store in a spice jar for up to 6 months.

IN THE PICKLE JAR

Beet slices, beet spears, tiny whole peeled beets: they all make wonderful pickles. However, for people accustomed to the soft, sweet, acidic flavor of vinegar-pickled beets, these are a surprise, as the beets stay quite firm — their texture is that of raw beets. Slice them thinly.

Beet Kvass (*Russel*)

yield: about 1 quart
(fermenting vessel: 2 quarts)
technique used: Mastering Brine Pickling (page 77)

One of our market regulars always requested jars of straight beet brine to purchase. She wanted to have this elixir whenever her mood was low. One day she brought a small paperback cookbook to show us a recipe for *russel*. That was the first time we'd heard of this traditional Jewish cooking brine. The pages of *The Complete American-Jewish Cookbook*, by Anne London and Bertha Kahn Bishov (1952), were yellow with age.

The recipe was simple: 12 pounds of beets in water (no salt) for 3½ weeks. Our recipe isn't much different — just less time and a bit of salt.

Try this as a base in your favorite borscht recipe. The rough chop in this recipe gives the beets enough surface area to ferment without breaking down the sugars too quickly, thus leading to alcohol; don't grate the beets.

1½ **pounds (2–3 medium) beets, scrubbed or peeled**
1 **quart unchlorinated water**
2 **teaspoons unrefined sea salt**

1. Chop the beets into ½-inch pieces, and put them in a ½-gallon jar. Add water to fill and mix in the salt. You won't need any followers or weight. Cover loosely.

2. Set aside on a baking sheet to ferment, somewhere nearby and out of direct sunlight, in a cool spot for 5 to 7 days, stirring daily. You will see some bubbling. Remove any scum as it appears.

3. You can start to taste the liquid on day 5. It will have effervescence, like soda; an acidic quality, like lemonade; and a slight saltiness; it will, of course, taste like beets. If you want something more like a vinegar, ferment for 1 week longer,

About Beet Kvass

Beet *kvass* is the sour salty liquid that comes from fermenting beet cubes. Depending on the region or ethnicity, this same liquid is also called *russel*, which is the Yiddish or Slavic word for brine, and brine it is. It's a fermented, ruby-colored beet "vinegar" used to flavor soups, preserve and color horseradish, and make drinks. This brine has a reputation as a tonic, cleanser, appetite builder, and hangover cure.

The word *kvass* comes from the old Slavic word meaning "yeast" or "leaven." It's a common brew throughout Eastern Europe, usually made by fermenting dark rye bread. In Russia, *rassol* is cucumber brine, pickle juice touted for the same virtues as kvass, and is the identifying ingredient in *rassolnik*, a traditional soup made with meat and barley.

taste again, and repeat until it's just right. Pour the liquid off the beets into a clean jar. *Note:* The beets themselves are a by-product of the process; however, they can be used to make a second batch of *russel*.

4. Store in the refrigerator. This tonic is meant to be made regularly and consumed quickly. It will keep, refrigerated, for about 5 days.

Golden Ginger Beet Kvass with Meyer Lemon

yield: about 2 quarts
(fermentation vessel: 2 quarts)

This is Tiffani Beckman-McNeil's recipe for beet kvass with a lemon twist. It is one example of a kvass that is a little less beet-y. (You can meet this fermentista and her husband Mike on page 306.) The process is the same as for the Beet Kvass above, but a gold tone replaces the ruby jewel tone. Make a more savory kvass by substituting onion, carrots, even cabbage for a little of the beets. Or add orange peel and spices such as cinnamon sticks. Tiffani says, "It's fun playing with different spices and seeing how things change, yet still stay the same."

    2–3 golden beets (or Chioggia beets for a bright
         pink brew), cut into ½-inch pieces
      1 thumb-sized piece fresh ginger, unpeeled and
         chopped (more is optional)
      1 Meyer lemon peel, torn into pieces
         Brine (1 tablespoon unrefined sea salt to
         ½ gallon unchlorinated water)

1. Fill a jar one-third full with the chopped beets. (Tiffani doesn't peel the beets but scrubs them well to remove dirt and trims off the tops.) Add the fresh ginger and lemon peel. Pour in the brine. Cover the ferment with a towel.

2. Set the jar out of direct sunlight in a cool spot to ferment for 5 to 14 days. Stir daily. At around day 5, remove the lemon peel and begin tasting. When the flavor suits your palate, filter and refrigerate the kvass. It will keep, refrigerated, for about 5 days.

BROCCOLI

Broccoli is a versatile vegetable. Raw, steamed, sautéed? Yes. Lacto-fermented? You'd rather not. When we tried brine-pickling broccoli florets, we came up with a lot of comments that weren't exactly flattering. When we chopped the florets and stalks and added them to a basic cabbage sauerkraut, it had a nice-enough earthy flavor for the first few weeks, and then a strong broccoli-gas taste developed, almost like sulfur. As it aged, this became even more acrid. Fermentation just isn't a long-term preservation solution for broccoli.

> **FERMENTISTA'S TIP**
>
> ### Quick Ferments
> *You can peel and then shred broccoli stems and add them to a sauerkraut, but make just a small batch and eat it within a few days — it's not a keeper. Or you can quick-ferment broccoli for an instant pickled salad. The fermentation process breaks down some of the sugars and starches in the vegetable, making it easier to digest.*

BRUSSELS SPROUTS

A fruit is a vegetable with looks and money. Plus, if you let fruit rot, it turns into wine, something Brussels sprouts never do.
— P. J. O'ROURKE, HUMORIST

Pickling Brussels sprouts came early in our fermentation experimentation. Kirsten's sister loves Brussels sprouts. We used to think she was the only one who held such affection for them, but now it seems everyone we meet loves them. We hoped to surprise her with a new way to enjoy them and eagerly prepared a jar of whole Brussels sprouts, decorated with herbs and bathed in brine. The jar sat in our fermentation cave, bubbling away in the company of 10-gallon crocks of varieties of sauerkraut. After a week, the color had turned the dull olive green of a pickle.

Kirsten began the process of taste-testing while Christopher watched. She took a sprout out of the jar; she spat it out. "These aren't ready," she said. A few days later, the result was the same. They were disgusting.

Even though we knew that in Eastern Europe barrels of whole cabbages are fermented, we suspected that the tight leaves were too dense to allow the acidification to penetrate to the centers. We briefly entertained the idea of shredding them for a sprout kraut, but the thought of scraping all those tiny Brussels sprouts back and forth across a grater for a wee bit of kraut was not appealing.

We've since learned that cutting the sprouts in half or into quarters and pickling them in a brine creates a delicious product.

YOUR RAW MATERIAL

Brussels sprouts are one of the few vegetables that aren't available fresh year-round. They're a cold-season crop found in markets as fall approaches — usually available from September through January.

Hot Smoky Sprouts

See photo on page 152

yield: about 1 quart
(fermentation vessel: 1 quart)
technique used: Mastering Brine Pickling (page 77)

This recipe is inspired by our love for Brussels sprouts sautéed with plenty of bacon. We use a small amount of smoked salt in the brine, as it can become overpowering.

4–5 cloves garlic
   1 tablespoon peppercorns
   1 tablespoon chile pepper flakes
   1 pound Brussels sprouts, halved
2–3 jalapeños, cut into strips or rounds
   1 grape leaf (optional)

BRINE (MAKES 2 QUARTS)
   ½ gallon unchlorinated water
   2 tablespoons unrefined sea salt
   2 tablespoons smoked salt

1. Put the garlic cloves, peppercorns, and chile pepper flakes in the bottom of a 1-quart jar or crock. Arrange the Brussels sprouts and the jalapeños so they're wedged below the shoulder of the jar. For a crock, make sure you have 4 inches of headspace. Pour in enough brine to cover the vegetables. Store any leftover brine in the fridge (it will keep for a week; discard thereafter and make a new batch, if needed).

2. Place a grape leaf, if using, or piece of plastic wrap over the vegetables. For a crock, top with a plate that will rest atop the pickles, and a weight, such as a sealed, water-filled jar, to keep things in place. For a jar, use a sealed, water-filled jar or ziplock bag as a follower-weight combination.

3. Set aside on a baking sheet to ferment, somewhere nearby, out of direct sunlight, and cool, for 7 to 14 days. During the fermentation period, monitor the brine level and top off with the reserved (or fresh) brine solution, if needed, to cover. You may see scum on top; it's generally harmless, but consult the appendix if you're at all concerned.

4. As the vegetables ferment, they begin to lose their vibrant color and the brine will get cloudy; this is when you can start to test your pickles. Begin tasting after a week. They're ready when the sprouts are sour enough for your palate.

5. When they're ready, store in jars, with lids tightened, in the fridge. These Brussels sprouts will keep, refrigerated, for 6 months. *Note:* The sprouts continue to ripen over time; the heat takes on more character.

Create Your Own Recipes

You can pickle Brussels sprouts in a number of ways — on their own in regular brine, with other vegetables in a medley, and with curry.

Brussels sprouts are versatile. Slice them thin and let the sprouts make a brine for a kraut, or add garlic and ginger to make a kimchi. Follow basic cucumber-pickling recipes, with or without the dill. Just be sure to cut the sprouts in half or into quarters.

BURDOCK (GOBO)

The largest green leaf here in the country is certainly the burdock leaf: if you put it round your little waist it is like an apron; and if you lay it upon your head when it rains, it is almost as good as an umbrella, for it is extremely large. One burdock never grows alone; where one grows there are several more, making quite a splendid sight.

— FROM "THE HAPPY FAMILY," BY HANS CHRISTIAN ANDERSEN, 1847

The reputation of burdock, or, as it's called by its botanical name, *Arctium lappa*, bounces between nuisance weed to flower gardeners and essential to herbalists and chefs. Its Japanese name is *gobo*.

Burdock has anti-inflammatory, antioxidant, and antibacterial properties. It's said to aid digestion and alleviate arthritis and some skin disorders. This list goes on, and the reason is that this "weed" belongs to the class of herbs known as adaptogens, which work to balance the system. This group of highly nutritive and medicinal broad-spectrum plants includes perilla, spikenard, nettle, and ginseng.

Burdock originated in the Siberian region of northern Asia. In Europe it was used during the Middle Ages both as a medicinal herb and as a vegetable. It's a popular vegetable in Japan and is important in the Chinese herbal pharmacy.

YOUR RAW MATERIAL

Though it's a biennial, most gardeners and farmers cultivate burdock (*Arctium lappa* var. *edule*) as an annual and harvest it for the long, thin taproot, which may be 4 feet long and with a 1-inch diameter. If you let it go to seed, in the "right" environment garden burdock will quickly get away, at which point you have the "pesky" wild burdock.

You'll find it in the vegetable section of natural-foods stores. Look for roots that are still firm, not limp like an old carrot. Select those that are about the thickness of your thumb; any bigger and they tend to be woody.

Burdock, or gobo, is a wonderful addition to sauerkraut. It imparts a mild sweetness, only subtly perceptible against the stronger taste of the cabbage.

Burdock Leaves

If you are a gardener or a wildcrafter and come across burdock, it's good to know that its tender leaves make a nice salad green (if you don't mind the small hairs on them). Shred a leaf or two — they're big — and add to a kraut; that will take care of the fuzzy texture.

IN THE CROCK

Burdock oxidizes to an unappetizing gray-brown when shredded and exposed to the air. Although in the beginning the color makes you think the burdock must have been scraped off the forest floor, after some hours in the anaerobic, soon-to-be-acidic environment of the brine, the brighter color of the freshly shredded root returns.

Shredded burdock works nicely with other vegetables, but if you're working with a lot of it, as in the recipe for kimchi (page 130), it's better to cut the roots into thin slices. They become a little too starchy when shredded for use by themselves.

✳ When I first started working with this plant, I wanted to make a burdock-only ferment. The peeled and shredded root soon began to oxidize. I added fresh-squeezed orange juice; I thought the flavor would complement that of the burdock and was hoping the acidity would balance the color, much in the way lemon juice does with sliced apples.

As it fermented it became increasingly starchy and thick, and there was no recognizable brine. The orange juice did nothing for the color or flavor; it was slightly alcoholic, and that was the least of its problems. It all went straight to the compost bin.

So much for an all-burdock ferment.

Burdock Kraut

Follow the directions for Naked Kraut (page 132), and add 4 large or 5 medium burdock roots, peeled and shredded. For a spicier kraut, also add ¼ cup minced horseradish root (see page 185 for handling tips). For a more colorful sauerkraut, add a grated carrot with the burdock.

Burdock Kimchi

yield: about 1 quart
(fermentation vessel: 2 quarts or larger)
technique used: Relishes, Chutneys, Salsas, and Fermented Salads (page 66)

This root never bubbled to the top of our gotta-have-it list — until fermentation. After much experimentation, we found this condiment to be a perfect (and tasty) way to incorporate burdock into our diet. It's a satisfying snack in the middle of the afternoon — a dollop of Burdock Kimchi and a few slices of cheese.

This kimchi is traditionally spicy, but we leave just how hot up to you.

2 carrots, thinly sliced
1 bunch scallions, greens included, cut into 1-inch slices
1 bunch mustard greens, thinly sliced
2 cloves garlic, minced
1 tablespoon finely grated fresh ginger
2 pounds burdock root
  Zest and juice of 1 lemon
1 tablespoon sesame seeds
  Chile pepper flakes or salt-free *gochugaru* to taste (a pinch for a mild flavor and up to 1 tablespoon for fiery-hot)
1–2 teaspoons unrefined sea salt or ½ cup fish sauce

1. Combine the carrots, scallions, mustard greens, garlic, and ginger in a large bowl. Mix well and set aside.

2. Peel the burdock root and thinly slice crosswise; then quickly squeeze on the juice of the lemon, to help the root retain its color. Add the burdock, lemon zest, sesame seeds, and chile flakes to the bowl, mixing to combine.

3. Sprinkle in the salt or fish sauce, and work it in with your hands; if you are not getting much brine, let sit, covered, for 30 to 45 minutes. Then toss and massage again for a few minutes to get everything mixed. At this point you should see brine at the bottom of the bowl.

4. Transfer your vegetables into a jar or crock, a few handfuls at a time, pressing to remove air pockets. More brine will release, and you should see brine above the veggies. Top the ferment with a 1-quart ziplock bag. Press the open bag down onto the top of the ferment, fill it with water, and seal.

5. Set aside on a baking sheet to ferment, somewhere nearby, out of direct sunlight, and cool, for 7 to 14 days. Check daily to make sure the vegetables are submerged, pressing down as needed to bring the brine back to the surface. You may see scum on top; it's generally harmless, but consult the appendix if you're at all concerned.

6. You can start to test the ferment after 1 week. You'll know it's ready when it's pleasingly sour, the flavors have mingled, and the pungency of the kimchi spices have developed.

7. Store in jars, with lids tightened, in the fridge. This ferment will keep, refrigerated, for 1 year.

VARIATION: Burdock-Carrot Kimchi

See photo on page 152

Follow the Burdock Kimchi recipe above, adding 2 pounds of thinly sliced carrots and omitting the mustard greens and sesame seeds.

CABBAGE, GREEN AND SAVOY

Cabbage, n: a familiar kitchen-garden vegetable about as large and wise as a man's head.

FROM

— AMBROSE BIERCE, *THE DEVIL'S DICTIONARY*, 1906

The lowly cabbage, round and plain and generally inexpensive in the market bins, turns out to be the Queen of the Crock! This simple-looking vegetable in the grocery store is one of the most beautiful in the garden — a magnificent "flower" when surrounded by all its deeply colored leaves peeling back as the plant appears to bloom.

This vegetable is the basis of most of the traditional ferments around the world. Fermented cabbage under its many names — German *sauerkraut*, Dutch *zuurkool*, Russian *kislaya kapusta*, Korean *kimchi*, Japanese *tsukemono*, Chinese *suan cai*, French *choucroute*, Swedish *surkål* — has been, and continues to be, an important staple in keeping people around the globe nourished through the lean winter months.

YOUR RAW MATERIAL

Winter cabbages are as beautiful as they are welcome for their freshness. January King, with outer leaves that are a deep fuchsia, matures just when we're in the darkest of days, reminding us it's time to make kraut to get us through the bleak months of February and March and to savor with thick hot soups. *Note:* These winter cabbages tend to release less brine.

In spring, nature brings us flowers and salad greens, but the big, overwintered cabbage heads you see are ready to do what's in their genetic makeup: bolt and go to seed.

Summer and fall cabbages are the archetypal pale green. They're crunchy and moist, perfect for putting up a year's supply of kraut. Savoy, beautiful and crinkly, is a late-fall variety. Its taste is generally milder than that of other cabbages; fermented, it has a similar flavor but the leaf has a thinner quality. When we made Lemon-Dill Kraut with savoy for our business, it was different enough that we renamed it Lemon-Dill's Curly Cousin. It's somewhat drier and produces less brine.

In general, for the recipes in this section, 1 cabbage head equals 2 to 3 pounds.

> **FERMENTISTA'S TIP**
>
> ### A Note on Goitrogens
>
> *Crucifers (the backbone of the canon of fermented vegetables) contain goitrogens, which some people with hypothyroid conditions should avoid, as the goitrogen suppresses thyroid function. Cooking breaks down goitrogen compounds; fermentation will not, so we spent time testing krauts and kimchis based on vegetables not from the cabbage family.*
>
> *To balance or counteract too much goitrogen, add sea vegetables (see Natural Iodine, page 135) to crucifer-based ferments.*
>
> *Alternatively, try Escarole Kimchi (page 176) and celeriac or carrot krauts — a few examples of ferments in other families that have just as much pizzazz and flavor as does anything with cabbage.*
>
> *The ferments pictured on pages 216–17 are all free of goitrogen.*

IN THE CROCK

Naked Kraut

See photo on page 122
yield: about 2 quarts
(fermentation vessel: 2 quarts or larger)
technique used: Mastering Sauerkrauts (page 53)

This is pure cabbage deliciousness. Just remember the kraut mantra: shred, salt, submerge.

3½ **pounds (1–2 heads) cabbage**
1–1½ **tablespoons unrefined sea salt**

1. To prepare the cabbage, remove the coarse outer leaves. Rinse a few unblemished ones and set them aside. Rinse the rest of the cabbage in cold water. With a stainless steel knife, quarter and core the cabbage. Thinly slice with the same knife or a mandoline, then transfer the cabbage to a large bowl.

2. Add 1 tablespoon of the salt and, with your hands, massage it into the leaves, then taste. You should be able to taste the salt without it being overwhelming. Add more salt if necessary. The cabbage will soon look wet and limp, and liquid will begin to pool. If you've put in a good effort and don't see much brine in the bowl, let it stand, covered, for 45 minutes, then massage again.

3. Transfer the cabbage to a crock or 2-quart jar, a few handfuls at a time, pressing down on the cabbage with your fist or a tamper to work out air pockets. You should see some brine on top of the cabbage when you press. Leave 4 inches of headspace for a crock, or 2 to 3 inches for a jar. Top the cabbage with one or two of the reserved outer leaves. Then, for a crock, top the leaves with a plate that fits the opening of the container and covers as much of the vegetables as possible; weight down with a sealed, water-filled jar. For a jar, use a sealed, water-filled jar or ziplock bag as a follower-weight combination.

4. Set aside the jar or crock on a baking sheet to ferment, somewhere nearby, out of direct sunlight, and cool, for 4 to 14 days. Check daily to make sure the cabbage is submerged, pressing down as needed.

5. You can start to test the kraut on day 4. You'll know it's ready when it's pleasingly sour and pickle-y tasting, without the strong acidity of vinegar; the cabbage has softened a bit but retains some crunch; and the cabbage is more yellow than green and slightly translucent, as if it's been cooked.

6. Ladle the kraut into smaller jars and tamp down. Pour in any brine that's left. Tighten the lids, then store in the refrigerator. This kraut will keep, refrigerated, for 1 year.

Three Cs

See photo on page 257
yield: about 3 quarts
(fermentation vessel: 1 gallon or larger)

The three Cs are cabbage, carrots, and celeriac. This kraut combination was one of the first products we sold at the market. Each of the vegetables provides a subtle flavor that doesn't overwhelm the others.

Follow the directions for Naked Kraut (page 132), adding 1 packed cup each of shredded carrot and celeriac with the cabbage and ¼ to ½ teaspoon additional salt.

Curtido

See photo on page 231
yield: about 1 gallon
(fermentation vessel: 1 gallon or larger)

Curtido tied Lemon-Dill Kraut for our best seller, and people who were adamant that they didn't like fermented vegetables liked Curtido.

Curtido comes from the Spanish verb *encurtir,* which means "to pickle." It is traditional in the cuisine of El Salvador, and it's as versatile in Latin American food as sauerkraut is in Eastern European. It's a refreshing replacement for pico de gallo salsa, which helps your efforts to eat local, as it's not reliant on the fresh tomato that travels 900 miles to get to your winter table.

　2　**heads (about 6 pounds) cabbage**
1–2　**carrots, thinly sliced**
　1　**onion, thinly sliced**
　4　**cloves garlic, grated**
　2　**tablespoons dried oregano, crumbled**
　1　**tablespoon chile pepper flakes**
　½　**teaspoon ground cumin, or to taste**
2½　**tablespoons unrefined sea salt**

Follow the directions for Naked Kraut (page 132), adding the carrot, onion, garlic, oregano, chile flakes, cumin, and salt to the shredded cabbage.

Juniper-Onion Kraut

See photo on page 152
yield: about 1 gallon
(fermentation vessel: 2 gallons)

This variation on Naked Kraut (page 132) was our first foray into beyond-cabbage kraut; we had no idea what would lie ahead. Kraut and onions are a delicious combination on their own, but the sweet piney notes of juniper really bring the flavors together. Some people love to bite into the whole berries for an intense bite — not unlike a shot of gin.

- 8 pounds (3–4 heads) cabbage
- 2 large sweet onions, thinly sliced
- 2 tablespoons juniper berries, lightly crushed
- 3 tablespoons unrefined sea salt

Follow the directions for Naked Kraut (page 132), adding the onions, juniper berries, and salt to the shredded cabbage. *Note:* Lightly crush the berries with the handle of your knife to release the flavorful oils.

Greek Lemon-Mint Kraut

yield: about 1 quart
(fermentation vessel: 2 quarts or larger)

Lemon is a player in this sprightly kraut as well as in the lemon-dill one that follows, but in this recipe we accentuate it even more with the use of the zest. The cooling quality of the mint and the freshness of the lemon make this a superb summer kraut. It's particularly nice on a Mediterranean platter and is a traditional accompaniment to lamb. Try lamb burgers topped with feta and this kraut.

- 1–2 heads cabbage
- ½ cup finely chopped fresh mint leaves, such as spearmint (see We Are Family: Mint, page 113)
- 1 lemon, juice and zest
- 1 tablespoon unrefined sea salt

Follow the directions for Naked Kraut (page 132), adding the mint, lemon juice and zest, and salt to the shredded cabbage.

Lemon-Dill Kraut

See photo on page 256
yield: about 1 gallon
(fermentation vessel: 1 gallon or larger)

One of our sons was going backpacking and wanted to bring a kraut, something refreshing that would provide some electrolytes to go along with the cheese, crackers, and trail mix that make up his standard fare. The sauerkraut we came up with soon became our best seller. Many of our students have come to our kraut school just to learn this recipe, and this is the kraut we recommend to those who say, "I don't like sauerkraut." It'll win them over.

- 2 heads (about 6 pounds) cabbage
- 1½–2 tablespoons unrefined sea salt
- 4 tablespoons lemon juice
- 1–2 tablespoons dried dill (to taste)
- 4–5 cloves garlic, finely grated

Follow the directions for Naked Kraut (page 132), adding the lemon juice and the dill with the salt. When the cabbage is glistening and you have a small pool of liquid in the bottom of the bowl, mix in the garlic.

Kirsten Writes

We received an e-mail from a customer off-season, right before Christmas, asking if we had any Lemon-Dill Kraut (above). Her seven-year-old had written to Santa and requested only two things: a bathrobe and a jar of our lemon kraut.

Natural Iodine

Consumption of large quantities of the goitro-gens in raw cruciferous vegetables is not recommended for those with a sensitive thyroid. The best way to consume them is fermented with seaweed (see page 232). It naturally contains iodine, which the body does not produce on its own, and which is important for the proper function of the thyroid.

Although some say iodine inhibits fermentation, we've never had a problem with it, nor do we know anyone else who has.

Scape Kraut

yield: about ½ gallon
(fermentation vessel: 2 quarts or larger)

This was one of our best sellers, especially in the fall — maybe it was its deep golden color. You'll find scapes, the curly flowering stalks of the garlic bulb, at farmers' markets in early summer. (See Garlic Scapes, page 183.)

- 2 heads (about 6 pounds) green cabbage
- ½ pound garlic scapes, thinly sliced
- 1 cup grated carrots
- 1 small fresh turmeric root, finely grated
- 1 teaspoon ground coriander
- 1 teaspoon red chile flakes
- 2 tablespoons unrefined sea salt

Follow the directions for Naked Kraut (page 132), adding the scapes, carrot, turmeric, and spices to the shredded cabbage before salting.

Smoky Kraut or Hot and Smoky Kraut

yield: about 2 quarts
(fermentation vessel: 2 quarts or larger)

Follow the directions for Naked Kraut (page 132), but replace half of the regular salt with smoked salt. After you've shredded the cabbage, add 1 sliced onion and 1 diced red bell pepper for a mild smoky kraut; for the hot version, add 2–3 diced jalapeños instead.

ABOUT SMOKED SALTS

There are many varieties of smoked salts, which impart different character and smoky notes. We use applewood, as it is delicious and readily available where we live. We encourage you to start with your region's specialty, such as alder, hickory, or mesquite. Some smoked salts are quite strong — in that case, use half smoked and half regular salt. The goal is for the smoky flavor to be noticeable but not overwhelming.

Wine Kraut

See photo on page 173
yield: about 2 quarts
(fermentation vessel: 2 quarts or larger)

We wanted to make a lacto-fermented wine sauerkraut that retained the flavor of the wine. Wine added to raw cabbage at the beginning of the ferment time became vinegary. Not bad, but not wine. We thought of trying to infuse the flavor by fermenting in an old barrel from one of the local wineries, but 55 gallons of kraut was a larger-scale experiment than we were up for. In smaller trials, we learned to add the wine at the end of the fermentation.

Ferment Naked Kraut (page 132) for 2 weeks, then add 1 cup of a good red wine. Because the kraut is already fermented, just let it sit on the counter with the wine infusion until you like the flavor. It will taste like a wine kraut immediately, but a day or two on the counter lets the flavors commingle and deepen.

Za'atar Kraut

yield: about 2 quarts
(fermentation vessel: 2 quarts or larger)

Za'atar is a blend of herbs used in Middle Eastern cooking. In the Mediterranean countries east of Italy, *za'atar* is believed to make one's mind alert and the body strong, and it is often incorporated into breakfast to prepare for a big day. If you'd like a bold kraut as part of your morning meal, this one's nice in an omelet.

Follow the directions for Naked Kraut (page 132), adding 2 tablespoons of the *za'atar* blend with the salt.

ABOUT SUMAC

Sumac, a red-flaked spice with a tart flavor reminiscent of lemon, is an essential spice in much of the Middle East. It has a long culinary history: it served as the tart, acidic element in food before the ancient Romans brought lemons to the region.

MAKE-YOUR-OWN
Za'atar Spice Blend

- ¼ cup ground sumac
- 2 tablespoons dried marjoram
- 2 tablespoons dried oregano
- 2 tablespoons dried thyme
- 1 tablespoon roasted sesame seeds

Combine all the ingredients, and there you have it!

Large-Batch (Homesteader) Kraut

yield: about 4 gallons
(fermentation vessel: 5 gallons)
technique used: Mastering Sauerkraut (page 53)

The basic process is the same for a large batch as for a small one. The differences have to do in part with the equipment needed to manage a vast pile of cabbage, especially before it breaks down, but the bigger factors are that the fermentation time is usually longer and the brine management duties are less (this is because the weight of the shredded vegetables with the resultant larger quantity of brine achieves a critical mass that helps keep a properly weighted follower in place). It is interesting to note that large batches need less manipulation for the cabbage to release its juices. If the cabbage is evenly salted, the mass, weight, and gravity help this happen on its own in a few hours.

Prep the cabbage in the largest bowl you have or try a Tubtrug, which is a large food-grade plastic vessel. Add salt as you go. This jump-starts the breakdown of the cell walls, releasing juices even before you begin to work at it.

40 pounds cabbage

1 cup unrefined sea salt

1. To prepare the cabbage, remove the coarse outer leaves. Rinse a few unblemished ones and set them aside. Rinse the rest of the cabbage in cold water. Quarter and core each cabbage with a stainless steel knife. Using the same knife, a mandoline, or a rotary slicer, shred or thinly slice the cabbage and transfer it to a very large bowl or food-grade tub; if you don't have another large vessel, you can mix right in the crock. As you slice, transfer the cabbage to the vessel, sprinkling a little of the salt onto each batch, then give the cabbage a toss to distribute the salt evenly.

2. When all the cabbage is shredded, continue to massage with your hands to evenly distribute the salt, then taste. It should taste slightly salty without being overwhelming. If it's not salty enough, continue adding salt and tasting, until it's to your liking. You should see plenty of brine accumulating in the bottom of your vessel. Cover the bowl with clean cloths and set aside for 1 to 3 hours to allow more brine to release.

3. Put 2 to 3 inches of cabbage into the bottom of the crock and press with your fists or a tamper to remove air pockets. Repeat with the remaining cabbage. When the vessel is packed, you should have pressed out all the air pockets and see a layer of brine on top. Leave at least 4 inches of space between the top of the brine and the rim of the crock. Arrange the reserved leaves, or another primary follower, on top. Add a plate that fits the opening of the container and covers as much of the cabbage as possible; weight down with a sealed water-filled 1-gallon jar. Usually this is enough, but after 1 to 2 days, you may need two or three jars.

4. Set the crock aside to ferment, somewhere nearby, out of direct sunlight, and cool, for 2 to 4 weeks. Check daily for the first few days to make sure the vegetables are submerged, pressing down to bring the brine back to the surface. If the cabbage is "lifting" above the brine or if it seems your brine has decreased, add more weight. You may see scum on top; it's harmless, but check the appendix if you are concerned. Later in the process you may also see yeasts bloom (consult the Scum Gallery, page 358, to identify); generally these can be left undisturbed until you're ready to test your kraut.

5. You can start to test after 2 weeks (see The Taste Test, page 73). You'll know it's ready when it's pleasingly sour and pickle-y tasting, without the strong acidity of vinegar; the flavors have mingled; the cabbage has softened a bit but still has some crunch; and the cabbage is more yellow than green and slightly translucent, as if it's been cooked.

6. When it's to your liking, spoon the ferment into smaller jars and tamp down, leaving as little headspace as possible. Pour in any remaining brine to cover. Tighten the lids, then store in the fridge. This kraut will keep, refrigerated, for 1 year.

Large-Batch (Homesteader) Curtido

yield: about 8 gallons
(fermentation vessel: 10 gallons)

This is a super-sized batch of Curtido. The process is a variation of the Large-Batch Kraut, but this recipe is larger still.

- 60 pounds cabbage
- 10 pounds carrots, thinly sliced
- 10 pounds onions, thinly sliced
- 4 heads garlic, cloves separated and grated
- 1 cup dried oregano
- ½ cup chile pepper flakes
- ⅓ cup ground cumin
- 1 pound (about 1 pint) unrefined sea salt, plus more to taste

Follow the Large-Batch Kraut directions (page 136), mixing the cabbage with the carrots, onions, garlic, oregano, chile flakes, and cumin, then adding the salt.

Large-Batch (Homesteader) Lemon-Dill Kraut

yield: about 8 gallons
(fermentation vessel: 10 gallons)

This recipe makes enough for a big family (a very big family) to last the year — as in, once fermented, it will take 40 quart jars to store it! It's somewhat labor-intensive; it'll take two people at least 2 hours to cut and prepare the cabbage.

- 80 pounds cabbage
- 3 cups lemon juice
- 1¼ pounds unrefined sea salt
- 1–1½ cups dried dill weed (to taste)
- 7 heads garlic, cloves separated and grated

Follow the Large-Batch Kraut recipe (page 136), adding the lemon juice and dill with the salt. When the cabbage is glistening and you have a small pool of liquid in the bottom of the bowl, add the garlic.

OlyKraut's Eastern European Sauerkraut

yield: about 1 gallon
(fermentation vessel: 1 gallon or larger)
technique used: Mastering Sauerkraut (page 53)

This recipe, one of OlyKraut's favorite traditional-style caraway krauts, in 2012 won the Good Food Award from the Seedling Project in San Francisco. It seamlessly blends the crisp, fresh taste favored by the modern palate with the deep, traditional flavor of sauerkraut and caraway. The recipe is based on one that OlyKraut founding member Kai Tillman learned from her grandmother. The OlyKraut women tasted batch after batch, adjusting as they went, until it was just right. Kai is no longer with OlyKraut, but this recipe won't be going anywhere.

- 5 pounds cabbage
- 1 large yellow onion
- 2–3 carrots
- 1 tart apple
- Juice of 1 grapefruit
- 3–4 tablespoons unrefined sea salt
- Sprinkling of caraway seeds

OlyKraut

We met the women from OlyKraut — Sash Sunday and Summer Bock — a year after they began making kraut commercially. It was around the same time we launched our farmstead kraut business. When we asked Sash what put her on the journey to fresh real sauerkraut, she said it was her home garden.

One year she grew a lot of cabbage and decided to try making sauerkraut. She liked it. She made more. "I gave a lot away," she said. "I was a kraut charity."

At that time Sash was a student at Evergreen State College, in Olympia, Washington, with her focus on food and nutrition. She and other agricultural students put together a farm-based business plan for Evergreen's organic farm. According to the plan, they would grow cabbage, make kraut, and sell it to the student-run cafeteria and at a farm stand. The school implemented the plan, and OlyKraut grew in part from that experience.

Meanwhile, in another part of town, Summer Bock, a holistic nutrition counselor, was part of a group called the Fermented Veggie Club. It was through the club that she met Sash. In 2008 circumstances, among them a great commercial kitchen space, aligned just right for the women to establish OlyKraut.

The white wood building that houses the business was originally built as a cannery in 1934. Inside, a 25-foot-long stainless steel table dominates the vast space. There's also an insulated fermenting "cave," as the main room gets quite chilly. The worst days, Sash told us, aren't when you don't feel the difference walking in and out of the cooler; it's when you want to work in the cooler in order to get warm.

Health — both of the local population and of the local economy — is the driving force behind the flavors of OlyKraut. "We hope raw fermented vegetables reclaim their essential place at the American table and will play an important role in healing our people, our food system, and even the environment," Sash said. "Don't underestimate the lowly lactobacillus."

Sash and Summer developed their first recipes through trial and error in small batches in their home kitchens. Now they use 55-gallon stainless steel barrels. OlyKraut's seasonal approach captures the peak of taste and abundance at harvest time in the Pacific Northwest, so all of their flavors are balanced and delicious.

Sash Sunday (left) and Summer Bock (right)

1. Slice the cabbage and onion into a large bowl. Grate the carrots and the apple into the bowl, then add the juice and the salt and sprinkle on the caraway seeds.

2. Using your hands, mix everything together, then pack it into a crock.

3. Weight, cover, and store on the shelf until it's delicious!

4. Ladle the kraut into smaller jars and tamp down. Pour in any brine that's left. Tighten the lids, then store in the refrigerator. This kraut will keep, refrigerated, for 1 year.

Create Your Own Recipes

So many krauts, so little time. Cabbage is the base for just about anything you can think of, kraut-wise. A good formula is 3 parts cabbage to 1 part other fresh veggies.

How about a salsa kraut? Use cabbage, cilantro, garlic, a serrano or two, sweet red peppers, lime zest, and juice.

Or a wasabi-nori kraut. Add 2 to 3 tablespoons of nori, cut into small pieces, plus 3 tablespoons of wasabi powder to Naked Kraut (page 132).

Use your imagination, and have fun!

CABBAGE, NAPA OR CHINESE

Napa, or Chinese, cabbage is the main ingredient of kimchi. It is a staple throughout Asia. Napa leaves are typically more tender, juicy, and delicate than those of other types of cabbage. Depending on the recipe you may use it whole, slice it diagonally or lengthwise, quarter it or halve it, roll it, or stuff it.

Whole-cabbage kimchi is a traditional winter dish — it's strong and made to last until springtime. A typical stuffing consists of radishes, scallions, mustard leaves, watercress, garlic, ginger, anchovy juice, pickled or fresh shrimp and oysters (the seafood protein causes the ferment to develop essential amino acids), and a chile pepper powder known as *gochugaru*.

Other whole-cabbage kimchis are lighter and sweet. One stuffing calls for a small amount of anchovy juice and red pepper but includes apple, Asian pear, chestnuts, jujubes, pine nuts, and ginger.

YOUR RAW MATERIAL

There are many varieties of Chinese cabbage. Some are short and stalky; some, long and thin. All work well as long as they're fresh. Choose cabbages with a tight body and light green outer leaves. The inner leaves should be almost white, with no browning on the edges. Sometimes the darker green outer leaves are left on the cabbage as protective wrapping. That's fine, but remove them when you're ready to prepare the cabbage.

When we were making kimchi commercially, sometimes we'd get a box of cabbages and when we cut them open, all were bolting. You can't tell if they're bolting until you split them open and see a tight-curling sprout with cruciferous-type flowers. We tried cutting out the sprouts, but that sent almost half the cabbage weight to the cows instead of the crocks. Then we tasted them.

When we realized the sprouts were mild, neither bitter nor tough, the cows were out of luck and the crocks were full again.

Kimchi

See photo on page 231
yield: about 1 gallon
(fermentation vessel: 1 gallon or larger)
technique used: Mastering Kimchi Basics (page 87)

This is our basic kimchi recipe. We make it in the fall in a 3-gallon batch, which almost lasts through the winter. It's a good basic recipe to use as a springboard for experimentation. Remember to plan ahead, as this recipe requires a brining period, 6 to 8 hours or overnight.

In traditional kimchi making, after brining, the cabbage can be sliced in a variety of ways: chopped, quartered, halved, or left whole. In the United States, it's most commonly cut into bite-size pieces, but slice it however you like. The pickling is usually done in onggi pots (see page 35).

1 gallon	Kimchi Brine (1 cup unrefined sea salt to 1 gallon unchlorinated water)
2	large napa cabbages
½ cup	chile pepper flakes or salt-free *gochugaru*
½ cup	shredded daikon radish
¼ cup	shredded carrot
3	scallions, greens included, sliced
½–1	head garlic, cloves separated and minced
1 tablespoon	minced fresh ginger

1. In a crock or a large bowl, combine the brine ingredients and stir to dissolve. Remove the coarse outer leaves of the cabbages; rinse a few of the unblemished ones and set aside. Rinse the cabbages in cold water, trim off the stalk end, and cut in half. Submerge the cabbage halves and the reserved outer leaves in the brine. Use a plate as a weight to keep the cabbages submerged. Set aside, at room temperature, for 6 to 8 hours.

2. Drain the cabbage for 15 minutes, reserving about 1 cup of the soaking liquid. Set the separated outer leaves aside.

3. Meanwhile, combine the chile pepper flakes, daikon, carrot, scallions, garlic, and ginger in a large bowl, and blend thoroughly.

4. Chop the brined cabbage into bite-size pieces, or larger if you prefer, and add them to the bowl. Massage the mixture thoroughly, then taste for salt. Usually the brined cabbage will provide enough salt, but if it's not to your liking, sprinkle in a small amount, massage, and taste again.

5. Transfer the vegetables, a few handfuls at a time, into a crock, jar, or onggi pot, pressing with your hands as you go. Add reserved brine as needed to submerge the vegetables and leave about 4 inches of headspace for a crock or onggi pot, or 2 to 3 inches for a jar. Cover with the brined leaves. For a crock, top with a plate and weight down with a sealed water-filled jar. For a jar or onggi pot, you can use a sealed water-filled jar or ziplock bag as a follower-weight combination.

6. Set aside on a baking sheet to ferment, somewhere nearby, out of direct sunlight, and cool, for 7 to 14 days. Check your ferment daily to make sure the vegetables are submerged. You may see scum on top; it's generally harmless, but consult the appendix if you're at all concerned.

7. You can start to test the kimchi after 1 week. It will taste mild at this point, like a half-sour pickle. The cabbage will have a translucent quality and the brine will be an orange-red color.

Kimchi is often quite effervescent; it's normal whether it's bubbly or not.

8. When it's ready, spoon the kimchi into smaller jars, making sure the veggies are submerged; screw on the jar lids, and store in the fridge. This kimchi will keep, refrigerated, for 9 months.

> **FERMENTISTA'S TIP**
>
> ### Salting with Sea Vegetables
>
> *Seaweed brings its own salt to the mix, and that sodium is unrefined, full of minerals, and bioavailable. For these reasons, many omit some salt for a ferment heavy with seaweed. If you're adding a significant amount to, say, a sauerkraut, cut the additional salt by half. That way, you get a bit of both.*
>
> *You don't have to presoak dried seaweed, but keep in mind that when it reconstitutes in the ferment, it will swell to five times the size. See Seaweed Primer (page 232) for more information.*

Sea-Chi (a.k.a. Sea Kimchi)

See photo on page 172
yield: about 1 gallon
(fermentation vessel: 1 gallon or larger)

This is a mild variation of our basic kimchi recipe, using two sea vegetables instead of the chile pepper flakes. *Sea vegetables* is the culinary-savvy term for what's commonly known as seaweed, a type of ocean algae. Despite all the great health reasons one should eat seaweed, some people find little about the ocean smell appealing. This kimchi uses two mild sea vegetables that when fermented do not smell "fishy." Dulse comes in small flakes and adds pretty purple flecks to the ferment. Sea palm has a mild flavor; when rehydrated in kimchi or another ferment, it retains a nice crunch. If you can't imagine kimchi without a little heat, feel free to add 1 to 2 tablespoons of chile pepper flakes.

You'll need to plan ahead for this recipe, as it requires a brining period, 6 to 8 hours or overnight.

1 gallon Kimchi Brine (1 cup unrefined sea salt to 1 gallon unchlorinated water)
2 large heads napa cabbage
½–1 head garlic, cloves separated and minced
1 tablespoon minced fresh ginger
3 scallions, sliced
½ cup shredded daikon radish
¼ cup shredded carrot
½ cup sea palm fronds, broken or cut into bite-size pieces
1 tablespoon dulse flakes

Follow the recipe for Kimchi (page 141), adding the sea palm and dulse when you add the seasonings, radish, and carrot.

Spirit Creek Farm

In 2006 Andrew Sauter Sargent picked up *Salt: A World History,* by Mark Kurlansky (a great read that we highly recommend). Reading about the sailors who stayed healthy by eating sauerkraut inspired Andrew, a sailor himself. Meanwhile, Jennifer Sauter Sargent, passionate about gardening, had a bumper crop of cabbage.

They harvested the cabbages and other vegetables, and they worked together to ferment them for their family. The first inkling of a business plan came when Andrew mentioned to Jennifer that if they made 30,000 jars of sauerkraut and netted a dollar on each, they'd have a profit of $30,000.

By the next year they'd talked themselves into starting a farmstead kraut business, and in 2007 Spirit Creek Farm was born. The couple's off-the-grid, solar-powered farm sits on 70 acres on the south shore of Lake Superior. They source their ingredients from sustainable organic farms in the Upper Midwest. They're committed to stewardship of their land and their community.

Jennifer recently participated in a farm-to-school program in which she taught the art of fermentation to 100 schoolchildren. Clad in rubber gloves, the children salted, hand-mixed, and pounded cabbage; when it was ready to ferment,

Andrew and Jennifer Sauter Sargent

the kids took turns pressing and pummeling the cabbage in a huge bucket. Jennifer said, "It was some of the best-pounded weeping kraut I've ever seen."

Different regions seem to have their own preferences for kraut taste. "All of our krauts are tailored to the palate of the northern Midwest," Jennifer says. "Our population is heavily Scandinavian and German, so we keep our flavors mellow." Once a year, though, Andrew steps up the amount of spices, adds seaweed, and makes a kimchi for family and friends. It's distinctive because their commercial kimchi is made with green cabbage, not napa cabbage, which they find difficult to source locally.

Andrew's Private Reserve Kimchi

yield: about 2 quarts
(fermentation vessel: two 2-quart jars)
technique used: Mastering Sauerkraut (page 53)

Andrew Sauter Sargent's recipe (see Meet the Fermentistas on page 143) is a bit different from the other kimchi recipes in this book in that he prepares kimchi like a kraut, without the extra brining step.

- 1 head napa cabbage, chopped
- 3 carrots, shredded
- 1 large daikon radish, shredded
- 1 large onion, chopped
- ¼ cup dulse seaweed flakes (or any other shredded sea vegetable; see page 142)
- 1 tablespoon chile pepper flakes
- 1 tablespoon minced garlic
- 1 tablespoon minced fresh ginger
- 1 tablespoon sesame seeds
- 1 tablespoon granulated sugar
- 2 teaspoons unrefined sea salt
- 1 teaspoon fish sauce

1. Mix all the ingredients together and let sit for at least 30 minutes.

2. Pound into two 2-quart jars, and cap loosely or top with a water-filled ziplock bag to seal off oxygen. Set aside to ferment, at room temperature, for at least 3 days. Taste for the degree of sourness you want, then refrigerate.

3. This kimchi will last for almost forever, but it will be long gone before forever comes!

Tsukemono (Japanese Pickled Cabbage)

yield: about 1 gallon
(fermentation vessel: 1 gallon or larger)
technique used: Mastering Sauerkraut (page 53)

This recipe and the next use the same ingredients. What makes them different is how you prepare the cabbage. For the Japanese *tsukemono*, you slice it before fermenting; for the Chinese *suan cai*, leave the cabbages whole.

The literal translation of *tsukemono* is "pickled things." Traditionally, this recipe calls for the cabbage to be "layered in salt," which is just too much for our taste. In Japan this ferment is made in a special container called a *tsukemono* press (see the resources, page 360); it has a lid that when screwed down acts as the follower and weight.

- 2 napa cabbages
- 2–4 tablespoons unrefined sea salt

1. Remove the coarse outer leaves. Rinse a few unblemished ones and set them aside. Rinse the rest of the cabbage in cold water. With a stainless steel knife, cut the cabbages in half lengthwise, then crosswise into ½-inch slices.

2. In a large bowl, mix the cabbage with 2 tablespoons of the salt, then taste. It should taste slightly salty without being overwhelming. If it's not salty enough, continue salting until it's to your liking. The napa will soon look wet and limp, and liquid will begin to pool. This cabbage tends to weep more quickly than green cabbage.

3. Transfer the cabbage to a 1-gallon crock or jar, several handfuls at a time, pressing down with your fist or a tamper to remove air pockets. You should see some brine on top of the cabbage when you press. When the vessel is packed, leave 4 inches of headspace for a crock, or 2 to 3 inches for a jar. Top the cabbage with one or two of the reserved outer leaves. For a crock, top the leaves with a plate that fits the opening of the container and covers as much of the vegetables as possible; then weight down with a sealed water-filled jar. For a jar, use a sealed water-filled jar or ziplock bag as a follower-weight combination.

4. Set aside on a baking sheet to ferment, somewhere nearby, out of direct sunlight, and cool, for 7 to 14 days. Check daily to make sure the cabbage is submerged, pressing down as needed to bring the brine back to the surface.

5. You can start to test the *tsukemono* on day 7. The fermented napa will have the same limp yet still somewhat crisp texture as kimchi and will smell a lot like sauerkraut but a bit stronger. Keep tasting; it could take up to 2 weeks to reach the proper degree of sourness.

6. When it's pleasing to your palate, it's ready. Ladle the ferment into smaller jars and tamp down. Pour in any brine that's left. Tighten the lids, then store in the fridge. This ferment will keep, refrigerated, for 8 to 12 months.

Suan Cai (Chinese Sour Cabbage)

yield: 1–2 gallons
(fermentation vessel: 2 gallons or larger)
technique used: Mastering Brine Pickling (page 77)

The literal translation of *suan cai* is "sour vegetable." This traditional napa "sauerkraut" comes from the northern part of China. Pickle the cabbages whole, without any other vegetables or spices. Use a few whole cabbages and wedge them into the crock; one would just float around and be difficult to weight down. Once fermented, they are used as an ingredient in stir-fries. Or you can use them as you would any other kraut.

Use these whole pickled leaves as a fun wrapper with your favorite sandwich filling. Just remove a leaf from the head and pat dry with a clean towel before wrapping.

2–4 napa cabbages
1–2 gallons Basic Brine (½ cup unrefined sea salt to 1 gallon unchlorinated water)

1. Rinse the cabbages in cold water and wedge them whole into the crock, leaving about 4 inches of headspace. Pour in enough brine to cover the cabbage completely. Remember the mantra: *Submerge in brine and all will be fine.* Top the cabbage with a plate and a weight such as a sealed water-filled jar.

2. Store any leftover brine in the fridge (it will keep for a week; discard thereafter and make a new batch, if needed). Set aside on a baking sheet to ferment, somewhere nearby, out of direct sunlight, and cool, for 2½ to 3 weeks.

3. During the fermentation period, monitor the brine level and top off with the reserved brine solution, if needed, to cover. You may see scum on top; it's generally harmless, but check the appendix if you are concerned. As the cabbage ferments, it will begin to lose its vibrant color and the brine will get cloudy.

4. You can start testing after about 2½ weeks by plucking a leaf from the whole head. It will be done when it tastes sour and kraut-y, and the leaves are somewhat translucent and have the limp yet somewhat crisp texture of kimchi.

5. To store, you can transfer the whole cabbages into clean gallon jars and pour in the brine, adding fresh brine to cover if needed. Or you can coarsely chop the cabbage and pack it into a gallon jar, or a few quart jars, like a kraut. This pickle will keep, refrigerated, for 8 months.

Kirsten and Christopher Write

We found one reference to this type of vegetable ferment accomplished as a dry-salting process. It seems part of the unique flavor of this method comes from the time it takes for the salt to break down the cell walls of whole cabbages to create the brine. We tried it.

We used four napa cabbages. The thinking was that whole cabbages would supply the critical mass necessary to make enough brine and weight. We rinsed them in cold water. Because we wanted to compact the cabbage for packing into the crock and to give the salt a place to start its work, we then tried to crush each base with the palm of a hand. Not easy. We sprinkled salt among the leaves as best we could.

The recipe called for stoneware pots and to weight the cabbage with a large rock. Instead, we used a 3-gallon crock and pressed in the cabbage as firmly as we could. We then weighted with 16 pounds in the form of two water-filled gallon jugs.

Then we waited.

After three days we had 1 inch of brine at the bottom of the crock. Hmmm. We rotated the cabbages, putting the top ones into the (wading) pool of brine. Two days later there was 2 inches of brine; the smell, however, was clearly headed toward a unique flavor that was, let's say, beyond our interest. We let it continue to ferment for a few weeks in the name of science, but it never developed enough brine to immerse the cabbage. It landed in the compost pile.

CABBAGE, RED

Red cabbage is not a go-to vegetable. Many people simply don't know what to do with it. Perhaps their only experience with it are the shreds thrown into a salad-bar mix to add color and texture to the iceberg lettuce. Red cabbage has so much more to offer.

Beyond a mild, pleasantly sweet flavor and a great color, it's packed with nutritional elements. During the Middle Ages, botanists encouraged the red pigment, which we now know as *anthocyanin*. The amounts of anthocyanin and vitamin C in red cabbage are superior to those of green cabbage. Studies suggest that certain anthocyanins have anti-inflammatory, antiviral, and antimicrobial properties.

YOUR RAW MATERIAL

When fermented, the violet-red of the raw cabbage is modified by a cooling blue hue that makes the whole affair a fuchsia-infused purple, the color of royalty, military honors, religious ceremonies, and the '60s haze of psychedelic drugs. For the artist of the crock, this cabbage adds allure to any dish.

The leaves of the red cabbage are different from those of the green. How to describe them? We hesitate to use the word *tough,* which gives the sense of a chewy texture, which is not the case. Red cabbage is sturdier than is the green; it keeps longer under cool storage and has a different texture than regular sauerkraut.

Because it stores well, look for heads that are crisp and brightly colored; avoid cabbage that looks old or wilted. Choose the heads with the deepest red, as this pigment is what gives nutritional value. A dull color indicates that the cabbage is no longer fresh. A fresh cabbage will still have some outer leaves — if it doesn't, or if you turn it over and the leaves are beginning to separate from the stem, you're looking at an old cabbage.

IN THE CROCK

Blaukraut

See photo on page 256

yield: about 1 gallon
(fermentation vessel: 1 gallon or larger)
technique used: Mastering Sauerkraut (page 53)

The flavor is decidedly more acidic than the traditional, Bavarian sugar-sweetened cooked version, but it's delicious and a satisfying accompaniment to meat and potatoes. Serve as a side dish just as it is, dress it up with blue cheese and walnuts (page 318), or turn it into Braised Blaukraut (page 340). It also makes a nice layer in a sandwich or wrap.

2–3	heads (about 6 pounds) red cabbage
2–3	crisp tart apples, cored, quartered, and sliced thin
1	medium onion, thinly sliced
2	tablespoons caraway seeds (or to taste)
1½–2	tablespoons unrefined sea salt

1. Remove the coarse outer cabbage leaves. Rinse a few unblemished ones and set them aside. Rinse the rest of the cabbage in cold water. With a stainless steel knife, quarter and core the cabbage. Thinly slice with the same knife or a mandoline, then transfer the cabbage to a large bowl. Add the apples, onion, and caraway to the cabbage.

2. Add 1½ tablespoons of the salt and, with your hands, massage it into the leaves, then taste. It should taste slightly salty without being overwhelming. Add more salt if necessary. Quickly the cabbage will glisten and liquid will begin to pool. If you've put in a good effort and don't see much brine in the bowl, let it stand, covered, for 45 minutes, then massage again.

3. Transfer the cabbage, several handfuls at a time, to a 1-gallon jar or crock, pressing down with your fist or a tamper to remove air pockets. You should see some brine on top of the cabbage when you press. When the vessel is packed, leave 4 inches of headspace for a crock, or 2 to 3 inches for a jar. Top the cabbage with one or two of the reserved outer leaves. For a crock, top the leaves with a plate that fits the opening of the container and covers as much of the vegetables as possible; then weight down with a sealed water-filled jar. For a jar, use a sealed water-filled jar or ziplock bag as a follower-weight combination.

4. Set aside your vessel on a baking sheet to ferment, somewhere nearby, out of direct sunlight, and cool, for 7 to 14 days. Check daily to make sure the kraut is submerged, pressing down to bring the brine back to the surface.

5. You can start to test the kraut on day 7. You'll know it's ready when it's pleasingly sour and pickle-y tasting, without the strong acidity of vinegar, and the veggies have softened a bit but retain some crunch.

6. To store, ladle the kraut into smaller jars and tamp down. Pour in any brine that's left. Tighten the lids, then store in the fridge. This kraut will keep, refrigerated, for 1 year.

Create Your Own Recipes

For amazing color, make a beet–red cabbage kraut. Our neighbor used a dynamite combination of these two red veggies and added chopped jalapeño for even more excitement.

CARROTS

The day is coming when a single carrot, freshly observed, will set off a revolution.

— PAUL CÉZANNE, POST-IMPRESSIONIST FRENCH PAINTER

You can't go wrong putting carrots in any ferment, at least as far as taste, color, and crunch are concerned. In other words, it makes a beautiful, crisp ferment that begs to be eaten. You'll find recipes throughout this A-to-Z section that include carrots (maybe even more than include cabbage). Curtido is a cabbage kraut punctuated by carrot coins (page 133), sliced carrots are featured in Burdock-Carrot Kimchi (page 131), and shredded carrots make an appearance in a number of krauts and kimchis.

Carrots also brine-pickle well. Our first introduction to pickled carrots were the ones prepared by a Ukranian neighbor. She never got used to the abundance in our American supermarkets and could not help saving every scrap of food. She would even ferment the miniscule carrots gleaned from thinning the garden. It took her hours to clean and prepare them. They were adorable in the jar and scrumptious too, but while we adopted the practice of fermenting carrots, we still feed all the tiny ones to the goats and horses.

YOUR RAW MATERIAL

Carrots come in myriad colors, they're available year-round, and they'll transform any ferment by adding a hint of sweetness. And they pair with any other vegetable. What more can you ask?

FERMENTISTA'S TIP

Yeasty Business

Ferments that contain a significant quantity of carrots are more susceptible to yeasts. This is also true for other roots with a high sugar content, such as beets. It isn't a problem, just something to be aware of. Keeping the level of the brine consistently above the vegetables will hold yeast at bay (see Scum You Can Ignore, page 356).

IN THE CROCK

Carrot Kraut

yield: about 1 gallon
(fermentation vessel: 1 gallon or larger)
technique used: Mastering Sauerkraut (page 53)

This is an adaptation of Sally Fallon's gingered carrots. Though it's a colorful and refreshing side dish, we like it best in carrot cake. The kraut adds moisture, and with the cream-cheese frosting, life is good. *Note:* Due to its high sugar content, this kraut continues to ferment in the refrigerator and will sour more with time.

FERMENTISTA'S TIP

To Peel or Not to Peel?

It's not always necessary to peel carrots. If they're young and sweet, just scrub them and grate. If the carrots are large with darker, bitter peels, pare them before you grate.

- 8 **pounds carrots, grated**
- 1–2 **tablespoons grated fresh ginger**
- **Juice and zest of 1 lemon**
- 1½–2 **tablespoons unrefined sea salt**

1. Combine the carrots, ginger, lemon juice, and zest in a large bowl. Add 1½ tablespoons of the salt and, with your hands, massage it into the veggies, then taste. It should taste slightly salty without being overwhelming. Add more salt if necessary. Carrots get briny almost immediately and liquid will pool.

2. Transfer the carrot mixture to a 1-gallon jar or crock, a few handfuls at a time, pressing down with your fist or a tamper to remove air pockets. You should see some brine on top of the carrots when you press. When the vessel is packed, leave 4 inches of headspace for a crock, or 2 to 3 inches for a jar.

3. Cover the carrots with a piece of plastic wrap or other primary follower. For a crock, top the carrots with a plate that fits the opening of the container and covers as much of the surface as possible; then weight down with a sealed water-filled jar. For a jar, use a sealed water-filled jar or a ziplock bag as a combination follower and weight.

4. Set aside on a baking sheet to ferment, somewhere nearby, out of direct sunlight, and cool, for 7 to 14 days. Check daily to make sure the carrots are submerged, pressing down as needed to bring the brine back to the surface.

5. You can start to test the kraut on day 7. You'll know it's ready when it has a crisp-sour flavor and the brine is thick and rich.

6. When it's ready, transfer the kraut to smaller jars and tamp down. Pour in any brine that's left. Tighten the lids, then store in the fridge. This kraut will keep, refrigerated, for 1 year, but is better within 6 months.

IN THE PICKLE JAR

Vietnamese Pickled Carrot and Daikon

yield: about ½ gallon
(fermentation vessel: 2 quarts or larger)
technique used: Mastering Brine Pickling (page 77)

This is a variation on a pickle that's an important ingredient in the Vietnamese *banh mi*, which is the cuisine's version of a hoagie, a hero, or a sub. The traditional ingredient is a vinegar pickle, but this lacto-fermented one carries itself just as well in this and other sandwiches. Because these pickles are Asian style, you'll be making the brine with some sugar.

BRINE

- ½ cup unrefined sea salt
- 2 tablespoons sugar
- 1 gallon unchlorinated water

- 2 pounds carrots, peeled and julienned
- 2 pounds daikon radishes, peeled and julienned
- 1–2 grape leaves (optional)

1. For the brine, add the salt and sugar to the water, and stir to combine.

2. Arrange the carrots and daikon, wedging them under the shoulder of a jar or with 4 inches of headspace in a crock. Pour in enough brine to cover the vegetables completely. Reserve any leftover brine in the fridge. (It will keep for 1 week; discard thereafter and make a new batch, if needed.)

3. Place grape leaves, if using, over the vegetables. For a crock, top with a plate that will rest atop the pickles; weight down the plate with a sealed water-filled jar. If using a jar, no follower or weight is needed if the pickles are wedged in place under the shoulder; just cover loosely.

4. Set aside on a baking sheet to ferment, somewhere nearby and out of direct sunlight, in a cool spot for 7 to 14 days. During the fermentation period, monitor brine level and top off with the reserved brine, if needed, to cover. You may see scum on top; it's harmless, but if you see mold, scoop it out.

5. As the vegetables ferment, they begin to lose their vibrant color and the brine will get cloudy; this is when you can start to test your pickles. They're ready when they're pleasingly sour and pickle-y tasting, without the strong acidity of vinegar.

6. Store in jars, with lids tightened, in the fridge. These will keep, refrigerated, for 12 months.

Fermented Carrot Sticks

See photo on page 152

This is a kid-friendly variation on the above recipe. Pickled carrot sticks can be a child's gateway into fermented food. They're crunchy and so convenient; just pull them out of the jar and serve with peanut butter.

Follow the process for Vietnamese Pickled Carrot and Daikon, using only the carrots and cutting them into sticks. For a less sour ferment, omit sugar from the brine. For a little more flavor, add a sprig of rosemary or 3 or 4 lemon slices to the jar.

CAULIFLOWER

Cauliflower is nothing but cabbage with a college education.

— MARK TWAIN, *PUDD'NHEAD WILSON*, 1894

Cauliflower, as its name suggests, is a bundle of flowers. It probably developed in Asia Minor, from wild cabbage, which grew in gardens of that area around 600 BCE. Botanists believe it looked somewhat like today's collards.

It made a mark on the culinary scene in the 16th century as *cauli-fiori*, from Genoa, then made its way to France, where it was grown in gardens and called *chou-fleur*. It was prized for its delicacy of flavor.

YOUR RAW MATERIAL

Cauliflower's head is called a *curd*. In making your selection, it is great to see thick, dark green leaves surrounding it. They serve as protection and keep the cauliflower fresh. However, these have usually been trimmed off, so when you examine the curd, it should be compact. Separation in the bud clusters, or a rough or loose texture, means the head has matured past its prime. The curd should be creamy and white, not dull. Don't bother with spotted cauliflower, as the spots are another sign of age.

Varieties other than the usual cream-white ferment well too. Orange cauliflower was developed in Canada in the 1970s; it has a sweeter taste and boasts 25 percent more vitamin A than its pale counterpart. The origins of the purple cauliflower are unclear, but it's said that it developed naturally. The color comes from anthocyanin, which is considered to be a beneficial antioxidant.

For us, green cauliflower and Romanesco are hit-or-miss in the crock, probably because these varieties are a cross between cauliflower and broccoli, and broccoli is our crock problem child (see page 127).

FERMENTED CARROT STICKS,
page 151

TOMATILLO SALSA,
page 240

HOT SMOKY SPROUTS,
page 128

BURDOCK-CARROT KIMCHI,
page 131

JUNIPER-ONION
KRAUT, *page 133*

PICKLED CRANBERRIES,
page 274

CAULIKRAUT, *page 154*

PRESERVED LIMES,
page 271

GARLIC PICKLE SLICES,
page 169

I've hidden, puréed, and disguised many a cauliflower floret into family meals. Cauliflower has a hefty amount of vitamins C and K. Raw, a serving fulfills 77 percent of the daily C requirement; cooked, that number is reduced to 46 percent. "Eating yucky food is a big price to pay for vitamins," to quote a member of my family. But fermented raw cauliflower is a whole other story.

About five years ago, I proudly traded some of my homemade feta for a big box of cauliflower. (My family didn't share my enthusiasm.) That year our garden produced an abundance of jalapeños. I brined the cauliflower with the jalapeños plus onions, carrots, and a lot of garlic. Crisp and spicy, the cauliflower took on all those flavors beautifully. In this new guise, cauliflower became a new family favorite.

IN THE CROCK

CauliKraut

yield: about 1 quart
(fermentation vessel: 1 quart or larger)
technique used: Relishes, Chutneys, Salsas, and Fermented Salads (page 66)

When making this tasty kraut, the key is to slice the cauliflower ribbon-thin. Use a mandoline slicer or the slicing option on a microplane grater. The latter works well enough, but be aware that the brittle cauliflower bits tend to snap and fly off the counter — just corral them and toss them back into the bowl.

>   1 **head (1½ pounds) cauliflower**
>   2 **jalapeños, minced**
> 1–1½ **teaspoons unrefined sea salt**

1. Rinse the cauliflower in cold water. Cut it into florets and slice as thinly as you can. Place in a bowl with the jalapeños. Sprinkle in 1 teaspoon of the salt, working it in with your hands; let rest for 30 minutes. It may seem too dry, but don't worry, it's fine.

2. Toss and massage the salted cauliflower again for a few minutes just to get everything mixed. Press tightly into the jar. It may still feel too dry, but the cauliflower will continue to weep as fermentation begins. Go ahead and tuck it in. Top the ferment with a ziplock bag, pressing the plastic down onto the top of the ferment, then fill the bag with water and seal; this will act as both follower and weight. If you don't feel there's enough brine, wait about 8 hours, remove the bag, and press down to get the brine to the surface. Then replace the bag.

3. Set aside on a baking sheet to ferment, somewhere nearby, out of direct sunlight, and cool, for 4 to 8 days. Check daily to make sure the vegetables are submerged, pressing down as needed to bring the brine to the surface. You may see scum on top; it's generally harmless, but consult the appendix if you're at all concerned.

4. You can start to test the ferment on day 4. You'll know it's ready when it's pleasingly sour and pickle-y tasting, without the strong acidity of vinegar; and the flavors have mingled.

5. Tamp down to make sure the kraut is submerged, screw on the lid, and store in the fridge. This ferment will keep, refrigerated, for 10 months.

Curried CauliKraut

yield: about 1 quart
(fermentation vessel: 1 quart or larger)

This is an ocher-yellow, Indian-spiced variation of CauliKraut. Toasting the curry spice seeds intensifies their flavor, but in a pinch you can substitute 2 teaspoons of curry powder instead (page 124).

- 1 teaspoon mustard seed
- ½ teaspoon coriander seed
- ½ teaspoon cumin seed
- 1 head (1½ pounds) cauliflower, cut into florets and sliced very thin
- 2 carrots, shredded
  Juice of 1 orange (⅓ cup)
- 1 spring onion, greens attached, sliced
- 1½–2 teaspoons unrefined sea salt

1. In a dry skillet, toast the mustard, coriander, and cumin seeds until fragrant. Set aside.

2. Follow the recipe for CauliKraut (at left), omitting the jalapeño and adding the rest of the ingredients to the bowl with the sliced cauliflower, including the toasted seeds.

IN THE PICKLE JAR

Cauliflower is a natural choice to brine-pickle in any vegetable medley. To prepare it for pickling, first remove the outer leaves. Turn the curd upside down and remove the core or stem with a paring knife. Discard the core.

Pull apart the curd and separate the florets into bite-size pieces. When you get to the big stems, use the paring knife to cut them apart, then continue to break apart into bite-size pieces. What you want is to retain those nice flowery shapes.

FERMENTISTA'S TIP

Fresh Is Best

Always use fresh veggies in your ferments. Old vegetables provide less energy, have fewer nutrients, and don't taste as fresh, resulting in less power in the crock or jar.

Edgy Veggies

See photo on page 257

yield: about 1 gallon
(fermentation vessel: 1 gallon or larger)
technique used: Mastering Brine Pickling (page 77)

This medley can range from spicy to fiery, depending on the jalapeños. The recipe was inspired by the pickled carrots and jalapeños served in many Mexican restaurants. They often appear on our winter table, dressing up stews, soups, and beans. A gallon might seem like a lot, but you'll see they go quickly.

- 1 head cauliflower, cut into florets
- 5 or more cloves garlic, whole or halved
- 2 pounds carrots, peeled and sliced
- 1 onion, cut into wedges
- 1 pound jalapeños, cored and cut into rounds (in the off-season, substitute 2 tablespoons chile pepper flakes and add a few more carrots and cauliflower florets)
- 1–2 tablespoons dried oregano, crumbled
- 1 gallon Basic Brine (½ cup unrefined sea salt to 1 gallon unchlorinated water)
- 1–2 grape leaves (optional)

1. Combine the veggies and spices in a large bowl and mix to distribute the ingredients. Pack into a crock or jar, wedging them under the shoulder of the jar or with 4 inches of headspace in a crock. Pour in enough brine to cover the vegetables completely. Remember your mantra: *Submerge in brine and all will be fine.* Reserve any leftover brine in the fridge. (It will keep for 1 week; discard thereafter and make a new batch, if needed.)

2. Place a grape leaf or a piece of plastic wrap over the top to keep the spices and vegetables from floating. For a crock, top with a plate that will rest atop the veggies, and a weight such as a sealed water-filled jar to keep things in place. If using a jar, no follower or weight is needed, as the vegetables are wedged in place by the shoulder; just cover loosely.

3. Set aside on a baking sheet to ferment, somewhere nearby, out of direct sunlight, and cool, for 7 to 21 days. During the fermentation period, monitor the brine level and top off with the reserved brine solution, if needed, to cover. You may see scum on top; it's generally harmless, but consult the appendix if you're at all concerned.

4. As the vegetables ferment, they begin to lose their vibrant color and the brine will get cloudy; this is when you can start to test your pickles. In the summertime this may be as soon as 1 week; in a cooler environment it will be closer to 2 weeks. They're ready when they're pleasingly sour and pickle-y tasting, without the strong acidity of vinegar; the flavors have mingled; and they're softer than they were when fresh but retain some crispiness.

5. When the vegetables are ready, store in jars, with lids tightened, in the fridge. After about 1 day check to be sure the pickles are still submerged, topping off with the reserved brine, if necessary. These pickles will keep, refrigerated, for 1 year.

CELERIAC

Unfortunately everyone seems to be completely baffled by celeriac, but it's beautiful in soups or thinly sliced into salads. When roasted it goes sweet and when mixed with potato and mashed it's a complete joy.

— JAMIE OLIVER, *HAPPY DAYS WITH THE NAKED CHEF*, 2001

YOUR RAW MATERIAL

Celeriac, though lacking in conventional beauty (it's really not pretty), is delicious fermented, but even more important, it's one of our favorite bases for crucifer-free kraut (good for the crucifer intolerant; see page 132). The shreds hold up to the fermentation and provide good consistency. It has a mild celery flavor, which other vegetables and spices complement, so it's a nice addition to krauts.

Working with Celeriac

Celeriac is a bit difficult to peel. The top and the sides, however, are straightforward enough. Using a paring knife, carefully cut off the skin. The bottom of the root is where it gets confusing: there's a tangled mass of roots with bits of dirt wedged in. Either spend a lot of time trying to salvage most of the tangle of roots or cut off the bottom and move on.

Kirsten Writes

Celeriac, or celery root, is rare on the American table. In Europe, on the other hand, it's quite common. I grew up eating it as a warm salad, somewhat like a traditional warm potato salad. My mother boiled it, then peeled it while still warm. She sliced it thin, added some raw onion, and dressed with vinegar, oil, salt, and pepper. And this is how I prepared it for my husband and kids. The children tolerated it.

A couple of years ago, when we began experimenting with fermenting celeriac, we were stunned by how delicious it is.

IN THE CROCK

Naked Celeriac Kraut

yield: about 1 quart
(fermentation vessel: 1 quart or larger)
technique used: Mastering Sauerkraut (page 53)

This is fermented celeriac, plain and unassuming. Like Naked Kraut (page 132), it is delicious and versatile. This recipe is shredded for a krauty consistency; however, for an alternative "salad," slice celeriac thinly on a mandoline.

2 pounds celeriac root, cleaned, peeled, and shredded
1–1½ teaspoons unrefined sea salt

1. In a large bowl, combine the celeriac with 1 teaspoon of the salt and massage well, then taste. It should taste slightly salty without being overwhelming. Add more salt, if necessary, until it's to your liking. The celeriac will become limp and liquid may begin to pool. The dry quality of these roots means sometimes the brine isn't obvious until the celeriac is pressed into the vessel.

2. Transfer a few handfuls at a time to a 1-quart jar or a 1-gallon crock. Press down on each portion with your fist or a tamper to remove air pockets. You should see some brine on top when you press. When the vessel is packed, leave 4 inches of headspace for a crock, or 2 to 3 inches for a jar. Top with a primary follower — a piece of plastic wrap or grape leaves, if you have some. For a crock, follow this with a plate that fits the opening of the container and covers as much of the vegetables as possible; then weight down with a sealed water-filled jar. For a jar, use a sealed water-filled jar or ziplock bag.

3. Set aside your vessel on a baking sheet to ferment, somewhere nearby, out of direct sunlight, and cool, for 5 to 10 days. Check daily to make sure the celeriac is submerged, pressing down as needed to bring the brine back to the surface. You may see scum on top; it's generally harmless, but consult the appendix if you're at all concerned.

4. You can start to test the kraut on day 5. It's ready when it's pleasingly sour. *Note:* The texture will be softer than that of a cabbage-based kraut.

5. When the kraut is ready, store in jars, with lids tightened, in the fridge. This kraut will keep, refrigerated, for 1 year.

Hungarian Celeriac

See photo on page 217
yield: about 2 quarts
(fermentation vessel: 2 quarts or larger)

In our hands-on krauting classes the vegetables are piled high for students to choose from. We start by tasting krauts so that people get a sense of what they like. This kraut never ceases to surprise and delight students, not only because it's delicious but also because most people have never thought to ferment celeriac. Often when it's time to make the kraut there's a mad dash to the vegetable pile for this gnarled root.

> 2 **pounds celeriac root, shredded**
> 5–6 **wax peppers (use Hungarian for heat, banana for sweet), thinly sliced**
> 1 **generous tablespoon caraway seeds**
> 1 **teaspoon ground paprika**
> 1–1½ **teaspoons unrefined sea salt**

Follow the directions for Naked Celeriac Kraut (page 157), adding the peppers and spices with the celeriac.

Create Your Own Recipes

Incorporate celeriac spears into a vegetable pickle medley.

CELERY

The best way to find out what others are doing in the celery business, is to take a bunch of your celery of an average grade, tie a bunch of damp peat moss upon the butts, then wrap all in paper to protect from the air and getting marred, and take the early train for your nearest city; inquire for the fancy grocer of the town, and show up to him just what you have.

— HOMER L. STEWART, *CELERY GROWING AND MARKETING A SUCCESS*, 1891

Where does celery fall on the nutritional scale? Urban legend has it that celery takes more calories to consume than it contains, and that it's all water, which leads some to think of it as a diet food and others to think of it as an empty food. Instead, celery boasts a number of health benefits. Got sleeplessness, mild anxiety, high blood pressure, arthritis, kidney stones, or gallstones, anyone? Need relaxation, a cancer preventive, a sexual stimulant? Celery. Nothing empty about it.

YOUR RAW MATERIAL

For fermenting, find the freshest celery available. We use locally grown heirloom celery; the stems are greener and there are more leaves. The stems are also denser, which means a stronger flavor and crunchier texture.

Homegrown celery has less moisture than store-bought. When packing it into the crock, with patience and massaging perseverance it *will* weep enough to create its own brine. But this same low moisture content gives homegrown celery ferments a more robust flavor and texture.

Celery "Stuffing"

See photo on page 217

yield: about 1 quart
(fermentation vessel: 1 quart or larger)
technique used: Relishes, Chutneys, Salsas, and Fermented Salads (page 66)

This "bready" name seems ridiculous for a vegetable ferment, but you'll be surprised. It's not a relish, a kraut, a kimchi, a pickle, or a paste. It is, though, a substantial presence in the mouth, and the thyme and sage suggest a turkey dinner. Whether you call it stuffing or dressing, this can be a gluten-free option to stuff poultry or to eat alongside as a dressing.

1½	pounds celery, including the leaves, chopped
8–10	fresh sage leaves, thinly sliced
1	tablespoon chopped fresh thyme
1	teaspoon unrefined sea salt
1–2	grape leaves (optional)

1. Combine the celery, sage, and thyme. Sprinkle in the salt, a little at a time, tasting as you go, until it's slightly salty, but not overwhelming. Massage the mixture and let sit, covered, for 30 minutes.

2. Pack the mixture, a few handfuls at a time, into a 1-quart jar, pressing as you go to remove air pockets and release brine; because of the texture, it will take some effort to get it tightly packed. This pressure will release more brine. When the jar is packed, leave 2 to 3 inches of

headspace. With store-bought celery there will likely be a noticeable layer of brine, while with homegrown the brine may just barely cover the vegetables. Add a grape leaf, piece of plastic wrap, or other primary follower. Because of the low brine content, make sure this is weighted well with a sealed water-filled jar or ziplock bag to act as a combination follower and weight.

3. Set aside to ferment, somewhere nearby, out of direct sunlight, and cool, for 5 to 10 days. Check daily that the celery is submerged, pressing down as needed to bring the brine back to the surface. You may see scum on top; it's generally harmless, but consult the appendix if you're at all concerned.

4. Start testing the ferment on day 5. When it's ready, this ferment will be crunchy, will taste of sage, and will have a mild, light sour flavor, very different from the sour boldness of most krauts.

5. When it's sour enough for your palate, tamp down the ferment under the brine, screw on the lid, and store in the refrigerator. Because of its high natural nitrate content, celery keeps well, if it remains submerged, and will last over 1 year, but you will want to eat it well before then.

Celery-Mint Salad

yield: about 1 quart
(fermentation vessel: 1 quart or larger)
technique used: Relishes, Chutneys, Salsas, and Fermented Salads (page 66)

Cool, bright, and lively, this is a summery-tasting variation on the Celery "Stuffing" recipe above. Serve on its own or add to a mixed-green salad.

1½ pounds celery, including the leaves, thinly sliced

1 bunch scallions, greens included, finely chopped

6 sprigs mint, thinly sliced

1 teaspoon unrefined sea salt

1–2 grape leaves (optional)

Follow the Celery "Stuffing" recipe (page 159), adding the scallions and mint to the celery before adding the salt.

Create Your Own Recipes

Celery, onions, and carrots make up the "holy trinity" known as *mirepoix*. They're used as the flavoring base for many French dishes. The French-inspired Creole cuisine of Louisiana replaces the carrot with bell pepper; celery, onion, and garlic are the basis for much Italian, Portuguese, and Spanish cookery. Each of these vegetables ferments delightfully. Try fermenting these celebrated triads alone or with herbs and spices.

Pickle whole celery sticks in the Basic Brine (½ cup unrefined sea salt to 1 gallon unchlorinated water) with or without spices. If you keep the stalks intact, be sure to remove the strings — otherwise it's like eating fermented dental floss.

CHARD

Have a huge crop of chard and want to preserve it? We can help you with the stems, but sorry, the leaves on their own just don't shine.

Our goal is to help you bring each vegetable to new flavor heights, not to ferment everything. If you'd like to add a few leaves of chard to a cabbage-based combination in the crock, be sure to chop them fine and treat them like an herb.

IN THE PICKLE JAR

Chard stems taste, well, like pickled stems, but they take on the flavors of any herb you ferment with them, and with the rainbow of color options — ruby, fuchsia, orange, yellow, and white — they look delightful in a jar. Use your favorite pickling flavors and follow the directions for brine pickling (page 77).

CILANTRO (CORIANDER)

Some people love cilantro. Some don't. If you dislike it intensely — okay, you loathe it — just skip to collard greens. If you're in the I-love-cilantro camp, keep reading.

YOUR RAW MATERIAL

In the grocery store, you'll usually find cilantro next to its cousin parsley. The herb is more tender than parsley, and that's evident in that it doesn't last as long at home in the crisper. Select bunches that show bright leaves with no signs of yellow or wilting. To make it last a bit longer, store it like a bouquet, with the stems submerged in a glass of water.

In the United States, the dried seeds are called coriander. You'll find them both ground and whole in the spice section. Coriander is indispensable in a pickling spice mix.

We like to ferment green coriander seeds, an ingredient for which you'll probably need a garden or a planter box, as you most likely won't find it in stores. To harvest, pluck the seeds before they develop fully, when they're still green. The flavor is somewhere between the coriander it's becoming and the cilantro that it was. The seeds are in this magical state for only a few days.

IN THE PICKLE JAR
Pickled Green Coriander

yield: about ½ pint
(fermentation vessel: 1 pint)
technique used: Mastering Brine Pickling (page 77)

These tiny green pickles are delicious, and the size of your batch is a testament to your patience. The best way we have found to bring some efficiency to the task of removing the small round seeds from the stalk of the seedhead is to use a pair of scissors. You will not need to make much brine, so if it's possible to time it with another pickle project you can just take a little brine for your itty-bitty coriander pickles.

½–1 cup green coriander seeds
1 cup Cucumber Brine (2 teaspoons unrefined
     sea salt to 1 cup unchlorinated water)
Grape leaf (optional)

1. Place the seeds in a small jar, leaving a few inches of headspace. Pour in enough brine to cover the seeds completely. Place a grape leaf, if using, over the seeds. Top with a sealed water-filled ziplock bag or jar.

2. Set aside, somewhere nearby, out of direct sunlight, and cool. Ferment for 4 to 7 days. Check daily to make sure the seeds stay submerged. You may see scum on top; it's generally harmless, but consult the appendix if you're at all concerned.

3. As the seeds ferment, they begin to lose their vibrant color and the brine will get cloudy; this is when you can start to test the seeds. They will be pleasingly sour and taste like tiny pickles with a cilantro finish.

4. Store these in a small jar with a tightened lid. They will keep, refrigerated, for 6 months.

Kirsten Writes

As a gardener, I'm always sad when the cilantro plants begin to bolt. The leaves are sparse as the plant reaches up to flower and go to seed, and they're no longer available for snipping and adding to recipes at will. When the plants are producing well, there are extra leaves that I could preserve, but the sensitive aromatic oils that give cilantro its flavor disappear when dried.

One summer I decided to try fermenting the green coriander seeds and leaves. It was astonishing — and thrilling — how well it worked. This was the beginning of my journey down the path of fermented flavor bases and pastes.

Whole-Leaf Cilantro

yield: about ½ pint
(fermentation vessel: 1 pint)
technique used: Whole-Leaf Ferments (page 72)

Fermented cilantro is slightly salty with a touch of lemon flavor and is powerful, pure, concentrated cilantro. This recipe uses the leaf whole, which when finished can be chopped and used for a garnish, as you would the fresh leaf. You can also make a cilantro paste by putting the leaves and stems through a food processor, following the steps for making pastes and bases in chapter 5 (page 69).

2–3 bunches (about ½ pound) cilantro
½ teaspoon unrefined sea salt

1. Remove the leaves from the stems. Put into a bowl and sprinkle with the salt. Mix in the salt, and the leaves will immediately start to sweat. Using your hands, gently toss and massage the salt into the leaves. The leaves will wilt quickly and start to brine. Don't expect a lot of brine; this is almost a dry ferment. It should taste salty but still pleasing; if not, then add a bit more salt.

2. Press the leaves into a pint jar. Top the ferment with a quart-sized ziplock bag. Press the plastic down onto the top of the ferment, then fill it with water and seal.

3. Set aside on a baking sheet to ferment, somewhere nearby, out of direct sunlight, and cool, for 4 to 7 days. Check daily to make sure the leaves are submerged, pressing if needed to bring the brine back to the surface. You may see scum on top; it's generally harmless, but consult the appendix if you're at all concerned. The leaves will become a deep green wilted color.

4. You can start to test the ferment on day 4. When you taste-test it, the sour is not as obvious as the salt. Ferment longer if more acidity is desired.

5. For storage, press a small round of plastic wrap or wax paper directly onto the surface of the ferment. Screw on the lid and store in the refrigerator, checking periodically that the ferment is submerged. This ferment will keep, refrigerated, for 6 months.

CILANTRO MEDICINE

As is the case with many aromatic herbs, cilantro has several medicinal properties. Incorporating foods-as-medicine into meals is a wonderful way to support your family's health.

Cilantro is said to cleanse the body of heavy metals. Its compounds bind to heavy metals, such as mercury, and release it from tissues.

Cilantro "Salsa"

yield: about 1 pint
(fermentation vessel: 1 pint)
technique used: Pastes and Bases (page 69)

This condiment adds interest to wraps and stir-fries. Peanuts, peanut oil, and sugar are added post-ferment so it's not a long keeper, but try it for a zippy change of pace.

2 bunches (about ½ pound) cilantro
4 cloves garlic
1–2 chiles, serrano or jalapeño
1 tablespoon grated fresh ginger
1 teaspoon unrefined sea salt
3 tablespoons lemon juice

  ¼ **cup roasted peanuts, minced in a food
     processor (optional)**
  2 **tablespoons peanut oil**
  ½ **teaspoon sugar**

1. Place the cilantro, garlic, chiles, and ginger in a food processor and blend to a paste consistency. Sprinkle in the salt and add the lemon juice. Press into a pint jar and top with a quart-sized ziplock bag. Press the plastic down onto the top of the ferment, then fill it with water and seal.

2. Set aside on a baking sheet to ferment, somewhere nearby, out of direct sunlight, and cool, for 4 to 7 days. Check daily to make sure the vegetables are submerged, pressing if needed to bring the brine back to the surface. You may see scum on top; it's generally harmless, but consult the appendix if you're at all concerned. The leaves will become a deep green wilted color.

3. You can start to test the ferment on day 4. When you taste-test it, the sour is not as obvious as the salt. Ferment longer if more acidity is desired.

4. After fermentation, stir in the peanuts, peanut oil, and sugar. This can be eaten immediately or stored in the refrigerator for about 1 week. Without the post-ferment additions, this paste can be stored in the refrigerator for 6 months.

COLLARD GREENS

Fermented collards are somewhat chewy, though not so much that they are unpleasant. Just be aware they don't soften the way cooked collards do. We like to ferment these greens with aromatic and pungent spices.

YOUR RAW MATERIAL

Collards are available year-round, but in cold climates they're best in the winter months, when they're sweet and juicy. During the heat of summer, they tend to be tough and slightly bitter. Select leaves that are deep green and pliable; they'll be more tender than leaves that feel brittle.

Christopher Writes

❋ We were on the road with seven hours of driving ahead of us and the morning was already blazing at 110°F. When we stopped at a small farmers' market at a rest area to get provisions for lunch, the vegetables and flowers were as wilted as the farmers who grew them.

At one stand, a woman was preparing Eritrean food. (It's similar to Ethiopian food, but lighter.) Many of the meals are based on a spongy fermented teff flatbread called *injera*, with spicy sauces and stews poured over it. On her menu that day was a meal with three sauces and collard greens as the foundation.

We explained we were traveling. "Oh," she said, smiling. "Well, you don't have to worry about it spoiling in this heat. We don't have refrigerators in Africa. The spices will do the work and keep it good."

Hours later, the food was indeed delicious, perfect for that sweltering day.

Ethiopian-Inspired Collard Ferment

See photo on page 172

yield: about 1 quart
(fermentation vessel: 1 quart or larger)
technique used: Relishes, Chutneys, Salsas, and
Fermented Salads (page 66)

In Ethiopian cuisine there's a stewed collard dish known as *gomen*. There are variations on the herbs that flavor it, so we played with the quantities and came up with this recipe.

It's a spicy ferment, and in Ethiopia it might be served with buttermilk curds or yogurt and a flatbread to temper the heat. At our table, it's a strongly flavored side dish to serve with a lentil or lamb stew.

2	bunches (about 1½ pounds) collard greens
1–1½	teaspoons unrefined sea salt
5	cloves garlic, minced
2	jalapeños or other hot chiles, minced
1	large onion, chopped
2–3	tablespoons finely grated fresh ginger
½–¾	teaspoon ground cardamom

1. Rinse the collard leaves and remove the stems. Place the leaves in a pile and roll them into a tight bundle, then slice thin. Transfer to a large bowl. (*Note:* Rolling the leaves makes it easier to get a thin slice.)

2. Sprinkle in 1 teaspoon of the salt, working it in with your hands, then taste. It should taste slightly salty without being overwhelming. Add more salt, if desired. The collards don't produce as much brine as their cousin the cabbage, but you'll have enough to submerge the veggies.

3. Add the garlic, jalapeños, onion, ginger, and cardamom. Toss and massage again to get everything mixed. At this point there is brine building at the bottom of the bowl.

4. Press the vegetables into a jar or crock. More brine will release at this stage, and you should see brine above the veggies. Top with a quart-sized ziplock bag. Press the plastic down onto the top of the ferment, fill with water, and seal; this will act as both follower and weight.

5. Set aside on a baking sheet to ferment, somewhere nearby, out of direct sunlight, and cool, for 5 to 10 days. Check daily to make sure the vegetables are submerged, pressing down as needed to bring the brine back to the surface. You may see scum on top; it's generally harmless, but consult the appendix if you're at all concerned.

6. You can start to test the ferment on day 5. It's ready when the flavors have mingled and it tastes mildly acidic.

7. Store in the same jar or transfer to one if you used a crock. Tamp down to submerge the collards, screw on the lid, and store in the refrigerator. This ferment will keep, refrigerated, for 6 months.

CORN

Our "next-door" neighbors (a mile of wooded ridge separates our farms) John and Frances have a big open stand along the highway sporting a sign year-round that announces CORN, a sad reminder that for ten months it's not sweet-corn season. Their stand comes alive with the vegetables of early summer. Then one day you'll see a single ear of corn wired to the sign and you know it's on.

Fresh sweet corn has such a fleeting season, the season of long lazy days and golden sunshine — perhaps that is why it's a national favorite for fresh eating and preserving. The usual choices for capturing this bit of summer are freezing and canning. In our experience lacto-fermented corn relish also stretches the season but isn't a long keeper. We have learned, however, that you can use frozen sweet corn to ferment any time of year.

YOUR RAW MATERIAL

Since there are over 200 varieties of sweet corn, let's just assume your local farmer is growing the best variety for your region. Your job is to make sure you choose fresh ears. Start with the husks — you want green, not dry, papery, or brown. The silk should be pale and a bit sticky. The good ears will feel plump when you pick them up. The next step (which may not be appreciated by the grower) is to peek at the kernels inside. The corn is fresh when the kernel has a milky juice. That is the sweet sign of tender corn, and this sugary juice happens to be turning into starch as soon as the corn's been picked. So the sooner you eat that corn (or get it fermenting), the less tough it will be.

IN THE CROCK

Sweet Corn Relish

yield: about 1 quart
(fermentation vessel: 1 quart)
technique used: Relishes, Chutneys, Salsas, and Fermented Salads (page 66)

This tangy relish has a Tex-Mex flavor that goes well atop nachos or in a chimichanga. The short fermentation time retains the sweetness of the corn but does not allow for long-term storage; over time, the sweet notes will be replaced by the sour.

For a different flavor, omit the cilantro and chile and sprinkle in ½ teaspoon of celery seed.

- 3 cups raw sweet corn kernels (from 5 or 6 ears); if using frozen add 1 tablespoon of fermented sauerkraut brine or pickle juice
- 1 red bell pepper, finely diced
- 1 red onion, finely diced
- ½ cup finely diced zucchini
- 1 serrano or jalapeño chile, finely diced (optional)
- 3 tablespoons chopped cilantro
- 1–1½ teaspoons unrefined sea salt

AFTER THE FERMENT
- 1 tablespoon raw honey

1. Combine the corn, bell pepper, onion, zucchini, serrano, and cilantro. Sprinkle in 1 teaspoon of the salt, working it in with your hands. At this point there is brine building at the bottom. (If you don't have enough liquid, add a bit of brine from a previous ferment, or some lemon or lime juice.)

2. Press the mixture into a jar or crock. More brine will release at this stage, and you should see brine above the veggies. Top the ferment with a quart-sized ziplock bag. Press the plastic down onto the top of the ferment, fill it with water, and seal; this will act as both follower and weight.

3. Set aside on a baking sheet to ferment, somewhere nearby, out of direct sunlight, and cool, for 3 to 4 days. Check daily to make sure the vegetables are submerged, pressing down as needed to bring the brine to the surface. You may see scum on top; it's generally harmless, but consult the appendix if you're at all concerned.

4. You can start to test the ferment on day 3. It's ready when it tastes slightly sour but retains some of the sweetness of the corn. When it's ready, add the honey.

5. If you don't serve it right away, store in a sealed jar in the fridge. This ferment will keep, refrigerated, for about 1 month.

Create Your Own Recipes

In our research we've found many old-school preservation references to crocks of cobs floating in salt brine — pickled corn on the cob! We have yet to conduct this culinary experiment, but if you're up to the challenge: the cobs are cleaned and cut crosswise into halves or quarters and then submerged in Basic Brine (page 78). Remember the mantra: *Submerge in brine and all will be fine.*

CUCUMBERS

Light, water, salt, bread,
dill and mustard seed:
Our cucumber has gingerly
matured into a pickle.
It has absorbed the elements.
The child of nature and of art.
— "XENIA," BY GYÖRGY PETRI, TRANSLATED BY
ROBERT AUSTERLITZ, FROM *CONTEMPORARY EAST*
EUROPEAN POETRY: AN ANTHOLOGY, 1983

Pickled cucumbers appeared on the culinary scene around 4,000 years ago in India. Modern Indian cuisine boasts hundreds of pickles and chutneys, and many recipes call for cukes to be cooked in oil and suspended in vinegar, with antimicrobial herbs and spices. We suspect these pickles were born from a lactic-acid process.

YOUR RAW MATERIAL

The most difficult aspect of making traditional lacto-fermented dill pickles might be finding the cucumbers. Although you can pickle any cucumber, pickling cucumbers are best. They're smaller and more uniform in size, and they have a thicker skin that's less likely to be bitter and is never waxed.

They're a challenge to find in a grocery store, but if you happen on some, inspect them carefully. They must be firm and crisp: in a word, fresh. Pickling cucumbers last only a few days before they show signs of age; dull, wrinkly skin is a sure sign that they were picked too long ago. Don't buy ones that have yellowed, either; they've been left too long on the vine.

The best place to find pickling cucumbers is at the farmers' market. They should be available for a few weeks in late summer. Ask farmers early in the season if they'll have them. Because they require daily picking, have a brief shelf life, and are a specialty crop, many growers don't want to take the risk that they'll be tossing them onto the compost pile.

> ### FERMENTISTA'S TIP

Cucumbers pickle quickly because the juice contains certain elements that encourage the growth of Lactobacillus plantarum.

One year we worked with a cucumber called the White Wonder. Our neighbor Josh, an organic farmer, introduced us to this ivory-white-skinned variety. We thought it was a brand-new hybrid. It was brand-new all right — in 1893, when it was introduced. It's an open-pollinated heirloom acquired by the seedsman W. Atlee Burpee from a customer in western New York State. We've made a lot of pickles, but we were impressed with the way it holds a sweet flavor and a crisp texture.

If you don't have the garden space, grow your own White Wonders, or one of the many other compact varieties, in pots.

IN THE PICKLE JAR

In this country, the archetype for the lacto-fermented cucumber pickle is the kosher dill — the cool, crisp, garlicky deli dills that came out of a barrel and were sold in New York as "full-sours" and "half-sours." Often the first business an immigrant from Eastern European could start was that of a pushcart vendor. Pushcarts were cheap to rent and mobile, and the market for pickles was good. Many of these vendors eventually bought their own carts, then stores. In New York, these were concentrated in Manhattan's Lower East Side and the area became known as the pickle district. Most of these shops are long gone.

That said, salt-brine pickling came from Europe much earlier. Dutch settlers in the seventeenth century pickled Brooklyn cucumbers, which they sold in Manhattan.

Bitter Cucumbers

Cucumbers can be bitter, and pickling doesn't solve the problem. All cucurbits (members of the gourd family, such as squash) produce bitter organic compounds called *cucurbitacins*. They hang out in the leaves, but if the plant is stressed (by, for example, deep fluctuations in temperature, uneven watering, or extreme heat) they enter the fruit. Unfortunately, once a plant starts to produce bitter fruit, it will continue to do so.

Commonly, cucumbers are left whole for pickling, so how do you know if they're bitter? Just taste one or two; that should tell you if you have a bitter batch. Occasionally the bitterness is in just the ends of the cucumber. If that's the case, slice them off and you're good to go. If a cuke is bitter, don't try to ferment it anyway — you'll be very disappointed.

New York Deli–Style Pickles

yield: about 1 gallon
(fermentation vessel: 1 gallon or four 1-quart jars)
technique used: Mastering Brine Pickling (page 77)

When the cucumber matures to a pickle, the white interior flesh turns a waxy and translucent color as the air is forced from the cells. The half-sours usually look mottled: the translucent flesh of the pickle mixes with the fresh white flesh of the cucumber. Full-sours are fully translucent inside.

> 20 **pickling-type cucumbers (not waxed)**
> 15 **cloves garlic**
> 1–2 **dried red chiles**
>   6 **bay leaves**
>   2 **tablespoons pickling spice,** *or*
>   **1½ teaspoons mustard seed, 1 teaspoon dill seed (or, better, 2 fresh dill seed heads), and 1 teaspoon coriander seed**
>   1 **gallon Cucumber Brine (¾ cup unrefined sea salt to 1 gallon unchlorinated water)**
>   **Grape, oak, or horseradish leaves, enough to top the jar or crock (optional)**

1. Scrub the cucumbers in water. Trim off the stems and scrub off the blossom ends, as they contain an enzyme that will soften the pickles.

2. Lightly mash the garlic cloves with the back of a knife, just enough to break them.

3. Pack the cucumbers, incorporating the garlic, chiles, bay leaves, and spices as you go, into four wide-mouth quart jars or a 1-gallon jar or crock. Pour in enough brine to cover the them. Tuck the grape leaves, if using, or a piece of plastic wrap over the cucumbers. Cover the jar loosely.

Store any leftover brine in the fridge (it will keep for a week; discard thereafter and make a new batch, if needed).

4. Set aside on a baking sheet to ferment, somewhere nearby, out of direct sunlight, and cool, for 3 to 6 days. During the fermentation period, monitor the brine level and top off with reserved brine, if needed, to cover. You may see scum on top; it's generally harmless, but consult the appendix if you're at all concerned.

5. The cucumbers begin a vibrant green — the colors look almost larger than life. As the cukes start to ferment, they turn a drab olive, the result of the acids interacting with chlorophyll. The brine will become cloudy as lactic acid is produced. In 3 to 4 days you'll have half-sours; in about 6 days you'll have full-sours. Taste until the pickles are as sour as you'd like them to be.

6. When the pickles are ready, cover with fresh grape leaves, if you have some, screw on the lids, and store in the refrigerator. These will keep, refrigerated, for 1 year.

IPA Pickles

yield: 1 gallon
(fermentation vessel: 1 gallon or four 1-quart jars)

If you have fresh hops, which bloom, conveniently, when the cucumbers are on, use those. They impart a lovely floral flavor, one not as evident in dried hops. Dried, however, will still give you an IPA Pickle.

Look for hops in the local health-food store, in the herb section, and at brewing-supply stores.

A student of ours gave us the idea for this recipe. We came up with these effervescent and hoppy pickles.

20 or so pickling cucumbers

3–4 cloves garlic

2 tablespoons pickling spice, *or*

   1½ teaspoons mustard seed,

   1½ teaspoons whole black peppercorns,

   1 teaspoon coriander seed, and 1–2 dried

   red chiles, such as cayennes

10–12 hop blossoms

1 gallon Cucumber Brine (¾ cup unrefined sea

   salt to 1 gallon unchlorinated water)

Follow the directions for New York Deli–Style Pickles (at left).

Hop Vines

Here in the Northwest, many people grow hops for the shade they provide. We have a few vines on the south side of our house. In the spring they may grow more than 12 inches a day, and by the time it's hot, we have a pretty green wall where the house gets the most direct sunlight. In the late summer, the smell is entrancing.

As the days chill, the vines die back. We then cut them down and toss into the compost, and the winter sun is free to warm the house.

FERMENTISTA'S TIP

Slices Are Nice

Some cucumbers are too big and a few are too soft (Armenian cucumbers, for example) to ferment whole. The solution? Preserve slices! Just make sure the cukes aren't so big that the seeds are large and well developed, as the seeds (like the blossom end) also contain enzymes that will soften the slices.

Garlic Pickle Slices

See photo on page 153

yield: about 2 quarts

(fermentation vessel: 2 quarts)

technique used: Mastering Brine Pickling (page 77)

This recipe is all about the garlic, but you can certainly add dill, dried hot peppers, curry — use your imagination. Slice cucumbers crosswise for rounds, lengthwise for spears, depending on the shape and size of the jars. Spears require uniformity in length, so that you can fit them tightly in a jar.

1¾ cups cucumber slices, about ½ inch thick

1 medium onion, sliced lengthwise into eighths

2 heads garlic, cloves separated and halved

1 teaspoon whole peppercorns

1 teaspoon mustard seeds

½ gallon Cucumber Brine (6 tablespoons

   unrefined sea salt to ½ gallon unchlorinated

   water)

A few grape leaves (optional)

1. Toss the cucumbers together with the vegetables and spices. Put into a ½-gallon jar or crock. Wedge in the cucumbers so they stay in place. Pour in enough brine to cover the vegetables. These slices won't stay wedged like whole pickles, but tucking a few grape leaves over the top will help keep everything under the brine. If you don't have any leaves, use plastic wrap. Store any leftover brine in the fridge (it will keep for a week; discard thereafter and make a new batch, if needed).

2. For a crock, top the leaves with a plate that fits the opening of the container and covers as much of the vegetables as possible; weight down with a sealed water-filled jar. For a jar, use a sealed water-filled jar or ziplock bag as a combination follower and weight.

3. Set aside on a baking sheet to ferment, somewhere nearby, out of direct sunlight, and cool, for 4 to 7 days. Check daily to make sure the slices are submerged, pressing down as needed to bring the brine back to the surface, and scoop out any scum that develops.

4. You can start to test it on day 4. You'll know this is ready when it tastes like pickles; at first it will be like a mild half-sour and will develop into a full-sour — it's done when you like it.

5. Store in jars, with lids tightened, in the fridge. This will keep, refrigerated, for 6 months.

Troubleshooting Cucumber Pickles

Cucumbers make the quintessential pickle. They have a few nuances not associated with the other vegetables. One is that they require a higher-salinity brine. If you follow the recipes, you'll have delicious, crispy pickles every time. But read on for an explanation of some typical cucumber pickle problems.

» **Hollow.** The cukes were too big or there was a long delay between harvest and brining. Hollow pickles are perfectly *safe* to eat.

» **Shriveled.** Too much water evaporated during the osmosis process. Either the brine was too salty or the cukes were too old at brine time. Shriveled pickles are unappetizing, but they're *safe* to eat. In fact, make them into a relish (for a recipe, see the facing page).

» **Mushy or slimy.** The brine didn't contain enough salt or the temperature during fermentation was too high (60–65°F is ideal). Other possibilities: The cukes came up over the level of the brine, or the blossom ends hadn't been scrubbed off. Discard.

» **Discolored.** This can come from water that is too hard. Changes caused by hard water are *safe*. Sometimes discoloration is only the result of the spices you chose, especially ground spices. Vegetables, too, can cause color changes. For example, red onions will turn the brine pink. Discoloration from spices or other veggies is *harmless*.

Bite-Size Pickles

Mature lemon cucumbers are too seedy for pickles, but when you're overwhelmed by the amount you have in the garden, you can pickle the babies. Trim off the stems and make sure to scrub off the blossom ends, as they contain enzymes that will soften the pickles. Use the seasonings for New York Deli–Style Pickles (page 168) or whatever pickling spices strike your fancy.

Kirsten Writes

I was commissioned to ferment a 10-gallon crock of dill pickles for the grand opening of an artisanal butcher shop. To source the local cucumbers I had responded to an online post for organic pickling cucumbers. They had been picked that morning and were firm, crunchy, and sweet — they were not a pickling variety, but immature slicers instead.

A week later when I opened the crock I found pickles that were incredibly tasty, as expected, but many were flat, squishy, and limp. Not in a rotten way, just in an unattractive way. They certainly couldn't be seen in public. That's when I learned: small cucumber ≠ pickling cucumber.

I sorted out the unusable ones, but the size of the pile bothered me. I didn't want to waste this otherwise good food. I chopped the pickles in a food processor. They were still delicious, and no longer visually unappealing. I divided the batch and came up with two great recipes: a superior hot dog condiment and a sweet pickle relish.

Sweet Dill Relish (or Save-the-Pickle Relish)

yield: about 2 quarts
(fermentation vessel: 2 quarts)

Sometimes a fermentista has to do what a fermentista has to do to help along a less-than-stellar ferment, and why not a sweet pickle relish? This is a great way to use flat pickles — and you can even use perfect ones!

- 4 **pounds lacto-fermented dill pickles, chopped in a food processor**
- 1 **cup finely chopped onion**
- 2 **tablespoons raw cane sugar**
- 1 **teaspoon mustard seeds**
- 1 **teaspoon ground turmeric**
- 2–3 **tablespoons raw apple cider vinegar**

1. Mix all of the ingredients in a large bowl. Taste. Add more sugar or vinegar if either isn't strong enough. When it's pleasing, put the mixture in a 2-quart jar.

2. Make sure the vegetables are submerged, then cover loosely with the lid. Set aside for 1 day, for the flavors to ripen and the onions to ferment.

3. Screw on the lid, put in the refrigerator, and wait a few days for the flavors to enhance.

IN THE CROCK (BEYOND PICKLES)

Pickle Kraut

Why choose between relish and kraut when you can have both? Turn both hot-dog favorites into one great condiment. Simply add chopped fermented pickles to a batch of Naked Kraut (page 132) after fermentation; pack in jars, tamp under the brine, and refrigerate the same as kraut.

RUTABAGA KRAUT, *page 225*

SEA-CHI (a.k.a. Sea Kimchi), *page 142*

GARLIC PASTE, *page 181*

ETHIOPIAN-INSPIRED COLLARD FERMENT, *page 164*

CURRIED GOLDEN BEETS, *page 124*

WINE KRAUT, *page 135*

HABANERO JICAMA, *page 188*

PEAS AND CARROTS, *page 211*

PICKLED SHIITAKE, *page 194*

EGGPLANT

When I was alone, I lived on eggplant, the stove-top cook's strongest ally. I fried it and stewed it, and ate it crisp and sludgy, hot and cold. It was cheap and filling and was delicious in all manner of strange combinations. If any was left over I ate it cold the next day on bread.

— LAURIE COLWIN, IN *ALONE IN THE KITCHEN WITH AN EGGPLANT: CONFESSIONS OF COOKING FOR ONE AND DINING ALONE*, 2007

For at least a year, a 2-quart jar of fermented eggplant sat patiently in our refrigerator. It remained steadfastly in its place while hands reached past it for other jars — even though a 2-quart jar took up a lot of real estate in our crammed refrigerator. The kids tend to ignore unknown things in jars, as they're wary of their mother's experiments. Their mother also looked at this somewhat gray ferment and thought, "Maybe tomorrow."

We'd never even tasted the lacto-fermented eggplant and the unappetizing color was a hurdle. One day Kirsten reached in the refrigerator and pulled out the patient jar of fermented eggplant and tasted it. We were all surprised — after fermentation, the texture was not mushy and it had an unexpected, pleasant lemony flavor; we liked it and hope you do, too!

YOUR RAW MATERIAL

Eggplant, or aubergine, is botanically a fruit (seeds inside). This member of the nightshade family is believed to have originated in India. Eggplant was brought to Europe in the Middle Ages by Spanish explorers, where it was mostly used as an ornamental, because it was thought to bring on fever or madness; the nightshade-family association with the poisonous belladonna made it difficult for it to land on the plate. When Thomas Jefferson brought the eggplant seed from Europe to his Monticello garden, it was to be decorative.

The late-summer farmers' baskets at the market are beautiful filled with the small round, large oblong, and long slim varieties of eggplant in shades of green, white, yellow, striped, and, of course, purple. While all of these varieties can be used, for fermenting we prefer the smaller ones that contain fewer seeds.

It is also important to know that once picked the fruit degrades quickly, so make sure your eggplant is fresh. Look for smooth, shiny skin that's free of blemishes of any kind. It is simple to detect aging fruit: the skin gets wrinkly and has a saggy quality.

Fermented Eggplant

yield: about 1 quart
(fermentation vessel: 1 quart or larger)
technique used: Mastering Sauerkraut (page 53)

Eggplant can leave a bitter taste on the tongue. In Mediterranean dishes the eggplant is salted to remove this quality. We don't know whether it's the salting or the breakdown caused by the fermentation process, but there is no bitter flavor in fermented eggplant.

1½	**pounds eggplant, peeled and cut into 1-inch cubes**
1	**scant tablespoon unrefined sea salt**
2–3	**cloves garlic, minced (optional)**
1	**sprig fresh whole basil leaves**
	Grape leaf (optional)

1. Put the eggplant in a large bowl; sprinkle in half the salt and, with your hands, massage it into the eggplant, then taste. It should taste slightly salty without being overwhelming. If it's not salty enough, add more salt, a little at a time, until it's to your liking. The eggplant will begin to sweat and then slowly release an amber-brown brine. If you've put in a good effort and don't see much brine in the bowl, let it stand, covered, for 45 minutes, then massage again. Add the garlic, if using, and mix in thoroughly.

2. Transfer half the eggplant to a 1-quart jar or 1-gallon crock. Press down with your fist or a tamper. You should see some brine on top when you press. Add the basil and the remaining eggplant and press again. When the vessel is packed, leave 4 inches of headspace for a crock, or 2 to 3 inches for a jar. Top the ferment with a grape leaf or a piece of plastic wrap. For a crock, top this with a plate that fits the opening of the container and covers as much of the vegetables as possible; then weight down with a sealed water-filled jar. For a jar, use a sealed water-filled jar or ziplock bag as a follower-weight combination.

3. Set aside the jar or crock on a baking sheet to ferment, somewhere nearby, out of direct sunlight, and cool, for 4 to 14 days. Check daily to make sure the eggplant is submerged, pressing down as needed to bring the brine back to the surface. You may see scum on top; it's generally harmless, but consult the appendix if you're at all concerned.

4. You can start to test the eggplant on day 4. You'll know it's ready when it's pleasingly sour and pickle-y tasting, without the strong acidity of vinegar.

5. Store in jars, with lids tightened, in the fridge. This ferment will keep, refrigerated, for 1 year.

Garlic Eggplant Wedding Pickles

yield: about 2 quarts
(fermentation vessel: 2 quarts or two 1-quart jars)
technique used: Relishes, Chutneys, Salsas, and Fermented Salads (page 66)

Dan Rosenberg and Addie Rose Holland (see Meet the Fermentistas on page 179) named these in honor of the four pairs of their dear friends who got married on four consecutive weekends in the summer of 2010. It took a brainstorming session to come up with a gift idea that would be efficient, tasty, and appreciated. As has happened on many an occasion, pickles saved the day.

The couple spent a day preparing a variety of pickled delights (including this one), and after 3 weeks of fermentation, they packaged the goodies into small mason jars and made up special labels. Some of the newlyweds claimed this was their favorite gift.

- 2 **pounds eggplant**
- 9 **ounces onion, finely chopped (about 2 medium onions)**
- 3½ **ounces garlic, minced (about 1 head)**
- 2 **ounces basil (about 1 bunch), chopped**
- 1 **pint unchlorinated water**
- 2 **tablespoons unrefined sea salt, plus more for salting the eggplant**

1. Peel the eggplant, then cut into ½-inch cubes, salt, drain, and rinse. Transfer to a large mixing bowl. Add the rest of the ingredients and stir to thoroughly mix the salt. Let stand for 30 minutes as the vegetables soften and the liquid is drawn out.

2. Pack into the mason jar(s). Make sure all the air is pushed out and the vegetables are submerged in the liquid. Screw on the lid(s).

3. Set the jar in a bowl or pie plate (to catch any juices that escape) in a spot where the temperature is a constant 60 to 75°F.

4. After 3 days, slowly loosen the cap(s) to release some of the built-up pressure. Try not to let any liquid escape.

5. Let ferment for at least 2 weeks before tasting. Eggplant cubes should be soft but not mushy and pleasantly sour — and garlicky! Refrigerate until ready to use as a relish or a chutney.

ESCAROLE

We were in deep winter, but thanks to the incredibly long growing season in the Kalahari were still getting greens out of the nethouse, albeit only escarole, and only escarole as tough as sacking. Nelson wanted it exclusively in salads nevertheless. . . . I don't know how many times I said, "This belongs in soup, minced, with onions." But no, we had to endure it in salads, and why exactly? Because people should eat something live and raw at every meal.

— NORMAN RUSH, *MATING*, 1992

Escarole is a broad-leafed member of the chicory family that tastes like a less bitter endive. The chicories have been an important food crop for centuries; they're native to the East Indies, spreading first to Egypt, then into Greece and the rest of Europe. Escarole makes a wonderful kimchi.

YOUR RAW MATERIAL
A cool-season green, escarole is best from December through April. The young plants are tender and are nice in a fresh salad; the more mature plants are perfect for fermenting. Escarole is also a great base for krauts and kimchis that are made without members of the cabbage family.

When shopping for escarole, make sure the leaves are bright green and fairly uniform in color. Pass by the escarole with yellowing outer leaves or coarse stems.

IN THE CROCK
Escarole Kimchi
See photo on page 217
yield: about 3 quarts
(fermentation vessel: 1 gallon or larger)
technique used: Mastering Kimchi Basics(page 87)

This brassica-free kimchi has generous amounts of garlic and chile that make it pungent and bold. We leave out the traditional ginger but if you'd like to add it, use 1 tablespoon grated. You'll need to plan ahead for this recipe, as it requires a brining period, 6 to 8 hours or overnight.

1 gallon Kimchi Brine (1 cup unrefined sea salt to 1 gallon unchlorinated water)

2 large heads escarole

2 large carrots, shredded

6–8 cloves garlic, minced

3–4 tablespoons chile pepper flakes or salt-free *gochugaru* (less if you prefer a milder flavor)

1. In a crock or a large bowl, combine the brine ingredients and stir to dissolve. Rinse the escarole in cold water and remove any wilted or damaged outer leaves; reserve a few unblemished outer leaves. Cut the escarole in half lengthwise. Submerge the escarole and reserved leaves in the brine solution. Use a plate as a weight to keep submerged. Set aside, at room temperature, for 6 to 8 hours.

2. Transfer the escarole to a colander to drain for 15 minutes, reserving about 1 cup of the soaking liquid. Set the separated outer leaves aside.

3. Meanwhile, combine the carrots, garlic, and chile pepper flakes in a large bowl, and blend thoroughly.

4. Chop the escarole into 1-inch pieces, and add them to the bowl. Massage the mixture thoroughly, then taste for salt. Usually the brined escarole will provide enough salt, but if it's not to your liking, sprinkle in a small amount, massage, and taste again.

5. Transfer the vegetables, a few handfuls at a time, to a crock, jar, or onggi pot, pressing with your hands as you go. Add any liquid left in the bowl, and if you need more to submerge the veggies, top with the reserved soaking water. Leave about 4 inches of headspace in your crock or onggi pot, or 2 to 3 inches for a jar. Cover with the reserved leaves. For a crock, top with a plate and weight it down with a sealed water-filled jar. For a jar or onggi pot, you can use a sealed water-filled jar or ziplock bag.

6. Set aside on a baking sheet to ferment, somewhere nearby, out of direct sunlight, and cool, for 7 to 14 days. Check daily to make sure the vegetables are submerged, pressing down as needed to bring the brine back to the surface. You may see scum on top; it's generally harmless, but consult the appendix if you're at all concerned.

7. Test the kimchi after 1 week. It will be quite mild at this point, like a half-sour pickle. The cabbage will have a translucent quality. The brine will be an orange-red hue. Kimchi is often quite effervescent; it's normal whether it's bubbly or not. If it's not sour enough, continue to ferment, keeping the veggies submerged.

8. When it's ready, spoon the kimchi into smaller jars, tamping down the veggies under the brine. Screw on the jar lids to seal, then store in the refrigerator, where it will keep for 9 months.

Create Your Own Recipes

Try different combinations of the chicory greens in kimchi. We make a medley of escarole, endive, and radicchio we affectionately call "Chic-chi."

FENNEL

The fennel is beyond every other vegetable, delicious. It greatly resembles in appearance the largest size celery, perfectly white, and there is no vegetable equals it in flavour. It is eaten at dessert, crude, and with, or without dry salt, indeed I preferred it to every other vegetable, or to any fruit.

— THOMAS JEFFERSON, IN *CONSUMING PASSIONS*, ED. JONATHAN GREEN, 1985

A member of the parsley family (along with caraway, cumin, and dill), fennel is native to southern Europe and grows all over the continent and in the Middle East, India, and China.

According to Anglo-Saxon herbal tradition, fennel is one of the nine sacred herbs and is associated with longevity, courage, and strength, perhaps from its powerful and plentiful flavonoid antioxidants — and as a cure for hiccups.

YOUR RAW MATERIAL

The entire plant is edible. Snip the leaves when they're young and add to salads and krauts. The celery-like stems are good as soon as they begin to fatten; however, when fully mature, the stalks can cause a tougher texture in a ferment. Fennel seed has a slight anise flavor, milder than that of the bulb, and somewhat nuttier.

IN THE CROCK

Fennel Chutney

See photo on page 123
yield: about ½ gallon
(fermentation vessel: 2 quarts or larger)
technique used: Relishes, Chutneys, Salsas, and Fermented Salads (page 66)

Fennel stalks finish a bit woody, but you could slice some very thin and add to the mix, if you like. This chutney goes well on turkey sandwiches, in cream cheese wraps, or as a condiment in a brunch spread.

> 10 fennel bulbs
> 2 sweet onions (but any type is fine), diced
> 1–2 tablespoons unrefined sea salt
> 1 cup dried cranberries
> ½ cup raisins
> 5–6 cloves garlic, minced

1. Thinly slice the fennel bulbs and cores with a knife or mandoline. (For a finer texture, chop the slices.) Put the fennel in a large bowl and add the onions. Mix well. Sprinkle in 1 tablespoon of the salt, working it in with your hands, then taste. It should taste slightly salty without being overwhelming. Add more salt if needed. You may need to pound this mixture a bit to get the brine; if it's stubborn, let sit, covered, for 30 to 45 minutes. Add the cranberries, raisins, and garlic. Toss and massage again for a few minutes to get everything mixed. You should see brine building at the bottom.

2. Pack the mixture, a few handfuls at a time, into a jar or crock, pressing to remove air pockets as you go. More brine will release and you should see brine above the veggies. Top the ferment with a quart-sized ziplock bag. Press the plastic down onto the surface of the ferment, fill it with water, and seal; this will act as both follower and weight.

3. Set aside on a baking sheet, somewhere nearby, out of direct sunlight, and cool, for 7 to 14 days. Check daily to make sure the vegetables

Real Pickles

We met the folks at Real Pickles through our daughter-in-law, Lydia. After she spent the summer working in our kraut kitchen she missed having so many fermented goodies there for the taking. When she was back at college, in Massachusetts, she found Real Pickles, based in Greenfield, Massachusetts. Lydia told us the product was great, just as fresh as ours.

When visiting the Real Pickles website and blog, we were struck by the company's deep commitment to the region's health and economy. Kirsten contacted Addie Rose Holland. She and Addie had a lot to talk about.

Besides a passion for a better world, we also had similar experiences with customers — especially the magic of flavor as revealed when standing by your sample tray watching someone experience a taste memory that transports them to another place and time.

"Many of our customers exclaim that our pickles (especially cucumber pickles) taste exactly like those their grandparents made," Addie says. "One woman was moved to tears by the memories. That kind of reaction makes us proud to know we're producing an authentic food, but also that we're helping to preserve part of our human culture by keeping these flavors alive."

The creation story: In 1999, Dan Rosenberg took his first fermented pickle lesson at a Northeast Organic Farming Association conference. Fermentation reinforced the very things Dan was passionate about as a young farmworker, social activist, and avid cook. Vegetable fermentation supported local agriculture and revived traditional

Addie Rose Holland and Dan Rosenberg

whole foods. Because of the exciting culinary possibilities, he came home and incorporated fermented vegetables into his daily routine, and soon his kitchen was full of stimulating smells and flavors.

Dan and Addie Rose moved to western Massachusetts the next summer and discovered a community bursting with appreciation for local foods, a strong interest in organic farming, and some of the best soils in the country. Addie and Dan felt it would be ideal to start a business dependent on local farmers and local consumers. Their company has been growing ever since.

"We try to ensure that our products appeal to a wide range of palates and incomes. Our products sell in a variety of markets, from Polish delis to natural-foods stores. Our flavor combinations tend toward simplicity, partly to feature traditional flavors, but also to keep production costs and shelf prices reasonable, so more people can afford them. Some of the combinations with more complex flavors and pricier ingredients remain relegated to our home kitchen."

are submerged. You may see scum on top; it's generally harmless, but consult the appendix if you're at all concerned.

4. You can start to test the ferment on day 7. It's ready when the flavors of the dried fruits have mingled with the slight sour of the ferment.

5. Store in jars, with lids tightened, in the fridge, leaving as little headroom as possible, and tamping the ferment down. This ferment will keep, refrigerated, for 8 months.

Fresh Fennel Kraut

yield: about 2½ quarts
(fermentation vessel: 1 gallon or larger)
technique used: Mastering Sauerkraut (page 53)

Fennel's flavor improves with fermentation, which makes it a simple addition to sauerkraut that imparts crispness and a complexity. Slice the bulbs very thin for this recipe, as it takes them longer to break down than the cabbage. If you don't have enough bulbs for the proper ratio, you can mince some of the fronds to add flavor.

3½ **pounds cabbage, shredded**
1 **pound fennel bulbs, sliced thin**
1–1½ **tablespoons unrefined sea salt**

Follow the directions for Naked Kraut (page 132), adding fennel to the bowl with the cabbage.

Create Your Own Recipes

» Add fennel slices to a mixed-vegetable pickle pot (see Edgy Veggies, page 155).
» Use fresh fennel bulb instead of seed in Farmhouse Culture's Apple-Fennel Kraut (page 268).
» Add fresh fennel and beets to Naked Kraut (page 132).
» Combine fennel seeds with Indian flavors, such as cardamom, in a beet kraut (page 120).
» Ferment green fennel seeds to capture their unique flavor; use the same method as Pickled Green Coriander (page 161).

GARLIC

There are five elements: earth, air, fire, water, and garlic.

— LOUIS DIAT, CHEF OF NEW YORK CITY'S RITZ-CARLTON, 1940S

Garlic contains a substance called allyl sulfide, which has strong sterilization power. It gets credit for some of the health magic of kimchi. It also adds great flavor.

We had to restrain ourselves at first from adding garlic to every ferment, but restraint became a lot easier when we began to produce commercial-sized batches — moving from cloves to heads, a few minutes became a few *hours* of peeling. Now that we are making small batches again, garlic has crept its way back into our ferments; for long-term storage, flavor, and getting through winter colds, nothing beats garlic.

YOUR RAW MATERIAL

The word *garlic* comes from the Old English *gar-leac,* meaning spear leek. It is harvested in midsummer and hung to dry in barns and sheds. Fresh garlic is available year-round in most markets. Choose heads that are firm to the touch; soft cloves indicate age or spoilage.

There are an estimated 300 varietals with great names like Nootka Rose and Persian Star, but there are only two types: hard necks and soft necks. The soft necks are longer keepers and are the type you often see braided. Garlic flavors range from mild, nutty elephant garlic (closely related to the leek) to the much spicier porcelain varieties. Check with your local farmer for the Aglio Rosso di Sulmona (an Italian heirloom Creole type), as we have been told that it is pretty special when pickled.

IN THE CROCK

Garlic mellows during fermentation. Fermented garlic paste is delicious. It's curious, though: The first thing you'll notice is that the "sauer" or acidic taste is mild and sweet. The bite, or heat, of raw garlic also disappears, but the flavor is still intense and decidedly, well, garlicky. The second thing you'll find is that fermented garlic is a great way to eat it "raw," because it doesn't linger on the palate in the way raw garlic does.

Garlic Paste

See photo on page 172
yield: about 1 pint
(fermentation vessel: 1 quart)
technique used: Pastes and Bases (page 69)

You'll want to have this on hand year-round. When you don't feel like peeling and mincing fresh cloves, this paste adds instant garlic flavor to any dish. Fair warning: Plan on about an hour of peeling time. It's worth the effort, though, as the paste is invaluable as a finishing garnish for dishes that otherwise call for fresh garlic. We love it mixed with a little fresh parsley and tossed with fresh homemade oven-fries just before serving.

6–8 heads garlic, cloves separated
2 teaspoons unrefined sea salt

1. Process the garlic to a paste consistency in a food processor. This paste has a sticky, thick, gooey consistency (a plus, as it makes it easier to keep it submerged). Sprinkle in the salt. Not much will change after salting, which makes it difficult to distinguish the brine. Don't worry — it will work. (*Note:* If available, add 1–2 tablespoons of fermented brine. This will add a little juice and jumpstart the process. Do *not* add water.)

2. Press the paste down into a quart jar. Top with a quart-sized ziplock bag. Press the plastic down onto the surface of the ferment, fill it with water, and seal.

3. Set the jar aside on a baking sheet to ferment, somewhere nearby, out of direct sunlight, and cool, for 14 to 21 days. Check daily to make sure the paste is submerged. You may see scum on top; it's generally harmless, but consult the appendix if you're at all concerned.

4. You can start to test the ferment on day 14. It's ready when the garlic is milder than when it was raw and has some acidity.

5. When it's ready, tighten the lid, then store in the fridge; it will keep, refrigerated, for 1 year, though you will use it up much sooner than that.

Moroccan Garlic Paste

yield: about ½ cup
(fermentation vessel: 1 pint)

Use this spicy paste to add bold flavor to just about any dish. It's especially good as a meat or vegetable rub. It's quite salty, which is good for seasoning meat and coating roasting veggies; just add a bit of olive oil.

> 2 **heads garlic, cloves separated and minced in a food processor**
> 2 **tablespoons lemon juice**
> 2 **teaspoons freshly ground black pepper**
> 2 **teaspoons ground cumin**
> 2 **teaspoons unrefined sea salt**

Follow the Garlic Paste recipe (page 181), combining all the ingredients before salting.

FERMENTISTA'S TIP

My Pickled Garlic Is Blue!

It's rare that a clove of garlic turns blue or bluish-green, but it does happen. Although it looks wrong, it's harmless and will taste normal.

According to the September 2004 issue of the America's Test Kitchen Newsletter, *"Under acidic conditions, isoallin, a compound found in garlic, breaks down and reacts with amino acids to produce the blue-green color. Visually, the difference between garlic cooked with and without acid can be dramatic, but a quick taste of the blue garlic proved that the color doesn't affect flavor."*

Brine-Pickled Garlic

technique used: Mastering Brine Pickling (page 77)

Most whole-vegetable pickles use garlic as a flavoring: several cloves swim in the brine among the rest of the vegetables. We usually dice these leftover fermented cloves and use them in salad dressings — if someone hasn't already popped them in their mouth.

So why not make a whole jar of these useful little delicacies? Having whole pickled garlic on hand gives you a secret ingredient to dress up dishes quickly — a little mincing, and *voilà!* Mellow garlic goodness. Like many good things, it doesn't come easy. Sit down with a good beverage, perhaps some music, a friend, and a pile of garlic — peeling takes time.

For a variation, add herbs or spices; try dried red peppers, whole peppercorns, or tarragon leaves.

> **Any quantity of garlic cloves**
> **Basic Brine (½ cup unrefined sea salt to 1 gallon unchlorinated water)**

1. Put into a jar or crock as many cloves as you're willing to peel.

2. Cover with brine and pickle as you would a whole brined pickle.

3. Set aside to ferment for 2 to 3 weeks. It's ready when the garlic is mild and has a light taste of vinegar.

GARLIC SCAPES

Scapes are the flowering stalks of garlic plants. Farmers cut off these stalks with their playful curl at the top to get the largest bulb development below-ground. Think of them as garlicky asparagus.

Scapes are delicious sautéed or steamed, and some cooks put them in pesto. We, of course, ferment them. They take well to the process but stay pretty crunchy. The strong flavor of scapes can be a nice substitution for garlic cloves in fermented krauts and kimchis. To ensure a seamless substitution, create a scape paste in a food processor; for a stronger taste, slice the scapes. They'll provide nuggets of garlic flavor. *Note:* Scapes tend to ferment firm, so slice them thin.

Christoper Writes

One summer we convinced our eldest son and his fiancée to work in the fermentation kitchen over their break while we were covering the farmers' markets. Since garlic scapes have a natural curl, Kirsten thought they'd look good as pickled ringlets. Honestly that's all she shared with the kids before heading out to a market, leaving them with a pile of scapes and five cases of pint jars. When we returned to the farm 12 hours later we found 50 jars of "celtic knots" — exquisitely coiled and twisted scapes in their jars with rosemary packed in the empty spaces. Fifty jars of artistic beauty, which when you factor the labor costs was extremely unprofitable, but a joy to display at the markets.

YOUR RAW MATERIAL

Garlic scapes arrive at farmers' markets and in CSA boxes in early summer. If you've planted garlic, cut them from your own patch early, when the curls are just poking above the leaves, to ensure tenderness.

Scapes should be firm but still flexible and free of blemishes, fading, and brown spots, which indicate age. They'll last about a week in the fridge.

IN THE CROCK

Garlic Scape Paste

yield: about 1 pint
(fermentation vessel: 1 quart or larger)
technique used: Pastes and Bases (page 69)

This is a strong, concentrated condiment, delicious as instant garlic seasoning or as a spread. It's a triple threat: it's easy to make, it uses a normally discarded part of the garlic plant, and it's a great time-saving condiment. Virtue number 4? No peeling!

- 1 **pound garlic scapes**
- 1 **tablespoon lemon juice**
- 1 **teaspoon unrefined sea salt**

1. Cut the triangular top off the bulbs, leaving the bulbs in place. (The top is dry and stringy and doesn't purée well.) Cut the stems into 1-inch pieces. Blend in a food processor, in two batches, to the consistency of pesto. Sprinkle in the juice and salt. The veggies will become juicy immediately.

2. Put the paste in a quart-sized jar or crock and press until brine covers the scapes. Put a piece of plastic wrap on the surface to keep the small bits submerged.

3. Set aside on a baking sheet to ferment, out of direct sunlight, somewhere nearby, and cool, for

5 to 10 days. Check daily to make sure the scapes are submerged. You may see scum on top; it's generally harmless, but consult the appendix if you're at all concerned.

4. You can start to test the ferment on day 5. It's ready when the garlic is mild and has a light sour taste, and the bright green color has faded.

5. Store in jars, with lids tightened, in the fridge. This ferment will keep, refrigerated, for 12 months.

IN THE PICKLE JAR
Pickled Garlic Scapes
See photo on page 122
Pickle scapes as you would asparagus (page 111), or use them as a flourish in a medley of pickled vegetables.

Note: For another scape ferment, see Scape Kraut (page 135).

GRAPE LEAVES

Most Americans in those days regarded ethnic food as a leftover from the past, eaten only by poor, simple folk who should have learned better. In the eyes of native-born Americans, tolma and grape leaf picking was shameful, unusual, a sign of desperate hunger. And there was a strong aversion to eating leaves. Anyone picking wild grape leaves from roadside vines must be in trouble, probably no better off than a homeless bum.
— IRINA PETROSIAN, *ARMENIAN FOOD: FACT, FICTION & FOLKLORE*, 2006

YOUR RAW MATERIAL
When you use grape leaves to top crocks of krauts and pickles, they do more than keep everything under the brine: they also release tannins, which help keep the veggies crisp. If you preserve the leaves in early summer, you have them on hand to use for pickles during winter fermentation.

Those of us with well-established grapevines are in good shape. We just grab what we need. If you don't have a vine and become a serious fermentista, you might end up planting one.

Or maybe you have a neighbor who grows grapes organically. As with all vegetables, the leaves are full of beneficial bacteria, and you don't want to be consuming chemical pesticides. The variety of grape doesn't matter; use whatever you can get your hands on: leaves from table grapes, Concord grapes, wine grapes.

Early-summer leaves are more tender, but you can harvest any time before their color changes, in the fall. If you're picking late in the season, select leaves near growing points; they're the youngest. Choose the largest ones, so that they are big enough to stuff.

IN THE PICKLE JAR
Preserved Grape Leaves
yield: about 1 quart
(fermentation vessel: 1 quart or two 1-pint jars)
technique used: Mastering Brine Pickling (page 77)

Use whole leaves to make Greek *dolmas* (stuffed grape leaves), or to top any crock of brine pickles in the off-season, when fresh leaves are unavailable.

2–3 dozen grape leaves

2–3 cups Basic Brine (½ cup unrefined sea salt to 1 gallon unchlorinated water)

1. Rinse freshly picked leaves in cool water. Put in a bowl, cover with the brine, and let soak for 1 hour. Remove the leaves and reserve the brine.

2. Stack the leaves in batches of eight or more — you can make one big pile or several smaller ones. Tightly roll each pile from stem end to tip. (Think cigars.)

3. Pack into a clean jar, wedging them under the shoulder of the jar. Pour in enough brine to cover the leaves completely. Cover loosely. Store any leftover brine in the fridge (it will keep for a week; discard thereafter and make a new batch, if needed).

4. Set aside on a baking sheet to ferment, somewhere nearby, out of direct sunlight, and cool, for 3 to 4 days.

5. The ferment is ready when the leaves go from a verdant green to a dark, dull green and the brine is cloudy. Store in the fridge in the same jar, lid tight. Make sure the leaves are covered in brine, adding reserved brine if needed. These will keep, refrigerated, for 12 months.

HORSERADISH

A worm lives in horseradish and thinks there is nowhere sweeter.

— SHOLEM ALEICHEM, *A TREASURY OF SHOLEM ALEICHEM CHILDREN'S STORIES*, 1996

Preparing fresh horseradish comes with pain. If you do not like the nose-burning, eye-tearing intensity that could succeed in driving you out of the kitchen, then fresh horseradish may not be for you. If you want a good story of the sacrifices you, the food artist, make to feed people amazing food, then this is the perfect veggie.

Prepared horseradish — the kind you find in most stores — always contains vinegar or citric acid, necessary for the stabilization of the volatile oils. As soon as the cells of the root are damaged by grinding or chopping, enzymes begin breaking down these oils. The sooner the introduction of acid, the more the sharp flavor is retained. A pure lactic acid–fermented horseradish condiment has a mellower flavor than that of typical commercial preparations because when we begin the procedure, we have to wait for the biological activity to change the sugars to acid. This takes more time than simply adding vinegar.

To get around this, we acidify the horseradish ferment with a little brine from a previous ferment. Although the acid helps to stabilize the heat, this ferment will continue to mellow over time. Make small quantities — more often.

YOUR RAW MATERIAL

In season, you'll find fresh roots in the produce section of the grocery store and at the farmers' market. The outside should be a khaki-earthy color, and a bit gnarled is fine. Look for roots that are firm and free of blemishes. When you peel or slice a root, it should be creamy white. The whiter the root, the fresher it is.

If you're a fermentista with plenty of garden space, consider a horseradish plant. The root can find its way into krauts, pickles, relishes, and chutneys. The leaves are large and flavorful, and we use them as primary followers on pickle crocks, as they contain tannins that keep ferments crispy.

To grow horseradish, choose a spot that won't be disturbed. It needs plenty of room to sprawl: it's a vigorous perennial that can hog an entire bed. It's hardy and disease-resistant; when you harvest the root, even the smallest bit left in the ground will sprout a new plant.

Kirsten Writes

Our horseradish clump withstood years of wet winters and hot dry summers. I wish I could recall what moved our two oldest boys, at ages 10 and 7, to harvest and grind some of the root. They didn't even like horseradish. I do remember the squeals of both agony and delight. I do remember the evacuation. The boys, wearing swimming goggles and bandannas across their faces like bandits, and the Cuisinart full of half-ground roots were escorted out to the porch.

Horseradish is rough on big people too. At Farmhouse Culture, in Santa Cruz (see page 269), gas masks are vital gear on prep days for their delicious Horseradish-Leek Kraut.

IN THE CROCK

Fermented Horseradish

yield: about ½ pint
(fermentation vessel: 1 pint)
technique used: Pastes and Bases (page 69)

Use this as you would any other prepared horseradish. Or make a horseradish cream sauce: add the fermented horseradish to a combination of sour cream and mayonnaise.

Note: We've made horseradish with salt only — that is, no brine, no lemon juice, no whey. Salt preserves the root as a condiment, but it won't be as hot. It's also much drier, so you'll have to press it firmly into the bottom of the container to ferment and store.

½ **pound horseradish root**
1 **teaspoon unrefined sea salt**
2–3 **tablespoons previously fermented brine or lemon juice**

1. Peel the horseradish, cut into small pieces, and process to a paste consistency in a food processor. Sprinkle in the salt and add brine or lemon juice.

2. Press the paste into a pint jar. Top the ferment with a quart-sized ziplock bag. Press the plastic down onto the top of the ferment, then fill it with water and seal; this will act as both follower and weight.

3. Set aside on a baking sheet to ferment, somewhere nearby, out of direct sunlight, and cool, for 3 to 7 days. Check daily to make sure the horseradish stays submerged, pressing down as needed to bring the brine back to the surface. You may see scum on top; it's generally harmless, but consult the appendix if you're at all concerned.

4. You can start to test the ferment on day 3. It's ready when it tastes like prepared horseradish.

5. Tighten the lid and store in the fridge. This ferment will keep, refrigerated, for 6 months.

VARIATION: Fermented Horseradish with Tomato and Garlic

Add ⅓ cup chopped dried tomatoes and 4 garlic cloves to the food processor with the horseradish.

Horseradish Kraut

Add fresh horseradish to a kraut after the kraut has fermented. This stabilizes the "hot" flavor; if you incorporate it early, the grated root loses its volatile oils and gets lost. To create Horseradish Kraut, add a 2- to 3-inch piece of root (peeled and grated) to every 2 to 3 pounds of Naked Kraut (page 132); to make Horseradish-Beet Kraut, add a 2- to 3-inch piece of root (peeled and grated) to 2 to 3 pounds of Simple Beet Kraut (page 120).

IN THE PICKLE JAR

Many traditional Russian pickles call for slices of horseradish root; add them to the brine of a cucumber pickle so their flavor infuses the brine.

JICAMA

Jicama has a mild sweetness and a clean, crisp texture somewhat like that of a water chestnut, and people often eat it raw. It grows mainly in parts of the Southwest, Hawaii, and Mexico, so you probably won't find it at a farmers' market in most of the United States. Supermarkets generally carry it.

Christopher Writes

Sometimes as a market vendor you find yourself in a place that is absolutely wrong for your product. One such time was a Saturday morning market at a winery. People did not want wine so early in the day, and they certainly did not want to try sauerkraut. We sold only one jar of sauerkraut that cold, dreary spring morning, but we were inspired to create something new. A couple stopped by who had just come home from Mexico, where they had tried a relish of pickled beets, cauliflower, and jicama; evidently it was fiery with habanero peppers. I have no idea what they ate, but Habanero Jicama (page 188) is what we crafted after hearing their story.

YOUR RAW MATERIAL

Select jicama roots that are firm and feel heavy for their size, but bigger doesn't mean better. In fact, the big ones end up woody and tough and contain little moisture, which is an issue if you plan to ferment.

Jicama contributes a nice crisp texture to a variety of pickle combinations. Just peel and cut the roots into spears about the size of French fries, or dice them.

IN THE CROCK

Grated and fermented, jicama retains its crispness and its light sweetness during fermentation. Because of its high starch content, the brine is usually thick and milky rather than watery.

Jicama makes a nice base for relishes and chutneys, as its mild flavor lends itself to many herb and spice combinations. To capitalize on the sweetness, add dried fruits.

To ferment it alone, follow the directions for Naked Kraut (page 132), substituting grated jicama for the cabbage.

Habanero Jicama

See photo on page 173

yield: about 1 quart

(fermentation vessel: 1 quart)

technique used: Mastering Brine Pickling (page 77)

Use as a condiment or a salsa, or sprinkle over a green salad.

1 large beet, peeled and diced
1 small head cauliflower, diced
1 jicama, peeled and diced
2 tablespoons diced sweet onion
1–2 dried habaneros (depending on how much heat you want)
1 quart Basic Brine (2 tablespoons unrefined sea salt to 1 quart unchlorinated water)

1. In a large bowl, combine all of the vegetables, then tightly pack them in a 1-quart jar, making sure the habaneros stay whole. Pour in enough

KALE

We are often asked if there are any vegetables we don't ferment. We always chuckle, thinking about our kale experience, and say, "Yep, kale." We have talked to a lot of people and have yet to hear a positive all-kale ferment story. There are so many vegetables that shine so much brighter in a ferment — make kale chips instead.

Our first experience with fermenting kale was in a long, wet spring several years ago in the Northwest, a La Niña year, and we had mulched with generous amounts of composted horse manure. This combination translated to amazing quantities of large kale leaves. We had recently purchased *Wild Fermentation* by Sandor Katz. The traditional Tibetan *gundru* recipe seemed to be the answer we were looking for. As seasoned fermenters we were excited by a new challenge and we didn't have any better ideas for preserving this bounty. (It would be a few years before we discovered kale chips.)

Every horizontal surface on the furniture of our porch was draped in kale leaves. The sun shone, the leaves wilted, we rolled and pounded. We stuffed leaves into gallon jars. The green juice streamed from the once lush leaves. We sealed the jars, placed them in the window, and waited.

In a few weeks, we enthusiastically opened our *gundru*. We peered into the jar — no mold or scum, and it smelled fermented. Then we tasted. We like strong flavors, but this was not a flavor we could work with. Interestingly, it was also extremely salty, even though there had been no salt added. We tried to flavor soup stock with it, but it was never palatable.

About six years later, new neighbors put in a huge garden. Our neighbor told Kirsten that she and her husband made *gundru* a few days earlier. Kirsten's eyebrows involuntarily rose. "Really?" she asked. "Let me know how that goes. We didn't have the best of luck with it. Could've been just us." A few weeks later, our neighbor told us she'd come home and the *gundru* jar had been emptied and dumped outside. Her husband hadn't even waited for her to try it.

brine to cover completely. Reserve any leftover brine in the fridge. (It will keep for 1 week; discard thereafter and make a new batch, if needed.)

2. Top the ferment with a quart-sized ziplock bag. Press the plastic down onto the top of the ferment, fill it with water, and seal; this will act as both follower and weight.

3. Set aside on a baking sheet to ferment, somewhere nearby, out of direct sunlight, and cool, for 7 to 14 days. During the fermentation period, monitor brine the level and top off with the reserved brine, if needed, to cover. You may see scum on top; it's generally harmless, but consult the appendix if you're at all concerned.

4. As the vegetables ferment, they begin to lose their vibrant color and the brine will get cloudy; this is when you can start to test your pickles. They're ready when the brine, cauliflower, and jicama are a deep red, the cauliflower has softened slightly (the jicama and beets will maintain their crisp texture), and the flavor is pickle-y, without the strong acidity of vinegar.

5. When they're ready, store in the refrigerator in the same jar with the lid tight. These pickles will keep, refrigerated, for 12 months.

Create Your Own Recipes

Pickle an equal amount of jicama and quarters of red onion with three or four thin slices of lime according to the process for brine pickling (page 77).

Try fermenting jicama with chocolate nibs, cinnamon, and chipotle powder. We made several attempts, but we couldn't perfect the ratio of nibs to the other ingredients: the bitterness of the chocolate dominated. Maybe you can figure it out!

KOHLRABI

This is rather a bastard vegetable. It is neither turnip nor cabbage and is seldom as tender and crisp as it should be. To me it is a mystery why people really care for it.

— JAMES BEARD, *JAMES BEARD'S AMERICAN COOKERY*, 1972

Though unfermented kohlrabi is sweet, unpretentious, and delicately flavored with hints of broccoli or cabbage, the fermented version is nicely acidic and tastes very similar to its cabbage counterpart. Make it plain or dress it up with the same flavors you would cabbage.

YOUR RAW MATERIAL

Despite its bulbous appearance, kohlrabi is actually a swollen stem. Peak season, when the flavor is sweetest, is spring through early summer, although kohlrabi is available year-round.

Look for deep green leaves with no yellowing. (Yellow is a sign the vegetable is past its prime.) Select small kohlrabi; the skin is still thin and you can use the whole vegetable. Larger ones have an inedible woody layer that you must peel; use a paring knife, as the skin is too fibrous for a potato peeler. If the globe is enormous, it will be quite woody inside so don't bother fermenting it.

Kohlrabi Kraut

yield: about ½ gallon
(fermentation vessel: 1 gallon)
technique used: Mastering Sauerkraut (page 53)

This is a straightforward sauerkraut à la kohlrabi. Try this recipe plain or feel free to jazz it up with any of the spices that work well in cabbage krauts.

3½ pounds kohlrabi
1–1½ tablespoons unrefined sea salt

1. Rinse the kohlrabi in cold water, peel, then shred with a knife or a mandoline. Transfer to a large bowl.

2. Add 1 tablespoon of the salt and, with your hands, massage it into the shredded kohlrabi, then taste. You should be able to taste the salt without it being overwhelming. Add more salt if necessary. The kohlrabi will soon look wet and limp, and liquid will begin to pool. If you don't see much brine in the bowl, let it stand, covered, for 45 minutes, then massage again.

3. Transfer the kohlrabi, several handfuls at a time, to a 1-gallon crock or jar. Press down on each portion with your fist or a tamper to remove air pockets. You should see some brine on top when you press. When the vessel is packed, leave 4 inches of headspace for a crock, or 2 to 3 inches for a jar. Top the kohlrabi with a piece of plastic wrap. For a crock, top with a plate that fits the opening of the container; then weight down with a sealed water-filled jar. For a jar, use a sealed water-filled jar or ziplock bag as a follower and weight.

4. Set aside on a baking sheet to ferment, somewhere nearby, out of direct sunlight, and cool, for 4 to 14 days. Check daily to make sure the vegetables are submerged, pressing down as needed to bring the brine back to the surface. You may see

scum on top; it's generally harmless, but consult the appendix if you're at all concerned.

5. You can start to test the kraut on day 4. You'll know it's ready when it tastes like sauerkraut made with cabbage (except it's not), it's pleasingly sour, and the kohlrabi has softened a bit but retains some crunch.

6. When it's ready, ladle the kraut into smaller jars and tamp down. Pour in any brine that's left. Tighten the lids, then store in the fridge. This kraut will keep, refrigerated, for 1 year.

Note: For another kohlrabi kraut, see Sauerrüben III (page 248).

Kirsten Writes

I was doing errands in town when my mobile phone rang. Christopher nervously told me to call the deli where I had dropped off a 5-gallon bucket of kraut the previous week.

"They say there's something wrong. The flavor is great but the texture is strange. You better call."

I talked with the owner. He didn't want it replaced. He just wanted us to know it was different, and wondered why. I talked about diversity in the local farmers' cabbages; varieties can make a difference, and so on. But the truth is I really wasn't sure why. He wasn't too concerned, so I never went to look at it.

A few months passed. I wanted to bring something new to market and I knew we had a batch of straight kohlrabi kraut I'd been holding back. I couldn't find the five-gallon bucket of shredded, fermented kohlrabi. I still didn't make the connection. It was months later when I burst out laughing and said to Christopher, "Remember the strange-textured sauerkraut? It wasn't cabbage at all — it was kohlrabi."

Clearly kohlrabi makes a fine substitute for cabbage.

LEEKS

Leeks originated in the Mediterranean basin and are one of the oldest cultivated vegetables. Egyptian writings show leeks as a barter currency (along with oxen and beer). Despite their warm, dry beginnings, leeks are a cold-weather crop.

Leeks are an important ingredient in many Asian cuisines and especially in kimchi. For example, there are kimchi recipes that call for a lot of them, as it is believed they reduce the speed of fermentation, which can allow more time for the flavor to develop beyond just the adicity. Asian recipes tend to use small leeks, the size of a scallion.

Like other members in the onion tribe, under fermentation the harsh pungency of the raw flavor is mellowed. Use them as a substitute for onions in a recipe or highlight them for their fine flavor, as we have in the Leek–Cracked Pepper Kraut on page 192.

YOUR RAW MATERIAL

Leeks available at the market are sizable and well developed, but you can eat them at any stage. The white shaft is more mildly flavored than is the green, but both ferment well. The outer leaves are often tough or stringy and won't soften enough during the ferment, so remove them and save for a stock.

Select leeks that are less than 1 inch in diameter. When pencil thin, they tend to be sweeter than scallions and make a good winter substitute for them.

As leeks grow, farmers pile soil around their bases to increase the length of the white part, and as a result soil often gets trapped between their layers. Sometimes this can pose a challenge when preparing. Remove any coarse outer leaves, and trim and discard the roots. Slice off the very darkest part of the stalk to the light green, more tender portion. Slice the stalk in half lengthwise and rinse under cold running water to remove the grit, taking care to rinse in between all the leaves.

Kirsten Writes

A number of years ago our neighbor Tina and I grew a garden together. We both were determined to feed our families largely from this garden. It was a substantial undertaking, and she and I practically lived in the garden. When we were not tending it, we were in the kitchen preserving the bounty. We were beyond tripling batches; we were making salsa recipes times twenty-two, or enchilada sauce times fourteen. Our jar count, pints and quarts, was already in triple digits halfway through the summer.

At one point the leeks were ready to bolt and all of them needed to be harvested at once. We had an overflowing wheelbarrow full of leeks pushed up to the kitchen door. The question was, what does one do with so many leeks? We called the university extension's food preservation hotline; they said jarring low-acid leeks would require cooking for 45 minutes in a pressure canner. That wouldn't do. Finally we sliced them, sautéed them in butter, and froze this "soup base" in usable portions. It ended up being a good use, though our freezers smelled like cooked leeks for months.

If only we had thought of fermenting them.

Leek Paste

yield: about 1 quart
(fermentation vessel: 1 quart or larger)
technique used: Pastes and Bases (page 69)

Leeks hold their flavor, so they make a versatile base to enhance soups, sauces, and salads. In fact, use this ferment as you would fresh leeks in any recipe.

1½ pounds leeks, light green parts included, cleaned and cut into 1-inch pieces
1 teaspoon unrefined sea salt

1. Put the leeks in a food processor and pulse until the leeks are finely chopped. Sprinkle in the salt; the leeks will become juicy immediately.

2. Press the leeks into a 1-quart jar. More brine will release at this stage, and you should see brine above the vegetables. Top the ferment with a quart-sized ziplock bag. Press the plastic down onto the top of the ferment, then fill it with water and seal; this will act as both follower and weight.

3. Set aside on a baking sheet to ferment, somewhere nearby, out of direct sunlight, and cool, for 5 to 10 days. Check daily to make sure the paste is submerged. You may see scum on top; it's generally harmless, but consult the appendix if you're at all concerned. You can start to test the ferment on day 5. It's ready when the verdant green becomes dull and the pungency of the leeks has softened and become slightly sour.

4. When the paste is ready, tamp down to make sure the leeks are submerged in brine, tighten the lid, then store in the fridge. This ferment will keep, refrigerated, for 6 months.

Leek–Cracked Pepper Kraut

See photo on page 230
yield: about 1½ gallons
(fermentation vessel: 2 gallons or larger)
technique used: Mastering Sauerkraut (page 53)

This kraut has more complexity than Naked Kraut (page 132), but it's still easy to make and versatile — a family favorite.

8 pounds green cabbage
2 pounds leeks, light green parts included
3–4 tablespoons unrefined sea salt
1–2 teaspoons cracked black pepper

1. To prepare the cabbage, remove the coarse outer leaves. Rinse a few unblemished ones and set them aside. Rinse the rest of the cabbage and the leeks in cold water. With a stainless steel knife, quarter and core the cabbage. Thinly slice the cabbage and leeks with the same knife or a mandoline, then transfer both to a large bowl.

2. Add 3 tablespoons of the salt and, with your hands, massage it into the leaves, then taste. You should be able to taste the salt without it being overwhelming. Add more salt if necessary. The cabbage and leeks will soon look wet and limp, and liquid will begin to pool. If you've put in a good effort and don't see much brine in the bowl, let it stand, covered, for 45 minutes, then massage again. Add the black pepper.

3. Transfer the vegetables, several handfuls at a time, to a 2-gallon crock. Press down on each portion with your fist or a tamper to remove air pockets. You should see some brine on top of the vegetables when you press. When the vessel is packed, leave 4 inches of headspace. Top the vegetables with one or two of the reserved outer leaves. Then top the leaves with a plate that fits the opening of the container and covers as much of the vegetables as possible; weight down with a sealed water-filled jar.

4. Set aside on a baking sheet to ferment, somewhere nearby, out of direct sunlight, and cool, for 14 to 21 days. Check daily to make sure the kraut is submerged, pressing down as needed to bring the brine to the surface. You may see scum on top; it's generally harmless, but consult the appendix if you're at all concerned.

5. You can start to test the kraut on day 14. You'll know it's ready when it's pleasingly sour and pickle-y tasting, without the strong acidity of vinegar and it's somewhat translucent and the color of cooked cabbage.

6. When it's ready, ladle the kraut into jars and tamp down. Pour in any brine that's left. Tighten the lids, then store in the fridge. This kraut will keep, refrigerated, for 12 months.

Leek Fun Fact

The tyrannical Roman emperor Nero loved leeks, and he believed they'd improve his singing voice. He ate them in soups and prepared in oil, and was called by some Porophagus, the leek eater.

Create Your Own Recipes

Leeks blend nicely with sauerkraut, and like their onion cousins, they're versatile.

 » Try leeks in the crock with cabbage and roots like carrots, horseradish, turnips . . .
 » Consider a leek-wine kraut: prepare a leek and cabbage kraut and finish the fermentation with a splash of white wine (see Wine Kraut, page 135).

MUSHROOMS

So here's to the mushroom family
A far-flung friendly clan
For food, for fun, for poison
They are a help to man.
— GARY SNYDER, "THE WILD MUSHROOM," FROM
LOOK OUT: A SELECTION OF WRITINGS, 2002

Mushrooms, contrary to our usual recommendation that fresh is best, ferment better when dried. Dehydrated, they retain the integrity of their texture, flavor, and nutrition. Dried mushrooms offer the fermentista a few advantages. The first is that the deep, fragrant, earthy flavor is intensified by dehydration, which helps the aroma stand up to fermentation. The second is that they are readily available year-round.

Don't rehydrate mushrooms before adding to a kraut — rehydration happens in the brine and all the concentrated flavor will stay in the kraut. Be sure to check for grit before adding mushrooms to a ferment. If you find some, wash or scrape it off.

YOUR RAW MATERIAL

When choosing dried mushrooms at the store, make sure the package and the mushrooms inside don't look faded. This is a sign they've been sitting on the shelf too long. The most widely available dried varieties are shiitakes, porcini, and chanterelles.

If you cannot find shiitakes in your regular market, check an Asian market. Look in the package (they are usually clear plastic); you want the mushrooms with thick, ridged caps and white cracks. These are grade-A mushrooms, sometimes called *hana*, which is Japanese for "flower." They are more flavorful than the thinner, brown-capped shiitakes. Chanterelles have a gold-apricot color that befits their fruity flavor. Porcini mushrooms are also large, meaty mushrooms that are generally sliced before they are dried. Look for chanterelles and porcini in specialty markets.

Of course there is always the option of dehydrating your own mushrooms. Whether you stumbled across a seasonal deal at the market or have wildcrafted your own (see Foraged Vegetables on page 258), you will be guaranteed fresh quality mushrooms.

IN THE PICKLE JAR
Pickled Shiitake

yield: about 1 quart
(fermentation vessel: 1 quart)
technique used: Mastering Brine Pickling (page 77)

These pickles are made with shiitake mushrooms, but the flavors in the recipe are versatile and other dried mushrooms can be substituted. When selecting dried mushrooms to brine-pickle, you want them whole. Sliced, crushed, or shriveled mushrooms could mean inferior quality and won't brine well.

3 cups dried shiitake mushrooms
1 quart unchlorinated water
1 tablespoon unrefined sea salt
2–3 cloves garlic
1 teaspoon peppercorns
2–3 whole dried red chiles
1 bay leaf
Grape, sour cherry, oak, or horseradish leaves (optional)

1. Place the dried mushrooms in a bowl with the water and set aside for 2 to 3 hours. The mushrooms will be plump and rehydrated, and the liquid will be a translucent earthy brown, like a broth. This is the liquid for the pickling brine. Drain this amber liquid into a large bowl, reserving the mushrooms, then strain the liquid for any grit. Stir the salt into this liquid. Inspect the now-plump mushrooms for bits of sand. Also check the stems: if they are woody, remove them and pickle just the caps.

2. Pack the garlic, peppercorns, chiles, and bay leaf into a quart jar, alternating with the mushrooms; pour in enough brine to cover. Store any leftover brine in the fridge (it will keep for a week; discard thereafter and make a new batch, if needed).

3. Add the grape or other leaves, if you have them, to keep the mushrooms from bobbing up. *Note:* Because mushrooms are soft, the leaves won't crisp the mushrooms but will help keep them somewhat firm. If you don't have leaves, top with a sealed, water-filled ziplock bag. Cover loosely.

4. Set aside on a baking sheet to ferment, somewhere nearby, out of direct sunlight, and cool, for 7 to 10 days. During the fermentation period, monitor the brine level, making sure the mushrooms are not bobbing out of the brine. If they are, press them down and top off with the reserved brine, if needed. If the problem persists, add a small weight, such as a sealed water-filled jar. You may see scum on top; it's harmless, but consult the appendix if you are concerned.

5. You won't see big color changes in this pickle, as the brine is dark. You can test on day 7, and you'll know it's ready when the brine tastes acidic, not just salty, and the mushrooms taste as if they've been marinated.

6. When they're ready, make sure the mushrooms are submerged, screw on the lid, and store in the fridge. This pickle will keep, refrigerated, for 2 months.

Create Your Own Recipes

Add dried mushroom slices to a kraut that has a strong earthy flavor, such as a cabbage-fennel kraut.

Kirsten Writes

Ilona was one of the first neighbors we met when we moved to our farm. She was from the Ukraine; she freely shared her time and her culture with unparalleled enthusiasm. Three times a week our two oldest sons, aged nine and six, would traipse across the narrow valley and spend the morning with Ilona learning to speak Russian and cook traditional meals. In payment the boys would bring Ilona the morning's fresh goat milk — warm, and sweet. Sometimes I would go over later with our two younger children to eat the lunch they'd prepared, and giggle as I saw my two boys with white kerchiefs fastened around their heads and white aprons around their waists — that would never have flown at home.

Ilona gave me a book that year, *The Art of Russian Cuisine*, by Anne Volokh. It was the first book that I used to brine-pickle vegetables, and it is still one of my favorite cookbooks. I read these types of cookbooks carefully, extracting nuggets of wisdom that go beyond the simple recipe, and I have learned a lot from this one. Ms. Volokh shares a delightful traditional method of fermenting mushrooms by layering them in salt in an oaken barrel. I recommend finding this book for more wisdom on traditional fermentation in Russia.

MUSTARD GREENS

Mustard greens have an ancient history. In the Himalayan region of India, it is believed people began consuming them some 5,000 years ago. Now the plant — greens, seeds, and stems — still plays a major role in the cuisine, especially in the area of the Punjab. The greens have spread to the cuisines of Italy, China, Japan, and Korea, and in more recent history Africa and the American South. In Italy they're braised with garlic; in Asia they're often pickled; and in the South, the greens are often slow-cooked with ham hocks.

And what about the seeds, brown and yellow? They're a nice addition to many of our pickling-spice mixtures. We also dry-roast them to put into kraut with other spices from the Indian spice palette.

FERMENTISTA'S TIP

Pickle Spice Recycling

When you reach the bottom of a jar of pickles, you will have two things: the brine and all those seeds and spices, plus a clove or two of mellow garlic. Save the brine (to make Brine Crackers, page 293), and if you need a spot of mustard or a little quick condiment, "recycle" the spices and garlic by putting them in the blender with a small amount of the brine and processing to a paste consistency. Remove any stems and anything else that is woody first. If you were heavy-handed with the peppercorns, you may want to take out a few of those as well.

YOUR RAW MATERIAL

The season for mustard greens is generally October through March. In the produce section of the supermarket or at a farmers' market, you'll find many varieties — from the huge, curly, peppery leaves to the delicate and fernlike mizuna. We use them all. Mustard greens have the best flavor and mouthfeel when harvested young. Then they're plump, crisp, and deep green. They have a stimulating, pepper-like flavor when raw and a slightly bitter taste when cooked.

IN THE CROCK

Salted and fermented mustard greens make a traditional salad, called *dakguadong*, in Thailand. Mustard greens are also a recurring ingredient in many traditional kimchi recipes.

These greens are tastiest as an ingredient in a mixed vegetable ferment — we have yet to create a single-ingredient mustard green recipe that we love. Incorporate mustard into kimchi and kraut ferments (see Burdock Kimchi, page 130, for a recipe using these greens).

BRIDAL PICKLES

In China's Sichuan province, lacto-fermented pickles (*zha cai*) are an important part of the culture and the cuisine. Traditionally, with the birth of a baby girl, her family put up *zha cai* in an earthen jar and continued every year until she married, when she would receive them as a gift. Twelve to fifteen pots indicated that the time had come.

Zha cai is a ferment made by salting the swollen green stem of a type of mustard, *Brassica juncea* var. *tsatsai*. (You may see it referred to as a tuber, but it's a stem.) The stem is lumpy and knobbed and looks a little like a green Jerusalem artichoke.

To make the ferment, the stem was salted and pressed until it dehydrated. Then it was rubbed with chile paste and put into an earthen pot to ferment — for years. It was usually rinsed before cooking.

OKAHIJIKI GREENS (SALTWORT)

How could you not order one packet each of saltwort, sneezewort, motherwort, and Saint-John's-wort, plus a sample of mad-dog skullcap, which the text said was once a folk remedy for rabies? At a buck a pop, how could you go wrong?

— KRISTIN KIMBALL, *THE DIRTY LIFE: A MEMOIR OF FARMING, FOOD, AND LOVE*, 2010

Also known as land seaweed and saltwort, this succulent green is a member of the goosefoot family. Okahijiki hails from Japan, where it adapted to soils with high levels of salt, as in a salt marsh, and is one of that nation's oldest vegetables.

In the spirit of diversifying your diet, here are some reasons to try okahijiki: It's rich in laminin, a protein necessary to the health of virtually every type of cell. It also boasts vitamins A and K, calcium, potassium, and iron.

YOUR RAW MATERIAL

Despite its name, saltwort isn't salty. (That's because the name comes from where it grows, not from its taste.) Nor is it rubbery, like seaweed, or fibrous and dry, which is how it feels to the touch. Its taste is juicy and crisp, with a hint of mustard.

Although this nutrient-dense leaf is popular in Japan, here in North America you've likely never heard of it. If you live where there's an Asian market, you may have a chance of finding it. There are farmers that grow it to sell at farmers' markets, but you may have to sweet-talk your favorite farmer into trying a small bed of it. Otherwise, go online and find a company that sells the seeds and then grow them yourself. They grow as easily as (tumble)weeds.

IN THE CROCK

Okahijiki Kraut

yield: about 2 quarts
(fermenting vessel: 2 quarts or larger)
technique used: Mastering Sauerkraut (page 53)

In this kraut, we wanted to evoke the flavors of Japan. It makes a great salad alongside sushi. Shiso leaves (see page 228) add a depth of flavor, but if you can't find them, this kraut will still be delicious.

- 1–2 **heads cabbage**
- 1–2 **cups chopped okahijiki greens**
- 1 **cup thinly sliced daikon radish**
  Handful of fresh or fermented shiso leaves, chopped
- 1–2 **tablespoons unrefined sea salt**
- 1 **tablespoon dried hijiki seaweed (optional)**

1. To prepare the cabbage, remove the coarse outer leaves. Rinse a few unblemished ones and set them aside. Rinse the rest of the cabbage in cold water. With a stainless steel knife, quarter and core the cabbage. Thinly slice the cabbage with the knife or a mandoline, then transfer to a large bowl. Add the okahijiki greens, radish, and shiso leaves.

2. Add 1 tablespoon of the salt and, with your hands, massage it into the leaves, then taste. It should taste slightly salty without being overwhelming. If it's not salty enough, add more until it's to your liking. The vegetables will soon look wet and limp, and liquid will begin to pool. If you've put in a good effort and don't see much brine in the bowl, let it stand, covered, for

45 minutes, then massage again. Add the hijiki, if using.

3. Transfer the vegetables, a few handfuls at a time, to a 2-quart jar or a 1-gallon crock, pressing down as you go with your fist or a tamper to remove air pockets. You should see some brine on top when you press. When the vessel is packed, leave 4 inches of headspace for a crock, or 2 to 3 inches for a jar. Top the kraut with one or two of the reserved outer cabbage leaves. For a crock, top the leaves with a plate that fits the opening of the container and covers as much of the vegetables as possible; then weight down with a sealed water-filled jar. For a jar, use a sealed water-filled jar or ziplock bag as a follower-weight combination.

4. Set aside on a baking sheet to ferment, somewhere nearby, out of direct sunlight, and cool, for 10 to 21 days. Check daily to make sure the vegetables are submerged, pressing down as needed to bring the brine back to the surface. You may see scum on top; it's generally harmless, but consult the appendix if you're at all concerned.

5. You can start to test the kraut on day 10. You'll know it's ready when the vegetables have turned a drab color and the cabbage is somewhat translucent; it's pleasingly sour and pickle-y tasting, without the strong acidity of vinegar; and the veggies have softened a bit but retain some crunch. Ferment longer if more acidity is desired.

6. Store in jars, with lids tightened, in the fridge. This kraut will keep, refrigerated, for 1 year.

WHEN THE GOING GETS TOUGH . . . THE TOUGH FERMENT!

Tumbleweed is a cousin of okahijiki and also edible. Sometimes called Russian thistle, tumbleweed was a valuable food in the driest period in American history, when our prairies were parched almost beyond imagination and were termed the Dust Bowl. At first tumbleweeds were fermented in salt as silage for animals, but after years of drought, tumbleweed kraut became food for humans. Timothy Egan writes in *The Worst Hard Time*, "Ezra and Goldie Lowery came up with the idea to can thistles in brine . . . they were good for you. High in iron and chlorophyll. Cimarron County declared a Russian Thistle Week, with county officials urging people who were on relief to get out to the fields and help folks harvest tumbleweeds."

OKRA

Sternest are the guardians of Hindi: can alien okra ever taste of bhindi?

— MUKUL KESAVAN, *CIVIL LINES: NEW WRITING FROM INDIA*, VOL. 4, 2001

Okra, a member of the mallow family, has its origins in Ethiopia, in Sudan, and along the Nile River. It's popular in the cuisines of western and northern Africa, the Middle East, and India. It came to the Americas and the West Indies via the slave trade and took hold in the warmer climates. You'll find it in any number of regional Southern stews as a thickener. In much of the English-speaking world, okra is known as lady's fingers.

Christopher Writes

My grandparents on my father's side lived on a small farm a few miles outside our farm town, but it seemed like the boonies to me. Grandpa Shockey retired from the Coca Cola bottling plant after 50 years. That's right, he worked the same job his whole life. When they retired, Grandpa focused on his big garden, which was over an acre and grew everything, including okra. For me, okra fell into the category of vegetables that are fine as long as they are breaded and fried within an inch of their lives. I would help Grandpa pick "a mess" of okra and then run it in to Grandma in the late morning so that she could start it soaking in buttermilk from the neighbor. By lunch the heat and humidity of a Missouri summer would force Grandpa and me into their small farmhouse, where Grandma would have a pile of fried okra draining on paper towels. Through trial and error I learned to favor the small ones that would be reliably cooked through.

YOUR RAW MATERIAL

Select okra pods that are bright green and hefty — 2 to 3 inches long. These are immature, but also tastier than their older mates in the bin. The fruit becomes fibrous and woody as it ripens (after all, okra belongs to the same family as jute and cotton). Stay away from pods that look dry and have blemishes or black spots. Make your pickles soon after you bring them home; even in the fridge, they start to degrade in a day or two.

IN THE PICKLE JAR
Curried Okra Pickles

yield: about 1 quart
(fermentation vessel: 1 quart)
technique used: Mastering Brine Pickling (page 77)

The curry powder gives this brine a unique yellow cloudy quality. When the pickles are all gone, use the leftover brine to make delicious crackers (page 293).

- **1** pound whole okra pods (or enough to fill a 1-quart jar)
- **2** cloves garlic
- **1** teaspoon coriander seed
- **1** teaspoon cumin seed
- **1** teaspoon peppercorns
- **4–5** dried tomatoes
- **½** red onion, cut lengthwise into a few wedges
- **1–2** teaspoons curry powder (page 124)
- **1** quart Cucumber Brine (3 tablespoons unrefined sea salt to 1 quart unchlorinated water)
- **1 or 2** grape leaves (optional)

1. Rinse the okra in cold water. Trim most of the stem from each pod, leaving just enough to keep the pod closed. Put the garlic, coriander, cumin, and peppercorns in the bottom of the jar, then arrange the okra, tomatoes, and onion on top. Mix the curry powder into the brine (this prevents the powder from lumping), then pour it into the jar. Make sure everything is submerged. Store any leftover brine in the fridge (it will keep for a week; discard thereafter and make a new batch, if needed).

2. Place the grape leaves, if using, over the vegetables as a primary follower (the tannins in the leaves keep the pickles crisp). *Loosely* cover the jar with the lid.

3. Set aside on a baking sheet to ferment, somewhere nearby, out of direct sunlight, and cool, for 5 to 7 days. During the fermentation period, monitor brine level and top off with the reserved brine solution, if needed, to cover. You may see scum on top; it's generally harmless, but consult the appendix if you're at all concerned.

4. As the okra ferments, it begins to lose its vibrant color and the brine will get cloudy; this is when you can start to test your pickles. They're ready when they're pleasingly sour and pickle-y tasting, without the strong acidity of vinegar; the flavors have mingled; the color of the okra is a muted, even dull green; and the brine is cloudy.

5. When they're ready, screw on the lids and store in the fridge. After about 1 day check to be sure the pickles are still submerged, topping off with the reserved brine, if necessary. These pickles will keep, refrigerated, for 6 months.

Spicy Okra Pickles

yield: about 1 gallon
(fermentation vessel: 1 gallon or four 1-quart jars)

Okra, with its roots in tropical soils, lends itself to heat. If you like spicy, increase the peppers in the jar. Dried cayennes work well; if you want heat and a slight smoky hint, use whole habaneros. This recipe is a variation of Curried Okra Pickles (page 199).

   3 **pounds okra pods, ends trimmed but still closed**
  15 **cloves garlic**
1–2 **dried red chiles**
   6 **bay leaves**
   2 **tablespoons pickling spice,** *or*
       1½ teaspoons whole black peppercorns,
       1½ teaspoons mustard seed,
       1 teaspoon coriander seed, and
       1 teaspoon dill seed (or, better, 2 fresh dill seed heads)
   1 **gallon Cucumber Brine (¾ cup unrefined sea salt to 1 gallon unchlorinated water)**
       Grape, oak, or horseradish leaves, enough to top the jar or crock (optional)

Follow the instructions for Curried Okra Pickles (page 199), leaving out the curry powder, and packing your okra, peppers, and other spices in a 1-gallon jar or four 1-quart jars.

ONIONS

An onion can make people cry but there has never been a vegetable invented to make them laugh.

— WILL ROGERS

Onions are often the "secret" to imparting a certain brightness to sauerkraut. In the crock for a basic cabbage kraut, they add a depth to the overall flavor without being oniony. Chunks of the bulb are a tangy component of pickled vegetable medleys as well. They not only look good in the jar but also taste great.

Onions are the only vegetable we know of that lack intrinsic lactic-acid bacteria. Combined with other vegetables in the sauerkraut crock, kimchi pot, or pickle jar, this is not a problem: the other veggies have plenty of the bacteria to jump-start the process. In onion-only relishes and chutneys, adding a little bit of sauerkraut brine is enough to inoculate the ferment, and it will acidify as well as anything else.

We have yet to meet a member of the onion clan that does not do a fantastic job in a ferment: red, yellow, white, sweet, shallots, chives (see sidebar, page 202), leeks (see page 191), scallions (see page 226), and ramps (see page 264).

Kirsten Writes

I put onions in just about every dish I make. However, I also realize that some people don't appreciate them as much as I do. The way I see it, there are two inherent problems. The first is the piquant raw onion. It is not only sharp-flavored but leaves one with strong breath and a powerful thirst the rest of the day. This is solved simply by cooking — but for some, the soft, slippery texture is not an improvement. Our son, who has an amazing ability to pick even the smallest fragment of cooked onion out of any dish, loves fermented onions. I suspect this has to do with the missing slime factor.

I have no proof, but I have read accounts of people who cannot eat raw onions at all yet can eat and enjoy fermented onions.

An Onion a Day

Most onions, especially the outer rings of the red onion, have a high supply of *quercitin*, a flavonoid that acts to block cancer cell formation. Some nutritionists recommend including a few ounces of raw onion in one's diet regularly to increase cancer protection. Researchers in Canada found that fermentation increased the levels of quercitin in onions (they used red onions), which elevates the antioxidant action. Quercetin also deactivates the growth of estrogen-sensitive cells often found to cause breast cancer. "An antioxidant/bio-flavonoid called quercetin is a prime anticancer weapon," says Terrance Leighton, a professor of biochemistry and molecular biology at the University of California at Berkeley. Leighton claims that "quercetin is one of the most potent anti-cancer agents ever discovered. It blocks cancer development and, if cancer is already present, its spread."

YOUR RAW MATERIAL

For the freshest onions, select bulbs that are firm and heavy. Old onions will not only be soft but will also have a potent odor. Onions store well in a cool, dark space, but sweet onions have a shorter storage life — unless you ferment them.

IN THE CROCK

Make relishes and chutneys by slicing or dicing the onions; it depends on the texture you'd like.

Slicing makes a more substantial condiment with a variety of applications — use in sandwiches and wraps, atop pulled pork, as a side. Dicing produces a softer, saucier texture, similar to that of a pickle relish (page 171) or a salsa.

The following recipes make 1 to 2 quarts of each condiment. Don't let that scare you off. Onion chutneys and relishes are excellent to have on hand.

We Are Family: Fermented Chives

yield: ½ pint
(fermentation vessel: 1 pint)
technique used: Whole-Leaf Ferments (page 72)

Chives, the smallest of the edible members of the onion tribe, are at their best in spring; by late summer the greens can be tough. Use any amount of chives you can snip or buy for this recipe. A 4-inch-diameter bundle yields less than 1 pint. Fermented chives tend to stick together. Just separate them with a fork and sprinkle them on anything you'd garnish with fresh chives.

Any quantity of chives in ¼-pound bunches
⅛ teaspoon unrefined sea salt per bunch

1. Finely chop the chives and add to a bowl. Sprinkle on the salt and work it in until the taste is slightly salty. The chives will create brine; however, the chopped chives will bunch and stick together and the brine will float on the outside. This is difficult to visualize, but you'll understand it when it happens.

2. Top the ferment with a ziplock bag, pressing it down onto the ferment, then fill it with water and seal. Set aside in a cool spot for 7 to 14 days. Check periodically that the chives are submerged, pressing if needed to bring the brine to the surface, and scooping out any mold. Start testing in 1 week. It will have a slight sour flavor and will be a very deep, dark green when ready.

3. To store, pack tightly in a jar and fill to the rim; tighten the lid, then store in the fridge for up to 8 months.

Simple Onion Relish

yield: about 2 quarts
(fermentation vessel: 2 quarts or larger)
technique used: Relishes, Chutneys, Salsas, and Fermented Salads (page 66)

    5 large onions
1–1½ tablespoons unrefined sea salt
    1 tablespoon mustard seed
    1 teaspoon ground cumin
    1 tablespoon sauerkraut brine (from your stash in the fridge)

1. With a stainless steel knife, trim the onions by making shallow, cone-shaped cuts on both ends. Peel away the papery outer layers of skin and any damaged or discolored layers. With the same knife or a mandoline, thinly slice the onions crosswise to make rings. Transfer to a large bowl and sprinkle in 1 tablespoon of the salt, working it in with your hands. Taste and sprinkle in more salt as needed to achieve a salty flavor that is not overwhelming. Add the mustard seed, cumin, and sauerkraut brine.

2. At this point there is brine building at the bottom. Press your onions into a jar or crock. More brine will release at this stage, and you should see brine above the onions. Top the ferment with a quart-sized ziplock bag. Press the plastic down onto the top of the ferment and then fill it with water and seal; this will act as both follower and weight.

3. Set aside on a baking sheet to ferment, somewhere nearby, out of direct sunlight, and cool, for 7 to 14 days. Check daily to make sure the onions are submerged, pressing down as needed to bring the brine to the surface. You may see scum on top; it's generally harmless, but consult the appendix if you are concerned.

4. You can start to test the ferment on day 7. It's ready when the onions are translucent, have lost their sharp bite, and are pickle-y tasting without the strong acidity of vinegar.

5. Store in jars, leaving as little headroom as possible, and tamping the onions down under the brine. Tighten the lids, then store in the fridge. This ferment will keep, refrigerated, for 18 months.

Onion and Pepper Relish

See photos on pages 122 and 230
yield: about 2 quarts
(fermentation vessel: 2 quarts or larger)
technique used: Relishes, Chutneys, Salsas, and Fermented Salads (page 66)

For this mild relish, use only bell peppers; if you want more heat, mix them with habaneros or jalapeños and add 1 tablespoon chile pepper flakes.

    5 large onions, sliced
    5 large red or green bell peppers, or a combination, thinly sliced
    1 tablespoon whole coriander seed, slightly cracked
    ½ teaspoon ground cumin
1–1½ tablespoons unrefined sea salt
    1 tablespoon sauerkraut brine (from your stash in the fridge)

Follow the directions for the Simple Onion Relish (above), adding the peppers along with the onions.

Onion Chutney

yield: about 1 quart
(fermentation vessel: 1 quart or larger)

    3 large onions, sliced or diced
    1 apple, diced
    ½ cup raisins
    1 teaspoon ground cumin
    1 teaspoon mustard seed
  1–2 teaspoons unrefined sea salt
    1 teaspoon curry powder (page 124)
    1 tablespoon sauerkraut brine (from your stash
       in the fridge)

Follow the directions for the Simple Onion Relish (page 203), adding the apples and raisins with the onions. *Note:* Mix the curry powder with the kraut brine before adding it; this prevents clumping.

"Onion Soup" Seasoning

yield: about 12 ounces

You'll need a dehydrator to make this versatile flavoring powder. Sprinkle it on any dish that could use a little zing — just like using onion soup mix as a seasoning. Try the classic chip dip by adding it to sour cream (see page 295).

    1 recipe Simple Onion Relish (page 203)

1. Loosely spread the fermented relish on non-stick or silicone drying sheets. Put into a dehydrator set at 100°F and dry for 14 hours.

2. Transfer the relish to a blender and process to a coarse powder.

3. Store in an airtight container. It will keep at room temperature for 6 months, or in the fridge or freezer for up to 1 year.

Cebollas Encurtidas (Pickled Onions)

See photo on page 217
yield: about 1 quart
(fermentation vessel: 1 quart or larger)

This recipe has its origins in Ecuador. It's a vinegar-pickled onion. There it calls for *cebolla paiteña*, a smaller and spicier onion than those we get in this country. Our fermented adaptation is delicious.

    3 red onions, sliced
    1 tablespoon lime zest (optional)
       Juice of 3 limes
    1 teaspoon unrefined sea salt

Follow the directions for the Simple Onion Relish (page 203), though this variation is even simpler as there are no spices to add. Add the lime juice in place of the sauerkraut brine. To increase lime flavor, include the zest.

Note: For a delicious onion kraut variation, see the Juniper-Onion Kraut recipe (page 133).

IN THE PICKLE JAR
Pickle thick wedges of onion in a salt brine. You can prepare them plain or — much more interesting — as a component of the seasoning for a vegetable medley. Thick slices or wedges stay firm and crisp. (Onions cut thin will be too soft and sort of lifeless.)

PAK CHOI (BOK CHOY)

This Asian green, a member of the vast cabbage clan, is a staple in kimchi. Whether of the large or "baby" variety, pak choi can be sliced into a kimchi as a replacement for, or supplement to, the napa cabbage (page 140). *Note:* The larger variety, with its succulent stalks, can cause the brine to take on a bit of a gelatinous quality. The fermentation process overcomes this with time, so if you find yourself with a gelatinous ferment, just tuck it back in for a little more curing time.

YOUR RAW MATERIAL

The commonly available pak choi has glossy, deep green leaves atop succulent, spoon-shaped white stems. It's compact, with a somewhat vertical habit, similar to that of celery. What's marketed as baby pak choi has short, chunky pale green stalks and is much smaller. It's also more supple and tender and has a milder flavor. Both varieties can be fermented. Choose pak choi that has bright glossy green leaves, with no yellowing and no bruising in the stalks.

GALANGAL

Used in many Southeast Asian cuisines, galangal root is becoming more widely available in specialty markets. This rhizome looks similar to ginger, but it is plumper and its pale orange-red skin is more translucent. Galangal has a distinctive flavor that lies somewhere between citrus and ginger, with a hint of eucalyptus. It adds wonderful notes to your ferments; use as you would ginger.

IN THE CROCK
Thai-Inspired Baby Pak Choi

See photo on page 257
yield: about 1 quart
(fermentation vessel: 2 quarts or larger)
technique used: Mastering Kimchi Basics (page 87)

Use the small "baby" variety of pak choi for this recipe. The heads remain whole and the remaining ingredients are made into a paste that is stuffed between the stalks. Serve one head as a side dish. You'll need to plan ahead for this recipe, as it requires a brining period, 6 to 8 hours or overnight.

- 1 gallon Kimchi Brine (1 cup unrefined sea salt to 1 gallon unchlorinated water)
- 6–7 heads baby pak choi
- 1 daikon root, shredded
- 1 cup Thai basil leaves
- 1 (1-inch) piece fresh galangal root (if unavailable, use fresh ginger)
- 1 teaspoon ground cayenne, chile pepper flakes, or salt-free *gochugaru*
- 1 stalk lemongrass, thinly sliced

1. In a crock or a large bowl, combine the brine ingredients and stir to dissolve. Rinse the pak choi in cold water and submerge the whole heads in the brine solution. Use a plate as a weight to keep the pak choi submerged. Set aside, at room temperature, for 6 to 8 hours.

2. Drain the pak choi for 15 minutes, reserving 1 cup of the soaking liquid.

3. Combine the daikon, basil, galangal, and cayenne in a food processor; pulse to a paste. Tuck small bits of this mixture between the stalks of the pak choi heads, as you would stuff an artichoke.

4. Spread the lemongrass in the bottom of your crock or jar. Lay the pak choi bundles in the crock, stacking and pressing as you go. When the bundles are all in the vessel, press until the brine covers them; use reserved brine as needed to submerge. Leave 4 inches of headspace for a crock, or 2 to 3 inches for a jar. For a crock, cover with a primary follower, such as a piece of plastic wrap, and top with a plate weighted down with a sealed water-filled jar. For a jar, you can use a sealed water-filled jar or ziplock bag as a follower-weight combination.

5. Set aside on a baking sheet to ferment, somewhere nearby, out of direct sunlight, and cool, for 4 to 5 days. Check daily to make sure the vegetables are submerged, pressing them down if necessary. You may see scum on top; it's generally harmless, but consult the appendix if you're at all concerned.

6. You may start to test on day 4. It's ready when the pak choi has completely wilted and the colors (and flavors) have mingled; it will be slightly sour and the vegetables will retain some crunch.

7. To store, press into the jar and seal the lid. This ferment will keep, refrigerated, for 2 months.

PARSLEY

Are you going to Scarborough Fair?
Parsley, sage, rosemary and thyme.
Remember me to one who lives there,
she once was a true love of mine.
— TRADITIONAL ENGLISH BALLAD

Parsley, another Mediterranean health food, is a strong source of vitamins K, C, and A and has folate, iron, and a whole host of good volatile oils. Parsley was used curatively prior to its use as a culinary herb. The ancient Greeks thought parsley sacred and, like us, used it as a garnish — though they garnished athletic champions and tombs of their departed with this herb.

YOUR RAW MATERIAL

While there are many varieties of parsley, the two common types you'll recognize are the curly-leafed and the Italian flat-leaf parsley. The flat-leaf variety is thought to be less bitter and more fragrant. Either is successful in fermentation, so use your favorite. Add minced parsley to any kraut or relish, and use the whole stems with leaves to enhance brine pickles.

Choose parsley that is not wilted. It should be deep green with no signs of yellowing.

Chimichurri

See photo on page 256

yield: about 1 pint
(fermentation vessel: 1 pint or larger)
technique used: Pastes and Bases (page 69)

This is our take on a traditional Argentinian condiment. In the original, the distinctive tang comes from wine vinegar; in our version, the lactic acid imparts the tang.

> 2 **cups fresh parsley leaves, well packed**
> ¼ **cup fresh oregano leaves (or 2–3 tablespoons dried)**
> 6 **cloves garlic**
> 1 **jalapeño or 1 teaspoon chile pepper flakes**
> 1 **small shallot**
> **Freshly ground black pepper, to taste**
> **Juice of 1 lime**
> 1 **scant teaspoon unrefined sea salt**

AFTER THE FERMENT
> ½ **cup extra-virgin olive oil**

1. Put the parsley, oregano, garlic, jalapeño, shallot, pepper, and lime juice in a food processor and blend into a paste. Sprinkle in the salt. The mixture will become juicy immediately.

2. Press the mixture into a pint jar. More brine will release at this stage and you will see brine above the paste. Top the ferment with a quart-sized ziplock bag. Press the plastic down onto the top of the ferment, then fill it with water and seal; this will act as both follower and weight.

3. Set aside on a baking sheet to ferment, somewhere nearby, out of direct sunlight, and cool, for 7 to 10 days. Check daily to make sure the herbs are submerged, pressing down as needed to bring the brine to the surface. You may see scum on top; it's generally harmless, but consult the appendix if you're at all concerned.

4. You can start to test the ferment on day 7. It's ready when the paste is slightly sour and dull green.

5. Stir in the olive oil. Eat immediately or store in the refrigerator in a sealed container for about a week. If you don't add olive oil it can be stored for 6 months in the refrigerator.

WE ARE FAMILY: ROOT PARSLEY

Root parsley is a variety of parsley grown for its large taproot instead of its greens. Despite their physical resemblance (like a humble, pale carrot), root parsley and parsnips are not alike. Parsnips are sweet; root parsley is not.

You'll find it under a variety of names, among them parsley root, Hamburg parsley, and Dutch parsley. It adds a mild parsley flavor to ferments and does not oxidize, so the white color is preserved during fermentation. Use it as you might a carrot. Add it to any ferment — kraut, kimchi, condiments, or pickles — sliced or shredded.

PARSNIPS

Before the potato there was the parsnip. Before sugar there were parsnips. In Europe, the parsnip was used as the starch of choice before the introduction of the potato. Parsnips also had an important role in dessert: before sugar was widely available in Europe, this pale tuber was used to sweeten cakes and puddings.

Kirsten Writes

During our first year as commercial fermentistas we sold our ferments in a roadside farm store. The owner of the farm store, Mary, had a surplus of parsnips. She talked me into trying to find a fermented outlet for parsnips. We decided to try some test batches: parsnip kimchi, parsnip-carrot pickles, and parsnip-carrot kraut. (Mary also had an abundance of carrots.)

We didn't care for the kraut, the pickles were decent, and the kimchi was our favorite, though it got off to a rocky start.

We let the kimchi age for three weeks. When we opened the crock it tasted good, yet the brine was viscous. That is a nice way of saying it was gooey and slimy; however, it wasn't the least bit rotten. We know now that it wasn't quite done, and that gooeyness is just a stage in the progression of the process. We hadn't had the good fortune to experience this in any of the fermenting we had done thus far. We suspected the parsnips.

My mother, who works with Chinese herbs, suggested schisandra berries. Her reasoning was that medicinally schisandra works against mucous buildup and the flavor would complement the sweetness. Christopher and I looked at each other and shrugged our shoulders. "Why not?"

We put the kimchi into a large bowl, tossed in some schisandra berries, and put it all back into a crock. A week later, our kimchi was delicious, and the texture perfect. We made a few more batches that winter, always adding schisandra. Later we realized these herbal berries had nothing to do with the consistency, but that didn't matter; they were now part of the recipe.

SCHISANDRA BERRIES

Schisandra berries are native to northern China, where they grow on a vine called magnolia vine. They have been used traditionally in China, Korea, and Japan for their tangy flavor as well as in medicinal preparations and tonics. They are also called "five flavors berries." We encourage you to try a dried berry on its own, but also warn you these berries are not for a faint palate. If you are up for the challenge, bite into the berry and allow the flavors to move through your palate. You will taste sweet, sour, bitter, pungent (spicy), and salty.

This quality makes schisandra uniquely flavorful in a ferment, but the berries can quickly overpower it. Use this spice sparingly. Crush lightly to release the flavor. Dried berries can be found at herbal stores. If you shop online make sure you find a reputable source (see the resources, page 360).

YOUR RAW MATERIAL

Parsnips look like carrots with a creamy complexion. They're a cool-season crop, sweetest after a hard frost. For fermentation, you must take into consideration the high amount of sugar, so combine with an equal amount of other veggies.

Shop for parsnips as you would for carrots: select firm, medium-sized roots; large roots often have a woody core.

IN THE CROCK
Parsnip Kimchi

yield: about 1 gallon
(fermentation vessel: 1 gallon or larger)
technique used: Mastering Kimchi Basics (page 87)

Dried schisandra berries impart complex flavors; parsnips contribute sweetness. This ferment has a two-step process that requires a brining time of 6 to 8 hours, and the kimchi spends a little more time curing than most of our ferments.

    1 gallon Kimchi Brine (1 cup unrefined sea salt
        to 1 gallon unchlorinated water)
    2 heads napa cabbage

SEASONING MIXTURE

    1 cup grated and packed parsnips (3–4 medium)
    ½ cup chile pepper flakes or salt free *gochugaru*
    ½ cup grated and packed daikon radish
    ¼ cup grated and packed carrot (about
        1 medium)
    3 scallions, greens included, sliced
    ½–1 head garlic (to taste), cloves separated and
        minced
    1 tablespoon minced fresh ginger
    1 tablespoon dried schisandra berries, lightly
        crushed

1. In a crock or a large bowl, combine the brine ingredients and stir to dissolve. Rinse the cabbage in cold water. Remove the coarse outer leaves and set them aside. Trim the stalk and cut each cabbage in half through the core. Submerge the halves in the brine solution with the reserved leaves. Use a plate as a weight to keep the cabbage submerged. Set aside, at room temperature, for 6 to 8 hours.

2. Drain the cabbage for 15 minutes, reserving 1 cup of the soaking liquid. Set the separated outer leaves aside.

3. Meanwhile, combine the parsnips, chile pepper flakes, daikon, carrots, scallions, garlic, ginger, and schisandra berries in a large bowl, and blend thoroughly.

4. Chop the brined cabbage into bite-size pieces, or larger if you prefer, and add them to the bowl. Massage the mixture thoroughly, then taste for salt. Usually the brined cabbage will provide enough salt, but if it's not to your liking, sprinkle in a small amount, massage, and taste again.

5. Transfer the vegetables a few handfuls at a time into a crock, jar, or onggi pot, pressing with your hands as you go. You will see brine on top of the veggies as you pack; this indicates that you are pressing out air pockets. Continue until the vegetables are all tucked in. Add the reserved soaking liquid if needed to fully submerge the vegetables. Leave about 4 inches of headspace for a crock or onggi pot, or 2 to 3 inches for a jar. For a crock, top with a plate and weight it down with a sealed water-filled jar. For a jar or onggi pot, you can use a sealed water-filled jar or ziplock bag as a follower-weight combination.

6. Set aside on a baking sheet to ferment, somewhere nearby, out of direct sunlight, and cool, for 14 to 25 days. Check regularly to make sure the vegetables are still submerged; press down to bring brine to the surface if not. You may see scum on top; it's generally harmless, but consult the appendix if you're at all concerned.

7. Test the kimchi on day 14. It's ready when it has a pleasing sour quality and the brine is thick, but not gelatinous or gummy.

8. When it's ready, spoon the kimchi into smaller jars, making sure the veggies are still submerged. Screw on the jar lids and store in the refrigerator, where it will keep for 6 months.

Create Your Own Recipes

» Parsnips go well with members of the allium family: leeks, onions, shallots, garlic.
» Pair with aromatic woody seeds, such as cumin and caraway.
» Pickle parsnips, in rounds or spears, the same way you would a carrot.

PEAS

Four hundred years ago, if you had a single pea in your hand, you would have called it a pease. That old form of the word can still be heard in a children's rhyme: "Pease porridge hot, pease porridge cold, pease porridge in the pot, nine days old."

— MARK MORTON, *CUPBOARD LOVE 2: A DICTIONARY OF CULINARY CURIOSITIES*, 2004.

English peas are the ones from the pods you "unzip" by snapping the top and pulling the string, thus revealing the treasures: small, round, and sweet. If you've ever grown these, it takes a lot of snapping and pulling to get any significant quantity. For this reason, we haven't tried.

Sugar snap peas and snow peas, however, have an edible skin, and we've found that fermentation is a great way to preserve their crisp freshness far beyond their short growing season. Snow peas are flat with petite seeds hardly visible through the pods. Sugar snap pods are plump, with noticeable peas.

Ferment either with other vegetables to provide the brine. The flavor will have depth, and the peas will stay pleasantly crisp.

YOUR RAW MATERIAL

Choose peas that are emerald green. They should have smooth skin and be firm to the touch, and when bent they should feel rubbery but will still snap. Stay away from peas that are much longer than 3 inches, as they are likely overgrown and tough.

Both of these varieties of pea have a string. To remove, nip the tip of each snow or snap pea and pull the string that runs along the edge.

Peas and Carrots

See photo on page 173

yield: about 1 quart
(fermentation vessel: 1 quart or larger)
technique used: Relishes, Chutneys, Salsas, and
Fermented Salads (page 66)

Make this as the weather warms and you see the pea season coming to an end. This ferment is a tasty way to preserve this spring treat and enjoy peas as a summer condiment. The carrots are added to create enough brine to cover the peas, which don't release enough on their own.

- 2 **cups chopped sugar snap or snow peas, cut into ½-inch pieces**
- 2 **cups shredded carrots**
- 1 **scallion, sliced**
- 2 **cloves garlic**
- 1 **tablespoon grated fresh ginger**
- 1 **tablespoon ground turmeric**
- 1–1¼ **tablespoons unrefined sea salt**

1. Combine the peas, carrots, scallion, garlic, ginger, and turmeric in a large bowl. Add a scant tablespoon of the salt and mix thoroughly with your hands, then taste. It should taste slightly salty without being overwhelming. Add more salt if needed. Let stand, covered, for 30 minutes. At this point, you should have just enough brine to cover the veggies.

2. Press your mixture into a jar or crock. More brine will release as you press the veggies; you should see brine above the mixture. Top the ferment with a quart-sized ziplock bag. Press the plastic down onto the top of the ferment, and then fill it with water and seal; this will act as both follower and weight.

3. Set aside on a baking sheet to ferment, somewhere nearby, out of direct sunlight, and cool, for 5 to 10 days. Check daily to make sure the vegetables are submerged, pressing down as needed to bring the brine to the surface. You may see scum on top; it's generally harmless, but consult the appendix if you're at all concerned.

4. You can start to test the ferment on day 5. When it's ready, the flavor of the carrots and peas will have mingled and it will be pleasingly sour.

5. Store in jars, with lids tightened, in the fridge, leaving as little headroom as possible, and tamping the ferment down under the brine. This ferment will keep, refrigerated, for 6 months.

Create Your Own Recipes

» Toss whole or chopped edible-pod peas in with a napa cabbage kimchi or other ferment.
» Pickle whole peas in Basic Brine (page 78) with fresh thyme or spring herbs (see Mastering Brine Pickling, page 77).

PEPPERS

Jalapeno Hal was a rough, tough cowboy. He was tough as a boot. He was tough as nails. He was tough as a horned toad's hide in summer. His heart was made of stone, and he was proud of it. . . . He was mean and had mean breath . . . scorching-hot breath. This was because Jalapeno Hal ate so many jalapeno peppers.
— JO HARPER, *JALAPENO HAL*, 1997

We roasted, seeded, and peeled whole green chiles; loaded them in half-pint jars; and pressure-canned them for 35 minutes (the requirement for this low-acid vegetable). They looked beautiful as they waited to become stuffed chiles rellenos in the winter. Then it was time, and that's when we discovered that even though they looked right, inside they were so mushy they disintegrated when touched. Lesson learned. We still roast and peel whole green chiles at harvest season, but now we freeze them instead of canning them. All others are fermented.

Fermented chiles — now there's the triumph in the preservation canon! The process not only keeps the integrity of their flavor; it also enhances it. Peppers and chiles in fermentation are versatile. You can make them into pastes, salsas, sauces, pickles. They'll add another layer of flavor to kraut and kimchi. Most fermented peppers do soften, not to mush, but they don't retain the crisp

HANDLING HOT CHILES

What makes chiles hot and spicy is *capsaicin*. All peppers have it, to varying degrees, except the bell pepper.

The level of capsaicin, or what the mouth feels as heat or fire, depends on a number of factors, among them the climate in which a chile grew, how much water it got, its age, and the number of seeds. Capsaicin oil is in the white pith and in the tissue around the seeds. It can cause a reaction even when you touch it.

This is important to you, the fermentista. Because capsaicin is an oil, it's not easy to wash off. Before you cut any of the hot chiles, put on a pair of thin protective gloves or rub a small amount of cooking oil on your hands; either acts as a barrier. When you've finished handling the chiles, wash your hands in hot water with dishwashing liquid or an oil-cutting soap. If there's still a problem, rinse your fingers in lemon juice or rubbing alcohol, then rub in a little aloe vera or milk. The casein in milk, and in products made from it, such as buttermilk and yogurt, neutralizes the capsaicin.

The lungs are even more vulnerable. Airborne capsaicin irritates the mucous membranes, and inhaling this compound can cause breathing problems. You'll feel it as a tightening in the lungs or you'll start to cough. Use caution if you suffer from any breathing problems, particularly asthma. Be sure to seed, chop, or grind raw chiles in a well-ventilated area. Capsaicin is also active during cleanup.

clean crunch of a fresh pepper, which is why we don't preserve them whole for rellenos.

Ferments containing a lot of peppers usually develop a bloom of Kahm yeast. Pepper pastes, in particular, are susceptible. You may think the ferment isn't working, but rest assured, the yeast is harmless, and as long as there's enough brine, the peppers will be safe and tasty beneath the yeast.

YOUR RAW MATERIAL

Sweet peppers are not spicy hot even though they're botanically the same species (*Capsicum annuum*) as their spicy chile siblings. These sweet, often bell-shaped peppers contain a recessive gene that excludes the capsaicin. (See Handling Hot Peppers at left.)

The most common sweet peppers are the red and green bell peppers, but there is a color out there for everyone — yellow, orange, purple, brown, and even black. Don't let the purple, brown, or black lure you, as these three colors don't hold their pigment in fermentation — for vivid exquisite ferments, stick to yellow, orange, and the reds.

Jalapeños and other hot chiles add complexity of flavor and striking color to any ferment. Use a small amount to create depth; use more for eye-watering fire. Hot chiles are an important crayon in the ferment art box. They are, well, not to use the word lightly, exquisite when you ferment them.

Whether you are working with chiles or sweets, choose peppers that are fresh. They will be firm with taut, glossy skin, and no wrinkles.

IN THE CROCK
Pepper Paste

See photo on page 216
yield: about 1 quart
(fermentation vessel: 1 quart)
technique used: Pastes and Bases (page 69)

In addition to its visual appeal and the taste, the beauty of this paste is its simplicity.

We make a gallon of it every year. If the family ate this freely, it would never last, but we save it in small jars and dole it out. The bonus: It gets better over time. You can easily scale up this recipe to make a gallon-size batch.

Use whatever type of chile you have. Our favorite is the fire-engine red Fresno, in part because its color is so appealing. It's similar to a jalapeño but is usually hotter.

1½ pounds chiles, stemmed
2 teaspoons unrefined sea salt

1. Put the chiles, seeds and all, in a food processor and pulse until coarsely chopped. Remove the food processor blade and stir in the salt.

2. Press the mixture into a crock or jar (see the note below). For a crock, add a primary follower: food-grade plastic screening (see page 36), like that used in a dehydrator, cut to size, works best to keep the small bits under the brine; otherwise, top the ferment with a quart-sized ziplock bag. Press the plastic down onto the top of the ferment, then fill it with water and seal; this will act as both follower and weight.

3. Set aside on a baking sheet to ferment, somewhere nearby, out of direct sunlight, and cool, for 21 days or more. Check the chiles occasionally to make sure your weights are in place and the chiles are submerged. It is normal to encounter yeasts; you can leave them undisturbed. The chiles take at least 3 weeks to develop a flavorful acidity, then 3 to 6 months more for a delicious and complex flavor.

4. Store in an airtight jar in the refrigerator, where this paste will keep for 2 years or more.

Note: For a long-term ferment, use a water-seal crock (see page 34) to help control the growth of yeast.

VARIATION: Hot Sauce

To make a Tabasco-style hot sauce, strain the paste through cheesecloth to remove some of the brine. Splash a bit of raw apple cider vinegar into the brine and *voilà!* — hot sauce. The brine mixture makes a tangy flavoring to add to anything from refried beans to guacamole.

Return the paste to the jar, tamp it down to keep it moist, cover with a small sheet of plastic, and screw on the lid.

Sambal

yield: about 1 pint
(fermentation vessel: 1 pint)
technique used: Pastes and Bases (page 69)

Sambal is Southeast Asia's version of pepper paste. Traditionally, and at its simplest, it consists of chile peppers and salt ground with a mortar and pestle. Each region, however, has its variation: chiles may be cayenne, Thai bird's eye, or Spanish; recipes may call for lime juice or lemongrass, shrimp paste or molasses. What they have in common is that they're always hot!

This recipe comes from Auguste Wattimena Huwaë, who was born and raised on the Maluku Islands (the Moluccas) of Indonesia, famous for cloves, nutmeg, and mace — hence their nickname, the Spice Islands. The use of bouillon in the traditional recipe probably reflects the influence of several European cultures, from the Portuguese, to the Spanish and the Dutch.

   ½ **pound fresh hot red chiles**
   1 **onion, chopped**
   1 **teaspoon Garlic Paste (page 181) or**
        2–3 cloves garlic, minced
   1 **bouillon cube or ½–1 teaspoon unrefined**
        sea salt
   1 **tablespoon lemon juice**

1. Put the chiles, onion, garlic paste, bouillon cube, and lemon juice in a food processor and process to a paste consistency. The mixture will become juicy immediately.

2. Press into a pint jar. More brine will release as you press the veggies; you should see brine above the mixture. Top the ferment with a quart-sized ziplock bag. Press the plastic down onto the top of the ferment, then fill it with water and seal; this will act as both follower and weight.

3. Set aside on a baking sheet to ferment, somewhere nearby, out of direct sunlight, and cool, for 7 to 15 days. Check daily to make sure the chiles are submerged. You may see scum on top; it's generally harmless, but consult the appendix if you are concerned.

4. You can start to test the ferment on day 7. It's ready when it is spicy-hot. When your taste buds get past the heat, you will detect wonderfully sour undertones as well.

5. Tamp down to make sure the sambal is submerged in its brine, and then cover the jar with the lid. This ferment will keep, refrigerated, for 6 months.

Sweet Pepper Salsa

See photo on page 122

yield: about 2 quarts
(fermentation vessel: 1 gallon)
technique used: Relishes, Chutneys, Salsas, and Fermented Salads (page 66)

Under the name Pepper Solamente, this was one of the products we brought to market. It's all peppers, but it makes a perfect fermented salsa, with all the color and tang of a tomato salsa without tomatoes. This salsa is delightful as is, or use it as a tomato-salsa starter kit: just before serving, add diced fresh tomatoes and a little minced cilantro to the pepper mixture.

>   3   **pounds sweet red peppers (the thicker the walls, the better), roughly chopped**
>   1   **pound jalapeños, seeds removed, roughly chopped**
>   2   **medium sweet onions, roughly chopped**
>   4   **cloves garlic, minced**
> 1½–2 **tablespoons unrefined sea salt**

1. Put the bell peppers, jalapeños, and onions in a food processor and pulse to mince. Transfer to a large bowl and add the garlic and 1½ tablespoons of the salt. Mix well, and you'll have enough brine immediately; then taste. It should taste slightly salty without being overwhelming. Add more salt if needed.

2. Press the mixture into a 1-gallon jar or crock. More brine will release as you press, and you should see brine above the veggies. You will have more brine than usual in this ferment; as the peppers and onions soften, the vegetable mass will not be dense enough to hold the usual scheme of primary and secondary followers in place. If using a jar weight on a plate, it will constantly slide sideways. The finely chopped veggies will want to float above the plate. So, for a primary follower, food-grade plastic screening (see page 36) works best; it will help keep the bits submerged. Otherwise, use a piece of plastic wrap. Top with a plate if using a crock or a sealed water-filled jar if using a jar.

3. Set aside on a baking sheet to ferment, somewhere nearby, out of direct sunlight, and cool, for 14 to 21 days. Check daily to make sure the vegetables are submerged, and adjust your followers and weights as needed. You may see scum on top; it's generally harmless, but consult the appendix if you're at all concerned.

4. You can start to test the ferment on day 14. It's ready when it has developed a pleasingly sour acidity, like salsa. This salsa will stay vibrantly colored.

5. When it's ready, spoon the ferment into smaller jars, leaving as little headroom as possible, and tamp down under the brine. Pour in any remaining brine to cover. Tighten the lids, then store in the fridge. This ferment will keep a long time refrigerated, up to 2 years.

DILLY BEANS, *page 117*

PEPPER PASTE,
page 213

JICAMA, *page 187*

RADICCHIO-GARLIC KRAUT,
page 218

HUNGARIAN CELERIAC,
page 158

CEBOLLAS ENCURTIDAS
(pickled onions),
page 204

ESCAROLE KIMCHI, *page 176*

CELERY "STUFFING,"
page 159

RADICCHIO

If you see it, it's so nice. If you eat it, it's paradise, the radicchio of Treviso.

— CLIFFORD A. WRIGHT, *A MEDITERRANEAN FEAST*, 1999

Radicchio, a member of the chicory family, is a beautiful salad green with white-veined maroon leaves. Even though it's often grown as an annual, it's actually a perennial, which means you can harvest leaves year-round. In Italy, cooks sauté or grill them in olive oil. Here we eat radicchio raw in salads. Try them fermented: you're in for a treat.

YOUR RAW MATERIAL

Commonly available is radicchio di Chioggia, which looks like a grapefruit-size head of red cabbage, but the texture is more like iceberg lettuce.

IN THE CROCK

Radicchio-Garlic Kraut

See photo on page 216

yield: about 1 quart
(fermentation vessel: 1 quart or larger)
technique used: Mastering Sauerkraut (page 53)

In this recipe we use radicchio di Chioggia. This ferment makes a great simple condiment, or use it to create Radicchio Tapenade (page 296).

> 2 heads radicchio di Chioggia
> 8 cloves garlic, finely grated or minced
> 1–2 teaspoons unrefined sea salt
> 5–6 sprigs basil, leaves removed and chopped
>   (optional)

1. To prepare the radicchio, rinse in cold water and remove an outer leaf to use as a follower.

With a stainless steel knife, quarter and core the radicchio. Thinly slice, then transfer the radicchio to a large bowl.

2. Mix in the garlic, 1 teaspoon of the salt, and basil, if using; massage into the leaves, then taste. You should be able to taste the salt without it being overwhelming. Add more salt if necessary. The radicchio will soon look wet and limp, and liquid will begin to pool.

3. Transfer the radicchio to a 1-quart jar or crock, pressing down with your fist or a tamper as you work. You should see some brine on top of the radicchio when you press. When you pack the vessel, leave 4 inches of headspace for a crock, or 2 to 3 inches for a jar. Top the radicchio with the reserved outer leaf. For a crock, top the leaves with a plate that fits the opening of the container and covers as much of the vegetables as possible; then weight down with a sealed water-filled jar. For a jar, use a sealed water-filled jar or ziplock bag as a follower-weight combination.

4. Set aside on a baking sheet to ferment, somewhere nearby, out of direct sunlight, and cool, for 5 to 10 days. Check daily to make sure the radicchio is submerged, pressing down as needed to bring the brine back to the surface. You may see scum on top; it's generally harmless, but consult the appendix if you're at all concerned.

5. You can start to test the kraut on day 5. You'll know it's ready when the vibrant color is muted, the bitterness has softened, and the pickle-y sour taste has developed.

6. Store in jars, with lids tightened, in the fridge. This kraut will keep, refrigerated, for 6 months.

RADISHES

There are some oligarchs that make me want to bite them just as one crunches into a carrot or a radish.

— EVA PERÓN

Most people think of kimchi as synonymous with fermented napa cabbage. In Korea, the radish is an equally important ingredient in kimchi. Radishes come in many varieties, and each has its place in the different styles of kimchi. In fact, it may be the fermented radish that gives kimchi its, um, distinctive fragrance. We used to think that the odor some people find difficult came from the ginger and garlic, but radishes can pack a scented punch. Don't let that scare you away.

Fermented radishes lose their tangy bite, so if you're wary of their spiciness, this process may help you grow to love these pretty red globes.

Radishes aren't just for kimchi. In ancient times, they were a conventional crop in Greece and the Roman Empire. Nowadays, in Bavaria, the radish is one of the symbols of the city of Munich, where salted radishes are consumed with pretzels and beer. Throughout Europe, grain-based meals often include them. In Japan, a drink is made from carrots and daikon radishes that's useful to cleanse the body. Practitioners of traditional Chinese medicine advise people to eat radishes in the spring to rid the body of winter stagnation. They contain the enzyme diastase, which helps the body digest starches. They also help clear phlegm from the body and are chock-full of vitamins. That's a lot of good from so small a veg.

YOUR RAW MATERIAL

The many varieties of radish offer an abundance of potential for the artist of the crock. They come in many sizes, shapes, and colors. Leave 'em whole, grate 'em, slice 'em, dice 'em. Small varieties such as the common Cherry Belle, Champion, Plum Purple, and French Breakfast are some of the first vegetables to appear in temperate-climate gardens and fields, and in the market. They make beautiful spring pickles.

At market you may see them bundled as Easter egg radishes. Select the ones that are bright and firm; soft or woody radishes are old and don't ferment well. The leaves give a hint about freshness: young, they'll have a little fuzz on them. When you get them home, remove the leaves and the radishes will last longer.

The larger varieties appear later in the season. Common to our North American markets are the Black Spanish, daikon radish, and the colorful Watermelon. Without cutting into one, it's difficult to determine if the root is woody. Again, look for firm, unblemished flesh. At home, toss onto the compost heap any with a hole in the interior, which indicates age.

IN THE CROCK

For radish kraut, grate them, salt lightly, and ferment. There will be a sulfurous odor that might dishearten the fermentista (or the fermentista's family). Don't worry; the odor will eventually become innocuous and the kraut will be mild flavored. If someone in your household has a sensitive snout, she'll thank you if you ferment this in the closet.

Sliced Radish Ferment

yield: about 2 quarts
(fermentation vessels: 2 quarts or larger)
technique used: Mastering Sauerkraut (page 53)

This recipe will work with any radish you choose. The result is especially dramatic with red or Watermelon radishes. Daikon radishes also render a lovely ferment, in both taste and texture.

- **3 pounds radishes, thinly sliced**
- **1 tablespoon unrefined sea salt**

1. Combine the radishes and half the salt in a large bowl and massage the mixture well with your hands, then taste. You should be able to taste the salt without it being overwhelming. Add more salt if necessary. The radishes will soon look wet and limp, and liquid will begin to pool.

2. Transfer the radishes, a few handfuls at a time, to a 2-quart jar or a crock, pressing down with your fist or a tamper as you work. You should see some brine on top as you press. When you pack the vessel, leave 4 inches of headspace for a crock, or 2 to 3 inches for a jar. Top with a primary follower. Then, for a crock, top the follower with a plate that fits the opening of the container and covers as much of the vegetables as possible; then weight down with a sealed water-filled jar. For a jar, use a sealed water-filled jar or ziplock bag as a follower-weight combination.

3. Set aside on a baking sheet to ferment, somewhere nearby, out of direct sunlight, and cool, for 5 to 14 days. Check daily to make sure the radishes are submerged, pressing down as needed to bring the brine back to the surface. You may see scum on top; it's generally harmless, but consult the appendix if you're at all concerned.

4. You can start to test for flavor on day 5. You'll know it's ready when the radishes have a nice crispy crunch with pleasingly sour notes.

5. Store in jars, with lids tightened, in the fridge, leaving as little headroom as possible, and tamp down under the brine. This ferment will keep, refrigerated, for 6 months.

IN THE PICKLE JAR
Spring Radish Pickles

yield: 1 quart
(fermentation vessel: 1 quart)
technique used: Mastering Brine Pickling (page 77)

The chiles provide additional color and spice. They're optional, but they do give the pickles some nice punch.

- **1–2 bunches salad radishes, ends trimmed**
- **5 scallions, whites only, halved lengthwise**
- **3 slices fresh ginger**
- **2–3 small dried red chiles or 1–2 tablespoons chile pepper flakes (optional)**

BRINE
- **1 tablespoon unrefined sea salt**
- **1 teaspoon sugar**
- **1 quart unchlorinated water**

1. Rinse the radishes and scallions in cold water. Pack the radishes with the scallions, ginger, and chiles, if using, into a jar, wedging the vegetables under the shoulder of the jar to prevent the radishes from floating above the brine.

2. Dissolve the salt and sugar in the water to make the brine. Pour in enough brine to cover the vegetables completely. Store any leftover brine in the fridge (it will keep for a week; discard thereafter and make a new batch, if needed). Loosely cover the jar with the lid.

3. Set aside on a baking sheet to ferment, somewhere nearby, out of direct sunlight, and cool, for 7 to 10 days. During the fermentation period, monitor brine level and top off with the reserved brine solution, if needed, to cover. You may see foam on top; it is harmless, but if you see mold, scoop it out.

4. As the vegetables ferment, they begin to lose their vibrant color and the brine will get cloudy; this is when you can start to test your pickles. They're ready when the brine is somewhat cloudy and bright pink from the radish skins and the radishes are sour like a pickle.

5. When the pickles are ready, screw on the lid and store in the fridge. After about 1 day check to be sure the pickles are still submerged, topping off with the reserved brine, if necessary. These pickles will keep, refrigerated, for 6 months.

Create Your Own Recipes

» Combine radishes with a choice of herbs and spices: ground coriander, shredded fresh garlic, shredded fresh ginger, pepper flakes or whole dried Thai chiles, or lemon slices or zest.

» Pickle daikon spears in brine to use in sushi rolls.

» Add red shiso leaves to the pickles for color (pink!) and a different flavor.

RAPINI (BROCCOLI RABE)

Treat rapini in the crock as you would its cousin mustard (they're members of the venerable crucifer clan). Despite the "broccoli" in the common name (the Andy Boy company dubbed it that in 1964 and actually owns the name), it behaves well in the crock. *Rapini* is Italian for "little turnip" and reflects that it's a descendant of the wild turnip.

THE RAW MATERIAL

Rapini is a cool-weather crop, and it's much sweeter after a hard frost. Look for deep green leaves and stems; yellow leaves and blemishes are signs of age. Raw rapini has a short shelf life, so ferment it as soon as possible; the vegetable's bitter quality intensifies with age.

Rapini Kimchi

yield: about 1 pint
(fermentation vessel: 1 quart or larger)
technique used: Mastering Kimchi Basics (page 87)

This green, though somewhat bitter when cooked, isn't dominant when fermented. But this is a strong-flavored kimchi, so serve it as a condiment. It pairs nicely with white foods such as cream cheese, chicken, fish, or white beans.

> 1 quart Kimchi Brine (¼ cup unrefined sea salt to 1 quart unchlorinated water)
> 1–2 bunches rapini, cut into 1-inch pieces
> ½ cup grated or shredded radish
> 4 scallions, chopped
> 2 cloves garlic, minced
> 1½ teaspoons lemon juice
> ¼ teaspoon chile pepper flakes or salt-free *gochugaru*
> 1 teaspoon anchovy paste (optional)

1. In a crock or a large bowl, combine the brine ingredients and stir to dissolve the salt. Rinse the rapini in cold water, and then submerge the vegetable pieces (buds and all) in the brine for 1 hour. Drain and gently squeeze out excess liquid.

2. Put the rapini in a bowl and mix in the radish, scallions, garlic, lemon juice, chile pepper flakes, and anchovy paste, if using. Taste for salt content; you should be able to taste the salt without it being overwhelming. The brining process and the anchovy paste are generally enough, but if you can't taste the salt, sprinkle in a little bit more.

3. Transfer the vegetables into a quart jar, pressing with your hands as you work. Add any liquid left in the bowl and leave about 4 inches of headspace. Place a sealed water-filled ziplock bag over the vegetable for the follower-weight combination.

4. Set aside on a baking sheet to ferment, somewhere nearby, out of direct sunlight, and cool, for 3 to 5 days. Check daily to make sure the vegetables are submerged, pressing down as needed to bring the brine to the surface. You may see scum on top; it's generally harmless, but consult the appendix if you're at all concerned.

5. You can start to test the kimchi on day 3. It's ready when the flavors have combined to make a pungent, slightly sour, slightly bitter condiment.

6. When the kimchi is ready, transfer it into small jars for storage, making sure the veggies are submerged. Screw on the jar lids and store in the fridge. This kimchi will keep, refrigerated, for up to 3 months.

RHUBARB

While I still live, and before I die,
I want another piece of that rhubarb pie.
Now I've had pie of about every kind,
gooseberry, raspberry, and even lemon rind.
I've been privileged to sample pie over the years,
but gooseberry is sour and brings me to tears.
Now, some people's favorite two pies are hot
    and cold.
But mine is rhubarb, even if it's two weeks old.

— DAVID HOVIOUS, *ALL MY LIFE IS POETRY*, 2008

Rhubarb is complicated. The leaf will kill you, the root is a powerful medicinal, and the stalk lies in the realm of the culinary. Most people don't know it can be eaten raw. The flavor of pickled rhubarb is unexpected, with a less sour bite than cooked rhubarb.

YOUR RAW MATERIAL

Most people think of rhubarb as an unusual member of the fruit family, because we know it as an ingredient in strawberry-rhubarb pie. It is often referred to as "pie plant." It is, however, a vegetable.

Rhubarb is a cool-season perennial that sends up shoots in the spring; as summer temperatures climb, this plant slows its growth, sometimes to the point of dormancy. Look for long, fleshy, firm stalks in the spring and early summer.

Rhubarb Relish

yield: about 1 pint
(fermentation vessel: 1 quart)
technique used: Relishes, Chutneys, Salsas, and Fermented Salads (page 66)

When we decided to try fermenting rhubarb, the first thought was of sweetener. Adding honey or sugar would encourage alcohol development, so we added dried fruit and then a touch of honey at the end of the ferment. It turns out the honey isn't necessary at all. After playing around with chutney flavors — onions, curry, and the like — the rosemary shone above the rest.

5–6 rhubarb stalks
  1 heaping tablespoon minced fresh rosemary
1–1¼ teaspoons unrefined sea salt
  ½ cup dried cranberries
  ½ cup dried golden berries (a.k.a. Cape
      gooseberries; see sidebar, page 224)

1. Rinse the rhubarb in cold water. Cut thick rhubarb stems lengthwise once or twice (twice if they're very thick), then slice the sections crosswise. You want 2 cups of thin slices. Put the pieces in a bowl and stir in the rosemary. Sprinkle in 1 teaspoon of the salt, then vigorously massage it into the rhubarb to release the water. It will still be too dry; let the bowl sit, covered, for 10 minutes, then massage again. Mix in the cranberries and golden berries. Taste for salt and sprinkle in more if needed to achieve a slightly salty flavor that is not overwhelming.

2. Transfer the rhubarb mixture into a quart jar, pressing down with your fist or a tamper as you go to to remove air pockets. More brine will release at this stage, and you should see brine above the mixture. Top the ferment with a quart-sized ziplock bag. Press the plastic down onto the top of the ferment, and then fill it with water and seal; this will act as both follower and weight.

3. Set aside on a baking sheet to ferment, somewhere nearby, out of direct sunlight, and cool, for 5 to 7 days. Check daily to make sure the mixture is submerged, pressing down as needed to bring the brine to the surface. You may see scum on top; it's generally harmless, but consult the appendix if you're at all concerned.

4. You can start to test the ferment on day 5. You'll be surprised to find the puckering sourness of the rhubarb has mellowed; it will be pleasantly acidic, as though a splash of lemon juice were added.

5. Spoon the ferment into a smaller jar and tamp down to make sure the rhubarb is submerged in its brine; screw on the lid, then store in the fridge. This will keep, refrigerated, for 2 months.

Fermented Rhubarb Infused with Ginger and Cardamom

yield: about 1 pint
(fermentation vessel: 1 quart)

  1 **pound rhubarb stalks, sliced**
  1 **tablespoon grated fresh ginger**
  ½ **teaspoon ground cardamom**
  1 **scant teaspoon unrefined sea salt**

Follow the same procedure as Rhubarb Relish (page 223), adding the ginger and cardamom to the rhubarb with the salt.

Golden Berries

Golden berries, also called Incan berries, Cape gooseberries, and Peruvian ground cherries, are becoming widely available as they enjoy the status of "superfood," meaning they are nutritionally loaded with vitamins and antioxidants. They are from the mountains of Peru, where the Incan Empire traditionally cultivated them. They grow in a pod and are closely related to the tomatillo. They are available in health food stores and online. They are a delightful addition to ferments, adding a bit of sweetness and citrus. Use in relishes and chutneys.

RUTABAGA

Kirsten Writes

Despite its nutritional punch, I only remember rutabaga landing in my grocery cart a handful of times. When our third son, Dmitri, was three, he said he really wanted "wootabaga." I didn't know where it came from, but I thought, cool. I handed him a sizable specimen with a deep purple blush on the top. He held it all the way home. We cooked it. He didn't say much. Next time we were in the store, he said he did not want a "wootabaga." It was not the beginning of a trend.

Somehow or other, a wild cabbage and a turnip got together and produced the rutabaga. Perhaps the marriage took place in Sweden, whence the name comes. There are references to it in Europe during the Middle Ages, though as animal fodder as well as people food, which is a hint to its association with poverty. Though seemingly similar, rutabagas are not turnips. Turnips have a light radish flavor, whereas when eaten raw, the rutabaga has a crisp, sweet flavor. Once fermented, rutabaga tastes similar to its brassica cousins, yet stands out with a touch more sweetness and a nice pale orange-yellow hue. Rutabagas also have a little less water content and so produce less brine.

YOUR RAW MATERIAL

Rutabagas should be heavy, but not overly large, as these can be overgrown and woody or pithy inside. You want them firm and blemish-free — no large cracks or deep pits. Sometimes rutabagas come waxed, to keep them fresher longer; do a thorough job of peeling those.

IN THE CROCK
Rutabaga Kraut

See photo on page 172

yield: about 2 quarts
(fermentation vessel: 2 quarts or larger)
technique used: Mastering Sauerkraut (page 53)

Why not rutabaga kraut? After all, rutabagas are in the crucifer family, another cabbage cousin. Keep it plain, or dress it up with any of the herbs or spices that complement this root, such as rosemary or dried orange zest. Serve it any time you would serve sauerkraut.

3½ pounds rutabaga
1–1½ tablespoons unrefined sea salt

1. A substantial rutabaga requires a sharp, sturdy knife. Peel first with a vegetable peeler and then trim off the ends and cut into manageable wedges that you will grate on a grater or in a food processor. Transfer to a large bowl.

2. Add 1 tablespoon of the salt and, with your hands, massage it into the rutabaga, then taste. You should be able to taste the salt without it being overwhelming. Add more salt if necessary. The rutabaga will soon look wet and limp, and liquid will begin to pool. If you've put in a good effort and don't see much brine in the bowl, let it stand, covered, for 45 minutes, then massage again.

3. Transfer a few handfuls at a time to a 2-quart jar or 1-gallon crock, pressing down with your fist or a tamper to remove air pockets. You should see some brine on top of kraut when you press. When you pack the vessel, leave 4 inches of headspace for a crock, or 2 to 3 inches for a jar. Top with a piece of plastic wrap or other primary follower. For a crock, top the plastic wrap with a plate that fits the opening of the container and covers as much of the rutabaga as possible; then weight down with a sealed water-filled jar. For a jar, use a sealed water-filled jar or a ziplock bag as a follower-weight combination.

4. Set aside on a baking sheet to ferment, somewhere nearby, out of direct sunlight, and cool, for 4 to 14 days. Check daily to make sure the rutabaga is submerged, pressing down as needed to bring the brine back to the surface. You may see scum on top; it's generally harmless, but consult the appendix if you're at all concerned.

5. You can start to test the kraut on day 4. You'll know it's ready when the flavor has developed a nice sour quality.

6. Store in jars, with lids tightened, in the fridge. This kraut will keep, refrigerated, for 1 year.

Note: For another rutabaga kraut, see *Sauerrüben III* (page 248).

SCALLIONS (GREEN ONIONS)

My father liked stalks of green onions with sweet, white, bulbous roots. They sat in a plate in water, like celery; before a meal he'd pick and eat them like fruit, especially before meals containing turnip or collard greens. He would say he was laying down a bed of straw before the cows and pigs — the rest of the meal — came home.

— DEXTER SCOTT KING, *GROWING UP KING*, 2003

Scallions, also called green onions, are a staple in many types of kimchi. They're rich in vitamins A and C (in the green tops). Feel free to use scallions in just about any kimchi or kraut recipe. Slice them into 1- to 2-inch pieces. *Note:* The green part does get soft. If that's unappealing, slice them paper thin. That way you'll get the taste and the health benefits, without the larger limp pieces. Use the white bulbs in brine pickle medleys.

YOUR RAW MATERIAL
Supermarkets usually carry two types of scallion: one is the immature root bulb of an onion; the other is the Welsh onion, which never develops a large bulb. Most consumers will never know the difference. That's okay, because for the purposes of fermenting, either works well.

In Korea, the wakegi onion is the scallion of choice. It stays firmer through the pickling process, so if you're a serious kimchi maker and a gardener, try growing this variety.

Vietnamese-Style Pickled Scallions

See photo on page 231

yield: 1 pint to 1 quart, depending on the size of the onions
(fermentation vessel: 1 quart)
technique used: Mastering Brine Pickling (page 77)

Feasting is a significant part of the celebration of Tet, the Vietnamese New Year. Even if a family is poor and hungry all year long, everyone gets full during Tet. The rich, meat-centric meals often cause people to feel ill, however, and this is why *hanh muoi*, the dish this ferment is based on, is an indispensable part of the menu. The onions create balance and aid in digestion.

This pickle employs a double ferment, which means you'll be adding ingredients partway through the curing period.

- 1 pound scallions (or substitute shallots)
- 1 quart Basic Brine (2 tablespoons unrefined sea salt to 1 quart unchlorinated water)

ON DAY 3 OF FERMENTATION
- 1–2 tablespoons unrefined sugar or honey
- 2 tablespoons rice vinegar

1. Rinse the scallions in cold water and peel off any dry skin. Cut off the green tops; save them for another use. Pack into a 1-quart jar, wedging the onions under the shoulder of the jar. Pour in enough brine to cover the scallions completely. Store any leftover brine in the fridge (it will keep for a week; discard thereafter and make a new batch, if needed). Top the ferment with a quart-sized ziplock bag. Press the plastic down onto the top of the scallions and then fill with water and seal; this will act as both follower and weight.

2. Set aside on a baking sheet to ferment, somewhere nearby, out of direct sunlight, and cool, for 2 days. On day 3, add the sugar and vinegar, and ferment for 2 days longer. During the fermentation period, monitor the brine level and top off with the reserved brine solution, if needed, to cover. You may see scum on top; it's generally harmless, but consult the appendix if you're at all concerned.

3. As the vegetables ferment, they begin to lose their vibrant color and the brine will get cloudy; this is when you can start to test your pickles. You'll know they're ready when they have a vinegary, sour flavor.

4. Store in the fridge in the same jar with the lid tight. These pickles will keep, refrigerated, for 4 months.

SHISO

Shiso, or perilla (*Perilla frutescens*), is in the mint family, a close relative of basil. Its culinary history in Japan, Korea, China, southern Asia, Vietnam, and Laos indicates that it's as important in that part of the world as basil is in the Mediterranean basin. In addition to its culinary uses, it's medicinal.

If you've seen this leaf before, it was likely in umeboshi plums (pickled), to which it contributes the brick-red color and its own aroma. The leaves are added to *ume* vinegar, which is the salted brine from the plums, at the last step of the process, during which the dry, wrinkled plum transforms into a complex condiment.

Shiso is rich in vitamins and minerals. It's considered a warming herb and has anti-inflammatory properties. It also stimulates the immune system, aids digestion, and perhaps helps kill unwanted bacteria in other foods. For example, in Japan it helps in the preservation of raw fish (sashimi).

Kirsten Writes

Traditionally whole shiso leaves were preserved in salt. They have many uses, including as a substitute for the nori in a sushi hand roll. The concentration of essential oils makes for a strong taste described as anything from fennel to mint to cinnamon. I can't say that any of those fit my reaction to the flavor, but I suppose our individual chemistry may react differently. I can say that I do not care for it fresh; however, I love the change that comes over it with fermentation. The best description I have is a strong floral perfume briefly fills the mouth before biting into the leaf. I recommend experimenting with this herb.

YOUR RAW MATERIAL

It's a challenge to find fresh leaves at the supermarket. Try the farmers' market or grow them yourself (look in specialty seed catalogs) in the garden or in pots on a windowsill. Nip off the flower buds as soon as they appear; this promotes bushy growth, and therefore more leaves. Plants come with red leaves or green, with a dry, paper-like quality. Both ferment well.

IN THE CROCK

Fermented Shiso Leaves

See photo on page 123

yield: less than 1 pint
(fermentation vessel: 1 pint)
technique used: Whole-Leaf Ferments (page 72)

Fermentation does alter the flavor of this herb and not in a bad way. The process brings out a salty sweetness with floral notes. These leaves are wonderful little condiments to put on a cheese plate, in a sandwich, or, more traditionally, with sushi rolls (page 314). If you can find them, the leaves come in bundles. Pick up at least three bunches.

3 (4-ounce) bunches shiso leaves
¼ teaspoon unrefined sea salt

1. Rinse the shiso well, then pick the leaves from the stems. The tender whorls on top are good whole. Put into a bowl and sprinkle with the salt. The leaves will immediately start to sweat. Using your hands, gently toss and massage the salt into the leaves. Don't expect a lot of brine; this is almost a dry ferment. It should taste salty but still pleasing; if not, then you may need to add a bit more salt.

2. Press the leaves into a pint jar. Top the ferment with a quart-sized ziplock bag. Press the plastic down onto the top of the ferment, then fill it with water and seal.

3. Set aside on a baking sheet to ferment, somewhere nearby, out of direct sunlight, and cool, for 10 to 20 days. Check daily to make sure the leaves are submerged. You may see scum on top; it's generally harmless, but consult the appendix if you're at all concerned. The leaves will become a deep green wilted color.

4. You can start to test the ferment on day 10. When you taste-test it, the sour is not as obvious as the salt. Ferment further if more acidity is desired.

5. For storage, press a small round of plastic or wax paper directly on the surface of the ferment. Screw on the lid and store in the fridge, checking periodically that the ferment is submerged. This ferment will keep, refrigerated, for 18 months.

Shiso Kraut

See photo on page 256

yield: about 2 quarts

(fermentation vessel: 2 quarts or larger)

technique used: Mastering Sauerkraut (page 53)

Both shiso and sauerkraut are digestive stimulants, so this kraut does double duty. That shouldn't be your only motivation, though; this kraut has a wonderful subtly floral flavor. The leaves turn a dark and nondescript color, but beautiful pink halos the leaves in the kraut. It is the same hue of pink that normally would be a bad color for the kraut, but in this case it's not. Don't be alarmed — enjoy.

Add 1 bunch (4 ounces) shiso leaves to a batch of Naked Kraut (page 132), adding them to the cabbage when salting. *Note:* Because it's such a small quantity of leaves, the salt amount likely won't change, but taste it anyway before packing, in case you need a sprinkle more to achieve the proper saltiness.

Shiso Gomashio

yield: ¾ cup

Gomashio is a Japanese seasoning powder made of sesame seeds and salt. If you're looking for a flavor substitute in the saltshaker, give this a try. High in protein and calcium, sesame seeds combined with the digestive aid of the shiso leaf to make this a healthy sprinkle that tastes great. The concentrated salty, floral flavor of the shiso blends wonderfully with the roasted sesame seeds. Sprinkle on greens, broccoli, hash browns, or anything that you would dress up with salt. *Note:* You'll need a dehydrator for this recipe.

¼ **cup Fermented Shiso Leaves (page 228)**
½ **cup sesame seeds**

1. Spread fermented shiso leaves across the trays in a dehydrator. Dehydrate overnight at 100°F.

2. In the morning place the sesame seeds in a dry cast-iron skillet over medium heat. Roast for about 10 minutes, stirring constantly with a wooden spoon, until the seeds turn golden brown.

3. Place the sesame seeds and dried leaves in a mortar and pestle and grind together. The mixture will keep for several months on the shelf and up to a year in the fridge.

IN THE PICKLE JAR

Shiso leaves, or a stalk of the plant, can be added when packing whole vegetables in pickle brine.

ASPARAGUS PICKLES,
page 111

LEEK–CRACKED PEPPER
KRAUT, *page 192*

TURMERIC PASTE,
page 244

SAUERRÜBEN II (sliced
with black pepper),
page 247

ONION AND PEPPER RELISH,
page 203

CURTIDO, *page 133*

VIETNAMESE-STYLE
PICKLED SCALLIONS,
page 227

KIMCHI, *page 141*

SEAWEED PRIMER

Sea vegetables, a.k.a. seaweed, are loaded with bio-available minerals and sodium. Adding seaweed to fermented vegetables is a good way to maximize the benefits of this vegetable.

» If you're unfamiliar with seaweed, start small. Add just a tablespoon of chopped seaweed or a teaspoon of dulse to a quart-sized ferment. This will give you the opportunity to see if you like the flavor and texture in the crock.

» Rather than chop or cut seaweed with a knife, snip with scissors.

» Lacking roots, seaweed absorbs its nutrients from sea water; this means it picks up all that blows or washes out from land. So make sure your seaweed comes from a clean source — ask the vendor or distributor if you're unsure.

» Some people with hypothyroid conditions who should avoid the cabbage family can offset its effects by adding sea vegetables to crucifer-based ferments (see Natural Iodine, page 135).

DULSE (*Palmaria palmata*) comes from the culinary heritage of northern Europe. It's readily available as a coarse powder and is a favorite to sprinkle into a crock of kraut or kimchi. Dulse is a good gateway seaweed as it adds pretty purple-red flecks to the ferment and the mild flavor may go unnoticed. See the Sea-Chi recipe, page 142.

HIJIKI (*Sargassum fusiforme*) is a coarse-textured seaweed with a strong ocean flavor, but it presents the opportunity to work with another color in the fermentista's palette. It's a glistening black and provides quite an aesthetic contrast to a kraut or a kimchi.

ARAME (*Eisenia bicyclis*) is one of the most popular seaweeds in Japanese cuisine. It's a different variety than hijiki but interacts with a ferment very similarly and with a milder flavor.

KOMBU (*Saccharina japonica*) is nice to add to any vegetable pickle brine, like you would a sprig of dill, but kombu contributes its own salt as well as nutrients and iodine. (You may want to cut the added salt in your brine solution by ¼ teaspoon for every few ribbons of dried kombu.) This seaweed will double in size when rehydrated and will change the aroma of your ferment. The enhanced flavor will be that of the ocean's briny essence. Add strips of kombu to any vegetable pickle combination. It's especially good with added garlic, ginger, and chile pepper flakes.

NORI (*Porphyra* spp.) is high in protein and vitamin B_{12}. You may know it in the sheet form for sushi rolls, but in its whole dried state, it's a translucent greenish-purple. Slice it into a kraut or kimchi for some subtle beauty. It is a mild-flavored seaweed and will not add an overwhelming flavor. This seaweed is commonly available in most grocery stores.

SEA PALM (*Postelsia palmaeformis*), also called American arame, has a mild flavor and when rehydrated in kimchi or other ferment retains a nice crunch. It is one of our favorite fermentation friends. See the Sea-Chi recipe, page 142.

WAKAME (*Undaria pinnatifida*) is a sweet, mild, and tender seaweed, though there's a lot of variation in what you can buy. It's one of the most popular of all the sea vegetables. Its texture is slippery, so cut it into small pieces for a kraut or kimchi. It's not suitable for brine pickling. For a different flavor, carefully toast wakame in a dry skillet and then crumble into a powder to add to a ferment.

SPINACH

We'll be honest. The only reason we tried fermenting spinach was for this book. Cooked spinach has texture issues for some people, and we imagined fermented spinach as a dark green slimy goo — like overcooked spinach might be.

The day had come. We looked at the beautiful fresh spinach and thought, how can we be doing this? At this moment we did not trust the process at all. Kirsten forged ahead and thought about all the ways cooked spinach is tasty. Quiche Lorraine and spanakópita came to mind. Since she didn't think that fermenting spinach with bacon would work, she went with the spanakópita flavor: oregano, lemon, and sweet onions. This was part of the backup plan as well: if the ferment texture wasn't appetizing, then we could cook it between layers of buttered phyllo with a lot of feta. Turned out not to be a problem; the spinach was delicious fermented. The texture was not at all what we expected. It had some crunch, similar to a wilted spinach salad.

Since we had spent so much time imagining the melted feta and flaky pastry, we made our spanakópita anyway and the recipe (Kraut-a-kópita) is on page 332.

FERMENTISTA'S TIP

Fermentation and Oxalic Acid

Many dark leafy greens, among them red orach, chard, and parsley, contain oxalic acid, which is the sour taste in wood sorrel and rhubarb and the woolly feeling on your teeth after you eat spinach. The good news is that fermentation breaks down this compound.

Lemon Spinach

yield: about 1 quart
(fermentation vessel: 1 quart or larger)
technique used: Mastering Sauerkraut (page 53)

With cabbage and most other ferments, you manhandle the veggies to release brine. Not so with spinach. Here, use your lightest touch — you want the leaves bruise-free.

1	large sweet onion, quartered and then thinly sliced
1½–2	teaspoons unrefined sea salt
2	pounds spinach leaves, chopped
1	generous tablespoon dried oregano, crumbled
2	tablespoons lemon juice

1. Place the onions in a bowl. Add about 1½ teaspoons of the salt and, with your hands, massage it into the onions. This gives the onions a chance to begin to brine so that when you work with the spinach, you can be as gentle as possible.

2. Add the spinach, oregano, and lemon juice, gently working everything together, then taste. You should be able to taste the salt without it being overwhelming. Add more salt if necessary. At first the spinach may not appear to have enough brine, but when you start pressing it into a crock, you'll see plenty.

3. Transfer the spinach mixture a few handfuls at a time into a jar, pressing down with your fist or a tamper as you work. You should see some brine on top of the spinach when you press. When you pack a 1-quart jar, you will have plenty of headspace. Top with a primary follower such as a bit of plastic wrap, then weight down with a sealed water-filled jar or a ziplock bag.

4. Set aside on a baking sheet to ferment, somewhere nearby, out of direct sunlight, and cool, for 4 to 10 days. Check daily to make sure the vegetables are submerged, pressing down as needed to bring the brine to the surface. You may see scum on top; it's generally harmless, but consult the appendix if you're at all concerned.

5. You can start to test the kraut on day 4. You'll know it is ready when the dark spinach color is a lighter dull green. It will have a surprising light crunch and a slightly sour flavor.

6. Store in jars, with lids tightened, in the fridge, leaving as little headroom as possible, and tamp down under the brine. This ferment will keep, refrigerated, for 6 months.

WE ARE FAMILY: ORACH

Orach, also called mountain spinach and purple passion spinach, belongs to the goosefoot family, whose members include common beets, chard, and, yes, spinach. It's a common green in Europe, where it's been in cultivation for thousands of years — longer than spinach — in the Mediterranean countries. In Italy, cooks use it to color pastas.

Use orach as you would spinach. Red orach is a vibrant fuchsia that makes it stand out in the produce section of the supermarket, at the farmers' market, and, most important, on your plate.

Ferment orach on its own like spinach, or add a bundle of chopped red orach to Naked Kraut (page 132). It'll turn the batch a beautiful, soft pink.

Cultured Pickle Shop

Alex Hozven is one of the "elders" in the renaissance of fermented veggies, but not because of age; in the late 1990s, she was one of the first to push the culinary potential of vegetables by creating new flavors with this very old tradition. And she is a master.

Her creativity, her palate, and her passion for the art are evident. Alex and her husband Kevin Farley own Cultured Pickle Shop in Berkeley, California, and produce a line of ten krauts available in Bay Area stores. The regular income fuels their true passion — the creativity that comes from working with the local farmers to generate imaginative seasonal products based on the variability of that year's harvest.

Their desire to both break the boundaries of what Americans define as a pickle and operate within the local foodshed comes together poetically in their line of tsukemono pickles (see page 144). *Tsukemono* is the Japanese word for "pickled things." Alex and Kevin ferment a few varieties of traditional Japanese pickles including kasu-zuke, in which fresh vegetable are pressed in salt for two days and then buried in a paste made from the "microbially charged" lees or dregs of the sake-making process (basically the leftover rice mash). Luckily, a sake producer is only a few blocks away. After anywhere from three months to a year, the pickles emerge; they are drier, since they are not cured in a brine, and have a unique multifaceted flavor with hints of sake.

Cultured Pickle Shop feels like a huge family kitchen rather than a production facility. Many vessels contain vegetables, herbs, or flowers brewing

Alex Hozven and Kevin Farley

and bubbling. We asked Alex how she views the changes that have taken place around the art of fermentation.

"In the 15 years we have been fermenting vegetables professionally we have seen a tremendous increase in interest in these products," she said. *Products* is perhaps not even the most accurate term, as every jar that comes out of our shop is more process than product. By that I mean that it is still in process. We have bottled or jarred it at a particular point in time, but every jar is its own ever-evolving ecosystem, an amazing and diverse world that we have the honor to work with, and only a narrow human lens to seek to understand.

"Even with the increased interest, I think because our culture has become accustomed to a stagnant, uniform, industrial means of food preservation, there is often misunderstanding of how living foods operate — ever growing, ever breathing. That said, we continue, because enough people in our fabulous northern California bioregion love what we do."

SUNCHOKES

These edible tubers are also known as Jerusalem artichokes, earth apples, *topinambur*, or sun roots. A perennial member of the sunflower clan, indigenous to the eastern United States, sunchokes can be found in the wild, in the supermarket, and in many gardens. They are in a group of vegetables that contain larger amounts of nondigestible carbohydrates called *prebiotics*: when these vegetables are consumed, they promote increased levels and activity of beneficial gut bacteria. Other vegetables in this group include asparagus, garlic, onions, and jicama.

Sunchokes are deliciously crisp when eaten raw; they have a sweet, nutty flavor that holds up nicely in fermentation. Like many roots they are sweeter in the fall and winter, which is also when they are freshest.

THE RAW MATERIAL

You want the sunchokes to be firm, with smooth brown skin. Well, relatively smooth; there are all the bumps after all. Avoid any with bruises, which will feel like soft spots. Also avoid any with sprouts. Peeling sunchokes is a matter of personal preference. We always peel the skins. If you prefer not to peel, scrub them well, paying attention to any grit that might hide in the folds.

WE ARE FAMILY: SCORZONERA

Scorzonera hispanica, or black salsify, also a member of the sunflower family, has quite a few folk names; two of the more colorful are viper's grass and goatsbeard. Having sons, we saw viper's grass as an opportunity to entice the boys with a fermented creation — how about some Viper Kraut?

These roots are black, sticky, usually dirty, and a bit gnarled, so as a food, at first glance, unappetizing. When you clean and peel this root, your hands will turn sticky and black. The good news — it easily washes off.

Black salsify stays firm when you handle or cook it. Raw, it's crunchy, with a texture almost like coconut. That same crunch and texture make it an excellent candidate for fermentation. You can make a tasty, pure scorzonera ferment, but because of the small size of the roots, it's a lot of work for a small return. Instead, add this root to other ferments as you would burdock (see page 129).

Cultured Pickle Shop's Fennel and Sunchoke Kimchi

yield: about 6 quarts
(fermentation vessel: 2 gallons or larger)
technique used: Mastering Sauerkraut (page 53)

10	pounds sunchokes, washed and peeled
5	pounds fennel bulbs, both bulbs and greens, washed
	Garlic, fresh ginger, and chiles (to taste)
5–7	tablespoons unrefined sea salt

1. Slice the sunchokes and the fennel bulbs quite thinly and then mince the fennel greens. Mince the garlic, ginger, and chiles to taste. (*Note:* Alex is quite generous with the amounts of each. Use your judgment or start with 1 head garlic, 3–4 tablespoons minced ginger, and 2–3 fresh chiles or 1–2 tablespoons chile pepper flakes.)

2. Put all the ingredients in a bowl and mix well. The salt is 3 percent of the weight of the vegetables and should be the perfect amount to maintain a crisp texture. Cover the bowl and let it sit for a few hours, and when you come back to it the vegetables will have released quite a lot of moisture.

3. Pack the mixture into your fermentation vessel, add followers and weights, and monitor over the next 4 weeks or so until it has reached your desired point of sour.

SWEET POTATOES

Every major culture that has survived owes its survival to the sweet potato, including the South after the War Between the States.
— LYNIECE NORTH TALMADGE, *THE SWEET POTATO LOVER'S COOKBOOK*, 2010

Sweet potatoes or yams? Most tubers in the grocery stores in this country are indeed sweet potatoes, even when labeled yams. True yams (in the family Dioscoreaceae) are grown in Africa and in the Caribbean, and very few ever end up in our grocery stores — especially not in rural southern Oregon. If you happen to find true yams, you will know it: they are larger than sweet potatoes, they have rounded ends, their skin is tough — almost bark-like — and the flesh is sticky.

So why all the confusion? It is believed that when orange-fleshed, softer-textured sweet potatoes (in the family Convolvulaceae) were introduced in the southern United States, growers wanted to differentiate them from the more traditional white-fleshed types. The African word *nyami* was used by the slaves to describe the Southern sweet potato, as it reminded them of the starchy, edible root from the lily family of plants that they knew from their homeland. The name *nyami* was adopted as *yam* for these softer Southern sweet potatoes, which incidentally are in the morning glory family and most likely native to the Americas.

Sweet potatoes are considered the world's seventh most important food crop. A study was conducted in India to determine whether a lactic-acid sweet potato pickle would be viable for small-scale industries. The study concluded that sweet potatoes could be pickled as such and that the flavor was pleasing. We are going to say the flavor is more than pleasing — it is amazing.

YOUR RAW MATERIAL

Sweet potatoes are available year-round in most stores; however, as with most crops, the harvest is in the fall. This is when you will find the freshest tubers. At any time, you want to purchase tubers that are firm (not soft or wrinkly) and blemish free.

The most common varieties are the more mealy, pale-fleshed potatoes (colors range from creamy beige to yellow or pink), such as Jersey or the Japanese varieties. The types with deep copper-toned and orange flesh are sweeter, moister varieties, such as Beauregard, Jewel, and Garnett. And new to the scene is Stokes Purple, with deep purple-magenta flesh. These potatoes have a rich, dense texture and a sweet flavor that lies somewhere between that of the pale-fleshed varieties and the sweet dark orange.

IN THE CROCK

Use sweet potatoes as you would carrots (page 148). They respond and look quite similar in a ferment.

West African Sweet Potato Ferment

yield: about 3 quarts
(fermentation vessel: 1 gallon)
technique used: Relishes, Chutneys, Salsas, and Fermented Salads (page 66)

In this ferment there is no shredding. Instead we are slicing the sweet potatoes quite fine. This is best done with the slicer side of a grater or the slicing blade in your food processor.

- 5 pounds sweet potatoes (we use the orange-fleshed variety), peeled and thinly sliced
- 1 green bell pepper, diced
- 1 medium onion, diced
- 5 cloves garlic, finely minced
- 3–4 dried tomatoes, thinly sliced
- 1 tablespoon whole coriander seeds

GOOD AND GOOD FOR YOU

The authors of the India study, done in 2006, were interested not only in the nutritional benefits of sweet potato fermentation but also in the "hygienic" potential because it is a safe way to process food. S. H. Panda, M. Parmanick, and R. C. Ray deemed lactic-acid fermentation "an important technology" in developing nations. "Lactic-acid fermentation also has some other distinct advantages, e.g., the food becomes resistant to microbial spoilage and to development of toxins (Kalantzopoulos 1997). Sweet potato, in tropical regions, is consumed in the households of small farmers and poor people. Night blindness is a major physiological disorder among these people due to vitamin A deficiency, which can be alleviated by regular consumption of orange-flesh (ß-carotene-rich) sweet potato either fresh, boiled . . . or as lacto-pickles."

1 tablespoon grated fresh ginger

2 teaspoons ground cayenne

2–3 tablespoons unrefined sea salt

1. Put the sweet potato slices in a large bowl. Add the bell pepper, onion, garlic, dried tomatoes, coriander, ginger, and cayenne, and mix well. Add 2 tablespoons of the salt and, with your hands, massage it into the mixture, then taste. You should be able to taste the salt without it being overwhelming. Add more salt as necessary. The sweet potatoes respond well to salting and will quickly begin to develop a brine. If you've put in a good effort and don't see much brine in the bowl, let it stand, covered, for 45 minutes, then massage again.

2. Transfer the sweet potato mixture a few handfuls at a time to a gallon jar or crock, pressing down with your fist or a tamper as you work. You should see some brine on top when you press. When you pack the vessel, leave 4 inches of headspace for a crock, or 2 to 3 inches for a jar. Top the veggies with a primary follower, such as a bit of plastic wrap. For a crock, top with a plate that fits the opening of the container and covers as much of the vegetables as possible; then weight down with a sealed water-filled jar. For a jar, use a sealed water-filled jar or ziplock bag as a follower-weight combination.

3. Set aside on a baking sheet to ferment, somewhere nearby, out of direct sunlight, and cool, for 7 to 21 days. Check daily to make sure the vegetables are submerged, pressing down as needed to bring the brine back to the surface.

4. You can start to test the ferment on day 7. You'll know it's ready when it's pleasingly sour

and all the flavors have mingled. The bright orange color of the sweet potatoes will remain.

5. Store in jars, with lids tightened, in the fridge, leaving as little headroom as possible, and tamping the ferment down under the brine. This ferment will keep, refrigerated, for 12 months.

TOMATILLOS

Tomatillos are a staple of Mexican cuisine and have been for a long time. They are from Mexico and were cultivated originally by the Aztecs. The conquering Spaniards then introduced them to a broader audience by bringing them back to Spain. While tomatillos look like green tomatoes, they should not be confused with green tomatoes. They are more closely related to ground cherries, which are native to the Americas; a variation is the golden berry, which you can read about on page 224. These fruits all have a papery husk that grows first. The small fruit develops until it fills the space inside the husk.

YOUR RAW MATERIAL

When shopping for tomatillos, you want the husk and the fruit inside to be bright green. This will ensure your tomatillo has a crisp tart flavor. As it continues to ripen, the husk turns yellow to brown and the fruit turns a pale yellow. For fermentation it is best to stick with the brighter green fruit.

While it is always best to use the freshest vegetables, tomatillos will last a week or two in the refrigerator. If you know you will be storing them for a few days, remove the husk first.

Tomatillo skins are often sticky; this coating, soapy with bitter saponins, should be washed off before preparing the fruits.

IN THE CROCK

Tomatillo Salsa

See photo on page 152

yield: about 1 quart
(fermentation vessel: 1 quart or larger)
technique used: Relishes, Chutneys, Salsas, and Fermented Salads (page 66)

"This is hands-down my favorite one of your ferments. If they all tasted like this, I would eat more of them," one of our offspring told us. Is that a compliment?

This recipe is delicious as a quick condiment that you ferment over a few days and eat within a few weeks. It can also be a great summery salsa to eat over the course of a full winter. For a more developed acidic flavor with a wonderful lemon-vinegar quality, allow this salsa to ferment for 3 or more weeks.

- 1 **pound tomatillos**
- 1 **medium onion, diced**
- ½ **bunch cilantro, finely chopped**
- 2 **cloves garlic, minced**
  - **Juice of 1 lime (for extra lime flavor, include the zest)**
  - **Pinch of cracked pepper**
- 1–3 **jalapeños, diced (optional); include seeds for more heat**
- 1 **teaspoon unrefined sea salt**

1. Remove the husks from the tomatillos; rinse the fruits well in cold water. Dice the tomatillos and put them in a bowl. Add the onion, cilantro, garlic, lime juice, pepper, and jalapeños, if using. Sprinkle in the salt, working it in with your hands. Taste and sprinkle in more salt as needed to achieve a salty flavor that is not overwhelming.

2. The brine will release quickly. Press the salsa into a jar. More brine will release at this stage and you should see brine above the veggies. Top the ferment with a quart-sized ziplock bag. Press the plastic down onto the top of the ferment and then fill it with water and seal; this will act as both follower and weight.

3. Set aside on a baking sheet to ferment, somewhere nearby, out of direct sunlight, and cool, for 5 to 21 days. Check regularly to make sure the vegetables stay submerged.

4. You can start to test the ferment on day 5, or for a long ferment wait until day 21. It's ready when the flavors have mingled, becoming almost lemony-acidic. The onions will retain a fresh crispness while the rest of the vegetables will soften.

5. Store in jars, with lids tightened, in the fridge, leaving as little headroom as possible, and tamping the ferment down under the brine. The shorter ferment should be enjoyed within a few weeks; the longer ferment will keep, refrigerated, for 6 months.

TOMATOES

There are only two things that money can't buy, and that's true love and homegrown tomatoes.

— GUY CLARK, "HOMEGROWN TOMATOES"

Is not the homegrown tomato the aspiration of every gardener? From the cheery sweet cherry tomatoes growing in pots at lofty heights on a city balcony to the small patch of fat tomatoes in Grandpa's garden, gardeners measure their summer calendar by when the first red (or almost red) tomato is brought to the table with great pomp.

As the summer progresses, tomatoes are in everything. Turns out, planting 18 heirloom varieties in tomato-starved May was too much. By late September, fresh pico de gallo, Greek salads, and chilled tomato gazpachos have lost their charm. Sauces, juices, and ketchup have been canned by the quart, and the lovely red orbs still hang on the vine. The gardener secretly thinks about how nice a surprise killing frost would be.

What else can be done? Despite our efforts, not too much in the fermenting world, and why? Sugar — that sweetness we love — wants to become alcohol. Tomato wine might be a better option.

In our test kitchen we have tried many different ways to make a fresh salsa, which always ends up tasting like old salsa — like the stuff that you forgot in the back of the refrigerator. You get it out and it tastes a bit fizzy and a bit composted, and you throw it out. Despite the flavor, technically the pH is on target and nothing is "bad." We are aware that many people do make quick ripe-tomato ferments that are meant for immediate consumption.

One compromise to get your tomatoes and probiotics too is to ferment a salsa starter. Find your favorite fresh salsa recipe and ferment all of the ingredients except the tomatoes. Keep this in your refrigerator and add fresh ripe tomatoes when you are ready to serve.

Green tomatoes can be fermented, sliced, and brined. Follow the instructions for New York Deli–Style Pickles (page 168).

There are recipes for making a ketchup by fermenting tomato paste with whey; this works but won't require the quantity you'll need when trying to preserve the harvest.

Cherry Bombs

yield: about 1 gallon
(fermentation vessel: 1 gallon)
technique used: Mastering Brine Pickling (page 77)

Choose tomatoes that are not fully mature, any color from yellowish green to red, but firm. If the green ones are still quite green and firm, leave them on the vine; they will not lose their bitterness as they ferment. Don't use tomatoes more than 2½ inches in diameter; they become little effervescent bombs. There is no doubt that this food is alive.

You can also make a variation using dill, horseradish, and more parsley instead of basil.

4–5 pounds cherry tomatoes
  1 sprig parsley or the leafy tops of celery
5–6 leafy stems of basil
    Pinch of chile pepper flakes
  1 head garlic, cloves separated
  1 teaspoon peppercorns
  1 teaspoon coriander seeds
  1 teaspoon mustard seeds
  1 gallon Cucumber Brine (¾ cup unrefined sea salt to 1 gallon unchlorinated water)
  3 fresh grape or other tannin-rich leaves (optional)

1. Rinse the tomatoes. Arrange them in a 1-gallon jar, or divide among smaller jars, working the parsley, basil, chile pepper flakes, garlic, peppercorns, coriander seeds, and mustard seeds around the tomatoes. This ferment looks stunning, so have fun arranging the ingredients. Be gentle when packing the tomatoes to maximize the space and keep them tucked under the brine. The riper tomatoes may split occasionally; remove these as you go. Pour in enough brine to cover the tomatoes completely. Reserve any leftover brine in the fridge (it will keep for 1 week; discard thereafter and make a new batch, if needed).

2. Place grape leaves, if using, over the tomatoes as a primary follower (the tannins in the leaves keep the pickles crisp). If using other tannin-rich leaves (page 79), add them now. For a crock, top with a plate that will rest atop the pickles, and a weight such as a sealed water-filled jar to keep things in place. If using a jar, top with a light weight, such as an empty jar, to keep everything in place, as the tomatoes won't remain wedged in.

3. Set aside on a baking sheet to ferment, somewhere nearby, out of direct sunlight, and cool, for 6 to 8 days. During the fermentation period, monitor the brine level and top off with the reserved brine solution, if needed, to cover. You may see scum on top; it's generally harmless, but consult the appendix if you're at all concerned.

4. As the tomatoes ferment, they begin to lose their vibrant color and the brine will get cloudy; this is when you can start to test your pickles. They're ready when the brine has soured, like pickle brine, and the tomatoes are pleasingly sour and very soft inside with a champagne-like effervescence.

5. Store in jars, with lids tightened, in the fridge, adding fresh brine as needed to keep the tomatoes covered. Top each jar with a fresh grape leaf, if you have them.

6. Let sit for 1 to 2 weeks; then they're ready to eat. You can keep these tomatoes for about 6 months in the refrigerator. *Note:* These pickles do continue to gain effervescence even under refrigeration. The pressure is not in the jar, like other especially live ferments, but in the tomato.

TURMERIC

Each spice has a special day to it. For turmeric it is Sunday, when light drips fat and butter-colored into the bins to be soaked up glowing, when you pray to the nine planets for love and luck.

— CHITRA BANERJEE DIVKURUNI, *THE MISTRESS OF SPICES*, 1997

Turmeric has a long history with culinary and medicinal purposes in India, Indonesia, and China. Medically it is a food that has received a lot of attention in the Western world in recent years for its anti-inflammatory and cancer-fighting qualities, and many studies are focusing on turmeric's effect on other ailments such as arthritis, Alzheimer's, liver damage, and various digestive issues. The active ingredient, curcumin, is a powerful antioxidant. Interestingly, when turmeric and black pepper are consumed together, the active ingredient in the pepper, piperine, boosts our bodies' ability to take in and use the curcumin.

YOUR RAW MATERIAL

If you want color, this is your ingredient. With varying amounts of fresh or dry turmeric, you will be able to turn your ferments anything from chartreuse yellow to a deep gold. Most people know turmeric as the dried spice that adds the classic gold color to yellow mustard or the ocher of Indian curries.

The recipes here use fresh turmeric root. It is a brown-skinned rhizome with a deep orange flesh akin to ginger in its appearance. The flavor has a warm but almost astringent or bitter flavor. Some people find the flavor musty or earthy. Its aroma is decidedly Eastern and unusual for some palates, but it is worth exploring this flavor in your creations.

Turmeric Paste

See photo on page 230

yield: about ½ pint

(fermentation vessel: ½ pint)

technique used: Pastes and Bases (page 69)

This paste has a very strong presence. A little goes a long way in adding flavor to sauces and steamed or sautéed vegetables. Make this paste when fresh turmeric is available. Because this is a seasoning that won't be eaten straight, you may increase the salt content by about one-third to enhance flavoring qualities, though it's not necessary for the fermentation process.

> ½ **pound fresh turmeric, roughly chopped**
> ½ **teaspoon freshly ground black pepper**
> ¼–½ **teaspoon unrefined sea salt**

1. Put the chopped turmeric in the bowl of a food processor and pulse to a paste consistency. Remove the blade and sprinkle in the pepper and salt. The root will become moist immediately.

2. Press into a half-pint jar. More brine will release at this stage, and you should see a small amount of brine above the paste. Top the ferment with a quart-sized ziplock bag. Press the plastic down onto the top of the ferment, then fill it with water and seal; this will act as both follower and weight.

3. Set aside on a baking sheet to ferment, somewhere nearby, out of direct sunlight, and cool, for 5 to 10 days. Check daily to make sure the turmeric is submerged. You may see scum on top; it's generally harmless, but consult the appendix if you're at all concerned.

4. You can start to test the ferment on day 5. It's ready when the acidity has developed. It will be more salty than sour.

5. When ready to store, tamp down to make sure the paste is submerged in its brine, and place a small bit of plastic wrap or wax paper over the ferment. Screw on the lid, then store in the fridge. This ferment will keep, refrigerated, for 12 months.

Turmeric Pepper Kraut

See photo on page 256

yield: about 1 quart

(fermentation vessel: 2 quarts or larger)

technique used: Mastering Sauerkraut (page 53)

This cheery yellow kraut looks like sunshine in a jar and has a bright flavor to match. If you're looking for a little warmth on a gray morning, try this sunny kraut as a complement to sunny-side-up eggs.

> 1 **small head (1½–2 pounds) cabbage**
> ½ **onion, thinly sliced (optional)**
> 1–1½ **tablespoons unrefined sea salt**
> 1½ **tablespoons finely grated fresh turmeric root**
> 1 **large clove garlic, grated**
> ½ **teaspoon freshly ground black pepper**

1. To prepare the cabbage, remove the coarse outer leaves. Rinse a few unblemished ones and set them aside. Rinse the rest of the cabbage in cold water. With a stainless steel knife, quarter and core the cabbage. Thinly slice with the knife or a mandoline, then transfer the cabbage to a large bowl. Add the onion, if using.

2. Add 1 tablespoon of the salt and, with your hands, massage it into the veggies. Set aside for 15 minutes to allow the cabbage to weep.

3. Mix in the turmeric, garlic, and pepper. Taste. You should be able to taste the salt without it being overwhelming. Add more salt if necessary.

4. Transfer the cabbage mixture a few handfuls at a time to a jar or crock, pressing down with your fist or a tamper as you work. You should see some brine on top of the cabbage when you press. Top the cabbage with one or two of the reserved outer leaves. For a crock, top the leaves with a plate that fits the opening of the container and covers as much of the vegetables as possible; then weight down with a sealed water-filled jar. For a jar, use a sealed water-filled jar or ziplock bag as a follower-weight combination.

5. Set aside on a baking sheet to ferment, somewhere nearby, out of direct sunlight, and cool, for 7 to 21 days. Check daily to make sure the kraut is submerged, pressing down as needed to bring the brine back to the surface. You may see scum on top; it's generally harmless, but consult the appendix if you're at all concerned.

6. You can start to test the kraut on day 7. You'll know it's ready when it's pleasingly sour and the cabbage has a translucent, brilliant yellow quality.

7. Store in jars, with lids tightened, in the fridge. This kraut will keep, refrigerated, for 12 months.

Create Your Own Recipes

This spice is versatile and colorful and can be strong. Shred small amounts of fresh turmeric root into sliced cucumber and onion pickles for that classic electric green color.

TURNIPS

Diocles praises the turnip plant, declaring that it stimulates the amorous propensities. So too does Dionysius, who adds that its effects are even stronger when eaten with rocket.

— PLINY THE ELDER, ANCIENT ROMAN AUTHOR AND NATURALIST

As the manuscript of this book neared completion, we realized we had forgotten to complete the turnip section. As our friend Melissa quipped, "That's how it is with turnips. Everybody forgets turnips." She and her husband grow some of the prettiest turnips in the valley, with names like purple top and white globe turnips, pink and white salad turnips, and golden turnips.

Melissa's observations are not new; they lie deep in Western cultural fabric. Throughout much of European history turnips were poor-people food and animal fodder. While a humble root, turnips are nutritionally power packed. They have high levels of antioxidants, phytonutrients, and glucosinolates (which help the liver process toxins). Among other healthful properties, turnips are anti-inflammatory and support the digestive system and bone health. So remember the turnips!

The tastiest turnips are found in the springtime or during the second crop in the fall, when they are still small and sweet. Select small- to average-sized turnips; the smallest turnips can look like spring radishes. These smallish turnips should feel heavy for their size — this is a sign of freshness because of the high water content (good for producing brine). To that end, avoid lightweight, soft, or shriveled tubers. Young turnips with blemish-free smooth skin do not need to be peeled; older turnips can have tough skin that should be peeled.

IN THE CROCK

Lesser known than sauerkraut are "soured turnips," or *sauerrüben*. We have included three variations on the theme.

Sauerrüben I (Turnip Kraut, Shredded)

yield: about 1 gallon
(fermentation vessel: 2 gallons)
technique used: Mastering Sauerkraut(page 53)

In this kraut the turnips are shredded. This is the most traditional style of *sauerrüben*.

10 pounds turnips
3–4 tablespoons unrefined sea salt

1. To prepare the turnips, rinse in cold water. Evaluate the skins; often young turnips do not need to be peeled, and in the case of the colorful varieties the color lies in the peel. If your turnips' skins are russeted or coarse, go ahead and peel them. Shred the turnips on a grater or mandoline and place in a large bowl.

2. Add 3 tablespoons of the salt and, with your hands, massage it into the turnips, then taste. You should be able to taste the salt without it being overwhelming. Add more salt if necessary. The turnip will soon look wet and limp, and liquid will begin to pool.

3. Transfer a few handfuls at a time to a 2-gallon crock, pressing down with your fist or a tamper as you work. You should see some brine on top of the kraut when you press. When you pack the vessel, leave 4 inches of headspace. Top with a piece of plastic wrap. Top the plastic wrap with a plate that fits the opening of the container and covers as much of the surface as possible; then weight down with a sealed water-filled jar.

4. Set aside on a baking sheet to ferment, somewhere nearby, out of direct sunlight, and cool, for 7 to 21 days. Check daily to make sure the turnips are submerged, pressing down as needed to bring the brine back to the surface. You may see scum on top; it's generally harmless, but consult the appendix if you're at all concerned.

5. You can start to test the kraut on day 7. You'll know it's ready when it's pleasingly sour and the texture is slightly softer than cabbage sauerkraut. If you used red or pink turnips, they will have "bled" into the brine, turning it pink.

6. Ladle the kraut into jars and tamp down. Pour in any brine that's left. Tighten the lids, then store in the fridge. This kraut will keep, refrigerated, for 1 year.

Sauerrüben II (Sliced with Black Pepper)

See photo on page 230

yield: about 1 gallon
(fermentation vessel: 2 gallons)

In this kraut the turnips are sliced. This texture variation makes the *sauerrüben* seem more like a salad than a kraut.

We have added generous amounts of fresh black pepper, which is wonderful if you love black pepper. Feel free to use less and taste as you go.

10 pounds turnips, very thinly sliced
2–3 tablespoons freshly ground black pepper
3–4 tablespoons unrefined sea salt

This is a variation on Sauerrüben I (at left). Use the same method, but slice the turnips instead of grating and add the black pepper with the salt.

PICKLING ROMAN STYLE

In his book *Around the Roman Table: Food and Feasting in Ancient Rome* (1994), Patrick Faas quotes Roman agricultural writer Lucius Junius Moderatus Columella, who lived at the beginning of the last millennium, on the pickling of turnips:

"Take the roundest turnips you can find and scrape them clean if they are dirty. Peel them with a sharp knife. Then, with an iron sickle, make an incision in the shape of an X, as picklers do, but be careful not to cut all the way through. Then sprinkle the incisions with salt, not especially fine. Place the turnips on a basket or in a trough, with a little extra salt, and allow the moisture to dry out for three days. After three days a piece from the inside of one turnip should be tasted, to tell whether the salt has penetrated through. If it has been absorbed, remove the turnips and wash them in their own moisture. If not enough moisture has been secreted, add some salt liquor and wash them in that.

"Then place them in a square wicker basket, not too tightly woven, but strongly made with thick wicker. Then place a board on the turnips that can be pressed down within the opening of the basket if necessary. When the board is in place, put heavy weights on it and leave the turnips to dry overnight. Then place them in a jug treated with resin, or in a glazed pot, and pour vinegar with mustard over it, so they are submerged. You can use them after thirteen days."

1. To prepare the cabbage, remove the coarse outer leaves. Rinse a few unblemished ones and set them aside. Rinse the rest of the cabbage in cold water. With a stainless steel knife, quarter and core the cabbage. Thinly slice with the knife or a mandoline, then transfer the cabbage to a large bowl.

2. Add 2½ tablespoons of the salt and, with your hands, massage it into the leaves, then taste. You should be able to taste the salt without it being overwhelming. Add more salt if necessary. The cabbage will soon look wet and limp, and liquid will begin to pool. If you've put in a good effort and don't see much brine in the bowl, let it stand, covered, for 45 minutes, then massage again.

3. Shred the squash, with either a cheese grater or the shredder blade of the food processor. You should have about equal amounts of squash and cabbage. Combine the squash with the cabbage, then massage and knead the mixture. The juices will continue to release. Add the chipotle powder. Taste at this point, and adjust the salt and chipotle to taste. Don't be afraid of a little heat; it will mellow during the fermentation period (see the note below).

4. Transfer the vegetables a few handfuls at a time to a 2-gallon crock, pressing down with your fist or a tamper as you work. You should see some brine on top of the vegetables when you press. When you pack the vessel, leave 4 inches of headspace. Top the veggies with one or two of the reserved outer cabbage leaves. Top the leaves with a plate that fits the opening of the container and covers as much of the vegetables as possible; then weight down with a sealed water-filled jar.

5. Set aside on a baking sheet to ferment, somewhere nearby, out of direct sunlight, and cool, for 7 to 21 days. Check daily to make sure the vegetables are submerged, pressing down as needed to bring the brine back to the surface. You may see scum on top; it's generally harmless, but consult the appendix if you're at all concerned.

6. You can start to test the kraut on day 7. You'll know it's ready when it's pleasingly sour and pickle-y tasting, without the strong acidity of vinegar.

7. To store, spoon into smaller jars, and pour in any brine that's left. Tighten the lids, then store in the fridge. This kraut will keep, refrigerated, for 12 months.

Note: If the chipotle mellows too much for your liking during fermentation, you can toss in a bit more before transferring the kraut into storage jars.

Holiday Squash Kraut

yield: about 2 quarts
(fermentation vessel: 1 gallon)

The base of this sauerkraut is exactly the same as the above Chipotle Squash Kraut; however, its temperament is completely different. This kraut is lively and has whole cranberry pickles mixed throughout, which lavishly burst cranberry and spice into your mouth. Little jars of this kraut, polka-dotted with red berries, look festive on the table.

1 medium head (about 2 pounds) cabbage
2 pounds winter squash
2½–3½ tablespoons unrefined sea salt
1–2 cups Pickled Cranberries (page 274)

For this variation on Chipotle Squash Kraut (page 249), leave out the chipotle powder. Add the cranberries when you transfer the finished kraut to smaller jars for storage.

Squash Chutney

yield: about 1 quart
(fermentation vessel: 2 quarts)
technique used: Relishes, Chutneys, Salsas, and Fermented Salads (page 66)

This condiment is wonderfully thick, both sweet and sour, and its bright orange hue adds a spark to any plate.

1½ pounds winter squash halved, seeded, and peeled (see Peeling Winter Squash, page 249)
½ cup shredded carrot (optional)
1–2 teaspoons unrefined sea salt
2 cloves garlic, grated
1 tablespoon sweet curry powder (page 124)
½ cup chopped raisins

1. Shred the squash, with either a cheese grater or the shredder blade on the food processor. You should have about 4 cups. Transfer to a large bowl. Add the carrots, if using.

2. Sprinkle in 1½ teaspoons of the salt, working it in with your hands. Taste for salt and sprinkle in more as needed to achieve a salty flavor that is not overwhelming. Add the garlic and curry powder. Stir in the raisins. Let sit, covered, for 30 to 45 minutes, then toss and massage again for a

few minutes to get everything mixed. At this point there is brine building at the bottom.

3. Press your vegetables into a jar or crock. More brine will release at this stage, and you should see brine above the veggies. Top the ferment with a quart-sized ziplock bag. Press the plastic down onto the top of the ferment and then fill it with water and seal; this will act as both follower and weight.

4. Set aside on a baking sheet to ferment, somewhere nearby, out of direct sunlight, and cool, for 7 to 21 days. Check daily to make sure that the vegetables are submerged. You may see scum on top; it's generally harmless, but consult the appendix if you are concerned.

5. You can start to test the ferment on day 7. It's ready when the squash has softened and is pleasingly sour, with some lingering sweet notes. The color will remain bright orange.

6. Spoon the ferment into smaller jars, leaving as little headroom as possible, and tamping it down under the brine. Screw on the lids, then store in the fridge. This ferment will keep, refrigerated, for 12 months.

Kirsten Writes

In one of my experimental moods I had this big idea that spaghetti squash would be great fermented. I imagined cutting it in half and forking out the meat into little strings ready to salt. That was not what happened. It turns out that the strings do not freely come out until the squash is cooked. Raw spaghetti squash is a mess. There will be no spaghetti squash kraut in our house.

Create Your Own Recipes

Winter squash is also good in a ferment when sliced very thinly, as in the recipe for West African Sweet Potato Ferment (page 238). Winter squash is versatile, and its mood can completely alter the mood of your ferment . . . have fun with it.

Try these blends or make up your own:

» Sliced squash with scallions, ginger, garlic, and hot pepper — inspired by kimchi
» Sliced squash with thinly sliced apples, caraway seeds, and leeks
» Shredded squash with shredded root vegetables such as kohlrabi or turnips, which act similarly to the cabbage but may be more available in the winter

---

ZUCCHINI AND OTHER SUMMER SQUASH

Zucchini's terrific, like bunnies prolific.
— UNKNOWN

Despite the obvious Italian name, and being a stalwart ingredient of Mediterranean cuisine, zucchini-type squash is native to the Americas, as are all variations of summer and winter squashes. Seeds were brought back to Europe by explorers; what we know as zucchini was then developed in Italy, and it is thought that it did not hit the cuisine scene until the late 19th century.

Anyone who has grown even one zucchini plant knows the point in the summer when you wake up at dawn to clandestinely leave extra zucchinis on the neighbors' doorsteps, in their unlocked cars, in their mailboxes, or with their goats. When we teach our late-summer pickling classes, we bring a lot of joy to people when we tell them that they can solve this problem by making an abundance of wee little pickles that they can enjoy in February, when summer squash is just a distant dream.

YOUR RAW MATERIAL

Summer squash is different from winter squash only in that the ideal time to harvest and eat it is when it's immature — meaning that the skin has not hardened, nor have the seeds developed. There are many beautiful varieties of zucchini and summer squash; there is not much difference nutritionally in the varieties and most of the nutrients are right under the skin, so it's best not to peel them. When choosing squash at the market, make sure the sensitive skin is glossy and undamaged.

Whatever variety you have, use the small ones to make whole pickles (see Summer Squash Basil Pickles, page 254). For these, choose squash that are less than 1¼ inches in diameter. If you are getting your squash from the farmers' market, you may want to make a request to your favorite farm that they pick you a batch of extra-small ones. They can never be too small; some of our favorite "baby" pickles have come from tiny squash with unopened blossom ends. For squash that is slightly larger than ideal, cut into rounds to sink in brine. Make sure the center is still intact. These are softer, but they can still make a nice addition to a vegetable medley.

If you are a gardener with a plant or two, you will have many opportunities to ferment different sizes. At the market they are generally around 8 inches long. When selecting your zucchini or other summer squash to ferment, there are a few things to keep in mind: You can use the larger ones but not the baseball bat–sized ones for kraut. Bigger is not better. If the inside is developing seeds and the consistency of the center flesh is beginning to have a more spongy quality, it is too large.

Use fresh squash; they begin to degrade in the refrigerator after about three days. This will begin to show itself as pockmarks on the thin skin of the fruit. Squash that are no longer fresh will have a shorter fermented shelf life as well.

IN THE CROCK
Zucchini Kraut

yield: about 2 quarts
(fermentation vessel: 2 quarts)
technique used: Mastering Sauerkraut(page 53)

This is a soft kraut, but not so soft that it would be described as mushy. Instead it is delicate with a texture similar to shredded zucchini. It is also delicate once fermented, lasting only about 2 months under refrigeration. You'll see there is a wide salt range in this recipe. We have found that salting shredded zucchini is a balancing act. It absorbs the salt and can quickly taste quite salty; however, since it is a tender vegetable, fermenting zucchini requires a brine that has a higher salt percentage, more like the 3 percent salt concentration in a cucumber pickling brine. What that means is that in this recipe, when you taste

for salt, you want it to be saltier than a kraut — like a salty potato chip.

Interestingly, although there is a lot of brine (this vegetable is 95 percent water), it stays incorporated in the ferment, keeping the zucchini suspended in the brine.

This one ferments rather quickly; in our fermentation cave, where is stays 60 to 65°F, it's done in 3 to 4 days, though we often let it go 5 days. It is a matter of taste and tang preference.

5–6 medium (8–10 inches) zucchini
1½–3 teaspoons unrefined sea salt

1. Rinse the zucchini in cold water and then shred in a food processor or with a mandoline. Transfer to a large bowl and add 1½ teaspoons of the salt. Massage it into the shredded zucchini with your hands. Taste for salt; because of the soft nature of this kraut you will want it to be saltier than usual, like a salty potato chip. Sprinkle in more salt if needed to achieve a salty flavor, keeping in mind that the salt should not be overwhelming. The brine develops immediately when the salt is added.

2. After a bit of mixing, this kraut goes straight into the crock. Transfer a few handfuls at a time to a jar or crock, pressing down with your fist or a tamper to remove air pockets. You should see some brine on top of the vegetable when you press. When you pack the vessel, leave 4 inches of headspace for a crock, or 2 to 3 inches for a jar. Top with a primary follower, such as a bit of plastic wrap. For a crock, top that with a plate that fits the opening of the container and covers as much of the zucchini as possible; then weight down with a sealed water-filled jar. For a jar, use a sealed water-filled jar or ziplock bag as a follower-weight combination.

3. Set aside on a baking sheet to ferment, somewhere nearby, out of direct sunlight, and cool, for 3 to 7 days. Check daily to make sure the zucchini stays submerged, pressing down as needed to bring the brine back to the surface. You may see scum on top; it's generally harmless, but consult the appendix if you're at all concerned.

4. This kraut ferments quickly in summer kitchens. Check yours after 3 days; when ready, this kraut will be soft and have a lemony acidic quality to the sourness.

5. Store in jars, with lids tightened, in the fridge, leaving as little headroom as possible, and tamping the ferment down under the brine. This kraut will keep, refrigerated, for 2 months.

IN THE PICKLE JAR
Summer Squash Basil Pickles

yield: about 2 quarts
(fermentation vessel: 2 quarts)
technique used: Mastering Brine Pickling (page 77)

Allow your inner fermentista to have fun with these whole baby-squash pickles, arranging them to stand regally in special jars. Any variety of summer squash — zucchini, pattypan, crookneck — makes amazing pickles. If you truly have abundance, you can pickle the small ones with the blossoms — either unopened or recently bloomed, but pluck off any ragged, tired blossoms. The blossoms hold up to the brining. The effect is striking and has a taste to match. Something to awe your friends at a potluck — if you are willing to share, that is. You can also use dill pickle spices in this recipe instead of basil.

Note: Zucchini can be anywhere from the size of your pinky finger to about 5 inches long and 1 inch in diameter. It is best if all the vegetables in one jar are similarly sized.

½–1 **pound whole baby zucchini or summer squash, enough to fill the jar, with or without blossoms**
4–5 **cloves garlic**
2 **sprigs basil**
1–2 **whole dried red chiles, sweet or hot**
2 **quarts Cucumber Brine (⅜ cup unrefined sea salt to 2 quarts unchlorinated water)**
Grape leaves (optional)

1. Rinse the vegetables in cold water. Arrange the squashes, garlic, basil, and chiles in a jar or crock, wedging them under the shoulder of the jar or with 4 inches of headspace in a crock. Be careful to not bruise or damage the squashes' skin when packing them. Pour in enough brine to cover the vegetables completely. Reserve any leftover brine in the fridge. (It will keep for 1 week; discard thereafter and make a new batch, if needed.)

2. Place grape leaves, if using, over the vegetables as a primary follower (the tannins in the leaves keep the pickles crisp). If using other tannin-rich leaves (page 79), add them now. If using a crock, top with a plate that will rest atop the pickles, and a weight such as a sealed water-filled jar to keep things in place. If using a jar, the secondary follower is often not needed since the squash is wedged in place by the shoulder; loosely cover the jar with the lid.

3. Set aside on a baking sheet to ferment, somewhere nearby, out of direct sunlight, and cool, for 4 to 6 days. During the fermentation period, monitor brine level and top off with the reserved brine solution, if needed, to cover. You may see scum on top; it's generally harmless, but consult the appendix if you're at all concerned.

4. As the vegetables ferment, they begin to lose their vibrant color and the brine will get cloudy; this is when you can start to test your pickles. When they're ready, the colors will appear dull, they will taste pickle-y, and though softer, they'll retain some crispness.

5. Store in jars, with lids tightened, in the fridge, adding fresh brine as needed to keep the pickles covered. Top each jar with a fresh grape leaf, if you have them.

Create Your Own Recipes

The mild flavor of Zucchini Kraut (page 253) lends itself to many combinations of herbs and spices. Use zucchini as a base for blends. Think about texture and what you want your final product to be. Do you want it to be congruent with the gentle nature of the zucchini, or would you prefer to add vegetables that will increase the crunch in the crock?

BLAUKRAUT, *page 147*

TURMERIC PEPPER
KRAUT, *page 244*

CHIMICHURRI, *page 207*

SHISO KRAUT, *page 229*

CRANBERRY RELISH, *page 274*

LEMON-DILL KRAUT, *page 134*

THAI-INSPIRED BABY PAK CHOI, *page 205*

THREE Cs, *page 133*

EDGY VEGGIES, *page 155*

Foraged Vegetables

All of the people who work in the kitchen with me go out into the forests and on to the beach. It's a part of their job. If you work with me, you will often be starting your day in the forest or on the shore, because I believe foraging will shape you as a chef.

— DANISH CHEF RENÉ REDZEPI

Gathering small bits in the wild will not only diversify your diet but will also expand your worldview. Just the act of leaving behind the store and picking a handful of leaves that will grace your table is rewarding and grounding. You must study what you are picking to be sure you have the correct plant, and you must think about stewardship (see Harvest Considerations on the facing page).

This section only scratches the surface of what can be wildcrafted and then fermented. Some of the plants we have included grow on the West Coast, and some only on the East. Some of the greens cross the line of weed, turned cultivated. Nettles, lamb's-quarters, and dandelion greens, for example, are available at many farmers' markets. Burdock also makes this list; however, since the cultivated root is widely available, we have included it among the garden vegetables under its own heading. The young leaves can be wildcrafted in the spring.

Kirsten Writes

I took a wild-plant walk at a neighboring farm led by a local herbalist. What struck me most on this journey was a conversation about food and our eating habits.

As we walked along the edge between forest and stream, he told us that a nice trail nibble can be a brand-new tender spring leaf of the wild Oregon grape. (For those of you unfamiliar with an Oregon grape leaf, think spiky, tough Christmas holly.) My first thought was okay, good to know, but that will never be a meal. As though reading my mind, our guide said that we need to diversify our diets, as season after season we are eating the same foods. He feels that food allergies are caused by this very thing. Modern agriculture, shipping, and refrigeration have left us with no experience of seasonality in the grocery store. In short, we are no longer forced to eat different foods as they are available during the seasons.

As I drove home, I began to think about how to bring more wild into our meals. . . .

"Uh, Mom, why are there holly leaves in our salad?"

Harvest Considerations

Wildcrafting plants is wonderful when done with care, but often it can lead to overharvesting (admittedly not a problem for common weeds like dandelion or lamb's-quarters). When using wild plants that are more elusive in a kraut or kimchi, keep in mind that less is more.

As a member of the Native Plant Society, seed farmer and wild gardener Barbara Hughey offers the following harvesting considerations: "When we begin to include wild foraged foods in our menus, there are a few simple things to consider to ensure that those special gifts from nature are protected from overharvesting. The best way to wild harvest responsibly is to only pick what you need. Collect only where the plants are plentiful, and consider how those plants reproduce. If harvesting the whole plant, consider when its seeds are mature so that they may grow again next season. We can gather and scatter the seeds to expand the area where the plants are growing. Doing some commonsense things like this, with plant conservation in mind, can be our way of giving something back each time we take. In this way we can rest assured that those plants will be there to enjoy well into the future."

DANDELION FLOWERS, LEAVES, AND ROOTS

Dandelion is a common wild plant found growing along roadsides and in yards and vacant lots. Its name comes from the medieval French *dent de lions* (lion's teeth), which refers to the leaves' jagged edges. The wild dandelion's Latin name is *Taraxacum officinale*, to be confused with its distant cousin *Chicorium intybus* or Italian dandelion, a member of the chicory family, along with radicchio and endive.

One cup of dandelions greens is said to supply 112 percent of the USDA recommended daily allowance of vitamin A and 535 percent of vitamin K. This is all well and good, but the leaf, even when fermented, is still bracingly bitter. We, personally, do not ferment these bitter greens, wild or cultivated, and prefer to eat them sautéed in butter. Our relationship with the wild dandelion has been the closest with the flower: fritters and wine. As for the greens and the root, well, like many plants we know, they are good for us but we don't often go there.

YOUR RAW MATERIAL

Dandelions can be found everywhere (like in the sidewalk cracks) but you want to be picky about the location you choose. Dandelions growing in rich soil will have larger leaves and roots. It is most prudent to avoid roadside specimens and only harvest from lawns you are confident have not been sprayed or chemically fertilized in many years.

Early spring is the best time to harvest the leaves; they are the most tender and least bitter before the flower appears. As spring progresses you will want to move from the leaves to flower buds — that is, if you want to make flower bud pickles. The taproot is edible year-round but best when the plant is dormant — late fall to early spring.

If you are purchasing dandelion greens from the market, they are most tender in the early spring or late fall after the frost. Select ones that are vibrant deep green, not wilting or yellowing.

IN THE CROCK

The addition of aromatic herbs to ferments of bitter greens in our experience helps to balance the bitterness; dandelion greens fermented with these herbs are still quite bitter. If we haven't discouraged you yet, and you want to include dandelion's digestive-enhancing qualities, add a handful of greens to Naked Kraut (page 132) or Kimchi (page 141). The dandelion's roots are also a powerful medicinal whose qualities can be enhanced by fermentation.

Digestive Bitters

This combination is just as it sounds — bitter. With this recipe, we leave the realm of the purely culinary and enter the realm of digestive health, a boon to the enjoyment of good food. This recipe comes to us from Nadine Levie, Lac and Chinese herbalist.

To the Naked Kraut recipe (page 132) add:

- **1 tablespoon grated fresh dandelion root**
- **1 teaspoon grated fresh ginger**
- **½ teaspoon dried cardamom**
- **½ teaspoon dried citrus peel**
- **½ teaspoon dried gentian**

IN THE PICKLE JAR
Fermented Dandelion Flower Buds

yield: about 1 pint
(fermentation vessel: 1 quart or larger)
technique used: Mastering Brine Pickling (page 77)

When selecting flower buds to pickle, be sure to pick buds that are still tightly closed, not flowers that have simply closed for the night, which will have bits of petals sticking out. Use these small pickles as you would capers.

- **2 cups dandelion buds**
- **1–2 heads garlic, cloves separated**
- **1 onion, sliced in wedges**
- **1 (1–inch) piece fresh ginger, chopped**
- **2 tablespoons red goji berries**
- **1–2 cups Basic Brine (1 tablespoon unrefined sea salt to 1 pint unchlorinated water)**

1. Combine the dandelion buds, garlic, onion wedges, ginger, and goji berries in a bowl and mix well. Transfer to a quart jar and pour in enough brine to cover the mixture completely. The dandelion buds will want to float; place some of the larger onion wedges on top to keep everything under the brine. Reserve any leftover brine in the fridge. (It will keep for 1 week; discard thereafter and make a new batch, if needed.)

2. For this ferment, use a ziplock bag filled with water as the follower; it will prevent the small ingredients from floating over the brine. Remember: *Submerge in brine, and all will be fine.*

3. Set aside on a baking sheet to ferment, somewhere nearby, out of direct sunlight, and cool, for 5 to 7 days. During the fermentation period, monitor the brine level. Press buds back into the brine or top off with the reserved brine solution, as needed. You may see scum on top; it's generally harmless, but consult the appendix if you're at all concerned.

4. As the buds ferment, they begin to lose their vibrant color and the brine will get cloudy; this is when you can start to test your pickles. The buds will become dull green and the flavor of the buds and brine will be slightly sour, with ginger and garlic notes, when these pickles are ready.

5. Store in the fridge in the same jar, lid tight.

Goji Berries

Goji berries (*Lycium barbarum*), also called wolfberries, add bright red polka dots to your ferments. These small crimson berries have received a lot of press in the last decade as a superfood with myriad benefits. They are usually found in stores as dried fruit. Use as you would a raisin in ferments.

LAMB'S-QUARTERS

This prolific plant (*Chenopodium album*) can be found all through North America. Chances are you have worked to "weed" it out of your garden — although cultivars of the foraged plant have been developed for the garden and for seed. A distinguishing feature of this highly nutritious green is a grayish powder found beneath the young leaves that gives the greens a silver patina; this powder is innocuous and rinses off easily.

This plant is similar to red orach and spinach; if you like these two greens, you will probably enjoy lamb's-quarters.

YOUR RAW MATERIAL

Like dandelion, this green can be found in back alleys, empty lots, and lawns. Choose your harvest site away from roadways and places treated chemically. We allow a few of the volunteers to colonize our garden beds and harvest from those. As with many greens, the younger leaves early in the season are the most tender. For lamb's-quarters a good rule of thumb is to harvest from plants that are less than a foot tall.

IN THE CROCK
Thyme for Lamb's-Quarters Kraut

yield: about 3 quarts
(fermentation vessel: 1 gallon)
technique used: Mastering Sauerkraut(page 53)

This kraut started out as a little experiment just to see how lamb's-quarters would behave in the crock — inquiring minds (like our farmer friend Mary with her abundant crop) wanted to know. We made the first batch and took it to market, where it sold out immediately. The next week and the week after we had so many requests that we filled a crock, this time a big one.

2–3 heads (5–6 pounds) cabbage

2–2½ tablespoons unrefined sea salt

2 bundles (about 1 pound) lamb's-quarters, finely chopped

2–3 carrots, grated

1 red onion, thinly sliced

1 teaspoon dried tarragon (or 1 tablespoon fresh)

1 tablespoon dried thyme (or 2–3 tablespoons fresh)

1. To prepare the cabbage, remove the coarse outer leaves. Rinse a few unblemished ones and set them aside. Rinse the rest of the cabbage in cold water. With a stainless steel knife, quarter and core the cabbage. Thinly slice with the knife or a mandoline, then transfer the cabbage to a large bowl.

2. Add about 2 tablespoons of the salt and, with your hands, massage it into the leaves. Allow this to begin weeping while you add the lamb's-quarters, carrots, onion, tarragon, and thyme. Massage into the cabbage and taste. You should be able to taste the salt without it being overwhelming; add more salt if necessary. Everything will soon look wet and limp, and liquid will begin to pool. If you've put in a good effort and don't see much brine in the bowl, let it stand, covered, for 45 minutes, then massage again.

3. Transfer the cabbage mixture a few handfuls at a time to a 1-gallon jar or crock, pressing down with your fist or a tamper as you work. You should see some brine on top of the cabbage when you press; this ensures that you are pressing out the air pockets. When you pack the vessel, leave 4 inches of headspace for a crock, or 2 to 3 inches for a jar. Top the cabbage with one or two of the reserved outer cabbage leaves.

For a crock, top the leaves with a plate that fits the opening of the container and covers as much of the vegetables as possible; then weight down with a sealed water-filled jar. For a jar, use a sealed water-filled jar or a water-filled ziplock bag as a follower-weight combination.

4. Set aside on a baking sheet to ferment, somewhere nearby, out of direct sunlight, and cool, for 7 to 21 days. Check daily to make sure the vegetables are submerged, pressing down as needed to bring the brine back to the surface. You may see scum on top; it's generally harmless, but consult the appendix if you're at all concerned.

5. You can start to test the kraut on day 7. You'll know it's ready when it's pleasingly sour and pickle-y tasting, without the strong acidity of vinegar; the onion flavor has softened; and the veggies look like cooked vegetables.

6. Store in jars, with lids tightened, in the fridge. This kraut will keep, refrigerated, for 12 months.

WILD MUSHROOMS

There's a lot to learn about the various types of mushrooms, especially when wildcrafting. We recommend taking a class in your local area to learn the particulars — the types available and in what season, and how to make sure you have the right mushroom. And always play it safe. We know the forest out our back door has many delicious varieties, yet we are only confident in harvesting boletus, chanterelles, and oyster mushrooms in the fall and morels in the spring — with varying degrees of success. We do not ferment them unless they have been dehydrated (see page 193).

NETTLES

Fresh wild nettles can be combined with other vegetables in kraut or kimchi. This herb (or green) is so nutritionally valuable it would be worthwhile to ferment it even with dried leaves if that is all you have available. A local herbalist told us that wildcrafted dried nettles are often blackish-green when dried, which he felt was because of the high iron content.

YOUR RAW MATERIAL

If you are wildcrafting nettles for kraut, they are best in the spring before they have begun to flower. Leave plenty of tops to flower and produce seeds, and work with whatever you can harvest without depleting the supply.

Nettles are fun to work with as they have a dry rustling quality, like crinoline petticoats, when you are chopping them and then massaging them into the cabbage. But be sure to wear gloves when working with them; they will sting.

Fresh Nettle Kraut

yield: about 2 quarts
(fermentation vessel: 2 quarts or larger)
technique used: Mastering Sauerkraut (page 53)

The nettle quantity in the recipe is variable. Since the leaves reduce in volume so drastically, 1 cup or 3 cups will not make a big difference in the final quantity of kraut. Whether a large or small dose of these healthy greens, the nettles add pleasant flavor that does not overwhelm.

- 1–2 heads (3½ pounds) cabbage
- 1–1½ tablespoons unrefined sea salt
- 2 cups (more or less) chopped and lightly packed fresh nettles
- 1 sweet onion (or a bundle of spring onions with the greens), thinly sliced
- 6 cloves garlic, minced

1. To prepare the cabbage, remove the coarse outer leaves. Rinse a few unblemished ones and set them aside. Rinse the rest of the cabbage in cold water. With a stainless steel knife, quarter and core the cabbage. Thinly slice with the knife or a mandoline, then transfer the cabbage to a large bowl.

2. Add about 1 tablespoon of the salt and, with your hands, massage it into the leaves. Allow this to begin weeping while you add the nettles, onion, and garlic. Massage into the cabbage and taste. You should be able to taste the salt without it being overwhelming. Add more salt if necessary. Everything will soon look wet and limp, and liquid will begin to pool. If you've put in a good effort and don't see much brine in the bowl, let it stand, covered, for 45 minutes, then massage again.

3. Transfer the cabbage mixture a few handfuls at a time to a 2-quart jar or 1-gallon crock, pressing down with your fist or a tamper as you work. You should see some brine on top of the cabbage when you press; this ensures that you are pressing out the air pockets. When you pack the vessel, leave 4 inches of headspace for a crock, or 2 to 3 inches for a jar. Top the cabbage with one or two of the reserved outer cabbage leaves. For a crock, top the leaves with a plate that fits the opening of the container and covers as much of the surface as possible; then weight down with a sealed water-filled jar. For a jar, use a sealed water-filled jar or ziplock bag as a follower-weight combination.

4. Set aside on a baking sheet to ferment, somewhere nearby, out of direct sunlight, and cool, for 7 to 21 days. Check daily to make sure the vegetables are submerged, pressing down as needed to bring the brine back to the surface. You may see scum on top; it's generally harmless, but consult the appendix if you're at all concerned.

5. You can start to test the kraut on day 7. You'll know it's ready when it's pleasingly sour, the onion and garlic flavors have softened, the cabbage is somewhat translucent, and the flecks of nettle are deep green.

6. Store in jars, with lids tightened, in the fridge. This kraut will keep, refrigerated, for 12 months.

RAMPS

In the fairy tale, newborn Rapunzel is given to the witch to pay for the harvesting of the green ramp that her pregnant mother saw over the garden wall and thought she would die without. The ramp (*Allium tricoccum*) is called a spring onion or a wild leek. A forest dweller, its green leaves sprout from the bulb before the canopy shades the ground. This early arrival of green after winter's long hungry spell made it prized. In the Appalachian Mountains, a folk remedy claims ramp's power to ward off winter's ills. Ramps, like their cousins in the cultivated onion family, are not only green but high in vitamins and minerals. No doubt this was what Rapunzel's mother needed.

Onions are an important ingredient worldwide, and it is thought that there were wild onions on every continent. The onion's reputation has spanned everything from a food to be worshipped, as in Egypt, to places and times where it was considered a food for the poor, as it was too pungent for the gentry. It is a good thing that the wealthy are over that. It is incredibly beneficial in the diet. It was one of the first foods recognized for its medicinal value, across cultures.

YOUR RAW MATERIAL

Ramps appear early in the spring in the East, from Georgia to Quebec. As one of the first fresh green foods to appear after winter they are a welcome sign and taste of spring. They are also very popular and should be harvested carefully, as the populations have diminished in recent years. Although loosening the ground with a spade or knife allows you to easily lift the whole bulb out, this can affect the patch long term when over-harvested. It's better to harvest the green tops and leave the roots in place. This method does not kill the plant and provides delicious flavor and wild nutrients in your ferment.

IN THE CROCK

Use ramps in place of onions or leeks in any fermented creation — your kimchi becomes Ramp-Chi.

WATERCRESS

Though watercress is also a cultivated green, it is quite commonly wildcrafted. It is semiaquatic and has a very short shelf life. It has the distinction of being the oldest known leaf vegetable to be consumed by humans. It has been traced back to the Persians and the Greeks and has a venerable reputation throughout Western history. Watercress is a salad green and a medicinal herb. It is said to promote an appetite; because of this quality it finds its way into many traditional kimchi recipes. Use it to infuse into a kraut or kimchi.

YOUR RAW MATERIAL

Whether you are wildcrafting or buying watercress, it should be long, leafy, and fragrant. The stems should be thick and shiny. You can check the quality of the plant by breaking the stem; if it is older, a thread will show at the break. The peppery quality of the plant varies; mild or spicy is acceptable to use.

Radish Cube Kimchi with Watercress (*Kkakdugi*)

yield: about 2 quarts
(fermentation vessel: 2 quarts or larger)
technique used: Relishes, Chutneys, Salsas, and Fermented Salads (page 66)

This is a traditional Korean recipe. The *gochugaru* makes it quite beautiful. It can be fiery or mild, depending on your choice of pepper powder.

 3 **pounds radishes, chopped in ½-inch cubes (though typically a large Asian-type radish, any kind will do)**
 ½ **cup ground cayenne or salt-free *gochugaru* (for a mild flavor, use ground paprika)**
 1 **bunch scallions, sliced into 1-inch sections**
 1 **bunch watercress, coarsely chopped (about 1 cup, loosely packed)**
 2–3 **cloves garlic, minced**
 1 **tablespoon finely grated fresh ginger**

1 tablespoon sugar

2 teaspoons Korean pickled baby shrimp, minced

2–3 teaspoons unrefined sea salt

1. Mix the radishes and cayenne in a large bowl. Stir in the scallions, watercress, garlic, ginger, sugar, and pickled shrimp. Add 2 teaspoons of salt and massage the mixture well with your hands. You should be able to taste the salt without it being overwhelming. Add more salt if necessary. The radish mixture will soon look wet and limp, and liquid will begin to pool.

2. Transfer the radish mixture a few handfuls at a time to a 2-quart jar, pressing down with your fingers or a tamper as you work. More brine will release at this stage, and you should see brine above the veggies. Top the ferment with a quart-sized ziplock bag. Press the plastic down onto the top of the ferment and then fill it with water and seal; this will act as both follower and weight.

3. Set aside on a baking sheet to ferment, somewhere nearby, out of direct sunlight, and cool, for 10 to 14 days. Check daily to make sure the vegetables are submerged, pressing down as needed to bring the brine back to the surface. You may see scum on top; it's generally harmless, but consult the appendix if you're at all concerned.

4. You can start to test the kraut on day 10. It is ready when the desired sourness is reached.

5. Spoon the ferment into smaller jars, leaving as little headroom as possible, and tamping it down under the brine. Pour in any remaining brine to cover. Tighten the lids, then store in the fridge. This ferment will keep, refrigerated, for 6 months.

Fruits

Our farm was carved from a hillside of hard clay soils and old streambeds that hide their rock bones under a thin skin of topsoil. A tractor and a plow will never be an option for us. It is not farmland, but forestland that was cleared for grazing animals. As we began to understand our place, it became clear that we had the ideal setting to grow a food forest garden — perennial fruit trees, bushes, and herbs intermingled on thin terraces tracing along the slope.

Since we have not discovered perennial vegetable trees yet, our garden's bounty is fruit. Christopher, the cellar master, tenderly ferments most of this fruit. In his "fermentation cave" apples become hard cider, pears become perry, rose hips become wine.

This is fitting, since the high sugar content of the fruit doesn't work in the crock with the lacto-fermentation. A high-fruit ferment will often become alcoholic instead of the soured stable condiments of vegetables. Still, with planning and care it is possible to incorporate some fruit.

This small section will help you navigate which fruits will work successfully with vegetables.

APPLES

Apples grow well on our Oregon farm. We have seven trees that are around 80 years old. They're tall and stately and provide more fruit than we can pick. The physics of our orchard ladders perched on hillsides presents enough challenge to ensure that the birds get plenty of "top-shelf" apples. Alas, it's true: those out of reach are always bigger and brighter and lack any extra protein in the form of worms.

Still, we grafted 100 heirloom cider varieties onto hearty rootstock, and they grow slowly on the hillside as well. They should be in full production at about the same time our last child leaves home. (What were we thinking?) The apples that don't become food — applesauce, dried apple rings, apple strudel, apple pie, or an ingredient in kraut — go through the press for cider.

On cider pressing days, there is some jockeying among family members for what the nectar will become: sweet cider, the ambrosia that we freeze for warm winter drinks of mulled cider, or hard cider, Christopher's true fermentation love. The negotiations don't stop there — after the hard cider is bottled, Kirsten lobbies for a few gallons to feed the vinegar barrels.

When we began experimenting with flavor, apples were among the first things we added to sauerkraut.

YOUR RAW MATERIAL

Worldwide there are more than 7,500 varieties of apples, and you can ferment any of them. In Russia, for example, there's a traditional ferment for crab apples. We don't profess to know which apples respond best to fermentation, but we like the softening end-of-fall sugary Yellow Delicious in our kraut just as much as the crisp-tart Gravenstein in the summer; each imparts its own qualities, but both are delicious. For color you can't beat an Arkansas Black, sliced with the skin left on. Experiment and decide which varieties you like best.

IN THE CROCK

Fresh apples add appeal to kraut, but not for the reason you think. They don't mellow the acidity or incorporate sweetness. (Remember, our friends of the lactic-acid family feed on sugar and turn it into acidity; see page 25.)

You can add grated or thinly sliced apples to a ferment. Grating imparts a hint of apple taste and a certain lightness of texture. For more texture and greater apple flavor, slice them.

To retain an apple's sweetness, incorporate sliced dried apple rings into krauts and chutney ferments.

| FERMENTISTA'S TIP |

Sweetening the Crock

For a sweet-flavored kraut, add stevia to the ferment. Its sweetness is not "eaten" and converted to acid by the lactic-acid bacteria. Adding sugar doesn't add sweetness, it adds sour (a trick used in some Asian ferments).

Stevia is extremely sweet; a pinch will go a long way. Use the dried leaves, as these are still a whole food. The white powder has been processed.

Farmhouse Culture's Apple-Fennel Kraut

yield: about 1 gallon
(fermentation vessel: 2 gallons or larger)
technique used: Mastering Sauerkraut (page 53)

  3–5 tablespoons unrefined sea salt
  7½ pounds cabbage, shredded
  1¾ pounds apples, thinly sliced
  ½ pound onions, thinly sliced
  5 teaspoons fennel seeds

1. Add 3 tablespoons of salt to the shredded cabbage, massage it into the leaves, and then add the apples, onion, and fennel seeds. Taste, and add more salt if needed.

2. Set aside for 5 to 21 days. Start tasting at day 5; it's ready when it appeals to you. (Kathryn likes a 21-day ferment.)

3. Pack in clean jars with tight lids, then store in the fridge. This will keep, refrigerated, for 1 year.

Kathryn Lukas, of Farmhouse Culture

I (Kirsten) first met Kathryn in 2011, at the Freestone Fermentation Festival. We immediately had a lot to talk about, starting with our common passions for Germany and sauerkraut.

Kathryn's fermentation adventure began in the professional culinary world. She was an owner/chef of a restaurant in Stuttgart, Germany, when she discovered "real" sauerkraut. She, like most of us when we took our first bite of fresh raw kraut, was blown away by the flavor — complex and crisp and everything else the stuff in the can is not. A few years later she was in the Natural Chef program at Bauman College in Santa Cruz, California, and learned the science of lactic-acid fermentation. She was introduced to sauerkraut from the culinary rather than the health angle, which was the more common approach.

Her first flavor was a classic kraut, the timeless combination of cabbage and caraway seed. Then she tried smoked jalapeño before developing an apple-fennel kraut (see recipe at left).

Kathryn and I kept in touch. When I visited her in Santa Cruz, she showed me around her facility, which is housed in a historic mill. It's a long way from Kathryn's early days when she fermented sauerkraut in individual jars in a basement.

Like kraut sommeliers, we tasted in the fermentation cave. Kathryn has a discerning palate and catches all the nuances of flavor. On the day I was there, Kathryn was trying to decide whether to keep Farmhouse Culture's Lemon Ginger Carrot on board. It was delicious but not perfect: the ginger was too strong. This kraut was proving to be a

Kathryn Lukas

challenge. Both the carrots and the ginger tended to be inconsistent in their sugar content and essence from crop to crop, making it difficult to produce a consistent product.

We ate lunch on a park bench overlooking Monterey Bay. Sticking to what we love, we had Reubens from a sandwich shop that uses Farmhouse Culture's kraut. We talked about flavor and what herbs and spices have to offer to the senses. Kathryn prefers dried, concentrated herbs to fresh; she finds that they stand up well to the fermentation. Her favorite way to personalize sauerkraut is to use whole seeds as one of the simplest ways to impart a powerful aroma and mood. The seeds concentrate the flavor, which bursts forth when you take a bite.

One summer Farmhouse Culture produced what it called the Summer of Love Kraut, a seasonal ferment of summer squash infused with lavender. People loved it, and it was a delicious combination, but using lavender requires a delicate balance, and it's difficult to get the blend just right.

LAVENDER AND KRAUT

Culinary lavender is tricky, and people are usually in one of two camps. Some love it; some people think eating it is like eating potpourri and say it should stay tucked in sachets.

Lavender has a cool and refreshing flavor. Mellow the floral tones by quickly toasting the buds over a dry skillet before adding them to the ferment. To determine whether you like the fermented flavor before committing to a crock of it, take 1 cup Naked Kraut (page 132) and add a pinch (less than ¼ teaspoon of lavender). Mix thoroughly, then press into a jar. Let ferment for a day or two, then taste the developing flavor to decide which lavender camp you're in.

CITRUS FRUITS

The various species of oranges and lemons in Assam would astonish you. Lemons of the finest kinds are found wild throughout the forests, and are a great treat to a thirsty, feverish explorer. I often come on a loaded tree in the midst of a grass plain, with no water nearer than some miles. They are doubtless the remains of an ancient civilization.

— CAPTAIN LOWTHER, AGRI HORTICULTURAL SOCIETY OF INDIA, *THE CULTIVATED ORANGES AND LEMONS OF INDIA AND CEYLON*, 1857

Citrus juice or zest can find a happy home in many a ferment. It's a tangy way to alter the flavor or the acidity of a kraut.

The citrus flavor of the zest will stay intact and be recognizable as that of lemons, limes, or oranges, but subtle. OlyKraut's Eastern European Kraut (page 138) is an example of using grapefruit juice to provide a unique balance of flavor. The "lemony" quality of our Lemon-Dill Kraut (page 134) is very different from that in Greek Lemon-Mint Kraut (page 134), because the latter uses the zest as well as the juice.

Fruit juices often come in handy when you need a little more brine in a ferment.

The cuisines of Morocco and India make good use of pickled lemons and limes, and other cuisines from other traditions incorporate them as well.

YOUR RAW MATERIAL
Limes and Key Limes. The common lime, or Persian lime, is an important component of many cuisines, and its zest is more flavorful and potent than that of the Key lime. In India, Persian limes are pickled as an accompaniment to many dishes. They can be sweet, salty, or hot, depending on the additions, and they're also found in chutneys.

Key limes are smaller than Persian limes, and their shape is almost round. Most are green: that means they were picked prematurely, to have the more tart-acidic flavor they're known for. (When they ripen on the tree, they're yellow and sweeter.)

Because Key limes are immature and their skins are thin, they have a short shelf life; they will turn brown soon after you bring them home unless you eat them or preserve them by fermentation.

Lemons and Meyer Lemons. Meyer lemons have a little less pucker than regular lemons and more floral and fruity notes. Botanically, they're a cross between lemons and mandarin oranges. The peel of the Meyer lemon is richly yellow and thin and delicate. The fruits don't ship as well or last, so their season is shorter. This — and their mild flavor — makes them a great candidate for preservation.

At the supermarket, look for the smallest, roundest lemons. They have more juice.

Preserved Limes

See photo on page 153

yield: about 2 quarts
(fermentation vessel: 2 quarts)
technique used: Relishes, Chutneys, Salsas, and Fermented Salads (page 66)

This is an intensely flavored condiment, a little goes a long way. The pickles we eat at a local Indian buffet inspired this recipe. We'd been enjoying them for years before we finally asked for the ingredients. The chef didn't share much, just enough to let the experiments begin.

Serve alongside anything that needs a briny citrus punch, Indian cuisine or not.

- 2 **pounds Key limes**
- 5 **sun-dried tomatoes, thinly sliced**
- 3 **fresh Fresno chiles or 1 sweet red pepper, diced**
- 4–6 **cloves garlic, minced**
- 3 **tablespoons unrefined sea salt**

- 2 **tablespoons sugar**
- 1 **tablespoon coriander seeds**
- 1 **tablespoon fenugreek seeds, lightly crushed**
- 1 **tablespoon grated fresh ginger**
- 2 **teaspoons ground turmeric**
- ½ **teaspoon ground cumin (optional)**

1. Rinse the limes in cold water and scrub the skins. With a stainless steel knife, quarter the limes and remove the seeds; place in a large bowl and mix in the tomatoes, chiles, garlic, salt, sugar, coriander, fenugreek, ginger, turmeric, and cumin, if using.

2. Press the mixture into a jar or crock. More brine will release at this stage, and you should see brine above the mixture. Top the ferment with a quart-sized ziplock bag. Press the plastic down onto the top of the ferment and then fill it with water and seal; this will act as both follower and weight.

3. Set aside on a baking sheet to ferment, somewhere nearby, out of direct sunlight, and cool, for 1 to 6 months. Check periodically to make sure the limes stay submerged.

4. You can start to test the ferment on day 30. Because it started out as an acidic mixture, your readiness clue is a little more subtle: it is no longer the bright citrus of fresh lime but tastes instead of garlic and the other spices; the flavor has become pungent and the lime flavor is stronger as the oils from the zest have permeated the pickle.

5. Store in jars, with lids tightened, in the fridge, leaving as little headroom as possible, and tamping the limes down under the brine. This ferment will keep, refrigerated, for a long time, 18 months or more.

Christopher Writes

✴ On my first trip into the countryside of Andhra Pradesh, I learned two things right away: just how efficient a meal can be, and that preserved lemons in India are spicy.

We spent the morning shuttling among government projects in cramped taxis. The success of every project may have been narrated by a different official each time, but the message was always clear: with more money, they could do so much more. By noon I was exhausted from the heat and humidity, the montage of bright colors, the loud sounds, the strong smells.

As we washed our hands and gathered in an open concrete government building, I could only wonder how they would cater for the dozen of us waiting to be fed.

In walked a small man carrying in both hands beautiful stacked stainless-steel containers, one small man delivering enough food for a dozen people. Among the dishes was a preserved lemon pickle that blew my mind and almost melted my forehead.

Preserved Lemons

yield: about 1 quart
(fermentation vessel: 2 quarts)
technique used: Relishes, Chutneys, Salsas, and Fermented Salads (page 66)

This highly salted, acidic lemon is a flavoring ingredient. Take a bit of preserved lemon from the jar and cut into a fine dice. The lemony flavor you expect is actually mellow; the salty-sour elements enhance a hint of sweetness. *Note:* To tone down the saltiness, simply rinse the bit of preserved lemon before you use it.

8 whole lemons, regular or Meyer
½–1 cup unrefined sea salt, plus 2 tablespoons
Freshly squeezed lemon juice, as needed

1. Rinse the lemons in cold water. Trim about ¼ inch from the tip of each. Cut the lemons as if you were going to slice them in half lengthwise, starting from the tip, but end the cut before you're all the way through; in other words, keep the lemons attached at the base. Now make a cut in the other direction, so the lemons are in quarters but still attached at the base. Remove the seeds and put the fruit in a large bowl. Rub generous amounts of salt in and around each lemon.

2. Pack the lemons in a jar or crock, pressing so juice rises to the top. Make sure the lemons are submerged in the juice-brine. To fill to the brim and ensure immersion, add freshly squeezed lemon juice as needed. Sprinkle 2 tablespoons of salt over the surface. Top the ferment with a quart-sized ziplock bag. Press the plastic down onto the top of the ferment, fill it with water, and seal; this will act as both follower and weight.

3. Set aside on a baking sheet to ferment, somewhere nearby, out of direct sunlight, and cool, for 21 to 30 days. Check periodically to make sure the lemons stay submerged.

4. The lemons will be ready after 21 days but can go longer if you like. Taste and decide; the changes are in the richness of the thick brine and infusion of the zesty flavor.

5. To store, tamp down to make sure the lemons are submerged in brine. Screw on the lid, then store in the fridge. This ferment will keep, refrigerated, for at least 18 months.

Create Your Own Recipes

» Add spices to the lemons. Traditional additions are cinnamon sticks, peppercorns, whole cloves, coriander seeds, juniper seeds, and bay leaves.

» Think South America! Preserve limes or lemons with garlic, onions, coriander, cilantro, and plenty of hot pepper. Chop fine and add to fresh tomatoes for a salsa or to a ceviche.

» Use grapefruit juice in sauerkraut to add citrus notes to the acidic flavor.

» Add orange zest or orange juice to ferments and chutneys; they hold their flavor through the fermentation process.

CRANBERRIES

They sailed to the Western Sea, they did,
To a land all covered with trees,
And they bought an Owl, and a useful Cart,
And a pound of Rice, and a Cranberry Tart,
And a hive of silvery Bees.
— EDWARD LEAR, *THE JUMBLIES*, 1871

Cranberry relish might just be more American than apple pie. (*Gasp!*) Here's why. The cranberry, *Vaccinium macrocarpon* and *V. oxycoccus*, is one of the three commercial fruit crops indigenous to the North American continent. They're native from Maine west to Wisconsin and south along the Appalachians to North Carolina. They're an introduced crop in the Northwest (Oregon, Washington, and British Columbia). Cranberries are water-lovers: they grow in bogs and marshes.

Native Americans used the cranberry extensively, as food and medicinally as a poultice against food poisoning. They ate them raw, they used them in pemmican (a sort of beef jerky), they sweetened them with maple syrup.

Early colonists got into the act, and cranberries were on the first Thanksgiving table.

Today we know about the list of health benefits accrued to this tart red berry: they're loaded with antioxidants; they're anti-inflammatory; with regular consumption, they may protect against various cancers.

You get all this when you ferment the berries, but without all the sugar and other additives that go into a commercial bottle of cranberry juice. Oh, and you get the bright cranberry taste too.

YOUR RAW MATERIAL

Cranberry season generally begins in September and runs through December. They often go on sale the week before Thanksgiving, which is a good time to put in a crock or two. Why limit this fruit to the holidays? You'll want to enjoy this condiment all year long.

IN THE CROCK
Cranberry Relish

See photo on page 257

yield: about 1 quart

(fermentation vessel: 2 quarts)

technique used: Relishes, Chutneys, Salsas, and Fermented Salads (page 66)

This is a simple conversion of traditional cooked cranberries with oranges to a fermented relish. Adding juice-sweetened dried cranberries balances the tartness of fresh ones. If it's not sweet enough for your taste, simply splash in a bit of maple syrup or honey before serving. *Note:* Although it's always better to use fresh ingredients, you can make this relish with frozen cranberries. It'll have a softer consistency but is otherwise just as scrumptious.

- 2 oranges
- 2 (8-ounce) packages fresh cranberries
- ½ teaspoon unrefined sea salt
- 1 cup fruit juice–sweetened dried cranberries
- 1 tablespoon chopped candied ginger (optional)

1. Wash the oranges, and zest one of them. Peel and section both oranges, then remove the membranes from the sections (the chewy, sometimes bitter membranes can negatively affect the texture of the ferment). Chop the sections and set aside.

2. Wash the fresh cranberries and put them in a food processor; pulse until lightly chopped. Transfer to a bowl and massage in the salt for a minute to develop the brine. Then mix in the dried cranberries, the orange zest and sections, and the ginger, if using.

3. Press the mixture into a jar or crock, making sure there are no air pockets. The brine will be a little thick from the oranges. Top the ferment with a quart-sized ziplock bag. Press the plastic down onto the top of the ferment, then fill it with water and seal; this will act as both follower and weight.

4. Set aside on a baking sheet to ferment, somewhere nearby, out of direct sunlight, and cool, for 5 to 7 days. Check daily to make sure the fruits are submerged, pressing down as needed to bring the brine to the surface. You may see scum on top; it's generally harmless, but consult the appendix if you're at all concerned.

5. Test the ferment on day 5. It will be the same deep crimson color of cooked relish and will have two sour notes: one from the cranberries and one from fermentation.

6. Store in jars, with lids tightened, in the fridge, leaving as little headroom as possible, and tamping the relish down under the brine. This ferment will keep, refrigerated, for 6 months.

IN THE PICKLE JAR
Pickled Cranberries

See photo on page 153

yield: about 1 quart

(fermentation vessel: 1 quart or larger)

technique used: Mastering Brine Pickling (page 77)

The trickiest part about pickling cranberries is that they really want to float, which makes sense, as they're harvested by flooding the bogs and then scooping the berries off the surface. For the primary follower, use food-grade plastic screening (page 36) cut to the size of the jar or crock.

2 (8-ounce) packages fresh cranberries
5 slices fresh or candied ginger
2 cinnamon sticks
1 tablespoon whole cloves
1 gallon Basic Brine (½ cup unrefined sea salt
    to 1 gallon unchlorinated water)
  Grape leaves (optional)

1. Rinse the cranberries in cold water. Combine with the ginger, cinnamon, and cloves in a large bowl; mix thoroughly.

2. Pack the mixture into a crock or jar. Pour in enough brine to cover the cranberries completely. Reserve any leftover brine in the fridge. (It will keep for 1 week; discard thereafter and make a new batch, if needed.)

3. Place a primary follower such as a round of food-grade screening to keep the berries from floating out of the brine. For a crock, top with a plate that will rest atop the berries, and a weight such as a sealed water-filled jar to keep things in place. If using a jar, top with a sealed water-filled jar or ziplock bag.

4. Set aside on a baking sheet to ferment, somewhere nearby, out of direct sunlight, and cool, for 7 to 21 days. During the fermentation period, monitor the brine level and top off with the reserved brine solution, if needed, to cover. You may see scum on top; it's generally harmless, but consult the appendix if you're at all concerned.

5. As the mixture ferments, the berries begin to lose their vibrant color. The brine will become only slightly cloudy, unlike other ferments, but will instead be the color of a rich rosé wine. You can start to test as soon as 7 days. The ferment is ready when the brine tastes acidic, like spiced vinegar, and the berries taste pickled.

6. Store in jars, adding fresh brine to cover if needed. Top with clean grape leaves, if you have some, then screw on the lids and store in the fridge. These pickles will keep, refrigerated, for 12 months.

Part 4

On the Plate

Sauerkraut is tolerant, for it seems to be a well of contradictions. Not that it would preach a gastronomic neutrality that would endure all heresies. It rejects dogmatism and approves of individual tastes. It forms a marvelous combination with numerous spices: juniper berries, coriander seeds, peppercorns, cranberries, apples, stock, and wine. . . . Its flavor sustains various potato dishes. . . . The variety of meats to which it consents is infinite: sausages of all kinds, hams, bacon, quenelles, pickled and smoked pork, goose, pheasant, etc. It makes excuses for red wine, although it has a weakness for beer. . . . Each stomach may find its own happiness in it.

— JULIEN FREUND (1921–1993), FRENCH SOCIAL SCIENTIST

HERE YOU ARE: you've made or bought some ferments. You know these fermented vegetables are good for you, you know they taste good on your fork straight out of a jar, but that only goes so far. What else can you do with these "sauer" vegetables?

We hope that the recipes in this chapter not only bring flavor and joy to your table but also help you understand ferments as an ingredient like any other, and that you use these "new" ingredients, tossing them into a dish as readily as any familiar one.

The full probiotic benefits of lacto-fermented vegetables come when they are consumed raw. But we also believe that eating home-preserved local vegetables is a priority. While the probiotics may be lost in the process of cooking, the essential nourishment is not. "Sauered" cabbage came into being as a way to keep people fed through the lean months of winter. These traditional meals were cooked for hours not only to nourish, but also to warm souls on cold nights.

We offer recipes that are cooked, and we believe remarkable flavor is worth the cooking. We also include recipes where the ferment is added at the end of the cooking time — this will lightly warm the ferment, but not damage the probiotics. Keeping the temperature of the ferment under 110°F will preserve the integrity of the probiotic enzymes.

In general, when cooking significant quantities of fermented vegetables or fermented brine, use nonreactive cookware, because acidity can leach from the reactive metals, causing off-flavors and colors (see page 31). Examples of what not to use are aluminum, copper, and cast-iron pots. For meals using just a splash of brine, which is no different from cooking with a splash of vinegar or lemon juice, this is not an issue.

We have tried to balance meals that require time and thought with recipes that are designed to be simple and quick. There are days when you have time to cook and want to produce something special, and there are the everyday moments when you don't have much time to get a meal to the table but still want to eat fresh, healthy food. Ferments are perfect for building, or adding to, simple quick meals, exponentially improving health and flavor. To this end, at the start of most chapters you'll find our Quick and Easy section, which offers simple ideas for getting ferments into your meals without digging deep into a recipe.

The thread that binds the recipes is fermented vegetables, not a particular cuisine. We are foodies, and we love the food of many cultures, sometimes pure and traditional and sometimes mixed and matched. Many of these recipes are a fusion of places and flavors that some might think break some sacred culinary rules, like kimchi that lands in cheese, oatmeal, or latkes (and we know we're not alone; we've seen the kimchi taco truck). Lastly, we hope these recipes will inspire you to fashion your own new family favorites.

CHAPTER 9

Breakfast

CULTURE FOR THE GUTSY

When we worked the markets, some people couldn't imagine kraut in the morning; others couldn't start without it. Once tried, ferments for breakfast become almost an addiction. So many people, ourselves included, have felt our days start brighter with improved digestion. From elaborate weekend breakfasts to simple spreads to top your toast, we hope these ideas enhance your mornings.

Most of the ways we eat our ferments just happen; there are no recipes. Having a ferment on the table with any meal is as natural as the ever-present salt and pepper shakers.

There is a pantheon of regular flavors. These are the ones that we know will dress up the meals, whose flavors will blend and satisfy the simplest of foods. For us this is Curtido (page 133), Leek–Cracked Pepper Kraut (page 192) or Fresh Nettle Kraut (page 263), Edgy Veggies (page 155), a chile paste of some kind (page 213), and Kimchi (page 141). You'll find your favorites, and before you know it you will be just adding the ferments and not thinking twice.

Rancher Enchiladas, page 287

Hot Cereal

Make your favorite oatmeal, steel-cut or regular, soaked or instant. Just be sure to cook it in water, not milk.

Top with a pat of butter or a tablespoon of olive oil, and heap on a healthy dose of kimchi. Or substitute hot rice cereal for oats, add an egg, and top with fermented veggies.

Fruit and Green Smoothies

Don't forget to add fermented goodies to your smoothies. A tablespoon or two of Cranberry Relish (page 274) or Carrot Kraut (page 149) adds pizazz to fruit-based smoothies, both green and yogurt. If you are a savory green smoothie drinker, the field is wide open; pick any kraut or brine to liven it up.

Omelets, Scrambles, Breakfast Burritos, and Eggs

Any egg breakfast lends itself to the addition of a kraut or fermented vegetable. Toss a little kraut into scrambled eggs at the end of cooking. Pour Sweet Pepper Salsa (page 215) on top of over-easy eggs or huevos rancheros. And here are some of the endless omelet possibilities:

» Lemon-Dill Kraut (page 134), cheese, and sautéed mushrooms
» Onion and Pepper Relish (page 203) with cheese
» Salmon, sour cream, and Lemon-Dill Kraut (page 134) (or other kraut)

» Leek–Cracked Pepper Kraut (page 192) with ham
» Curtido (page 133), chorizo, and cheese

Schmears

"Schmear" is New York deli slang for a bagel topping, like cream cheese. These spreads can be schmeared on anything from a bagel or toast to tortillas or collard leaves.

The instructions are the same for each of these. Place room-temperature cheese in a food processor with the rest of the ingredients. Add brine as needed to achieve a creamy texture. These spreads will keep, covered, for 1 week in the refrigerator.

Herb Schmear

8 ounces cream cheese, softened
1–2 tablespoons fermented paste: chives
(page 202), basil (page 114), etc.
A few teaspoons fermented brine or lemon
juice

Combine the cream cheese and paste in the food processor and blend until combined. Add brine as needed to achieve a creamy texture.

KRAUTCHEESE,
page 284

HERB SCHMEAR,
page 282

GADO GADO SCHMEAR,
page 284

Kimcheese

- 8 ounces cream cheese, softened
- 4 tablespoons Kimchi (page 141)
- A few teaspoons fermented kimchi brine or lemon juice

Combine the cream cheese and kimchi in the food processor and blend until combined. Add brine as needed to achieve a creamy texture.

Krautcheese

- 8 ounces cream cheese, softened
- 3 ounces feta cheese
- ¾ cup kraut of choice: Lemon-Dill (page 134), Greek Lemon-Mint (page 134), or Lemon Spinach (page 233)
- A few teaspoons fermented brine or lemon juice

Combine the cream cheese, feta, and kraut in the food processor and blend until combined. Add brine as needed to achieve a creamy texture.

Cranberry Blue Cheese

- 8 ounces cream cheese, softened
- 3 ounces blue cheese
- ½ cup Pickled Cranberries (page 274)
- A few teaspoons extra cranberry brine or lemon juice

Combine the cream cheese, blue cheese, and cranberries in the food processor and blend until combined. Add brine as needed to achieve a creamy texture.

Gado Gado Schmear

- 1 cup peanut butter
- ½ teaspoon honey
- ½ teaspoon shoyu or soy sauce
- ½ cup Kimchi (page 141)

Combine the peanut butter, honey, and shoyu in a bowl. Lightly squeeze the kimchi to drain, saving the brine; chop finely. Add the kimchi to the peanut butter mixture. Stir until smooth, adding brine as needed to achieve a creamy texture.

Sauerkraut Frittata

serves 4

Gluten-Free, Vegetarian

Sauerkraut is a natural with meats and sausage, and it is just as well suited to eggs and cheese. A frittata is essentially a flat omelet that has the stuffing baked into it. It has the flamboyance of a quiche without the work or the gluten of the crust. Another advantage is that it is ready to be served all at once, with none of the hassle of keeping individual omelets warm.

The beauty of this recipe is that it can be varied easily just by changing the type of kraut or herbs. For a richer dish, add smoked salmon or Italian sausage.

1 medium onion, thinly sliced

2 tablespoons olive oil

6 eggs

Salt and freshly ground black pepper

Scant ¼ teaspoon freshly grated nutmeg

3 cloves garlic, minced

1½ cups Naked Kraut (page 132), or any other kraut, drained

2 tablespoons butter

2 tablespoons Parmesan cheese (optional)

1. Preheat the oven to 350°F.

2. Sauté the onion slowly in 1 tablespoon of the olive oil until caramelized; set aside.

3. Crack the eggs into a large bowl. Add salt and pepper to taste, nutmeg, the remaining 1 tablespoon of the oil, and the garlic. Beat lightly.

4. Gently squeeze the kraut to remove most of the liquid; it should be moist but not dripping. Stir the kraut and the cooled caramelized onions into the egg mixture.

5. Heat a 10-inch ovenproof sauté pan over medium-low heat. Melt the butter in the pan, turn off the heat, and pour in the egg-kraut mixture. Then transfer the pan to the oven.

6. Bake 20 to 25 minutes, or until set.

7. Remove from the oven and sprinkle with the cheese, if using.

Christopher Writes

Though it may seem an eternity when you're in the middle of it, the bountiful zucchini days are not all that long. During the zucchini storm, zucchini muffins are a standard at our farm, mostly because it's harvest season, which means breakfast comes between early-morning garden harvesting and midmorning in the fermentation kitchen.

We have tried to preserve the bounty through freezing and drying, and both work reasonably well. Kirsten has used the frozen shredded zucchini in sauces of various stripes in the winter, and the seasoned dried zucchini chips are popular straight out of the dehydrator, which means they don't last long. We were looking for something new when Kirsten gave fermentation a try, and the positive results gave us another preservation option for the abundance.

Now our muffin breakfasts extend into autumn, at least until our last crock of fermented zucchini is finished. I love all things sweet as much as Kirsten loves savory, so we have a recipe for both camps. If you have a favorite zucchini muffin recipe, try it with fermented zucchini. Our only suggested modification is to reduce the salt a bit, maybe by a third. You will also find these muffins rise wonderfully.

Savory Zucchini Muffins

yield: 12 large muffins

VEGETARIAN

These muffins are best eaten warm with a thick slab of butter in the middle or slathered with cream cheese.

- 6 tablespoons coconut oil, melted and cooled
- 2 eggs
- 2 cups unbleached all-purpose flour
- 2½ teaspoons baking powder
- ½ teaspoon salt
- 1 tablespoon minced fresh sage or 1 teaspoon dried sage
- 1 tablespoon minced fresh parsley
- 1 teaspoon minced fresh rosemary or ½ teaspoon dried rosemary
- 1–2 scallions, thinly sliced
- 2 cups Zucchini Kraut (page 253)

1. Preheat the oven to 350°F. Grease a 12-cup muffin pan.

2. Beat the coconut oil and eggs in a large bowl.

3. In another bowl, sift together the flour, baking powder, and salt. Add the herbs and scallions.

4. Alternate adding the fermented zucchini and the dry ingredients to the wet mixture.

5. Fill the muffin cups two-thirds full.

6. Bake for 35 to 40 minutes, or until a toothpick inserted in the center comes out clean.

7. Let the muffins cool for a few minutes before removing them from pan.

Spiced Zucchini Muffins

yield: 12 large muffins

VEGETARIAN

Little time is needed to get these muffins ready for the oven since the zucchini is already prepared.

- 6 tablespoons coconut oil, melted and cooled
- ⅓ cup sugar
- 2 eggs
- 1½ teaspoons vanilla extract
- 2 cups unbleached all-purpose flour
- 2½ teaspoons baking powder
- 1 teaspoon cinnamon
- ¾ teaspoon allspice
- ½ teaspoon ground ginger
- ½ teaspoon nutmeg
- ½ teaspoon salt
- 2 cups Zucchini Kraut (page 253)
- ½ cup raisins or currants
- ½ cup chopped walnuts

1. Preheat the oven to 350°F. Grease a 12-cup muffin pan.

2. Beat the coconut oil, sugar, eggs, and vanilla in a large bowl.

3. In another bowl, sift together the flour, baking powder, spices, and salt.

4. Alternate adding the fermented zucchini and the dry ingredients to the wet mixture. Fold in the raisins and walnuts.

5. Fill the muffin cups two-thirds full.

6. Bake for 35 to 40 minutes, or until a toothpick inserted in the center comes out clean.

7. Let the muffins cool for a few minutes before removing them from the pan.

Rancher Enchiladas

see photo on page 280

serves 6

Gluten-Free

Years ago, when we were still in college, a friend made a variation of this recipe. These were the enchiladas that her mom ate on the ranch she grew up on in Silver City, New Mexico. We dubbed them Rancher Enchiladas, and the recipe has traveled with us through the years and is now updated with the addition of curtido. This Latin American ferment shines here. Prepare this for a Sunday morning brunch or for any meal.

This recipe is simple, but it requires a bit of finesse at the end to put it all together and get the six plates to the table.

FILLING

- 1 onion, diced
- 1 tablespoon olive oil
- 1 pound ground grass-fed beef
- 1 tablespoon chile powder
- ½ teaspoon ground cumin

- 1 dozen corn tortillas
- ½–1 cup coconut or other frying oil
- 2 cups Curtido (page 133)
- 3 cups or 2 (16-ounce) cans red enchilada sauce
- 6 eggs
- Butter, for frying eggs
- ½ pound cheese, Cheddar or jack style, shredded

1. Preheat the broiler. Set six ovenproof plates on the counter.

2. Make the filling: Sauté the diced onion in the olive oil until translucent; add the beef. Sprinkle in the chile powder and cumin, and continue to fry until the beef is browned and cooked through. Keep the filling warm over low heat.

3. Fill the bottom of a small pan with enough oil to cover a tortilla. Heat the oil until very hot but not smoking, and fry the tortillas, one at a time, for about 5 seconds each, until softened but not crisp.

4. Using tongs, transfer the tortillas to a paper-towel-lined baking sheet to drain.

5. Place one tortilla on each plate. Evenly divide the beef filling among the tortillas. Spoon about ⅓ cup curtido over each one and top with another tortilla.

6. Using multiple pans, fry the eggs over-easy in the butter, and place one on top of each tortilla stack.

7. Divide the enchilada sauce evenly over the tortillas, sprinkle on the cheese, and place the plates under the broiler for 5 to 8 minutes to melt the cheese. Serve immediately.

Smoky Kraut Quiche

serves 6 to 8

VEGETARIAN

The smoky kraut gives this a rich "meaty" flavor, while remaining totally vegetarian. We often serve this at our class, Kraut Around the Clock. While our students are in the fermentation kitchen with Kirsten, Christopher is in the other kitchen preparing all things sauerkraut for lunch.

CRUST

1⅓ cups unbleached all-purpose flour
7 tablespoons cold butter, cut into small pieces
1 egg
Pinch of salt

FILLING

2 cups Smoky Kraut (page 135), with brine squeezed out
8 ounces Swiss cheese, shredded
3 eggs
1 cup half-and-half
¼ teaspoon nutmeg

1. Make the crust: Put the flour in a bowl and rub in the butter. Add the egg and the salt, and combine with a fork until the mixture resembles a coarse meal.

2. Transfer the dough to a floured work surface and knead lightly until the mixture holds together. Try not to overwork the dough.

3. Shape the dough into a 4-inch disc, wrap in plastic, and refrigerate for 30 minutes.

4. Meanwhile, prepare the filling: Put the drained kraut in a bowl and toss with the shredded cheese. In another bowl, whisk the eggs with the half-and-half; stir in the nutmeg.

5. Preheat the oven to 400°F.

6. Remove the dough from the refrigerator and let soften for 5 minutes. Roll out the dough on your work surface, flouring the rolling pin as necessary, to fit a 9-inch pie pan. Fit the crust in the pan and crimp the edge.

7. Spread the kraut/cheese mixture in the crust evenly, then pour the egg mixture over that.

8. Bake the quiche for 30 minutes, until set and nicely browned. Let cool for 5 to 10 minutes before serving.

SMOKY KRAUT QUICHE

CHAPTER 10

Snacks

A PICKLE A DAY KEEPS THE DOCTOR AWAY

Snack time is a good way to incorporate fermented vegetables into your children's (or any finicky eater's) diet. (Children's taste buds are more receptive and therefore more sensitive.) At our market booth we have observed young children who just cannot get enough Lemon-Dill Kraut, or even kimchi. We often wondered if these children's bodies might be craving fermented food.

This chapter starts with crackers, crisps, and dips and ends with snacks that can also be hors d'oeuvres — ferments sophisticated enough to be paired with wines.

Brine Crisps

yield: 1 pound crisps
Gluten-Free, Raw, Vegan

So now that you are a fermentista, your refrigerator contains many colors and flavors of kraut, kimchi, and pickles. You are setting out a fermented favorite with every meal.

But there is something else: a collection of small jars in the back of your refrigerator with leftover brine from the sauerkraut, kimchi, or pickles. As a fermentista you know to save all this wonderful elixir that is left at the bottom of your crock or jar. As purveyors of all things kraut, we ended up with very big jars of leftover brine. That is when we developed these popular crisps (and the crackers on the facing page).

These are like chips — unevenly sized and you can't stop putting them in your mouth. You can use either brown or golden flax seeds. We like to use a mix because it gives the crackers a textured look between the darker and duller-looking brown seeds and the shiny golden ones.

> 2 **cups flax seeds (a mix of brown and golden is nice)**
> 1½ **cups any fermented brine**
> 1 **cup spring water**

1. Mix the flax seeds and brine in a container that can hold them plus expansion as the seeds soak up the brine.

2. Cover the container with a lid and let soak for 12 hours, stirring occasionally if convenient (in other words, if you are starting the soak at night to make crackers the next day, no need get up through the night and stir).

3. Spread your gelatinous flax-seed goo evenly on dehydrator trays equipped with sheets for making fruit leathers. Don't try spreading this on the normal dehydrator screens (like we did our first batch) unless you have great patience for cleaning tiny ironed-on seeds out of the mesh. The thinner you spread, the thinner the crisps. With practice, you can get the seeds so thinly spread that when they are finished you can break them up with your hands to the size you like. If you decide to leave them a bit thicker, the crisps will work better for dipping into spreads.

4. Dehydrate at or below 103°F.

5. Check the crisps after 10 to 12 hours. When they are mostly dry, flip them over to finish evenly, about 1 hour longer.

6. When the crisps are completely dry and crispy, break the sheets apart to the desired size. Store in an airtight container. They will keep fresh for several weeks. If you want to re-crisp them, you can do this by dehydrating them for about an hour.

Brine Crackers

See photo on page 290
yield: 1 pound crackers
Gluten-Free, Raw, Vegan

This recipe is versatile and can be varied by using different nuts, or substituting part of the flax seeds with chia seeds. These crackers are a variation on the recipe at left but have a different consistency than the wispy Brine Crisps. They are cut into small squares and hold up to spreads. The crackers (and the crisps) take on the flavors of whatever fermented brine you soak the seeds and nuts in. Some of our favorites flavors include New York Deli–Style Pickle crackers (page 168), Kimchi crackers (page 141) with their hint of spicy-hot, and Curtido crackers (page 133).

- ¾ **pound flax seeds (a mix of brown and golden is nice)**
- ¼ **pound almonds**
- 1 **quart fermented brine**

1. Mix the seeds, nuts, and brine in a bowl or container with a lid and soak for 12 hours, stirring occasionally if convenient.

2. In a food processor, blend the mixture to a uniform consistency, then spread evenly on dehydrator tray sheets as described in the Brine Crisps recipe, at left.

3. Dehydrate at or below 103°F.

4. Check the crackers after 10 to 12 hours. When they are mostly dry, flip them over to finish them evenly, another 1 to 2 hours.

5. Transfer to a cutting board and cut to the desired size. Store in an airtight container. The crackers will keep fresh for several weeks.

CRISP AND CRACKER TIPS

» Flip your crackers or crisps over when they are still a little sticky but mostly dried. This way you will get both sides nicely dried.

» Better dehydrators can give you better results in terms of the evenness of the drying and preservation of the raw enzymes. Choose one with a thermostat and timer if possible.

» If using a household blender instead of a food processor, add a little cracker mixture at a time and empty into a large bowl as soon as the blades begin to struggle to process everything evenly.

» If using a Champion-style juicer instead of a food processor, be sure to use the blank to push everything straight through instead of the juicing screens.

» Your yield will equal the amount of seeds you start with, so 1 pound of seeds, mixed with a quart of brine, results in a little more than 1 pound of crackers.

» Walnuts can replace the almonds. The flavor is nice; however, the cracker may be a little more "oily."

» Try any brines: beet, dill pickle or any pickle brine, almost any kraut or kimchi, your own special combination . . .

» If you don't have enough brine for the recipe, use what you have and make up the difference with unchlorinated water. The flavor will be much more subtle but still delicious.

Pickled Almonds

yield: 4 cups

GLUTEN-FREE, VEGAN

Soaking nuts in salt water is important in increasing their digestibility. Nuts contain enzyme inhibitors and phytic acid; both are broken down by soaking. The salt neutralizes the enzyme inhibitors, allowing our bodies to absorb the nuts properly. So it was a natural for us to use ferment-enhanced salt water, or brine, to soak the nuts.

The best part is the sublime addictive flavor that this achieves — crispy with a hint of salt. Curried brine on cashews, Curtido brine on pumpkin seeds . . . let your imagination lead you.

This recipe calls for almonds. The process is the same for whatever nut you choose to soak: walnuts, pecans, cashews, hazelnuts, pine nuts, pumpkin seeds, or any other seed or nut.

4 cups almonds or other nuts
Enough fermented brine to cover the nuts

1. Soak the nuts in the brine for 12 hours.

2. Spread the nuts out on a dehydrator tray.

3. Dehydrate at 103°F or less for a total of 12 to 14 hours.

4. Check the nuts after 10 to 12 hours. If they are dry, they will be lightly crispy; if not, the mouth-feel will be soft and pithy. If the nuts are not dry, continue dehydrating for another couple of hours. It is important that your nuts are fully dry, or else they could become moldy when stored — that is, assuming they aren't gone as quickly as they are around here.

5. Store in an airtight container. They'll keep fresh for several weeks.

Chipotle Kraut Dip

See photo on page 290

yield: about 1 cup

GLUTEN-FREE, VEGETARIAN

Though recently "discovered" by celebrity chefs and mainstream culture, chipotle peppers are believed to date back to the Aztec civilization. The presumption is that smoke-drying the jalapeños came about as a way to solve the problem of how to preserve the fleshy-walled rot-prone chiles. Or perhaps the Aztec celebrity chefs realized that the smoky notes followed by the jalapeño's heat was a winning combination.

As we mentioned, the heat of the pepper comes from the alkaloid compound capsaicin (page 212). This capsaicin fire is "put out" (or at least mellowed) by the fats in the sour cream or avocado, making the dip a mild snack.

Serve this dip with chips, crackers, or veggies slices such as carrot, celery, and bell peppers.

½ cup Chipotle Squash Kraut (page 249)
½ cup sour cream

Simply mix the squash kraut with the sour cream in a bowl.

VARIATION: Vegan Dip

2 ripe avocados
½ cup Chipotle Squash Kraut
1 tablespoon lemon juice

1. Cut the avocados in half and remove the seeds. Scoop the avocado pulp into a bowl. Mash with a fork until a fairly smooth consistency.

2. Add the Chipotle Squash Kraut and the lemon juice. Stir until well mixed.

French Onion Dip

yield: 2 cups
GLUTEN-FREE, VEGETARIAN

This is not your grandmother's onion dip made with powdered soup mix; rather, it's an unprocessed probiotic dip that will satisfy that junk food desire, without the junk.

½ cup "Onion Soup" Seasoning (page 204)
1½ cups kefir cheese or sour cream
1 teaspoon paprika
Juice of 1 small lemon (2 tablespoons)
Pinch of salt

1. Put the dehydrated onion seasoning in a blender or food processor and pulse to break it up. Then add the kefir or sour cream, paprika, lemon juice, and salt. Pulse just enough to blend the ingredients.

2. Refrigerate the dip for a few hours to allow the flavors to mingle.

Sour Cream and Chives Dip

yield: 1 cup
GLUTEN-FREE, VEGETARIAN

It doesn't get simpler than this classic chip dip. If you are not one for potato chips, serve this on top of baked potatoes.

1 cup sour cream
1 tablespoon Fermented Chives (page 202)
Salt and freshly ground black pepper

Mix the sour cream with the chives, salt, and pepper, and serve.

Black Bean Salsa

See photo on page 290
yield: 2 cups
GLUTEN-FREE, VEGAN

When we have tortillas and cheese available, the go-to snack for our teenage children is quesadillas. Tortillas topped with cheese and Black Bean Salsa make a nutritious and robust enough snack to hold them until dinner. This salsa also works as a dip with corn chips.

1 cup cooked black beans
2 large tomatoes, diced
1 avocado, diced
½ bunch cilantro, chopped
½ cup fermented onions (page 201), chopped
1 teaspoon Garlic Paste (page 181) or
    1 clove garlic, minced
½ cup diced Edgy Veggies (page 155) or
    1 jalapeño, diced
Juice of 1 lime

1. Combine the beans, tomatoes, avocado, and cilantro in a bowl. Stir in the onions, Garlic Paste, Edgy Veggies, and lime juice.

2. Allow the salsa to sit, covered, at room temperature for an hour to let the flavors marinate.

3. Taste, and refrigerate when the flavors have blended. The salsa will keep for about a week refrigerated.

Radicchio Tapenade

See photo on page 290

yield: 2 cups

GLUTEN-FREE, VEGAN, RAW

If you want to ease into eating bitter vegetables, this recipe is perfect. The bitter element is softened by the strong flavors of the cured olives and capers. Enjoy this as a spread on your favorite substrate, such as crackers, crusty bread, or potatoes.

> 1 cup (packed) Radicchio-Garlic Kraut (page 218)
> 1 cup pitted kalamata olives, drained
> 1 (4-ounce) jar capers, drained
> 1–2 tablespoons olive oil (optional)

Put the kraut, olives, and capers into a food processor. Pulse until nearly smooth. Add the oil, if using, for a creamier texture.

Baba Ganoush

yield: 2 cups

GLUTEN-FREE, VEGAN, RAW

The beauty of this recipe is the speed with which it is carried out. No roasting and scraping hot eggplant, just measuring and blending. Since the fermented eggplant is already acidic, the lemon juice is also omitted.

This is good as a dip for pita triangles, chips, or crackers. It can be part of a Middle Eastern meze plate. And if you are looking for a hearty snack, it can also be used as spread on an open-faced sandwich or wrap.

> 2 cups Fermented Eggplant (page 174)
> ½ cup tahini
> 3 cloves garlic or 1 head roasted garlic

> 1–2 tablespoons chopped fresh or fermented parsley
> Pinch of salt
> Olive oil
> Smoked paprika

1. Put the eggplant, tahini, garlic, parsley, and salt in a food processor and purée.

2. Serve the dip in a shallow bowl, garnished with a drizzle of olive oil and a sprinkling of smoked paprika.

Kraut Balls

See photo on page 297

yield: 16 balls

Most of us can't resist something deep-fried, and these tangy, creamy balls are no exception. The history of sauerkraut balls lies somewhere in the area of Akron, Ohio. Being on the West Coast, we've never tasted authentic traditional ones, but our version is tasty. We do not specify what flavor kraut to use, having found that almost any one works well.

Serve as a hot hors d'oeuvre or a decadent side, with mustard sauce for dipping.

> 1 cup chopped ham
> 1 tablespoon butter
> 1 small onion, finely diced
> 1 cup unbleached all-purpose flour
> Pinch of dry mustard or ½ teaspoon prepared mustard
> 1 cup milk
> 2 cups sauerkraut, drained and finely chopped
> 1–2 tablespoons minced parsley
> ½ cup potato flour
> Enough coconut oil to deep-fry

KRAUT BALLS

KRAUT BALLS MUSTARD SAUCE

½ cup Dijon mustard
½ cup sour cream

1. Put the ham in a food processor and pulse until it is finely chopped.

2. Melt the butter in a skillet, and add onion and the ham. Sauté until the onion is translucent and lightly browned.

3. Stir in the flour, mustard, and milk. This will thicken quickly; keep stirring until the flour and milk are cooked. It will become a fluffy paste.

4. Take the pan off the stove and let cool. Mix in the sauerkraut and parsley.

5. When it is cool enough handle, roll the mixture into walnut-sized balls. They will be sticky, so roll them in a dish of potato flour, giving them a light coating. (This saves the step of rolling in beaten egg and breadcrumbs and gives the balls a crisp texture and a hint of French-fry flavor.)

6. Make the mustard sauce by mixing the mustard and sour cream together.

7. Heat the oil in a deep-fryer or saucepan. Drop the balls in the hot oil and fry until brown, about 5 minutes. Serve hot with mustard dipping sauce on the side.

Pickle in a Blanket

serves 6
GLUTEN-FREE

These are simple and satisfying, and they disappear quickly.

3–4 slices naturally cured pastrami
2–3 ounces chèvre or cream cheese, at room temperature
3–4 whole New York Deli–Style Pickles (page 168) (or other lacto-fermented dill pickle)

1. Lay out the slices of pastrami (the blankets) on a cutting board.

2. Spread a thin layer of chèvre across half of each pastrami slice.

3. Lay a pickle on the edge of each "blanket" and roll the pickle in it.

4. Slice the roll-ups into rounds.

Beet Kraut on Cucumbers

serves 6
GLUTEN-FREE, VEGETARIAN

This recipe definitely can be dressed up or down. Its fun color, crunchy and creamy texture, and slight sweetness please kids, but it also looks chic served on a wooden tray or beautiful plate as an hors d'oeuvre at a party.

4 ounces cream cheese or fresh chèvre, at room temperature
1 cucumber, sliced into rounds
½ cup Simple Beet Kraut (page 120), lightly drained
Dill weed, small sprigs (optional)

Spread the cream cheese on the cucumber rounds. Top each one with a dollop of beet kraut and garnish with a sprig of fresh dill, if you have some.

Smoky Dates

serves 6
GLUTEN-FREE

This hors d'oeuvre speaks for itself. Sweet, smoky, tangy! Omit the cheese and it becomes both vegan and raw.

   6 Medjool dates
   12 small, thin slices flavorful aged hard cheese (optional)
   ¼ cup Smoky Kraut (page 135), lightly drained, or Naked Kraut (page 132)

1. Slice the dates lengthwise. Remove the pits.

2. Stuff the dates with the cheese (if using) and top with kraut; otherwise omit the cheese and tuck a bit of kraut in each date.

CHAPTER 11

Lunch

FERMENTS ON THE GO

There is a proverb that goes: "Eat breakfast like a king, lunch like a prince, and dinner like a pauper." Many people believe this means your biggest meals should be enjoyed during the earlier parts of the day. While modern science tells us there is some truth to this old proverb, in many ways our modern lifestyle does not accommodate a rich, nutrient-dense lunch. This chapter will demonstrate simple ways that your midday meals can become nutritionally strong feasts. We'll begin with some quick and easy options for the road (like sandwich and wrap fillings, hand pastries, and salads) or meals that you can cook up at home without too much fuss.

Blaukraut with Blue Cheese and Walnuts, page 318
Tempeh Reuben, page 307

QUICK AND EASY LUNCH IDEAS

Sandwiches

While we've included specific recipes for sandwiches, any sandwich can take some kraut. And
don't let "sandwich" hold you back; all of the recipes in this chapter can be rolled up into your wrap
of choice. For hot sandwiches, add ferments after
grilling or near the end to avoid probiotic loss.

In this chapter we've got classics, healthy
twists, and some hearty, juicy, messy sandwich
fillings, because who can argue with the joy of a
messy sandwich? Enjoy these recipes on bread, in
a wrap, or just on their own with a green salad.

» Grilled cheese sandwich variations with
  kraut could be a whole chapter. Try Leek–
  Cracked Pepper Kraut (page 192) with
  sharp cheddar cheese, or Swiss cheese with
  horizontally sliced garlic dill pickles. Kathryn
  at Farmhouse Culture recommends fontina
  cheese melted over Farmhouse Culture's
  Apple-Fennel Kraut (page 268) on rye bread,
  paired with a glass of Sauvignon Blanc.
» Many ferments, not just dill pickles, are
  great chopped and tossed in a tuna salad,
  especially Curtido (page 133). Or make it
  salmon salad with OlyKraut's Eastern European Sauerkraut (page 138) and mayonnaise.
» Any pastrami or corned beef sandwich is a
  natural for kraut, especially the Reuben. Or
  try the Rachel: a Reuben made with turkey.
» Speaking of turkey, what about Cranberry
  Relish (page 274) and a little grilled Brie?

Wraps

Ethnic wrap breads — flatbreads, tortillas, pitas,
naan — have become vessels for myriad combinations: veggies, cheeses, meats, salads, ferments;
anything goes. The kraut, kimchi, relish, or pickles will provide the zing for anything you can
think up and wrap up.

Gluten-Free Wraps

For gluten-free wraps, use collard leaves. They are
sturdy enough to wrap like a burrito. Slice off the
thick stem at the base of the leaf, then run a rolling
pin quickly down the spine of the leaf to soften it
enough to fold or roll. If you want a bit more of a
tender wrap, wilt the leaf slightly by laying it quickly
on a hot, dry skillet.

Nachos, Quesadillas, Tacos, Burritos

Anything you would put salsa on can take a
ferment. Especially suited for this is Curtido
(page 133), Tomatillo Salsa (page 240), Chipotle
Squash Kraut (page 249), West African Sweet
Potato Ferment (page 238), or any of the pepper
and onion ferments. Using ferments for salsa is
particularly appealing in the winter months. They
add the much-needed bling to the winter array
when the fresh tomatoes are from far away and
the pico de gallo is crunchy.

Pizza

When we started asking people at the farmers' market how they ate sauerkraut, we were truly surprised at how many put sauerkraut on pizza as a topping. Though we admit to having a lot of unusual applications for kraut, it never even occurred to us to put it on pizza. Lacto-fermented olives yes, kraut nope.

It's great, in the same tangy way that pineapple is. Try it on your favorite combination of toppings. It works. Either dollop the kraut on top when the pizza comes out of the oven, or make sure the kraut is under the cheese. When exposed, the shreds of cabbage will burn before the pizza is done.

Sausages and Hot Dogs

Adding fermented condiments will up the culinary ante of a hot dog. To make this classic street food into an *haute* dog, choose the best-quality dog or brat you can find. Increasingly there are local producers making nitrate-free, all-grass-fed-beef hot dogs.

Don't forget the bun! Always warm your bun, and use good ones. Grocery store buns can melt or fall apart quickly from the moisture in the toppings. For a hardier bun, use thin baguettes. Cut the baguette to the length of your sausage. Slit it lengthwise, open, and remove a little bit of the soft center to create a nest for all the great toppings and to keep your dog from being too bready. (Our kids eat these soft bits immediately; if you don't have starving teenagers hovering, you can dip the soft bread in olive oil as a little snack.)

The topping arrangements that follow include our fermented takes on regional classics as well as combinations we dreamed up. Of course, adding any raw fermented kraut or vegetable to a hot dog and bun is delicious.

Christopher Writes

The scene: Produce market, busy street, person cautiously peering at the booth of the farmstead kraut purveyors.

"Would you like to sample some sauerkraut?"

"No, I forgot my hot dog," says the person as he walks away, laughing big belly laughs.

We heard this joke at least once every time we went to market. So here we go — we will say it anyway: kraut is amazing on a hot dog or bratwurst.

The Chicago Dog

Top with fermented onions (page 201), tomato wedges, a dill pickle spear, plenty of yellow mustard, Sweet Dill Relish (page 171), and a pinch of celery salt.

The Seattle Dog

Smear cream cheese on a bun. Add your dog and top with Onion and Pepper Relish (page 203), fermented jalapeños, or sliced Edgy Veggies (page 155) and a fermented hot pepper sauce (page 214).

All-the-Way Dog

This foot-long dog, found throughout the Southeast, has regional variations. The meat sauce in some regions is a beanless chili, and in others it is ground beef simmered for hours in ketchup, onions, and spices.

Slather your bun with yellow mustard. Top the dog with the meat sauce, fermented onions (page 201), and Coleslaw (page 320).

Chili Dog

Nest your hot dog in a bun. Top with chili, sharp cheddar cheese, and a generous dollop of Curtido (page 133). Garnish with chopped cilantro (fresh or fermented).

Bacon-Wrapped Dogs

A friend of ours who used to be a vegetarian calls bacon "the gateway meat." This combination of bacon and hot dog puts former vegetarians well over the carnivore threshold. Roll a medium-sliced uncured bacon strip around each hot dog and fry in a preheated heavy pan with the loose ends of the bacon tucked underneath the dog. Some people use toothpicks to hold the bacon in place; we don't. Just fry it slowly, turning the hot dog carefully, and the bacon will crisp into place.

» **WITH LEEK–CRACKED PEPPER KRAUT:** Top your bun with aioli, nest your bacon dog, and top with generous amounts of Leek–Cracked Pepper Kraut (page 192).

» **WITH WILTED SPINACH, ONIONS, AND BLUE CHEESE:** Line your bun with a bed of fresh baby spinach leaves. Place your bacon-wrapped dog in this. Top with Cebollas Encurtidas (page 204) and crumbled blue cheese.

Sweet Bratwurst Dog

Fry or grill a chicken bratwurst. Put it in a bun with sweet stone-ground mustard and aioli. Top with Apple-Fennel Kraut (page 268).

Eastern European Brat

Fry or grill your favorite local bratwurst. Put it in a bun with mustard. Top with grilled red pepper and a healthy dollop of OlyKraut's Eastern European Sauerkraut (page 138).

BACON-WRAPPED DOG

*Mike McNeil and
Tiffani Beckman-McNeil*

Backyard CSA

Tiffani Beckman-McNeil and her husband, Mike McNeil, promote local whole food in Sonoma County, California, where their business is Backyard CSA, a farm-to-table webstore. They are passionate about food, and this passion fuels a broader goal of healthier people and a healthier planet.

Mike spends a lot of time in the kitchen making good food, and he makes his own sausage from pastured pork.

Tiffani grew up in Kansas, her roots German, so sauerkraut was often on the table. It wasn't until her late 20s that she rediscovered this German cuisine staple through her exposure to the works of Weston A. Price, and in 2009 she made her first batch. Kirsten met Tiffani a few years later at the (then) Freestone Fermentation Festival where Tiffani was introducing people to Beet Kvass (page 125).

At that time Kirsten often asked people, "What is your favorite way to eat kraut?" Most often the answer involved a sausage. Tiffani's answer proved no different — except she uses Mike's homemade sausages, which they grill and top with raw shredded cheese and one of their ferments. She shared, "Mike's best achievement is our very popular dill pickle relish, made with fermented cucumbers and leeks. When we take it to shows, it sells out! I never liked relish until trying his concoction." Tiffani shares their recipe for Golden Ginger Beet Kvass with Meyer Lemon on page 126.

Tempeh Reuben

See photo on page 300

serves 6

VEGETARIAN

This is one of the first meals we made when we established our own kitchen during our vegetarian years, and it is one of the few recipes that has survived as our cooking style grew and changed.

This open-faced sandwich uses a few traditionally fermented ingredients, but it is definitely a fusion: tempeh from Indonesia, soy sauce from Japan, sauerkraut from the cold climes of Europe, and the concept of the Reuben sandwich from somewhat disputed origins in the early part of the twentieth century in the USA.

    1 (16-ounce) package soy tempeh
    ½ cup water
    ¼ cup soy sauce
  1–2 tablespoons canola oil
    1 medium onion, diced
    ½ cup mayonnaise (Homemade Sunflower
        Mayonnaise or Almonnaise; see page 320)
    1 tablespoon prepared horseradish
    6 pieces Jewish-style caraway-seeded rye
        bread
    2 cups Naked Kraut (page 132) or Simple Beet
        Kraut (page 120)
    2 cups grated Swiss cheese

1. Preheat the broiler.

2. Slice the tempeh thinly. Bring the water and soy sauce to a simmer in a skillet and add the tempeh slices. Simmer for 1 to 2 minutes on each side, cooking a salty flavor into the tempeh. Remove from the pan and set aside. Rinse the cooking liquid from the pan.

3. Return the pan to the stove and warm the oil over medium heat. Add the tempeh and onion to the pan and sauté until the onions are translucent and the tempeh is lightly browned. Remove from the heat and set aside.

4. Make the sauce by mixing the mayonnaise and horseradish together; slather this on the slices of bread.

5. Put the rye bread, sauce side up, on a baking sheet. Divide the tempeh mixture among the 6 sandwiches. Top each open-faced sandwich with a generous helping of sauerkraut and Swiss cheese.

6. Adjust the oven rack to the middle position and broil until the cheese is bubbling, about 5 minutes. Serve hot.

Tempeh Salad

serves 6

GLUTEN-FREE, VEGETARIAN, VEGAN

This sandwich filling is quite tasty and gives you a double dose of fermented foods. The fermented celery with sage and thyme, along with the pickle, gives this salad a fresh crunch.

    1 cup vegan chicken-flavored broth or chicken
        broth
    1 (16-ounce) block soy tempeh
  ½–1 cup mayonnaise, to taste (Homemade
        Sunflower Mayonnaise or Almonnaise;
        see page 320)
  3–4 tablespoons Celery "Stuffing" (page 159)
    1 New York Deli–Style Pickle (page 168), diced
    ¼ red onion, diced
      Salt and freshly ground black pepper

1. Bring the broth to a simmer and add the block of tempeh. Simmer 3 to 5 minutes on each side, allowing the tempeh to soak up the flavors. Watch the pan so that it does not run dry.

2. Remove the tempeh from the pan; let cool to the touch. Dice it into cubes and put them in a bowl with the mayonnaise, celery ferment, pickle, and onion, and add salt and pepper to taste.

3. Mix and serve on crusty bread, in a wrap, or on crackers (gluten-free if you wish), or rolled up in collard leaves.

VARIATION: Chicken Salad

Combine the same ingredients as above, using 2 cups cooked chicken meat instead of soaked tempeh.

Egg Salad 1

serves 6

GLUTEN-FREE, VEGETARIAN

This is the down-and-dirty version, meant to be on the table quickly.

- 1 **dozen eggs, hard-boiled and peeled**
- 1 **cup Simple Onion Relish (page 203), drained and chopped**
- 1 **New York Deli–Style Pickle (page 168) (or other lacto-fermented dill pickle), diced**
- ½ **cup mayonnaise (Homemade Sunflower Mayonnaise or Almonnaise; see page 320)**
  Salt and freshly ground black pepper

1. Put the eggs in a bowl, and chop them with a fork to the desired consistency.

2. Add the onion relish, pickle, mayonnaise, and salt and pepper to taste. Mix with the fork.

3. Spread the egg salad on rye bread or serve on a bed of lettuce.

Kirsten Writes

My Jewish grandmother made egg salad often. I loved it but thought she might kill me with the raw onions — at least socially. Once in a while she'd offer the onions sautéed in margarine with mushrooms. She would say it should be schmaltz, not margarine, but schmaltz wasn't available in rural Arizona and she would never have rendered her own chicken fat, unlike her traditionalist granddaughter. Could be that's why the onions were usually raw. I solved this problem with fermented onions.

MAKING SCHMALTZ

Schmaltz is rendered chicken fat that traditionally has been used much in the same way as butter — from frying potatoes to spreading on toast. The simplest way to make it is to chill the broth made from a whole chicken and then skim the yellow fat off the top of the broth. The other way is to collect the skins and any fat from your various chicken dishes and save them in the freezer until you have a pound or so. Once you have collected enough pieces, slowly sauté them, pouring off the grease as it melts. (Traditionally these leftover pieces were cooked with onions until crunchy and served as a dish in their own right.) Store schmaltz in a jar in the fridge for a month or in the freezer for 6 months.

Egg Salad 2

serves 6

GLUTEN-FREE, VEGETARIAN OPTION

This rich egg salad takes just a little more time to prepare.

    1 dozen eggs, hard-boiled and peeled
    2 cups sliced mushrooms
    2 tablespoons schmaltz (rendered chicken fat;
         see sidebar) or walnut oil
    2 cups Simple Onion Relish (page 203)
    ½ cup mayonnaise (Homemade Sunflower
         Mayonnaise or Almonnaise; see page 320)
       Salt and freshly ground black pepper

1. Put the eggs in a bowl, and chop them with a fork; set aside.

2. Sauté the mushrooms in the schmaltz or oil over medium heat until browned, then remove the pan from the heat.

3. Put the onion relish in the pan and toss with the mushrooms.

4. Add this mixture to the eggs, using a rubber spatula to blend thoroughly. Add the mayonnaise, salt and pepper, and mix.

5. Serve the egg salad chilled, preferably on dark rye bread or a bed of lettuce.

Fish Tacos

See photo on page 310

serves 8

GLUTEN-FREE

This recipe suggests three different ferments. Each lends its own mood to the tacos, and each version is delicious.

    4 (6-ounce) tilapia fillets
       Scant ¼ teaspoon salt, to rub on fish
    ¼ teaspoon black pepper
    1 tablespoon coconut oil
    8 corn tortillas
    2 cups Chipotle Squash Kraut (page 249) or
         Curtido (page 133); or 1 recipe Cabbage
         Salsa (page 321); or 1½ cups Chimichurri
         (page 207)
    4 jalapenõs, thinly sliced
       Lime wedges (optional)

1. Sprinkle the fish with salt and black pepper, and rub it in lightly.

2. Melt the coconut oil in a large skillet over medium-high heat, coating the pan. Lay the fish fillets in the pan, and cook for 3 minutes on each side or until the fish flakes easily.

3. Warm the tortillas on a dry, hot skillet until soft.

4. Divide the fish fillets, your chosen ferment, and the jalapeño slices evenly among tortillas. Serve with lime wedges, if desired.

SUSTAINABLE FISH

Fish can be a confusing food source. Which species are threatened? Which are are subject to heavy metal contamination? Which fish should be wild caught and which should be farmed? Then there are the nets and the dolphins. . . . Some farmed fish are proving to be a good protein choice for feeding an increasing population. Tilapia, tra, and barramundi can be produced sustainably in small-scale operations, feeding local economies. *Four Fish* by Paul Greenberg is an important book about our relationship with the sea and its food.

FISH TACOS, *page 309*

Classic Bierocks

serves 6 (2 bierocks per person)

Eastern European in origin, bierocks are traditionally meat-filled pastries. They can fall into the dinner or lunch category. The process takes a bit of time, but these handy stuffed hand rolls are excellent cold (for those who don't like warm sauerkraut) and easily taken on the go.

This recipe is a variation of a regional specialty from Kansas, thought to originate in German regions of Russia, where they are stuffed with cabbage. Substituting fermented cabbage seemed like a natural progression. We offer a few stuffing options below, but these are the perfect venue for playing with some of the creative flavors you come up with. Serve bierocks with mustard sauce.

DOUGH

- 2 (¼-ounce) packages active dry yeast
- 2 cups warm water
- ½ cup sugar
- 4 tablespoons butter, softened
- 1 egg
- 2 teaspoons salt
- 7 cups unbleached all-purpose flour

FILLING

- 1–2 tablespoons oil, for sautéing
- 1 medium onion, chopped
- 1 pound ground beef
- 2 cups sauerkraut, plain or mixture of choice, with the brine squeezed out
- Salt and freshly ground black pepper
- Pepper Paste (page 213) or red chile flakes, to taste (optional)

MUSTARD SAUCE

- ½ cup Dijon mustard
- ½ cup sour cream

1. Begin by making the dough: In a mixing bowl, dissolve the yeast in the warm water; let it proof in a warm place for a few minutes. Then mix in the sugar, butter, egg, salt, and half of the flour. Allow the sponge to rest for 10 minutes. Stir in the remaining flour 1 cup at a time by hand, forming a soft dough.

2. Put the dough in an oiled bowl, cover with plastic wrap, and refrigerate for 2 hours; or set it on the counter to rise at room temperature for 1 hour.

3. While the dough is rising, prepare the filling: Add the oil to a skillet and sauté the onions over medium heat until translucent. Crumble in the ground beef. When the meat is lightly browned, remove the pan from the heat. Add the sauerkraut, salt and pepper to taste, and pepper paste, if using.

4. When the dough has risen, punch it down, roll it out, and cut out about a dozen circles approximately 4 inches in diameter (we use the rim of a bowl for cutting). Repeat with the remaining circles of dough, gathering the scraps and re-rolling as needed to use up the dough.

5. Place about ⅓ cup of the stuffing mixture in the center of each circle of dough. Bundle the edges together and pinch closed.

6. Lightly grease a baking sheet. Lay the bierocks, pinched side down, on the baking sheet about 3 inches apart. Let rise in a warm, draft-free place for 30 minutes.

7. Meanwhile, prepare the mustard sauce: combine the mustard and sour cream and mix well.

8. Preheat the oven to 375°F.

9. Bake the bierocks for 20 to 30 minutes, until browned. Serve hot, with mustard sauce. Leftovers become pocket sandwiches the next day.

VARIATION: Greek Lamb Bierocks

Serve these Greek-inspired bierocks with a yogurt sauce.

FILLING

- 1 pound ground lamb
- 3 cloves garlic, minced
- 1–2 tablespoons olive oil, for sautéing
- 2 cups Greek Lemon-Mint Kraut (page 134)
- ½ cup crumbled feta cheese
- Salt to taste (*Note:* With salt in the kraut and in the feta, chances are you won't need additional salt)

YOGURT SAUCE

- 1 cup Greek yogurt
- 1 clove garlic, finely grated
- Salt to taste

1. Brown the lamb and garlic in olive oil over medium heat. Remove the pan from the heat. Add the drained sauerkraut and the feta.

2. Fill and bake the bierocks as in the main recipe (page 311). While they are baking, combine the ingredients for the yogurt sauce. Serve the bierocks hot with the yogurt sauce on the side as a dipping sauce.

VARIATION: Sweet Potato–Tofu Bierocks

VEGETARIAN

This variation of these tasty hand pastries is vegetarian.

FILLING

- 1–2 tablespoons coconut oil, for frying
- 16 ounces firm tofu, cut into cubes
- 1 medium onion, chopped
- 1 cup diced sweet potato, roasted until tender
- 2 cups Edgy Veggies (page 155), drained and pulsed briefly in a food processor
- ½ teaspoon salt
- Pinch of dried oregano, crumbled
- Chile pepper flakes to taste

CHIPOTLE MAYO

- 1 cup Homemade Sunflower Mayonnaise (page 320)
- ½ teaspoon chipotle powder, or to taste

1. Heat the oil in a skillet over medium heat, then carefully add the tofu cubes and fry until browned, 5 to 10 minutes. Add the onion and sauté until translucent, stirring constantly.

2. Add the sweet potato and stir until the pieces are coated and warmed through. Remove the pan from the heat. Add the Edgy Veggies, salt, and spices.

3. Fill and bake the bierocks as in the main recipe (page 311). While they are baking, combine the mayo and chipotle powder. Serve the bierocks hot with the chipotle mayo on the side for dipping.

Gazpacho

serves 6

GLUTEN-FREE, VEGAN (OMIT HONEY), RAW

This is a quick, healthy summer soup. It's a natural place to include fermented vegetables, herbs, or garlic. Pickled vegetables can be anything from summer squash to okra. Improvise with whatever you have. For strong spicy notes, stir in a bit of

Pepper Paste (page 213). We like our soup chunky, but all the ingredients can also be puréed.

     4 **cups tomato juice**
 1–2 **cups diced fresh tomatoes**
     2 **scallions, thinly sliced**
     2 **tablespoons olive oil**
     1 **teaspoon honey**
  1½ **cups diced Edgy Veggies (page 155), or a combination of pickled vegetables**
     3 **tablespoons Sweet Pepper Salsa (page 215)**
       Salt and freshly ground black pepper
     ¼ **teaspoon ground cumin**
     ¼ **teaspoon ground cayenne**

1. Combine the tomato juice, tomatoes, scallions, oil, and honey, in a large bowl. Stir in the ferments and seasonings, and mix well.

2. Chill for at least 1 hour. Serve with crusty bread for a light lunch or Sauerkraut Frittata (page 285) as part of a brunch menu.

Kirsten Writes

There is a clear division in our house — the mushroom lovers and those who will not have anything to do with a mushroom. Strangely enough, when we go on family mushroom hunts in the forest behind our farm, it is the non-eaters who find the most. I suspect the mushrooms know, and find them less threatening. While we don't find portobellos in the woods, I know I can always find them in the grocery store.

Stuffed Portobellos

serves 4
Gluten-free, Vegetarian

We made recipe cards to give to customers who wanted to know how to use kraut in recipes. This recipe was one of the first ones we came up with and remains one of our favorites. The earthy mushrooms, sharp cheese, and acidic kraut complement one another perfectly.

Crimini mushrooms or baby portobellos can be used to make this as an hors d'oeuvre instead of a main dish.

     4 **portobello mushrooms**
     1 **tablespoon butter**
     1 **tablespoon olive oil**
     4 **cloves garlic, minced**
     1 **cup drained and packed Lemon-Dill Kraut (page 134)**
     4 **ounces goat cheddar cheese, grated**
     1 **scallion, finely sliced**

1. Remove the stems from the mushrooms and chop. Set the caps aside, leaving them whole.

2. Heat the butter and oil in a large Dutch oven or other heavy pan with a lid. Add the mushroom stems and garlic and sauté lightly over medium heat.

3. Meanwhile, for the filling, loosely chop the drained sauerkraut and put it in a bowl. Add the cheese and scallions, then add the sautéed stems and garlic and toss together.

4. Leaving the oil in the pan, return it to the stove over low heat. Lay the mushroom caps in the pan, top sides down.

5. Divide the filling mixture into 4 portions and form patties. Place a patty on top of each portobello. Put the lid on the pan and continue to cook over low heat for 10 to 15 minutes. Preheat the broiler.

6. When the cheese has melted and the mushrooms are soft, place them under the broiler set on low to lightly brown the tops. Serve hot.

VARIATION

Put this filling on rye bread and toast slowly under a low broiler setting. Serve with a rice pilaf and fresh green salad.

Sushi-Norimaki

serves 4
GLUTEN-FREE, VEGAN

The first sushi was packaging for fermented fish. Cookbook author Madhur Jaffrey explains that records from sixth-century China describe preserving raw fish by wrapping it in boiled rice. Amino acids from the fermenting fish and lactic acids from the fermenting rice preserved the fish for as long as several years. The rice was thrown away when the fish was eaten. The same type of recipe showed up in eighth-century Japan, and eight centuries later the Japanese began eating both fish and rice that had been pickled over a few days. In the nineteenth century, vinegar replaced fermentation in the rice and fresh fish completed the transformation to the sushi we enjoy today.

Here, fermented vegetables bring the taste of fermentation back to sushi. This simple rolled sushi — norimaki — is made with a sheet of nori seaweed spread with vinegared rice and a line of filling.

VINEGARED RICE (SUMESHI)
- 1 cup sushi rice
- 3 tablespoons rice vinegar
- 1 tablespoon sugar
- 1 teaspoon salt

FILLING
- **Any fermented vegetables (whatever you have on hand), such as Fermented Carrot Sticks (page 151), Fermented Shiso Leaves (page 228), or Kimchi (page 141)**

ASSEMBLY
- 4 sheets nori
- 2 tablespoons sesame seeds
- 1–2 tablespoons pickled ginger
- 1–2 tablespoons wasabi paste
- Shoyu or soy sauce

1. For the vinegared rice: Soak the rice in cold water for 10 to 15 minutes; drain.

2. Transfer the rice to a saucepan and add 1 cup water. Cover and bring to a boil over high heat. Lower the heat and simmer, covered, for about 10 minutes, or until the water has been absorbed. (*Note:* The trick is not to remove the lid and yet know when the water has been absorbed; do your best, removing the lid to check quickly once.)

3. When the rice is cooked, remove the saucepan from the heat and set aside, covered, to rest for 10 minutes.

4. Meanwhile, mix the rice vinegar, sugar, and salt in a bowl until dissolved.

5. Place the rice in a shallow dish or casserole. Sprinkle the vinegar solution over the rice, then fold it in. Allow the rice to cool to tepid before you begin to roll.

6. Prepare your choice of pickled vegetables; you will want ½-inch-long matchstick pieces.

7. To assemble and roll the norimaki: Cut each sheet of nori in half crosswise. Lay a nori sheet on a sushi rolling mat. Place 2 to 3 tablespoons of

SUSHI-NORIMAKI

the rice on the middle of the sheet, spreading it evenly over the surface; leave a ½-inch margin on one side.

8. Sprinkle a thin line of sesame seeds along the center of the rice. Arrange the pickled veggies on top.

9. Pick up the mat, keeping your vegetables centered, then roll the mat over to meet the other side. Press and roll the mat over your roll lightly. The roll will stick together from the moisture in the rice. When the roll is tight, cut it into 6 even pieces.

10. Repeat the steps to assemble and cut the remaining 3 rolls. Arrange all the pieces on a plate and serve with pickled ginger, wasabi paste, and shoyu.

> ### FERMENTISTA'S TIP
>
> #### Storing Leftover Norimaki
> *The vinegar, which was added to this evolving recipe in the nineteenth century to replace the fermented rice, does provide a measure of preservation. Rolls should never be put in the refrigerator, as the rice will get hard. Keep them in an airtight container in a cool spot if you don't intend to eat them immediately, for up to 1 day.*

Tempura
serves 4 to 6
VEGETARIAN

We make these with Edgy Veggies (page 155). Since the pickled vegetables have a salty tartness on their own, the dipping sauce can simply be shoyu (soy sauce) with a splash of rice vinegar.

BATTER
- 2 egg yolks
- 1½ cups ice water
- 1¾ cups unbleached all-purpose flour

- 3–4 cups pickled vegetables, drained
  Quality high-heat oil, for deep-frying

TEMPURA OIL
Traditionally sesame oil is used in the frying of tempura. Interestingly, at the highbrow tempura establishments in Japan the oil is only used once. It is then sold to the lesser establishments, where it is used a few more times.

1. To make the tempura batter: Put the egg yolks in a bowl. Add the ice water, slowly stirring and blending it well as you go. If you are feeling a need to be authentic, stir with chopsticks.

2. Add the flour all at once and mix lightly; you don't want to wake up the gluten or warm the batter. The batter should be cold and lumpy.

3. Pour oil into a small saucepan or deep fryer to a depth of ½ inch and heat over high heat to about 360°F; you will know the oil is hot enough if the batter drops to the bottom, sizzles, and bounces up to the top. (*Note:* The temperature of the oil should be monitored constantly. If it cools too much, the batter will absorb the oil and your tempura will become soggy. To maintain the temperature, fry only a few pieces at a time.)

4. Pat the pickled vegetables dry with a paper towel.

5. Coat the vegetables in batter and fry about a minute on each side.

6. Serve immediately over a bowl of steamed rice, with a side of Vietnamese Pickled Carrot and Daikon (page 150).

Kirsten Writes

As much as I love cooking with fresh whole ingredients, there are days when I don't want to spend much time in the kitchen. Ferments in salads to the rescue!

Salads, where we expect to find tangy flavors, are a natural place to showcase fermented veggies. Adding a few fresh vegetables and some olive oil mellows out the acidity and transforms a kraut into a gourmet salad. Add a little mayo instead of olive oil, and you have a zingy take on traditional coleslaw. I share some of our favorites in this section, but any salad can be dressed up with a last-minute dollop of something fermented.

Bavarian Pickled Radish and Sausage Salad

serves 4 to 6 as a main-dish salad
GLUTEN-FREE

This salad is a full meal on a hot summer day when you just don't feel like cooking. It also travels well in a picnic basket — just don't forget the crusty bread.

4 precooked sausages, ideally Bavarian weisswurst (or bratwurst, if you don't have access to a German sausage maker)
2 cups Sliced Radish Ferment (page 220)
1 medium red onion, diced
1 New York Deli–Style Pickle (page 168) or other lacto-fermented dill pickle, diced
2–3 teaspoons capers
¼ cup minced parsley or 1 tablespoon Chimichurri (page 207)

DRESSING

2 tablespoons balsamic vinegar
2 tablespoons sweet mustard
2 tablespoons olive oil
Salt and freshly ground black pepper

1. Boil the sausages in water until warm.

2. Meanwhile, in a large bowl whisk together the dressing ingredients.

3. When the sausages are warm, slice them thinly and add to the bowl.

4. Lightly chop the fermented radish slices, and add to the bowl along with the onion, pickle, capers, and parsley.

5. Toss the salad and serve. For a warming indoor meal, serve with hearty bread or boiled Yellow Finn potatoes.

Blaukraut with Blue Cheese and Walnuts

See photo on page 300

serves 4 to 6

Gluten-Free, Vegetarian

This recipe is almost as simple as serving the kraut straight from the crock. In a few minutes you have dressed it up and created a gourmet salad, worthy of any occasion.

- 1 cup walnut pieces
- 1 tablespoon walnut oil
- 1 crisp sweet apple, cored and thinly sliced
- 2 cups Blaukraut (page 147)
- ½ cup crumbled blue cheese

1. Preheat the oven to 350°F.

2. Toss the walnut pieces with the oil. Spread them on a cookie sheet and toast in the oven. This should take 4 to 5 minutes; watch them carefully to avoid overbrowning.

3. Remove the nuts from the oven and allow them to cool.

4. Toss the apple with the blaukraut. Sprinkle the blue cheese and walnuts over the top and serve.

Celeriac Remoulade

serves 4

Gluten-Free, Raw, Vegetarian

This is a variation on the French salad of the same name. The acidity comes from the fermented celeriac instead of the traditional lemon juice. This creamy salad can be served alongside any main dish; try roast chicken or poached fish. It also makes a good sandwich filling.

- ¼ cup mayonnaise, preferably homemade (page 320)
- 2 tablespoons crème fraîche or sour cream
- 1 teaspoon Dijon mustard
- 1¼ cups Naked Celeriac Kraut (page 157)
- 1 tablespoon minced fresh parsley
- 1 tablespoon minced New York Deli–Style Pickle (page 168) or other lacto-fermented dill pickle
- ½ teaspoon minced capers
  Pinch of dried tarragon, crumbled
  Salt and freshly ground black pepper

1. In a small bowl whisk together the mayonnaise, crème fraîche, and mustard to create the dressing.

2. Mix in the celeriac kraut, parsley, pickle, capers, and tarragon. Add salt and pepper to taste. Serve as a side salad.

Beet and Celery Salad

serves 4

Gluten-Free, Raw, Vegan

This quick, magenta-colored salad fuses the fresh with the fermented deliciously.

- 1 cup Simple Beet Kraut (page 120)
- 4 stalks celery, thinly sliced on the diagonal
- ¼ cup apple juice or cider
- 3 tablespoons sunflower oil (if you can find the cold-pressed oil that tastes like sunflower, all the better)
- 4 scallions, finely sliced
- 2 tablespoons chopped fresh parsley
- 1 tablespoon apple cider vinegar

Combine the kraut, celery, and juice in a bowl. Add the oil, scallions, parsley, and vinegar. Mix well and let the salad marinate for an hour before serving.

Wilted Spinach Salad with Rhubarb Relish

serves 4 to 6
GLUTEN-FREE, VEGAN OPTION

The rhubarb relish adds a wonderful zing that brightens this classic salad. This can be made with bacon, in which case the hot bacon fat from frying is the first step in the warm dressing that will wilt the spinach.

For a lighter or vegan variation, omit the bacon (and its grease) and substitute olive oil. If using olive oil, remember to heat it gently; it does not do well with high heat.

    1 pound fresh spinach
  2–3 slices bacon (optional)
    1 red onion, thinly sliced
  2–3 tablespoons olive oil (if omitting bacon)
    2 tablespoons balsamic vinegar
   ½ cup Rhubarb Relish (page 223)
      Salt and freshly ground black pepper

1. Wash and dry the spinach. Place the greens in a salad bowl.

2. If using bacon, fry the slices until crisp. Remove the bacon from the pan and add the onions. If using olive oil, warm it in the pan and add the onion.

3. Sauté the onion slices until they begin to caramelize. Add the balsamic vinegar and continue to cook until the onions have caramelized completely and the balsamic has reduced and thickened.

4. Pour the hot onions and dressing over the spinach, then toss. Add the rhubarb relish, season with salt and pepper, and toss again.

5. If you used bacon, crumble the slices and sprinkle on top of the salad. Serve warm.

Tzatziki

serves 4 to 6
GLUTEN-FREE, VEGETARIAN

Tzatziki is a Greek cucumber salad that is a summer standard at our house. It is simple, quick to prepare, and easy to eat (as in: all the kids love it).

    1 fresh cucumber
    1 cup Greek yogurt or strained yogurt
    1 teaspoon Garlic Scape Paste (page 183)
   ½ teaspoon Mint Paste (optional; page 113)
      Salt

1. Peel and grate the cucumber using a mandoline or grater, then squeeze to drain the excess liquid.

2. Put the grated cucumber in a bowl. Add the yogurt, garlic scape paste, mint paste (if using), and salt to taste. Mix well. We use it as a side dish, a dip, or as part of a meze platter.

Coleslaw

serves 4
GLUTEN-FREE, RAW, VEGAN

This simple coleslaw has a tang from the kraut that blends nicely with the sweetness of the fresh carrots.

> 2 cups plain sauerkraut
> 1 cup grated carrots
> 1 cup Homemade Sunflower Mayonnaise or Almonnaise (recipes follow), or your favorite store-bought mayo

1. Put the sauerkraut in a sieve and gently squeeze out the liquid. Then put the kraut in a bowl with the shredded carrots.

2. Toss the vegetables together, then mix in the mayonnaise.

Almonnaise

yield: about 2 cups
GLUTEN-FREE, RAW, VEGAN

This is an eggless mayonnaise that we have been making since our vegetarian days in the early 1990s. Marilyn Diamond wrote the original recipe in *The American Vegetarian Cookbook*.

> ½ cup raw almonds
> ½–¾ cup water
> 1 generous teaspoon nutritional yeast
> ½ teaspoon salt
> 1–1¼ cups cold-pressed light oil
> 3 tablespoons lemon juice or brine
> ½ teaspoon apple cider vinegar

1. Put the almonds in a food processor, blender, or Vitamix. Grind until they are a fine meal.

2. Add about half of the water, along with the yeast and salt. Blend this first, and add the remaining water until you have a creamy consistency.

3. With the motor running on low speed, drizzle in the oil in a thin continuous stream until the mixture thickens.

4. Keep the machine running and add the lemon juice and vinegar; keep blending for about a minute, until the mayonnise thickens a bit more.

Homemade Sunflower Mayonnaise

yield: about 1 cup
GLUTEN-FREE, RAW, VEGETARIAN

Homemade mayonnaise is very simple to prepare and worth the effort. It has the reputation of being tricky, as it can be sensitive and every once in a while it will fail. Sometimes it will not get thick, and sometimes, if too much oil is added, it will separate and look as though it is curdled. Don't be disheartened if this happens. Just try again; the flavor of this fresh whole food is worth it.

> 1 whole egg
> 1 egg yolk
> Pinch of salt
> 1 cup cold-pressed sunflower or almond oil
> 1 tablespoon lemon juice or brine

1. Put the egg and the extra yolk into a blender or food processor, and blend for a few seconds.

2. With the motor running, begin to drizzle in the oil in a thin stream. When the mixture reaches the desired consistency, stop; you may not need the full cup of oil. With the motor running again, add the lemon juice. As soon as it is blended in and the mixture has thickened, your mayonnaise is ready.

VARIATION: Aioli

Use the same process to make aioli. Use olive oil instead of the sunflower oil. The aioli will have a rich color and olive flavor but will not set up quite as thick.

Cabbage Salsa

serves 4 to 6

Gluten-Free, Vegetarian, Raw

This coleslaw can be used as a chip dip, a side salad, or a dressing for a sandwich. Or try wrapping it up in a burrito or fish taco.

  1 cup shredded fresh cabbage
  1 cup Naked Kraut (page 132; there's no need to drain it)
  ½ cup finely diced red onion (fresh or fermented)
  2 tablespoons fermented cilantro leaf or paste (page 162)
  1 tablespoon Hot Sauce (page 214) or jalapeño brine
  1 clove garlic, minced
  ¾–1 cup Homemade Sunflower Mayonnaise or Almonnaise (page 320), or your favorite store-bought mayo
Freshly ground black pepper

Combine the cabbage, kraut, onion, cilantro, hot sauce, and garlic in a bowl, and mix well. Add the mayo, starting with ¾ cup and adding more as needed to reach the desired creaminess. Season with pepper to taste.

Ranch Slaw

serves 4

Gluten-Free, Vegetarian, Raw

This recipe includes a homemade ranch dressing. If you have leftovers, the dressing will keep in the refrigerator for a week, though it never lasts more than two days at our house.

  2 cups shredded fresh cabbage
  1½–2 cups light, refreshing kraut, like Three Cs (page 133)

RANCH-STYLE DRESSING
  ½ cup Homemade Sunflower Mayonnaise (page 320)
  ½ cup sour cream
  ¼ cup plain kefir or buttermilk
  1 tablespoon sauerkraut brine, or 1 tablespoon lemon juice with ¼ teaspoon salt added
  ½ teaspoon dried or fermented chives (page 202)
  ½ teaspoon dried dill
  ½ teaspoon garlic powder

1. Toss the cabbage and kraut together in a bowl.

2. For the dressing, whisk together the mayonnaise, sour cream, kefir, brine, chives, dill, and garlic powder.

3. Add about 1 cup of the dressing to the slaw, or more if you like your slaw "juicy."

CHAPTER 12

Happy Hour

CROCKTAILS

It all started with what's left at the bottom of the crock, which in large crocks can be a lot of brine. At first we fed it to the pig, but the brine was so delicious and frankly the pig didn't even like it; so we began to take it to the market to distribute one shot at a time (see sidebar, page 324).

We spent so much time joking about slinging back shots that it was only a matter of time before we thought about using brine as a mixer in cocktails. Before the word was even out of our mouths, somebody yelled out, "Crocktails" — of course.

The brine from pickling shredded vegetables is pure vegetable juice. Remember, this liquid is achieved by shredding your vegetables, often cabbage, and through the further breaking down of the cells with salt and pressing. When these concentrated vegetable juices undergo fermentation, they become a rich cloudy elixir containing not only the properties of the vegetable but increased vitamins C and B along with the additional beneficial bacteria (probiotics), enzymes, and minerals produced by the process. Kraut juice is also high in electrolytes. Folk remedies in many cultures have found healing in fermented vegetables and the resulting brine. So, bottoms up!

Kirsten Writes

Our crocktails are all about capturing the golden age of cocktails. Developed with our favorite bartenders, Ursula and Ted Raymond, they are a tasty postmodern twist on retro drinks. Serve them at parties, where they make great conversation starters.

2. Squeeze the juice from the lemon and orange into a shaker. Add the bourbon, cranberry relish, brine, and ice. Shake vigorously until chilled. Strain into the prepared glass.

Old-Fashioned

See photo on page 322

serves 1

This was one of the first American cocktails, showcasing the whiskey and bourbon around at the turn of the twentieth century.

This drink is made by "muddling" (or squishing) the fruit. As a fermentista you will recognize this as tamping. Your kraut tamper will get a chance to moonlight as a muddler.

> 1 tablespoon Cranberry Relish (page 274)
> 1 tablespoon simple syrup (see Brine-Ade, page 324)
> ¼ orange wedge
> Cracked ice
> 2 ounces bourbon
> ½ ounce sweet vermouth
> Soda water, enough to fill the glass (optional)

Combine the relish, simple syrup, and orange wedge in an 8- to 10-ounce glass. Use your muddler to mash the relish and orange into the syrup. Add ice, then pour in the bourbon and vermouth. Stir gently. Top off with soda water, if desired.

VARIATION: Old-Fashioned Spritzer

This version dilutes the alcohol to make a much lighter drink. Pour the mixture into a 16- or 20-ounce glass, add more ice, and fill with soda water.

Jalapeño Shots

serves 1

These are hot and spicy — get ready for a whole-body experience of warmth — and somehow the salt makes it all work.

> ½ ounce brine from a jalapeño ferment
> ½ ounce gin
> Dab of salt

1. Mix the brine and gin in a shot glass. Moisten the back of your hand between your index finger and thumb and sprinkle it with salt.

2. Lick the salt, then quickly drink the shot.

Kimchi Mary 1

See photo on page 322

serves 1

Kimchi brine is a natural fit for a spin on a Bloody Mary. In this drink brine replaces the tomato juice altogether. Since this drink typically has lots of veggies and pickles in the garnish, use lacto-fermented versions as adornments.

> ½ cup kimchi brine
> 2 ounces vodka
> ½ lemon
> Salt for the rim
> Cracked ice
> Edgy Veggie skewer (page 155)
> Fermented celery stick (page 160)

1. Combine the brine and vodka.

2. Rub the lemon half around the rim of the glass, then dip the rim in salt.

3. Add ice to glass, then pour in the kimchi-vodka mix.

4. Garnish with the skewered veggies and a fermented celery stick.

Kimchi Mary 2

serves 1

In this variation the brine is part of the tomato based mix. This version should also be decorated with fermented veggies as above.

- ½ **cup kimchi brine**
- ½ **cup tomato juice**
- 4 **drops Worcestershire sauce**
  - **Pinch of black pepper**
  - **Pinch of dried dill weed**
- 1 **teaspoon brine from Pepper Paste (optional; page 213)**
  - **Salt for the rim**
  - **Cracked ice**
  - **Edgy Veggie skewer (page 155)**
  - **Fermented celery stick (page 160)**

1. Stir together the kimchi brine, tomato juice, Worcestershire, pepper, dill, and chile brine, if using.

2. Follow the directions for Kimchi Mary 1 (left), but substitute this mixture for the straight kimchi brine.

The Pickle Back

serves 1

This is a way to drink your pickle juice if you are not ready for straight-no-chaser kraut shots — though sort of in reverse, as the pickle juice is the chaser. T. J. Lynch of the Rusty Knot, in Manhattan's West Village, is credited with originating this drink.

- 2 **ounces Jameson Irish whiskey**
- 2 **ounces fermented pickle brine**

You need two shot glasses. The Jameson leads, followed closely by the brine.

THE BEET-RED RUSSIAN

We wanted to blend the Russians' love of the beet with their passion for vodka. It seemed like a natural combination that had to work. We tried and we tried and we tried; the only way to get something drinkable was to add a lot of orange juice and a wee bit of beet brine to the vodka. It just ended up a salty red screwdriver — not fit for brown bread, sour cream, or a Russian winter.

CHAPTER 13

Dinner

BRINE AND DINE

At dinnertime we enjoy humble food with good conversation and the well-being that comes from sitting down together with family for a meal at the end of a long, varied day; we hope the recipes we have chosen to share will inspire this. Most of the dishes are warm and comforting, and many are variations of old-world, traditional, unassuming one-pot meals.

Blaukraut and Apple-Stuffed Pork Loin, page 332

QUICK AND EASY DINNER IDEAS

Our family enjoys meals that are based on building your own, which was born out of the desperation that can come with creating a balanced meal during the late-afternoon witching hour with a baby and three young children. Something simple like baked potatoes with five or six toppings was easy to put together, and for the kids a meal with à la carte toppings gave them a sense of ownership over what was on their plate. The kids could "build" their meal right at the table, and we knew that as long as a few of the toppings were our ferments, we had won the eat-your-veggies battle.

The kids are big, the parents are less tired, but we still have many meals like these.

Baked Potatoes

My Aunt Eleanor was visiting to help at our youngest son's birth and one night she made baked potatoes. The thing that was special is that after scrubbing and poking the potatoes with a fork, she rubbed a tiny bit of oil and some flaked salt on the skin. We like eating the potato skins, and this small step brought them to a new level.

For this meal we simply prepare the potatoes as above and bake. Right before serving we get out small bowls and fill them with three or four different ferments and a few non-fermented toppings. The ideas here are just to get you started — anything you love or happen to have on hand is probably perfect.

POTATO TOPPINGS

» Any kraut you have on hand: Sauerrüben 1, 2, or 3 (pages 246–48), Burdock Kraut (page 130), Naked Celeriac Kraut (page 157),

and Escarole Kimchi (page 176) are some favorites
» Chopped Preserved Limes (page 271)
» Any herb pastes, especially chive (page 202), or Chimichurri (page 207)
» Radicchio Tapenade (page 296)
» Shredded cheese or feta crumbles
» Sour cream
» Steamed broccoli

Chili

If you make chili, bring fermented condiments to the table — you will never eat chili (or a chili dog) without something fermented again!

CHILI (AND REFRIED BEAN) TOPPINGS

» Curtido (page 133)
» Simple Onion Relish or Onion and Pepper Relish (page 203)
» Chipotle Squash Kraut (page 249)
» Pepper Paste (page 213)
» Cilantro "Salsa" (page 162)
» Tomatillo Salsa (page 240)

Noodles, Fried Rice, and Stir-Fries

Top noodle bowls and fried rice with krauts or kimchi. For this we like Carrot Kraut (page 149), Burdock Kimchi (page 130), Pickled Shiitake (page 194), or Vietnamese-Style Pickled Scallions (page 227).

Whole-leaf ferments like shiso (page 228) or Thai basil (page 115) are wonderful to garnish a stir-fry or fried rice right before serving.

Refried Beans

yield: 12 cups

GLUTEN-FREE, VEGAN OPTION

Hands-down, our kids would tell you homemade refried beans are their favorite meal. Once soaked and simmered, a big pot of beans becomes a meal and countless snacks; in this recipe the fermented element comes in the soaking liquid, and because kraut is so delicious on beans, especially refried beans, we recommend you try making your own if you never have.

We learned to make them when we were in college in Tucson. At first we made them with lard as we had been taught. During our vegetarian years we made them with copious amounts of olive oil. Now we use lard when we have raised our own hog, and when we are out of that we use olive oil. We use a full cup of oil for a large pot of beans; however, you will still have a great pot of beans if you would rather use less.

This recipe is for a big pot of beans that will make two or more meals. Don't forget to start the day before you want to eat them.

         4 cups pinto or Anasazi beans
       1–2 tablespoons any fermented brine, if available
       4–5 cloves garlic, minced
         1 tablespoon salt, or more to taste
       ½–1 cup olive oil or good-quality lard, melted
           Any kraut or ferment for topping; try Smoky
           Kraut (page 135), Curtido Rojo (page 121),
           Curried CauliKraut (page 155), Naked
           Celeriac Kraut (page 157), Scape Kraut
           (page 135), Onion and Pepper Relish
           (page 203), or Tomatillo Salsa (page 240)

1. Put the beans in a large bowl or pot, and cover them generously with water. The beans will double in size as they soak, so use enough water to keep them all submerged. Add the brine, if using. Cover and set aside. After 12 hours, pour off the water and replace with fresh water.

2. When you are ready to cook the beans (ideally after 24 hours), pour off the soaking water and rinse the beans.

3. Put the beans in a pot and bring to a boil. Carefully skim off any foam that rises to the top. Reduce the heat and simmer until the beans are soft, about 1½ hours. Check occasionally to make sure there is plenty of water over the beans as they cook.

4. When the beans are soft, remove them from the heat and drain. Put the beans back into the pot with the garlic, salt, and oil. Mash with a potato masher. Add fresh water as needed. You are aiming for a smooth, creamy texture. Homemade refried beans are smoother and softer than canned.

5. When ready to eat, warm the beans over medium heat and serve in a bowl, in a burrito, or in a taco with any kraut you choose. Warm leftovers by adding more water to the pot and stirring often.

FERMENTISTA'S TIP

Fermentation and Beans

Adding fermented brine to soaking beans helps break down the complex sugars (raffinose and stachyose) and neutralize phytic acid, making the beans more digestible.

Blaukraut and Apple–Stuffed Pork Loin

See photo on page 328

serves 6 to 8

GLUTEN-FREE

Ted and Ursula Raymond came up with this recipe for kraut combined with chèvre and fresh apples. The flavors blend brilliantly, perhaps only to be out-done by the effect of the fuchsia-colored stuffing in the center of the roast. This meal tastes as good as it looks. Serve with any kind of potato dish — fried, mashed, or gnocchi — and a green salad.

> 1 (2- to 3-pound) whole pork loin
>   Salt and freshly ground pepper
>
> **STUFFING**
> 1 cup Blaukraut (page 147)
> 1 apple, peeled and diced
> 4 ounces chèvre
>
> **GRAVY**
>   Drippings from the roast
> 1 cup apple cider
> 2 teaspoons arrowroot or cornstarch

1. Preheat the oven to 350°F.

2. Cut the loin lengthwise, but not all the way through. Open this flap and flatten. Sprinkle with salt and pepper.

3. Combine the blaukraut, apple, and chèvre in a bowl and mix well. Spread the stuffing mixture over the center of the flattened pork loin, then fasten it shut with skewers or toothpicks (or truss the loin with a length of kitchen twine).

4. Lay the stuffed loin in a shallow baking pan. Roast uncovered for 1½ hours, or until cooked through, when the internal temperature reaches 145°F.

5. Transfer the pork to a platter, remove the skewers, and let the meat rest to absorb juices while you make the gravy.

6. In a saucepan, whisk together the pan drippings, cider, and arrowroot until smooth. Bring to a boil over medium-high heat, whisking constantly for 1 minute.

7. Pour the gravy over the top of the roast. Serve in thick slices.

Kraut-a-kópita (Spanakópita)

serves 6

VEGETARIAN

Spinach brings to mind Greek spanakópita: oregano, lemon, and sweet onions. With some misgivings — the family is divided about the texture — we tried to make a ferment with the flavors (page 233), and it's good! The spinach has some crunch, similar to that of a wilted spinach salad. But we've found its highest and best use is in a delicacy we've christened Kraut-a-kópita. This variation of the classic Greek spinach pastry is quick to prepare, as the fermented spinach is one of the main ingredients. We eat this as a hot main dish accompanied by a Greek salad. It makes a nice appetizer, too, alone or as part of a meze platter.

> 1 pound frozen phyllo pastry leaves (also called filo dough)
> 1½–2 sticks butter (or 1–1¼ cups olive oil or a combination)

3–4 **cups Lemon Spinach (page 233)**

4 **eggs**

1 **pound crumbled feta cheese**

1 **tablespoon unbleached all-purpose flour**

½ **teaspoon freshly ground black pepper, or to taste**

1. Preheat the oven to 375°F.

2. Defrost the phyllo pastry according to the directions on the package.

3. Melt the sticks of butter over low heat. Lightly brush the bottom and sides of a baking dish with a bit of the melted butter. (We use a chafing dish–sized casserole, but a 9 × 13-inch dish works, too; phyllo sheet sizes vary, so use a pan that fits the sheets you purchase or trim the phyllo to fit the pan.)

4. Put the fermented spinach in a colander for a few minutes to drain slightly.

5. Meanwhile, break the eggs into a bowl and beat lightly. Mix in the feta, then add the flour, spinach, and black pepper. Set aside.

6. Lay the phyllo sheets out and cover them with a slightly dampened clean tea towel or plastic wrap, as the sheets tend to dry out quickly and can be frustrating to work with. Lay down the first pastry sheet on the buttered pan. Brush this lightly with butter and add another sheet. Continue layering until you have used 8 to 10 sheets; this should be about half the package.

7. Spread the filling across the entire surface. Now, to form the top crust, repeat the layering process until the sheets are used up. If you are using a smaller pan, roll the edges under and

tuck them into the sides; this makes a nice, pie-like effect.

8. Bake for 45 minutes, or until crisp and golden. Let stand 10 minutes before cutting into squares. Serve warm or at room temperature.

Sauerkraut Strudel

serves 6

Vegetarian

Many cuisines wrap fillings, sweet or savory, into layers of dough. The High German word *strudel* literally means "whirlpool," which is what the wrapped dough looks like, swirling through a soft, warm filling.

1 **pound frozen phyllo pastry leaves (also called filo dough)**

1½–2 **sticks butter (or 1–1¼ cups olive oil or a combination)**

FILLING

3 **cups diced onions**

2–3 **tablespoons butter**

2 **eggs**

8 **ounces cream cheese, at room temperature**

4 **cups Naked Kraut (page 132) or any other favorite kraut**

1 **cup grated Swiss cheese**

½ **cup grated cheddar cheese**

1 **cup cooked white or brown rice (great use of leftovers)**

2 **teaspoons caraway seeds**

2 **teaspoons dried dill weed**

Salt and freshly ground black pepper

1. Preheat the oven to 350°F.

2. Defrost the phyllo pastry according to the package directions.

3. For the pastry, melt the sticks of butter over low heat. Lightly brush a baking sheet with a little of the butter.

4. For the filling, sauté the onions over low heat in the 2–3 tablespoons of butter until translucent.

5. In a bowl, mix the eggs with the cream cheese until smooth. Add to this mixture the onion, sauerkraut, Swiss and cheddar cheeses, rice, caraway, dill, salt, and pepper. Mix well, and set aside.

6. Lay the phyllo sheets out and cover with a slightly dampened clean tea towel or plastic wrap, as the sheets tend to dry out quickly and can be frustrating to work with. Lay the first pastry sheet on the prepared baking sheet; brush the pastry lightly with the melted butter and add another sheet. Continue layering until you have used 12 to 15 sheets.

7. Spread the filling lengthwise along the bottom third of the top sheet, in a 3-inch-wide swath, leaving a 3-inch border along the edge of the pastry. Gently fold the long sides over the filling and, starting with the short side nearest you, carefully roll up the dough until you have formed a log. Tuck the edges under the log and arrange seam side down in the middle of the baking sheet. Brush a little more melted butter over the surface.

8. Bake the strudel for 50 minutes, or until golden crisp on the outside and set on the inside.

9. Serve with applesauce and pickled vegetables, such as beets.

Rouladen

serves 4

Gluten-Free

The traditional version of this dish is one of the first meals Kirsten learned to cook from her grandmother. It is a perennial special birthday meal at our farm. While the conventional version uses pickles as a stuffing, we have also added sauerkraut to the mix. The kids think it breaks all the rules to mess with their favorite dish, but nobody turns it down.

The hardest part of this recipe is to get the meat cut right. If you happen to have a German butcher in the neighborhood, you are set. Just request a rouladen cut, which is usually from the bottom round. You will get a piece of beef that is anywhere from 8 to 10 inches long, around 4 inches wide, and about ¼ inch thick. To achieve this without an enlightened butcher takes a little more creativity. If left to your own devices, look at the cuts and choose one that will come the closest to the desired size with the least amount of extra steps at home. You don't have to worry too much if it is a tougher cut, as the acidic kraut and long roasting time will make it tender.

One possibility is to cut a sirloin tip, cutlet, or round steak into 4- to 6-inch slices and then pound them with a meat mallet. It can be helpful to place the meat between plastic wrap and butcher paper while pounding. The other way is to partially freeze the meat to make cutting it into thinner slices easier; it still may need some flattening. Remember, you are after long and thin.

½ cup minced onion

1½ cups drained **Naked Kraut** (page 132), brine reserved

2 **New York Deli–Style Pickles** (page 168), diced

4 slices grass-fed beef (see above notes), at least 8 inches long and ¼ inch thick (about 1½ pounds total)

4 slices bacon

2–3 tablespoons butter

Water or stock

1. Prepare the filling by mixing together the onion, sauerkraut, and dill pickle; set aside.

2. Lay the meat slices flat on a large cutting board and pat dry with a paper towel.

3. Arrange 1 bacon slice lengthwise across each piece of meat. Take a handful of the kraut mixture and place it on top of the bacon, extending an inch from the edge and about a quarter of the way up the length of the steak (how much will depend on the size of your cut). Any extra filling can be added to the broth for more flavor.

4. Start the roll by tightly tucking the short side over the kraut filling. Roll the steak end-to-end and secure with three toothpicks, one on the flap and one pinching each side closed.

5. The trick to great rouladen is in the searing. Melt the butter in a heavy-bottomed pot or Dutch oven over high heat until both pot and butter are hot and just about to brown. Lay the rolled bundles in the pot and thoroughly brown all sides, 2 to 3 minutes per side.

6. Add the reserved brine to the pot, then add enough water or stock to cover the rouladen. Bring to a simmer. Put a lid on the pot and continue to simmer on the stovetop (or in a 250°F oven) until tender. This usually takes 1½ to 2 hours.

7. Once the meat is tender, transfer the rouladen to a serving dish with a slotted spoon. Carefully remove the toothpicks. Put the pot back on a medium-high burner and remove the lid. Continue to cook until the sauce is reduced, and then spoon it over the rouladen.

Kimchi Latkes

See photo on page 337

serves 2 as a main course, or 4 as a side dish

VEGETARIAN, GLUTEN-FREE OPTION

Thanks to the slight acidity brought to these potato pancakes by the kimchi, they have a lighter flavor than their all-potato counterpart. This is a versatile fusion dish that can be a side or carry the meal with the addition of sauces — it's just as comfortable with sour cream as with an Asian-style peanut sauce.

1 cup peeled and shredded potatoes

1 cup drained and packed **Kimchi** (page 141)

3 tablespoons unbleached all-purpose flour or your favorite gluten-free blend

3 eggs, beaten

Pinch of salt to taste (the kimchi adds salt, so generally we don't add any)

½ cup peanut or coconut oil, for frying

1. Put the grated potatoes in a strainer or colander and push out any extra moisture.

2. In a medium bowl, stir together the potatoes, kimchi, and flour. The goal is to have a nice coating of flour on the potatoes and vegetables. Mix in the eggs, and add salt, if needed.

3. Heat the oil until hot over medium-high heat in a large skillet.

4. Place large spoonfuls of the potato mixture into the hot oil, pressing down on them to form patties ¼ to ½ inch thick. Brown the latkes on one side, then turn and brown the other side.

5. Serve hot with sour cream or peanut sauce.

Rösti

serves 2 to 3 as a main dish, or 4 to 6 as a side dish
Gluten-Free, Vegan

Rösti was originally a farmer's breakfast in Switzerland. It is generally made of potatoes and egg and fried like a pancake — very much like a latke. There are also *rösti*s made of shredded celeriac or kohlrabi, or a combination. Shredded was our hint to try *rösti* with fermented vegetables. The flavor is bright and tangy. We often put caraway in our celeriac, which rounds out the flavor.

> 1 cup Naked Celeriac Kraut (page 157)
> 1 cup Kohlrabi Kraut (page 190)
> 1 cup garbanzo bean flour
> 2 eggs
> 2–3 tablespoons coconut oil, for frying

1. In a medium bowl stir together the ferments, garbanzo flour, and eggs. In this recipe it is not necessary to squeeze out the brine; it provides the liquid for the batter.

2. In a large heavy-bottomed skillet over medium-high heat, heat enough oil to generously coat the bottom of the pan.

3. Drop spoonfuls of the *rösti* mixture into the hot oil, pressing down to form patties about ¼ to ½ inch thick. These can be small pancakes about 3 inches in diameter or larger pan-sized cakes, like a thick crêpe. Brown on one side, then turn and brown the other side.

4. Serve the *rösti* hot with a salad and tomato soup.

VARIATION
These are versatile pancakes that can also be topped with smoked fish and rolled.

KIMCHI LATKES, *page 335*

Zucchini Curry

serves 4

GLUTEN-FREE, VEGAN

This curry was born in order to use the tasty, albeit soft, fermented zucchini. It only takes about 20 minutes to prepare. The sauce is creamy and tasty; the ferment gives it a tang that is almost of lemon and limes.

Start by gathering your ingredients. In making curries, it is nice to have everything lined up when the sauce is moving quickly.

> 1 **medium onion**
> ½ **cup raw cashews**
> ½ **cup water**
> 2 **tablespoons oil**
> 1 **tablespoon whole cumin seeds**
> 2–3 **cloves garlic, grated, or 1 teaspoon Garlic Paste (page 181)**
> 1 **tablespoon grated fresh ginger**
> 1 **tablespoon Pepper Paste (page 213)**
> 1 **teaspoon ground coriander**
> 1 **teaspoon garam masala**
> 1 **teaspoon ground turmeric**
> 2 **cups Zucchini Kraut (page 253)**
> 3 **tablespoons tomato paste**

1. Prepare the onion by dicing it coarsely and puréeing it in a blender. Pour the onion purée into a bowl or measuring cup, and set it aside.

2. Put the cashews and water into the blender. Blend into a smooth, thick cream; set aside.

3. Heat a heavy-bottomed skillet over medium-high heat. Add the oil and cumin seeds; toast them about 1 minute, stirring constantly. Add the onion purée, and sauté until browned; it will look almost pink.

4. Turn the heat down to medium. Stir in the garlic, ginger, and chile paste. Give it a moment to brown, then stir in the coriander, garam masala, and turmeric.

5. Stirring constantly, add the kraut and tomato paste. Simmer for about 5 minutes, stirring often. The zucchini will break down immediately.

6. Stir in the cashew cream. When the sauce is thoroughly mixed and warm, serve over freshly cooked brown rice.

Polish Pickle Soup

serves 4

GLUTEN-FREE, VEGAN OPTION

It was a glorious spring day, in the way that only May can deliver in southern Oregon. The fields and mountains were green, the apple blossoms sprinkled the ground with petals, and the scent of lilacs wafted through the air. We were at a gathering of neighbors, talking about, well what else, fermenting vegetables. Pickles, to be exact. Our neighbor shared that his ex-wife was Polish and she grated pickles into soups. Kirsten was intrigued and went home with some concepts, but mostly she wanted to grate a pickle.

> 6 **medium potatoes, peeled and cubed**
> 2 **medium carrots, sliced**
> 3 **cups rich chicken bone broth or vegetarian broth**
> 2 **tablespoons butter or sunflower oil**
> 6–7 **scallions, sliced**
> 2 **cloves garlic, minced**
> ½ **teaspoon mustard seeds**
> 1 **cup pickle brine**

2 large New York Deli–Style Pickles (page 168)
or other lacto-fermented dill pickles, grated
1 teaspoon dried dill weed or a couple of sprigs
fresh dill, chopped
Salt and freshly ground black pepper
Minced fresh chives
Sliced hard-boiled eggs (optional)

1. Put the potatoes, carrots, and broth in a medium-sized pot. Bring this to a boil, then reduce the heat and simmer until the potatoes are tender. Remove from the heat and set aside.

2. In a nonreactive soup pot (stainless is fine), heat the butter or oil. Toss in the scallions, garlic, and mustard seeds, stirring often, and cook over medium heat until the onions and garlic are soft, but not browned.

3. Transfer the potato-carrot mixture to the soup pot. Using a potato masher, gently mash the vegetables. You only want to break them up a bit. This will thicken your soup.

4. Add the brine, the grated pickles, and dill weed. Bring the soup to a simmer, and continue to cook for a few minutes, allowing the flavors to meld. If the soup is too thick, you may add a bit more brine or broth.

5. Add salt and pepper to taste and garnish with the chives and eggs, if using.

RICH BONE BROTH

There are many recipes for making soup stocks, truly a flavor foundation of your soups. Stocks are easy to make and then freeze for a more instant ingredient. They just require a bit of planning. We do not claim the final word on broths but will share how we make them.

Put a whole chicken in a stockpot with any "extra bits," although we've noticed many packaged whole chickens don't include the neck or giblets these days. Cover the chicken with cold water and bring it to a full boil, then turn the heat down immediately. This helps draw the flavor. Skim off any foam that develops, taking care not remove the fat.

Let simmer for about 1 hour, then remove the whole chicken from the broth. Remove the meat from the bones to use for another dish, like chicken salad (page 308). Then all the bits, skin, bones, and cartilage go back into the pot. At this point add some vegetables: half an onion, celery ends, and carrots. Add a tablespoon of vinegar to draw the minerals from the bones. Bring the pot to a simmer again and cook all day, about 6 to 12 hours.

Strain and use immediately, or cool and freeze in small portions.

Braised Blaukraut

serves 6
GLUTEN-FREE

In Kirsten's childhood this sweet and sour vegetable side dish was made with fresh cabbage, onions, and tart apples and sprinkled with a little sugar and vinegar. The acid of the added vinegar preserved the red color of the cabbage, which would otherwise turn blue with cooking. Our take on this recipe uses fermented red cabbage, onion, and apples, and the ferment's acidity preserves the beautiful color. It gets its sweetness from thick balsamic vinegar, and the flavor of the dish will be directly affected by the vinegar you use (see the note). This warm salad is rich enough as a light dinner served with potatoes.

Note: The quality and types of balsamic vinegars vary greatly, depending on where they're made, how long they're aged, and in what type of wood barrel. Some are thin and quite acidic, while others are thick and sweet, almost syrupy. In this recipe we use the longer-aged, thick, sweet type; it is concentrated, so you don't need much.

        6 slices bacon
        1 medium onion, diced
        2 cups Blaukraut (page 147)
    2–3 teaspoons aged balsamic vinegar
           Pine nuts, raw

1. Fry the bacon in a heavy-bottomed pan until brown and slightly crisp. With tongs or a fork, remove the bacon from the pan, allowing the drippings to stay in the pan. Let the bacon cool, then crumble and set aside.

2. Lower the heat and add the onion to the pan; sauté until translucent.

3. Turn off the heat, add the blaukraut, and braise in the heat remaining in the pan, stirring frequently.

4. When the blaukraut is warm, splash on the balsamic vinegar to taste and toss in the crumbled bacon.

5. Garnish with pine nuts before serving.

Au Gratin Potatoes

serves 6 as a main dish, or 8 or more as a side dish
GLUTEN-FREE, VEGETARIAN OPTION

This dish comes in many forms and has many names, including scalloped potatoes. The word *gratin* comes from the French word "to scrape," which means the vegetable is prepared in a flat dish and browned on top. It has been fun to come up with ferment-inspired variations of this dish.

For our purposes, not only does baking the gratin with different ferments give this dish surprising flavor, but it can also showcase a variety of ferments in one meal. Our favorite way to serve the gratin is flanked by a colorful array of ferments, each bit containing a new flavor. Radicchio-Garlic Kraut (page 218) complements the subtle flavors of the potato and leek, Lemon-Dill Kraut (page 134) with its bright quality balances the cream, and Fresh Nettle Kraut (page 263) or Cultured Pickle Shop's Fennel and Sunchoke Kimchi (page 237) can give a winter heartiness to the dish. Or some pickle slices for some zing. Try Three Cs (page 133) for a classic flavor combination, or any of your favorites.

        1 scant cup chicken or vegetable broth
    3–4 pounds potatoes, well scrubbed, skins left on, thinly sliced

½ cup Leek Paste (page 192)

2 cups half-and-half

¼–½ teaspoon freshly grated nutmeg

Salt and freshly ground black pepper

1. Preheat the oven to 350°F. Butter a large casserole dish and set aside.

2. Bring the broth to a boil in a large pan, then add the potatoes. Cook for a few minutes, then stir and cook for a few more, about 5 minutes. (*Note:* This little bit of boiling in the broth not only adds depth of flavor but reduces the baking time. Potatoes cook more quickly in the water-based broth than in the rich half-and-half.)

3. Add the leeks, half-and-half, nutmeg, and pepper to the pan and mix carefully. When the half-and-half is heated, transfer everything to your buttered dish.

4. Cover the casserole with aluminum foil. Bake for 1 hour.

5. When the potatoes are soft, remove the foil; bake for a few more minutes, until the top is golden.

VARIATIONS

» Add 1 cup Naked Celeriac Kraut (page 157) with the potatoes, or in place of the leeks.

» Mix in ½ to 1 cup blue cheese, or a smoked blue cheese.

» Replace the leeks with fermented onions.

Palestinian Lentils and Rice (a recipe from the West Bank)

serves 4 to 6

GLUTEN-FREE, VEGAN

The loft of our barn is a one-room off-the-grid space that has the charm of horses and goats rustling around underneath you as you sleep. Our dear friends Annaliese and Scott asked if they could live in this space after the birth of their son Zeke. They enjoyed the simplicity of the space and were able to spend three months putting all of their energy into bonding. We enjoyed having a baby around and sharing meals with Scott and Annaliese, who have traveled extensively and are wonderful cooks.

This dish, made by Annaliese, was our introduction to the Middle Eastern sumac-spice blend *za'atar* (page 136), which she included in the rice; we have modified her recipe by including Za'atar Kraut instead. This simple meal has become a staple comfort meal at home, and for our son now in college a quick, cheap meal he can eat all week.

1 onion, diced

2 cloves garlic, minced

½ cup olive oil

1 bay leaf

½ teaspoon ground cumin

¼ teaspoon ground turmeric

1½ cups uncooked basmati rice (brown if you have time, white if not)

1½ cups uncooked lentils

6 cups water

2–3 onions

½ cup slivered almonds

2 cups Za'atar Kraut (page 136)

1. In a heavy-bottomed pot, sauté the diced onion and garlic in half of the olive oil until translucent. Add the bay leaf, cumin, and turmeric, and sauté for 1 minute longer.

2. Add the rice and lentils, and stir until they are coated in oil. Add the water. Bring to a boil, then cover the pot and simmer over low heat until the rice and lentils are tender.

3. Meanwhile, slice the remaining onions into rounds and caramelize in the remaining ¼ cup olive oil.

4. Dry-roast the slivered almonds in a skillet over low heat.

5. When the rice-and-lentil mixture has finished cooking, keep it in the pot or scoop it onto a serving platter. Spread the kraut evenly over the rice and lentils. Then spread out the caramelized onions, and sprinkle the almonds on top. This is a one-pot meal but still wonderful to serve with a fresh salad or a vegetable dish.

Choucroute Garni

serves 8
Gluten-Free

Traditional dishes vary depending on the region they're from and the economics that shaped family recipes. Choucroute garni as a peasant dish is very simple — perhaps just bay leaves, juniper berries, apples, onions, and a little bit of meat in the form of pork knuckles or salt pork. As this meal climbs the economic ladder, it is outfitted with bacon and sometimes many types of sausage, ham, or wild game.

As sauerkraut marched west from Germany and Eastern Europe, it landed in the Alsatian region of France, where it got this elegant name that means "dressed sauerkraut" (*choucroute* is a French modification of the German-Alsatian *sürkrüt*). With this dressy name it also took on elements of the French cuisine, such as the use of goose or duck fat, or the addition of foie gras.

Humble or fancy, this dish is a mound of slowly stewed sauerkraut served on a platter piled high with various meats. The recipe here is what Kirsten grew up eating, in many variations. It is a one-pot meal served with plenty of mustard, Dijon or sweet.

    4 thick strips bacon
    2 medium onions, diced
    2 tart apples, sliced
 4–6 cups sauerkraut; try Naked (page 132),
        Juniper-Onion (page 133), or OlyKraut's
        Eastern European (page 138)
  2½ cups Riesling or fresh apple cider
    1 cup chicken stock
    2 teaspoons juniper berries
 3–4 bay leaves
    1 teaspoon whole peppercorns
        A few sprigs parsley and thyme, tied with
        a cotton string
    4 bratwurst sausages
    4 bockwurst sausages, or similar sausage

FERMENTISTA'S TIP

Rinsing Kraut
Traditional recipes call for rinsing the sauerkraut before adding. If you are using a very salty or canned kraut, you would definitely rinse the kraut, but if you are using your own freshly fermented kraut, there's no need to drain or rinse.

1. Preheat the oven to 250°F.

2. In a heavy-bottomed, nonreactive pot with a lid, fry the bacon strips until they start to brown and the fat is rendered.

3. Add the onion and apple slices and sauté these in the bacon fat until soft. Remove the bacon and chop into small pieces. Add the sauerkraut to the pot, stirring it into the bacon grease. Return the chopped bacon to the pot.

4. Add the Riesling or apple cider, the chicken stock, and the spices. Stir everything together and place the herb bundle on top of the kraut.

5. Simmer in the oven for 2 to 3 hours.

6. About 30 minutes before serving, discard the herb bundle. Fry the bratwurst and bockwurst; when they're browned on all sides deglaze the pan with a bit more wine or cider. Pour this liquid into the sauerkraut, then tuck the bratwurst and bockwurst into the kraut and continue to cook slowly for another 30 minutes.

7. Serve with plenty of mustard, crusty bread, and boiled potatoes.

VARIATION

Here's a stovetop version of this same dish, adding the kraut last to preserve the probiotics: Fry the bacon and bratwurst in large nonreactive pan. Remove the meat pieces as they brown and cook. Add the onions and apples to the fat. When the onions and apples are caramelized, deglaze the pan with the wine or apple cider; omit the chicken broth. Add the spices, omitting the herb bundle. Add the bockwurst and simmer until warm. Return the bacon and bratwurst to the pan; when everything is warm remove from heat and add the sauerkraut, stirring gently to warm.

Zuurkoolstamppot

serves 4

Gluten-Free, Vegetarian option

This Dutch dish is a mash of root vegetables such as potato, carrots, parsnips, or a combination of vegetables that are available. The beauty of *stamppot* is its versatility and also that it's warm, hearty, and easy to make. This is a very thick stew, not as smooth as mashed potatoes. It is often served as a main dish with sausage.

Kirsten Writes

Stamppot is one of the first things I think of when I think of Dutch cuisine. My family lived in Rotterdam when I was 16. It was proudly set before me when I was invited to meals with the families of new friends I made. If translated literally means "stamped pot," as in mashing the vegetables. It is warm comfort food.

3	pounds mealy potatoes, like russets, peeled and cut into ½- to 1-inch dice
2–3	stalks celery, sliced
2	carrots, cut into thick slices
½	teaspoon salt
2	cups milk or rich vegetable or chicken broth
½	pound bacon slices (optional)
2–3	cups sauerkraut
	A few sprigs parsley or celery leaves, minced

1. Put the potatoes, celery, and carrots in a soup pot and cover with water; add the salt. Bring to a boil over medium-high heat, then reduce to low and simmer until the potatoes and carrots are soft but not falling apart. Drain and mash the vegetables.

2. Return the cooked vegetables to the pot, add the milk, and mash lightly; some of the vegetables should still retain a chunky texture. Keep this warm on low heat or in a warm oven.

3. In a large, nonreactive skillet fry the bacon, if using, until just crisp. Turn off the heat. Remove the bacon and set it aside on paper towels to cool.

4. Put the sauerkraut in the hot pan with the bacon fat and allow it to warm. Meanwhile, chop the bacon. Mix everything together in the pan — the warm mashed vegetables, sauerkraut, and bacon. Serve warm, garnished with parsley.

Grilled Chicken with Fermented Sweet Potatoes and Peanut Sauce

serves 4
GLUTEN-FREE, VEGAN OPTION

This meal was inspired by the traditional West African groundnut stew, groundnut meaning peanut. We were introduced to it by a neighbor who had done Peace Corps work in Sierra Leone. This stew varies greatly but often is made with sweet potatoes, chicken, and peanut butter. It has a delicious complex flavor, as does this fermented take on the stew.

This meal is incredibly easy since the fermented ingredients are made in advance. Grilled chicken is placed on a bed of rice topped with fermented sweet potatoes and a peanut sauce. It can become a vegan meal simply by omitting the chicken.

PEANUT SAUCE
- ½ cup peanut butter
- ¾ cup vegetable or chicken broth
- ½ teaspoon Garlic Paste (page 181) or 1 clove garlic, minced

- 3–4 boneless chicken breasts
- 2 cups cooked rice
- 2 cups West African Sweet Potato Ferment (page 238)
- Fresh cilantro leaves

1. Prepare the peanut sauce: Put the peanut butter in a bowl and whisk in the broth, about ¼ cup at a time, until a creamy, smooth consistency. Stir in the garlic.

2. Grill or broil the chicken breasts.

3. When the chicken breasts are cooked, slice them thinly. Arrange the chicken over a bed of freshly cooked rice, and top with the sweet potato ferment. Drizzle the peanut sauce over the top, and garnish with cilantro leaves.

Zwiebelkuchen

serves 4 to 6

We first encountered *zwiebelkuchen* in the medieval German town of Bacharach, which hugs a strip of land between the Rhine and the steep vineyard-dotted hills of the valley.

There are a few weeks each year when the young white wine that is not finished fermenting can be bought. Called *Federweiss*, this wine is light and fruity and, we learned, packs in a higher alcohol content than usual. This is traditionally paired with *zwiebelkuchen* — an onion-rich pan pastry. We have improvised here by using fermented

GRILLED CHICKEN WITH
FERMENTED SWEET POTATOES
AND PEANUT SAUCE

onions, which give this pie a bright tart flavor that still pairs nicely with white wine.

DOUGH

- 1 (¼-ounce) package active dry yeast
- 1 cup warm milk
- 1½ cups unbleached all-purpose flour
- 4 teaspoons butter, at room temperature

FILLING

- 4 strips uncured bacon
- ½ cup sour cream
- 2 eggs
  Salt and freshly ground black pepper
- 1 cup Simple Onion Relish (page 203), drained and packed

1. Begin by making the dough: In a large bowl, dissolve the yeast in the warm milk (it should feel like a comfortable warm bath to your finger) and let stand until frothy, about 5 minutes.

2. Incorporate a cup of the flour with a wooden spoon. Add the butter and mix with your hands or a spoon to combine fully, then add enough of the remaining ½ cup flour to form a soft dough. Knead for a couple of minutes; the dough will be on the wet, sticky side.

3. Lightly grease the sides of the bowl and return the dough, flipping it over to oil its top. Cover with a damp kitchen towel and place in a warm spot to rise.

4. When the dough has doubled in size, make the filling: Fry the bacon strips until crisp. Drain the bacon, saving the fat, and set aside to cool.

5. In a bowl, whisk the sour cream into the eggs. Add the salt and pepper. Crumble the bacon and add it to this mixture along with the onion

relish. (For an extra-rich pie, you can stir in a tablespoon or two of the bacon fat.)

6. Preheat the oven to 375°F.

7. Punch down the dough. Then roll it out and place on a baking sheet. Crimp the edges a bit — imagine a galette meets a pizza crust.

8. Spread the filling evenly across the top of the dough.

9. Bake the pie for 30 minutes, or until nicely browned and a toothpick inserted in the center comes out clean.

Michaela Hayes

Michaela sees fermentation not only as a culinary art but also as a real part of local sustainable food systems. She founded Crock & Jar, a micro-krautery in New York City, and says a big part of their mission is to teach. "What do I do with it?" comes up all the time in her fermentation classes. Her fermentation journey gives her a unique perspective in answering that question. She loves giving people examples of how to use their ferments. She prefers to use ferments raw, but she feels that when cooked "there is a uniqueness of flavor that fermented vegetables lend to a dish. It is often subtle and sublime."

For a time, Michaela experienced vegetable fermentation like an artist-in-residence: She was charged with creating the pickling station at Gramercy Tavern in New York City. Her *job* was to experiment and invent distinctive flavors. It was her *job* to help chefs use the ferments and to taste what they made. Sounds like too much fun for a job.

Michaela had a restaurant walk-in refrigerator full of seasonal produce as her fermentation palette. She says, "I tore through books and researched other fermenters experimenting with recipes and devised my own. There were definite misses, but every project was a step leading to the next thing. A corner of the temperature-controlled wine room became my fermentorium."

One of the challenges Michaela encountered at Gramercy Tavern directly shaped how she thinks about eating and using fermented vegetables. While executive chef Mike Anthony was extremely committed to the entire pickling program, some of the cooks were resistant to using the fermented vegetables in dishes; she says, "I pushed to get the

Michaela Hayes

cooks to think about fermented produce as another tool in their belt. What it made me realize is that if talented, trained cooks don't see fermented vegetables as a welcome addition to their stockpile of wonderful ingredients, then how are less experienced cooks supposed to get comfortable using them?"

She continues, "Once the cooks began to use the ferments, they came up with super-cool ways to do it. In a restaurant dedicated to seasonal American cuisine, one of the highlights of my time on the pickling station was getting kimchi on the menu. The cooks blended it up, mixed it with a sweet, julienned carrot-and-daikon quick pickle, and used it as a base for a fried oyster salad — absolutely gorgeous."

You'll find the recipe she shared for Chocolate Sauerkraut Cake in the dessert section (page 351).

Northwest Gingered Carrot Cake

See photo on page 348

serves 12

VEGETARIAN

One of our traditions is that the birthday person gets to pick the three meals on his or her birthday as well as the "cake," which is in quotes because more than one person in our family is a fan of pie rather than cake. Still, among the cake side of our family, carrot cake rules. When we were brainstorming desserts for this book, we knew we needed to tackle carrot cake.

It wasn't difficult to get to a ginger-carrot ferment (the main ingredient of this cake) since the fermented version enhances the regular version — it's somehow lighter and richer than the original, which may come from the interaction of the baking soda and the ferment. The basic recipe is from a favorite baking book, *Williams-Sonoma Essentials of Baking*. It's incredibly moist and spicy, so you don't need much in the way of frosting. We sometimes frost with just a light spread of sour cream. Otherwise, use your favorite cream cheese frosting.

2 cups cake flour
2 teaspoons baking powder
2 teaspoons baking soda
½ teaspoon salt
1 teaspoon ground cinnamon
½ teaspoon ground mace
1½ cups sugar
4 large eggs
1¼ cups coconut oil, melted and cooled
Grated zest of 1 orange
3 cups Carrot Kraut (page 149)

½ cup walnuts or pecans, quickly browned in a pan and then chopped
½ cup dried cranberries or raisins

1. Preheat the oven to 350°F.

2. Butter and lightly flour either two 10-inch round pans or one 9-by-13-inch rectangular pan.

3. Sift the flour, baking powder, baking soda, salt, cinnamon, and mace into a medium bowl.

4. In a large bowl, whisk together the sugar, eggs, oil, and orange zest. Stir in the carrot kraut.

5. Using a rubber spatula, fold the dry ingredients into the wet ingredients until combined.

6. Finally, add the nuts and dried fruit. Pour the batter into the prepared pans.

7. Bake until a toothpick inserted in the center of the cake comes out clean, usually 30 to 40 minutes. As soon as the middle no longer looks different than the edges and begins to crack a bit, remove the pans from the oven to preserve the moistness of the cake.

Kirsten Writes

Discussion of the culinary virtues of sauer-kraut is not complete without the much-joked-about sauerkraut chocolate cake. So much so that according to the sauerkraut chocolate cake recipe in the book *America's Best Lost Recipes: 121 Recipes Too Good to Forget*, the cake was a popular April Fool's Day treat in the 1960s — as well as at my house growing up. My father, German and a professor, loves sauerkraut and chocolate, but not together. He likes his sauerkraut savory and his chocolate sweet. Every few years a student would think it was funny to bring him a sauerkraut choco-late cake.

Chocolate Sauerkraut Cake with Coconut Kefir Glaze

serves 12

GLUTEN-FREE, VEGETARIAN

This cake has bounced around in various iterations from the immigrant cuisines of the Germans and Eastern European countries. The acidic ferment provides the moisture much in the way that bak-ing with buttermilk does. Now Michaela Hayes has updated it as deliciously gluten-free. It has a complex nutty flavor from the addition of buck-wheat flour. The sauerkraut keeps the cake from drying out and becoming crumbly, which can be a problem for gluten-free foods.

Michaela and Kirsten talked about which krauts, beyond Naked, would work. She origi-nally used a turmeric-chile kraut; since we had a turmeric-pepper kraut in the refrigerator, we used it, though with a bit of trepidation. It was great. The turmeric did not stand out. How about

Chipotle Squash Kraut (page 249)? We agreed there are many flavors that might pair well.

- ⅔ cup buckwheat flour
- ⅔ cup millet flour
- ⅔ cup white rice flour
- ⅔ cup cocoa powder
- 1½ teaspoons baking soda
- 1¼ cups hot water
- ½ cup Earth Balance shortening or butter, melted
- 1 teaspoon vanilla extract
- 1⅓ cups sugar
- 1 large egg
- 1 cup Naked Kraut (page 132), puréed smooth

GLAZE

- 3 tablespoons coconut kefir (or coconut milk if you don't have coconut kefir available)
- 1 cup confectioners' sugar

1. Preheat the oven to 350°F.

2. Grease a 12-cup Bundt pan with the fat of your choice.

3. Combine the flours, cocoa, and baking soda and set aside. (*Note:* Feel free to substitute 2 cups all-purpose flour for the gluten-free mix.)

4. Mix together the hot water, melted shortening or butter, and vanilla and set aside.

5. In a large mixing bowl, beat the sugar with the egg until pale yellow and fluffy. Add to this the wet and dry mixtures, alternating and begin-ning and ending with wet ingredients.

6. Fold in the sauerkraut, and then pour the cake batter into the prepared pan.

7. Bake for 45 to 55 minutes, or until a tester inserted into the center of the cake comes out clean. Let cool in the pan for about 15 minutes, then turn out and cool on a rack.

8. Mix the coconut kefir and the sugar together to make a glaze, and drizzle it over the cooled cake. You can change the consistency of this glaze by using more or less sugar. For a special touch, use a thinner glaze as a base layer, then top with a thicker layer of glaze. This is a trick to give your glaze more texture. Your cake will look festive, and you will enjoy the more complex quality as it melts in your mouth.

Note: You will probably eat this cake too quickly to notice, but the kefir icing is also a live food and will continue to ripen (in other words, get more sour) as it sits.

Sauerkraut Coconut Macaroons

yield: 1 dozen
GLUTEN-FREE, VEGETARIAN

Rinsed and drained sauerkraut has the consistency of flaked coconut in baked goods, so it only seemed natural to give it a try in our favorite gluten-free cookies. We suggest you wait to tell them about the sauerkraut until after they rave.

These are moister than typical macaroons. You can use the same amount of shredded coconut in this recipe for a sturdier, denser macaroon. Baking on parchment paper helps with removal of the warm macaroons to a cooling rack or straight to mouth.

  1 **cup Naked Kraut (page 132)**
  4 **large egg whites**
  ¾ **cup sugar**
  ¼ **cup tapioca flour**
1½ **teaspoons vanilla extract**
  ¼ **teaspoon almond extract**
  2 **cups flaked coconut**

1. Preheat the oven to 325°F.

2. Line a large baking sheet with parchment paper.

3. Rinse and drain the sauerkraut in a colander. Squeeze to remove all the moisture you can. Chop the sauerkraut to roughly the same size as your coconut to aid in the visual deception.

4. In a large bowl, combine the egg whites, sugar, flour, and vanilla and almond extracts. Add the sauerkraut and coconut and mix until well combined.

5. Drop by rounded tablespoons, about 2 inches apart, on the prepared cookie sheet. Bake until lightly golden brown.

6. Let the macaroons cool for 1 minute, then transfer to a wire rack to cool completely, if you can leave them alone that long.

VARIATION: Chocolate-Beet Coconut Macaroons

Use Simple Beet Kraut (page 120) in place of Naked Kraut, and add some chocolate chips — or better yet, chunks — to the mix before forming the macaroons. These will bake off a nice toasted pink with the chocolate soft and gooey.

SAUERKRAUT COCONUT MACAROONS

Rhubarb Fool

serves 4 to 6

Gluten-Free, Vegetarian

Kirsten fermented rhubarb with cardamom specifically with a lacto-fermented variation of this iconic dessert in mind. Our daughter walked in the kitchen and saw the fresh strawberries and whipped cream on the counter next to where Kirsten was working. Her finger was headed for the cream when, mid-dip, she noticed the jar of fermented rhubarb. "Oh no, really?" she asked.

It turned out to be a hit and not nearly as heavy as its syrupy cooked counterpart.

1 cup Fermented Rhubarb Infused with Ginger and Cardamom (page 224)
2 cups fresh strawberries
3 tablespoons sugar
  Zest of 1 lemon
1 pint whipping cream

1. In a food processor blend together the fermented rhubarb, strawberries, sugar, and lemon zest. Set aside.

2. Whip the cream until stiff. (*Note:* We don't add any sugar, just a few drops of vanilla. Feel free to make the cream to your taste.)

3. To serve as a fool, fold the rhubarb-strawberry sauce into the whipped cream. Or, for more of a spectacle, layer the sauce and cream in tall parfait glasses.

MEET THE FERMENTISTA

Mary Alionis

The phone rings.
"Is this the fermentation hotline?"
"Hi, Mary."

There are people, and you know who you are, who open the back of a book and read the ending first. If this is you, well, you will meet this fermentista throughout this book — only not as a fermentista, but as an organic vegetable farmer.

Mary Alionis was often behind the scenes of our Mellonia product's originality by "pushing" vegetables that we would never have thought to ferment — okahijiki, for example. Her husband Vince stood by and often said, "The experiments must continue."

Beyond just egging us on, they supported the experiments wholeheartedly, not only selling our krauts in their farm store, but also schlepping the sometimes-finicky jars to the local farmers' markets.

When we stopped fermenting commercially, Mary decided to continue the experiments. Oregon's Farm Direct Law went into effect in 2012, which meant Mary could ferment vegetables grown on the farm without jumping through all of the certification hoops, with the caveat that all of the vegetables had to be grown on-site — so Mary's creativity was put to the test immediately. She began with recipes from our business, but about a month after she started, all the winter cabbages had been sold. Mary had an abundance of carrots, burdock, chicory, and other vegetables that didn't seem to go together. Many of our conversations were like the call-in cooking

Mary Alionis

shows where the caller tries to stump the chef with three incongruent ingredients from her pantry.

"So Vince just found a row of overwintered black Spanish radishes. He was going to till them in, but we tasted them first. They were super-spicy in the fall; now they are sweet and delicious. I wonder what I should do. I am thinking about cilantro and lime juice," Mary informs me.

"Radishes are a great tonic in the spring and it sounds yummy. You should try that . . . ," I respond.

Scum

THE GOOD, THE BAD, AND THE UGLY

Just about every recipe for sauerkraut, kimchi, or pickles nonchalantly mentions skimming scum off your jars daily. We would like to demystify this scum. What follows is a gallery of images meant to help you assess this scum and any other shady characters in your crock.

Foam Is Harmless

The first thing to appear on the surface is foam. It doesn't need removing unless the amount becomes thick and unwieldy. The less you touch your brine, the less likely you are to contaminate it. Most scum is safe, and not an indicator that your batch is spoiled.

Remove this foam if it's excessive. Otherwise, we normally leave it undisturbed until the ferment is finished, as it tends to settle down. We believe that a thick brine layer is important, and every time you dip into the crock, the brine level falls. When the ferment is finished, remove all the foam and other scum and enjoy the beautiful kraut underneath.

Scum You Can Ignore

Kahm yeast is harmless. When touched, this scum breaks apart into tiny floating flecks and can take a long time and a lot of patience to remove. And the next day it is back with a vengeance. In our experience, this scum is best left alone. To remove it daily would be to compromise your brine quantity and increase the potential for contamination. When left alone, it does not increase nearly as much. Over a long ferment it might affect quality, but over a short ferment cycle, as for most of the recipes in this book, it will be fine. Check it every few days for mold, which you will want to remove.

Remove Surface Mold

You will easily recognize the bluish furry stuff or sometimes spots of a brownish-orange gelatinous substance. Mold is no good, but as long as it stays on top of the brine, your veggies are safe and anaerobic. Simply spoon it off as it develops.

Every good fermentista learns that this task must be done silently and without an audience. Especially if that audience is the one to whom you plan to serve your beautiful pickles. We have been told by younger members of the family, "I don't want to know what goes on in the fermentation cave . . ."

Remove the mold by carefully ladling it out; wipe down the edges of the glass with a clean paper towel. You can also use the leaf, or whatever follower you have in place, to "catch" the mold. Toss the leaf, wipe the edges, and replace with a new leaf. If the brine level in this jar is getting a little low, top off with some fresh brine solution that you have made. Replace the cloth or lid with a clean one.

Watch Your Brine Levels

For krauts, kimchis, and condiments, if the brine level falls below the level of your vegetables, the exposed portion will be rotten and not safe to eat. It will appear discolored, soft, even a bit slimy, and sometimes dry with a white film or mold. Without brine yeasts, slime organisms and mold have been given a chance to move in. In general, though, your whole batch is not lost.

Remove the followers and the "ugly" kraut until you reach the level of the brine. The kraut under the brine should be crispy and vibrantly colored.

After you have removed the offending kraut, it is good to remove just a little more to make sure you got it all, especially in the presence of mold.

Carefully wipe the edges of the crock or jar, so the good kraut doesn't get tainted as you pull it out.

The Exposed Pickle

For brine-pickled vegetables, the whole vegetable will be lost if part of it pokes out of the brine. Here's how to handle that situation.

Early in the fermentation process, just poke the pickle back under the brine and add more brine if necessary.

Often, if you remove the brazen floater vegetables, the rest under the brine will be fine. Use a clean nonreactive utensil to check. Add brine if the level is low.

If you don't catch it early or this happens during the storage period, veggies can become so soft they will almost disintegrate.

Sometimes the whole batch is unsafe to eat and should be tossed. Look out for these signs:

» If the vegetables are a light pink, there was probably too much salt, meaning that the lactic acid–producing bacteria were unable to thrive and got overwhelmed by yeast. (*Note:* Some veggies are pink or bleed pink into the ferment, including beets, red onions, pink turnips, pink or red radishes, red cabbage, radicchio, and shiso leaves.)

» If the vegetables are soft or slimy, they are also unsafe, for one of the following reasons:

- fermenting temperature too high
- not enough salt to overwhelm the slime-producing organisms
- uneven salt distribution

Toss unsafe batches of brine-pickled vegetables and begin again. You want only crispy, bright-tasting pickles.

Watch your brine levels. The kraut on the left came out of the brine; the kraut on the right is still safe and tasty.

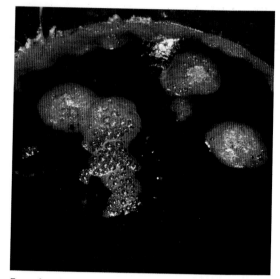

Foam forming early in the fermentation cycle.

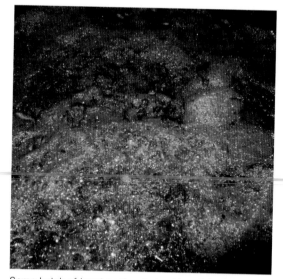

Same batch of kraut as the photo at top right 3 days later. Remove the foamy scum if you can do so without exposing the kraut.

Scum on top of the brine and grape leaf in a finished jar of pickles. Remove the leaf and scum, replace the leaf, add fresh brine as needed, and store.

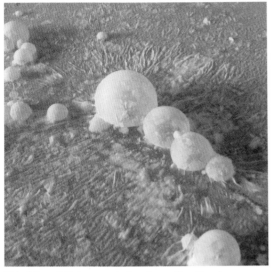

Thin layer of Kahm yeast. See Scum You Can Ignore, page 356.

Small flecks of mold formed on bits of escaped vegetables. Remove when you see them.

Remove surface mold with a strainer.

These beets continued to ferment in storage. When the lid was removed, they "climbed" out of the jar as the CO_2 was released. They are safe to eat.

Resources

For any fermenting supplies, check your local kitchen and cooking stores first. Thanks to the popularity of the fermenting arts, most of these stores carry a wide variety of supplies. You might just find everything you need. If not, here are some resources to get you started.

Crocks and Crock Accessories

For new, straight-sided Ohio Stoneware–type crocks, check your local hardware store. This will probably be your most cost-effective source, as shipping heavy stoneware can be expensive. Harsch Gärtopf (Gairtopf) fermenting crocks are widely available online, as is the TSM Polish version. We have seen this one in many brick-and-mortar cooking stores as well. As prices and shipping vary so widely, we cannot recommend one site over another. Japanese pickle presses, a.k.a. tsukemono presses, are great, and we suggest doing an Internet search if you are interested in these. Believe it or not, Sears (the online store) has a large selection; however, they are more expensive than presses from other sites that are associated with Amazon.

ACE HARDWARE
866-290-5334
www.acehardware.com
Generally has a good selection of crocks

ADAM FIELD POTTERY
720-244-5243
www.adamfieldpottery.com
Traditional onggi pots and a fun time-lapse video of the pot-making process

AMY POTTER
www.amypotter.com
Another clay worker who has put her creativity into the crock. Her pieces hold approximately 1.5 gallons of kraut.

BANDANA POTTERY
Michael Hunt and Naomi Dalglish
mhunt@mitchell.main.nc.us
www.michaelhuntpottery.com
Traditional onggi pots and a blog about their time in Korea

CANNING SUPPLY
Kitchen Krafts, Inc.
888-612-1950
www.canningsupply.com

COUNTER CULTURE POTTERY
Sarah Kersten
www.sarahkersten.com
Handmade crocks with water seals

877-469-1718

www.houserice.com

Japanese pickle presses, a.k.a. tsukemono presses

LEHMAN'S

888-438-5346

www.lehmans.com

A great place for many hard-to-find homesteading goodies. They have a nice selection of fermenting supplies and carry USA-made wooden followers, crock lids, and large tampers — which they call "stompers."

OGUSKY CERAMICS

Jeremy Ogusky

www.claycrocks.com

Jeremy is all about pickle pots. He has fun crocks for the small-batch fermentista.

REN BOURS CERAMICS AGENCY

www.sauerkrautpots.com

European-style crocks showing the old-world artistry

THE SAUSAGEMAKER

888-490-8525

www.sausagemaker.com

Polish-style fermenting crocks, the split-style stone-weighted followers, and a few hand-crank cabbage shredders

Vegetables, Herbs, and Spices

AGROHAITAI LTD.

www.agrohaitai.com

Stem mustard as well as other Oriental vegetable seeds

BULK HERB STORE

877-278-4257

www.bulkherbstore.com

MOUNTAIN ROSE HERBS

800-879-3337

www.mountainroseherbs.com

High-quality, certified-organic herbs and spices from a source with sustainable agricultural practices. A good place to find schisandra berries if you can't get them locally.

pH Strips, Airlocks, and Supplies for Jar Fermentation Systems

For the DIY fermentista, the parts to make your own airlock and jar systems (and pH indicators) are available at brewing supply stores and the following online retailers.

CULTURES FOR HEALTH

800-962-1959

www.culturesforhealth.com

Informative website with water seal–style crocks as well as lids with airlocks and pH strips. Their specialty item is glass-weighted followers for mason jars.

PERFECT PICKLER

941-276-2007

www.perfectpickler.com

The Perfect Pickler is basically a plastic wide-mouth lid with a hole and gasket to accommodate an airlock. The system uses a stainless steel follower to use with your own mason jars. The website is informative and has many great recipes.

603-722-0189

www.pickl-it.com

The Pickl-It system uses an airlock affixed directly to the glass lid of a bail-type jar in sizes from 1 liter to 5 liters. They also sell glass weights.

TREE BONE POTTERY

Joshua Ratza

www.treebonepottery.com

Jar-sized ceramic split-style weighted followers perfect for a mason-jar ferment.

Informational Websites

PICKLES

Science of Cooking

www.exploratorium.edu/cooking/pickles

PICKLE RECIPES

Awesome Cuisine

www.awesomecuisine.com/categories/vegetarian/pickles

PLANTS DATABASE

Natural Resources Conservation Service

http://plants.usda.gov

VECTIS ROAD ALLOTMENTS

www.veraveg.org

History of vegetables, including asparagus, carrots, dill, garlic, mint, and onions

Metric Conversion Charts

Unless you have finely calibrated measuring equipment, conversions between U.S. and metric measurements will be somewhat inexact. It's important to convert the measurements for all of the ingredients in a recipe to maintain the same proportions as the original.

GENERAL FORMULAS	
Ounces to grams	multiply ounces by 28.35
Grams to ounces	multiply grams by 0.035
Pounds to grams	multiply pounds by 453.5
Pounds to kilograms	multiply pounds by 0.45
Cups to liters	multiply cups by 0.24
Fahrenheit to Celsius	subtract 32 from Fahrenheit temperature, multiply by 5, then divide by 9
Celsius to Fahrenheit	multiply Celsius temperature by 9, divide by 5, then add 32

APPROXIMATE EQUIVALENTS BY WEIGHT	
US	**Metric**
¼ ounce	7 grams
½ ounce	14 grams
1 ounce	28 grams
1¼ ounces	35 grams
1½ ounces	40 grams
2½ ounces	70 grams
4 ounces	112 grams
5 ounces	140 grams
8 ounces	228 grams
10 ounces	280 grams
15 ounces	425 grams
16 ounces (1 pound)	454 grams
0.035 ounces	1 gram
1.75 ounces	50 grams
3.5 ounces	100 grams
8.75 ounces	250 grams
1.1 pounds	500 grams
2.2 pounds	1 kilogram

APPROXIMATE EQUIVALENTS BY VOLUME	
US	**Metric**
1 teaspoon	5 milliliters
1 tablespoon	15 milliliters
¼ cup	60 milliliters
½ cup	120 milliliters
1 cup	230 milliliters
1¼ cups	300 milliliters
1½ cups	360 milliliters
2 cups	460 milliliters
2½ cups	600 milliliters
3 cups	700 milliliters
4 cups (1 quart)	0.95 liter
1.06 quarts	1 liter
4 quarts (1 gallon)	3.8 liters

Bibliography

Affairs of Living (blog). "Cultured Vegetables: Pickled Kohlrabi Spears with Dill and Craway (gluten free, raw, vegan, ACD)." June 27, 2009. christensenka.squarespace.com/imported-20100106014405/2009/6/27/cultured-vegetables-pickled-kohlrabi-spears-with-dill-and-ca.html.

Allen, Zel, and Reuben Allen. "Onion Aficionados Weep." *Vegetarians in Paradise.* www.vegparadise.com/highestperch312.html

Atkinson, Catherine, and Trish Davies. *East European Kitchen.* New York: Hermes House, 2001.

Barrangou, Rodolphe, Sung-Sik Yoon, Frederick Breidt Jr., Henry P. Fleming, and Todd R. Klaenhammer. "Characterization of Six *Leuconostoc fallax* Bacteriophages Isolated from an Industrial Sauerkraut Fermentation." *Applied Environmental Microbiology* 68, no. 11 (2002): 5452–58.

Barrett, Francis. "Pepper and Peppers." *Iberia Nature.* www.iberianature.com/material/peppers.html.

Battcock, Mike, and Sue Azam-Ali. *Fermented Fruits and Vegetables: A Global Perspective.* FAO Agricultural Service Bulletin no. 134. FAO, 1998. www.fao.org/docrep/x0560e/x0560e00.htm#con.

Belleme, John, and Jan Belleme. *Japanese Foods That Heal: Using Traditional Japanese Ingredients to Promote Health, Longevity & Well-Being.* Tuttle Publishing, 2007.

Bergqvist, S. W., Ann-Sofie Sandberg, N. G. Carlsson, and Thomas Andlid. "Improved Iron Solubility in Carrot Juice Fermented by Homo- and Hetero-Fermentative Lactic Acid Bacteria." *Food Microbiology* 22, no. 1 (2005): 53–61.

Bisakowski, Barbara, Avtar S. Atwal, Nancy Gardner, and Claude P. Champagne. "Effect of Lactic Acid Fermentation of Onions (*Allium cepa*) on the Composition of Flavonol Glucosides." *International Journal of Food Science and Technology* 42, no. 7 (2007): 783–89.

Bitterman, Mark. *Salted: A Manifesto on the World's Most Essential Mineral, with Recipes.* Berkeley: Ten Speed Press, 2010.

Body Ecology. "5 Unusual Leafy Green Vegetables You Should Know (and Eat!)." July 23, 2008. www.bodyecology.com/articles/5_unusual_leafy_green_vegetables_you_should_know.php.

Braverman, Lewis E., and David S. Cooper, MD, eds. *Werner & Ingbar's The Thyroid: A Fundamental and Clinical Text.* 10th ed. Lippincott Williams & Wilkins, 2013.

Bremness, Lesley, and Jill Norman. *The Complete Book of Herbs & Spices.* Viking Penguin, 1995.

Caruso, Frank L., Peter R. Bristow, and Peter V. Oudemans. "Cranberries: The Most Intriguing Native North American Fruit." *APSnet.* www.apsnet.org/publications/apsnetfeatures/pages/cranberries.aspx.

Cohen, H. W., S. M. Hailpern, J. Fang, and M. H. Alderman. "Sodium Intake and Mortality in the NHANES II Follow-up Study." *American Journal of Medicine* 119, no. 3 (2006): 7–14.

Davis, Jeanine M., and Jacqulyn Greenfield. "Cultivating Ramps: Wild Leeks of Appalachia." In *Trends in New Crops and New Uses,* edited by J. Janick and A. Whipkey, 449–52. ASHS Press, 2002. www.hort.purdue.edu/newcrop/ncnu02/v5-449.html.

Dosan, Adina. "Red Orach: A Delicious Plant for a Delicious Spring Soup." Dave's Garden. April 18, 2012. http://daves-garden.com/guides/articles/view/3692/#ixzz2LkLWMniC.

Dworkin, Martin, Stanley Falkow, Eugene Rosenberg, Karl-Heinz Schleifer, and Erko Stackebrandt. *The Prokaryotes: A Handbook on the Biology of Bacteria: Proteobacteria: Alpha and Beta Subclasses.* 3rd ed. Vol. 5. Springer Science+Business Media, 2006.

Eastman, Quinn. "Beneficial Bacteria Help Repair Intestinal Injury by Inducing Reactive Oxygen Species." Emory Woodruff Health Sciences Center. May 10, 2011.

Espsäter, Anna Maria. "Slow Food in Korea: An Introduction to Korean Cuisine — From Kimchi to Bibimbap." *Transitions Abroad.* www.transitionsabroad.com/listings/travel/travel_to_eat/slow_food_in_korea.shtml.

Fallon, Sally, and Mary G. Enig. *Nourishing Traditions.* 2nd ed. New Trends Publishing, 2001.

Fleming, H. P., R. F. McFeeters, and M. A. Daeschel. "Fermented and Acidified Vegetables." *Compendium of Methods for the Microbiological Examination of Foods* (1992): 929–51. (http://ajph.aphapublications.org/doi/abs/10.2105/MBEF.0222.056.

Floyd, Keith. *Keith Floyd's Thai Food.* HarperCollins, 2006.

Halász, Anna. *Lactic Acid Bacteria.* In *Food Quality and Standards,* ed. Radomir Lasztity, 70–82. Vol 3, *The Encyclopedia of Life Support Systems.* Eolss Publishers, 2009.

Hartke, Kimberly, ed. "Traditional Chinese Sauerkraut Recipe Contributed by Blog Reader." *Hartke Is Online* (blog). March 12, 2009. http://hartkeisonline.com/whole-and-natural-foods/traditional-chinese-sauerkraut-recipe-contributed-by-blog-reader.

Hayes, Michaela. "Wedding Pickle." *Crock & Jar* (blog). August 31, 2012. www.crockandjar.com/wedding-pickle.

Henderson, Judy, Rose Massey, Carrie Thompson, and Lillie Tunstall. "Pickle and Pickle Product Problems." FCSW-497-05. North Carolina Cooperative Extension Service, 2001.

Hui, Y. H., Sue Ghazala, Dee M. Graham, K. D. Murrell, and Wai-Kit Nip, eds. *Handbook of Vegetable Preservation and Processing.* Marcel Dekker, 2004.

Jaffrey, Madhur. *A Taste of the Far East.* Pavilion, 1993.

Kallas, John. "Making Dandelions Palatable." *Backwoods Home Magazine,* July/August 2003. www.backwoodshome.com/articles2/kallas82.html.

Katz, Sandor Ellix. *Wild Fermentation: The Flavor, Nutrition, and Craft of Live-Culture Foods.* Chelsea Green Publishing, 2003.

Kurlansky, Mark. *Salt: A World History.* Penguin, 2003.

Lewin, Alex. *Real Food Fermentation: Preserving Whole Fresh Food with Live Cultures in Your Home Kitchen.* Quarry Books, 2012.

Manay, N. Shakuntala, and M. Shadaksharaswamy. *Foods: Facts and Principles.* 2nd ed. New Age International, 2001.

Manjoo, Farhad. "Tipping the Balance for Kitchen Scales." *New York Times,* September 13, 2011.

Martin, Geoffrey. *Industrial and Manufacturing Chemistry: A Practical Treatise.* 6th ed. Philosophical Library, 1955. First published 1913 by Appleton.

Merritt, Marlene. "Your Patients Are Malnourished . . . And So Are You." *Acupuncture Today* 12, no. 9 (September 2011).

Miller, Greg. "Mind-Altering Bugs." *Science NOW.* August 29, 2011. http://news.sciencemag.org/sciencenow/2011/08/mind-altering-bugs.html

Mollison, Bill. *The Permaculture Book of Ferment and Human Nutrition.* Tagari Pubications, 1993.

Mueller, Kristen, Caroline Ash, Elizabeth Pennisi, and Orla Smith. "The Gut Microbiota." *Science* 336, no. 6086 (June 2012): 1245.

Nicholson, Jeremy K., Elaine Holmes, James Kinross, Remy Burcelin, Glenn Gibson, Wei Jia, and Sven Pettersson. "Host-Gut Microbiota Metabolic Interactions." *Science* 336, no. 6086 (June 2012): 1262–67.

Panda, Smita H., Mousumi Parmanick, and Ramesh C. Ray. "Lactic Acid Fermentation of Sweet Potato (*Ipomoea batatas L.*) into Pickles." *Journal of Food Processing and Preservation* 31, no. 1 (February 2007): 83–101.

Pederson, Carl S., and Margaret N. Albury. *The Sauerkraut Fermentation*. Bulletin 824. New York State Agricultural Experiment Station, 1969.

Pennisi, Elizabeth. "Do Gut Bugs Practice Mind Control?" *Science NOW*, January 31, 2011. http://news.sciencemag.org/sciencenow/2011/01/do-gut-bugs-practice-mind-control.html.

Plengvidhya, Vethachai, Fredrick Breidt Jr., Zhongjing Lu, and Henry P. Fleming. "DNA Fingerprinting of Lactic Acid Bacteria in Sauerkraut Fermentations." *Applied and Environmental Microbiology* 73, no. 23 (2007): 7697–702.

Price, R. H. *Sweet Potato Culture for Profit: A Full Account of the Origin, History and Botanical Characteristics of the Sweet Potato.* Texas Farm and Ranch Publishing Co., 1896.

Rennie, Helen. "Rhubarb in the Raw: How Not to Cook Rhubarb." Culinate. May 3, 2007. www.culinate.com/columns/front_burner/Rhubarb+in+the+raw.

Roberts, J. S., and D. R. Kidd. "Lactic Acid Fermentation of Onions." *LWT—Food Science and Technology* 38, no. 2 (March 2005): 185–90.

"Sauerkraut: Problems and Solutions." Oregon State University Extension Service, March 2013.

Schmutz, P H., and E. H. Hoyle. "Common Pickle Problems." JGOC 3101. Clemson Cooperative Extension, revised August 2000. www.clemson.edu/extension/hgic/food/food_safety/preservation/hgic3101.html.

Schultheis, Jonathan R., and L. George Wilson. "What Is the Difference between a Sweetpotato and a Yam?" North Carolina Cooperative Extension Service. Revised January 1998. www.ces.ncsu.edu/depts/hort/hil/hil-23-a.html

Shibamotot, Takayuki, and Leonard F. Bjeldanes. *Introduction to Food Toxicology*. Academic Press, 1993.

Stein, Rob. "Microbes May Play Crucial Role in Human Health, Researchers Discovering." *Washington Post*, October 9, 2011.

Stern, Jane, and Michael Stern. *The Lexicon of Real American Food.* Lyons Press, 2011.

Tezla, Albert, ed. *Ocean at the Window: Hungarian Prose and Poetry since 1945*. University of Minnesota Press, 1980.

Trail, A. C., H. P. Fleming, C. T. Young, and R. F. McFeeters. "Chemical and Sensory Characterization of Commercial Sauerkraut." *Journal of Food Quality* 19 (1996): 15–30.

Van d'Rhys, Darius. "Growing the Tasty, Exquisitely Fiery Hot Wasabi!" Dave's Garden. August 6, 2008. http://davesgarden.com/guides/articles/view/1167.

"Virtuous White Produce." *The Week*, October 7, 2011: 22.

Volokh, Anne, and Mavis Manus. *The Art of Russian Cuisine.* Macmillan, 1983.

Vorbeck, Marie L., Leonard R. Mattick, Frank A. Lee, and Carl S. Pederson. "Volatile Flavor of Sauerkraut. Gas Chromatographic Identification of a Volatile Acidic Off-Odor." *Journal of Food Science* 26, no. 6 (November 1961): 569–72.

Wood, B. J. B., and W. H. Holzapfeland, eds. *The Genera of Lactic Acid Bacteria.* Vol. 2. Blackie Academic and Professional, 1995.

Yoon, Sook-ja. *Good Morning, Kimchi! Forty Different Kinds of Traditional & Fusion Kimchi Recipes.* Hollym International, 2005.

Acknowledgments

We would like to thank all those who came to our farmers' market booth, tasted our creations, and told us their stories. We thank our students, who taught us so much. Customers and students, you inspired this work.

There comes the point when you think you can't possibly ask your friends to hear one more word about sauerkraut or fermentation. Many of them, though, continued to read and reread our words and are still our friends. It's because of them that this book came into existence. Some of our most dedicated readers are themselves busy farmers; we thank all of you for your patience and time.

Heartfelt thanks go to Gianaclis Caldwell, who not only read but also supported us and cheered us on from the beginning to the end — especially during the hardest part, the middle, when progress almost stalled. To Barbara Hughey and Dennis Clancy, who were part of the project from the first pages. To Vicki Hames, who sharpened her red pencil time and time again as she went painstakingly through each page. And to Susanne Petermann, Carol Hoon, Maud Powell, and Melissa Matthewson, who took turns reading our words.

We want Mary and Vince Alionis to know how much we've appreciated their generosity and support in all phases of our fermenting journey. From selling our product to pushing our creativity, they always had another vegetable for us to try: first, while we produced, and then when Mary started fermenting her family's farmstead krauts. Thanks, guys.

Thank you to Nadine Levie, who was not only one of biggest cheerleaders but also helped us learn and understand the medicinal quality of herbs in the ferments. Thanks, Mom.

Lydia Wren Shockey, thank you for all the special artwork you've done for us.

For the crocktails, we thank Ursula and Ted Raymond, who taught us the basics and the terminology for mixing drinks, and, more important, for being co-inventors of the probiotic cocktails. And thank you to Neil Clooney and Dee Vallentyne, owners of Smithfield's Restaurant and Bar in Ashland, Oregon, for providing support and the bar space to mix up the drinks.

We're lucky to have gotten to know the following fermentistas from around the country. These pioneers of nouveau vegetable fermentation are passionate about sustainable food systems and in their approaches to the art and the cause. We feel deep gratitude for the support of Kathryn Lukas and Sash Sunday, not only with the book, but also as fellow kraut purveyors and friends. We're thrilled that Alex Hozven, Addie Rose Holland, Jennifer Sauter-Sargent, Tiffani Beckman McNeil, and Michaela Hayes took part in this project; *Fermented Vegetables* is richer for your insight and recipes. We also want to recognize Helen Bartels for sharing her mother's recipe. Thank you all so much.

And then we found Storey Publishing and all the great folks who have brought this book to a tangible reality. We are deeply grateful to everyone on Team Storey whom we worked with directly or indirectly. Margaret Sutherland and Alethea Morrison's expertise and vision combined with our own to create a strong, beautiful book — we thank you both. And a special thank-you to our editor Molly Jackel, with whom we enjoyed working. Molly spent countless hours molding and forming our words and then asking for a few more here and there — until *Fermented Vegetables* was truly a complete guide. Thank you, Molly.

A glimpse into the world of food photography was just plain fun. Thank you to everyone at both of the photo shoots. And thank you, Erin Kunkel; your exquisite photography brought out the culinary artistry that this food has to offer.

Index

italic = photograph of food dish

C

cabbage
  with apples, 268
  with beets, 119–21, 124
  Cabbage Salsa, 321
  with fennel, 180, 268
  in kimchi, 87–89, 91
  with lamb's-quarters, 261–62
  with leeks, 192–93
  with nettles, 263–64
  with okahijiki, 197–98
  outer leaf as follower, 36, 56
  with parsnips in kimchi, 209–10
  preparing, 41–42
  in sauerkraut, 53–60, 61–63
  with winter squash, 249–250
cabbage, green and savoy, 131–40
  Curtido, 133, *231*
  Greek Lemon-Mint Kraut, 134
  Juniper-Onion Kraut, 133–34, *152*
  Large-Batch (Homesteader) Curtido, 138
  Large-Batch (Homesteader) Kraut, 136–37
  Large-Batch Lemon-Dill Kraut, 138
  Lemon-Dill Kraut, 134, *256*
  Naked Kraut, *122*, 132–33
  OlyKraut's Eastern European Sauerkraut, 138–40
  Scape Kraut, 135
  Smoky Kraut or Hot and Smoky Kraut, 135
  Three Cs, 133, *257*
  Wine Kraut, 135–36, *173*
  Za'atar Kraut, 136
cabbage, napa or Chinese, 140–46
  Andrew's Private Reserve Kimchi, 144
  Chinese Sour Cabbage (*Suan Cai*), 145–46
  Kimchi, 141–42, *231*
  Sea-Chi (a.k.a. Sea Kimchi), 142, *172*

Tsukemono (Japanese Pickled Cabbage), 131, 144–45, 235
cabbage, red, 147–48
  Blaukraut, 147–48, *256*
Cabbage Salsa, 321
cake
  Chocolate Sauerkraut Cake with Coconut Kefir Icing, 351–52
  Northwest Gingered Carrot Cake, *348*, 350
carrots, 148–51
  Burdock-Carrot Kimchi, 131
  Carrot Kraut, 149–50
  Fermented Carrot Sticks, 151, *152*
  peelers for, 43
  Vietnamese Pickled Carrot and Daikon, 150–51
cauliflower, 151–56
  CauliKraut, *153*, 154
  Curried Caulikraut, 155
  Edgy Veggies, 155–56, *257*
Cebollas Encurtidas (Pickled Onions), 204, *217*
celeriac, 156–58
  Celeriac Remoulade, 318
  Hungarian Celeriac, 158, *217*
  Naked Celeriac Kraut, 157–58
celery, 158–60
  Beet and Celery Salad, 318
  Celery "Stuffing," 159, *217*
  Celery-Mint Salad, 159–60
chard, 160, 233, 234
Cherry Bombs, 242–43
chicken
  Chicken Salad, 308
  Grilled Chicken with Fermented Sweet Potatoes and Peanut Sauce, 344, *345*
  rich bone broth, 339
chili
  Chili Dog, 304
  quick dinner ideas, 330
Chinese Sour Cabbage (*Suan Cai*), 145–46
Chipotle Kraut Dip, *290*, 294

Chipotle Squash Kraut, *123*, 249–50
Chi-tini, 325
chives, 201
  Fermented Chives, 202
  Sour Cream and Chives Dip, 295
Chocolate Sauerkraut Cake with Coconut Kefir Glaze, 351–52
Chocolate-Beet Coconut Macaroons, 352
Choucroute Garni, 342
chutneys, 38, 43, 65
  basic steps, 66
  Fennel Chutney, *123*, 178, 180
  Onion Chutney, 204
  Squash Chutney, 251
  visual guide, 67–68
cilantro (coriander), 160–63
  Cilantro "Salsa," 162–63
  Pickled Green Coriander, 161
  Whole-Leaf Cilantro, 162
citrus fruits, 270–73
  Preserved Lemons, 272
  Preserved Limes, *153*, 271
cleanliness, 50–51, 98
CO2 air bubbles, 28, 36, 56–57, 63
coconut
  Chocolate Sauerkraut Cake with Coconut Kefir Glaze, 351–52
  milk, 69, 115
  Sauerkraut Coconut Macaroons, 352, *353*
Coleslaw, 320
collard greens, 163–64
  Ethiopian-Inspired Collard Ferment, 164, *172*
commercial production, 12–13
condiments, 64–75
  pastes and bases, 69–71
  relishes, chutneys, salsas, salads, 66–68
  seasonings, 75
  whole-leaf ferments, 72–74
coriander. *See* cilantro
corn, 165–66
  Sweet Corn Relish, 165–66

Preserve the Bounty with More Books from Storey

Nan K. Chase and DeNeice C. Guest
Make and preserve your own fresh juices, wines, teas, and more from fruit, vegetables, and herbs. From strawberry juice to dandelion wine, citrus peel tea, or watermelon mint syrup, this guide teaches you how to make nutritious drinks year-round.

Hannah Crum & Alex LaGory
Learn everything there is to know about this popular fermented tea, including flavoring ideas, health benefits, and, of course, how to brew it. Then put your kombucha to work with more than 100 recipes for baked goods, cocktails, condiments, snacks — even beauty products!

Matthew Weingarten & Raquel Pelzel
Forage wild ingredients from the sea, forests, and rivers, and preserve them for your own kitchen using old-world methods. Dozens of delicious recipes teach you how to cure, can, smoke, and pickle your foraged bounty.

Sherri Brooks Vinton
This spiral-bound Q&A volume is the perfect companion to all your preserving projects. Accessible information and illustrated tips will help you safely can, dry, ferment, freeze, and infuse all your favorite foods.